Labor Autonomy and the State
in Latin America

THEMATIC STUDIES IN LATIN AMERICA

Series editor: Gilbert W. Merkx,
  Director, Latin American Institute,
  University of New Mexico

THE POLITICAL ECONOMY OF
REVOLUTIONARY NICARAGUA
by Rose J. Spalding

WOMEN ON THE U.S.–MEXICO BORDER:
RESPONSES TO CHANGE
edited by Vicki L. Ruiz and Susan Tiano

THE JEWISH PRESENCE IN LATIN AMERICA
edited by Judith Laikin Elkin and Gilbert W. Merkx

POLICYMAKING IN MEXICO: FROM BOOM TO CRISIS
by Judith A. Teichman

LAND, POWER, AND POVERTY:
AGRARIAN TRANSFORMATION AND
POLITICAL CONFLICT IN CENTRAL AMERICA
by Charles D. Brockett

PINOCHET: THE POLITICS OF POWER
by Genaro Arriagada. *Translated by* Nancy Morris

SEARCHING FOR AGRARIAN REFORM IN LATIN AMERICA
edited by William C. Thiesenhusen

THE CHILEAN POLITICAL PROCESS
by Manuel Antonio Garreton. *Translated by* Sharon Kellum

LABOR AUTONOMY AND THE STATE IN
LATIN AMERICA
edited by Edward C. Epstein

Additional titles under preparation.

Labor Autonomy and the State in Latin America

edited by
Edward C. Epstein

Boston
Unwin Hyman
London   Sydney   Wellington

WESTVIEW PRESS * BOULDER, COLORADO

© 1989 by Unwin Hyman, Inc.
This book is copyright under the Berne Convention.
No reproduction without permission. All rights reserved.

Unwin Hyman, Inc.
8 Winchester Place, Winchester, Mass. 01890, USA

Published by the Academic Division of
Unwin Hyman Ltd
15/17 Broadwick Street, London W1V 1FP, UK

Allen & Unwin (Australia) Ltd,
8 Napier Street, North Sydney, NSW 2060, Australia

Allen & Unwin (New Zealand) Ltd in association with the
Port Nicholson Press Ltd,
Compusales Building, 75 Ghuznee Street, Wellington, New Zealand

First published in 1989

ISBN 0-8133-1275-2 (Westview)

Library of Congress Cataloging in Publication Data

Labor autonomy and the state in Latin America.
– (Thematic studies in Latin America)
1. Latin America. Trade unions, to 1986
I. Epstein, Edward C.   II. Series
331.88'098

ISBN 0-04-445331-0

British Library Cataloguing in Publication Data

Labor autonomy and the state in Latin America/edited by
Edward C. Epstein.
p. cm. – (Thematic studies in Latin America)
Includes index.
ISBN 0-04-445331-0
1. Trade-unions – Latin America – Political activity –
Case studies.
2. Labor policy – Latin America – Case studies.
I Epstein, Edward C., 1943– .   II. Series.
HD6530.5.L33 1989
322'.2'098 – dc 19   88-30377 CIP

Typeset in 10 on 12 point Palatino by
Computape (Pickering) Ltd, North Yorkshire
and printed in Great Britain at
the University Press, Cambridge

WESTVIEW PRESS
Frederick A. Praeger, Publisher
5500 Central Avenue
Boulder, Colorado 80301

To Tessa and Rosalyn,
the women in my life

Contents

Chapter 1

A Historical Introduction

Edward C. Epstein

*T*he focus of the present volume is an examination of the con- temporary relationship of organized labor and the state in the nine most urbanized Latin American countries – Argentina, Brazil, Chile, Colombia, Cuba, Mexico, Peru, Uruguay, and Venezuela. Specifically, the degree of political autonomy attainable by the trade unions and, with it, the possibility of meaningful political participation for most of the urban work force are explored.

With the growth of unions in the region near the beginning of the twentieth century, workers' efforts to use their collective numbers to make up for individual weakness vis-à-vis their employers aroused great concern. The common preoccupation of Latin American conservatives has been with factors such as the effect of unrestrained wage claims on the economy and fears of the supposed radicalism of labor movements headed first by Anarchists and Anarcho-Syndicalists and later by Communists and Socialists. Others of a less status quo inclination saw the possibility of converting the existing unions into a base for a middle-class dominated populist political coalition capable of inducing the traditional elites to share power. Under either of these two scenarios, influential political groups saw an autonomous labor movement as undesirable. Regardless of their different upper or middle class origins, such groups would look to the state as an instrument to be used to control labor, given the state's access to the means of coercion.[1]

The centralized state has long played a significant role in overseeing economic growth and political order throughout Latin America.[2] With the rise of national labor movements, those controlling the state in each country responded to labor's increasing presence with the passage of legislation governing various aspects of trade union activity. Typical action included the promulgation of (1) regulations concerning the type of worker eligible for membership and the minimum number needed to form officially recognized unions, (2) obligations to submit detailed financial records to regular government scrutiny, (3) conditions under

1

which internal elections might be held and those eligible to compete as officers, (4) rules for engaging in collective bargaining with management, (5) minimum time limits for engaging in government-supervised conciliation of differences, (6) cases where union-management differences had to be submitted to binding arbitration, and – last, but obviously not least – (7) the requirements needed to constitute a legal strike. The failure to follow any of these regulations could be legal grounds for overturning union elections, suspension or cancellation of official union recognition (required for collective bargaining rights), or the illegalization of a strike. In the instance of a strike being officially proclaimed illegal, those participating usually lost whatever job protections they had and were subject to the possibility of immediate dismissal without right of appeal or compensation. Although state rules and regulations could be justified as needed to maintain order, all had the common effect of limiting trade union autonomy.

The restrictions placed on union activity not only meant that total autonomy was virtually impossible, but also that labor would have to contend with opposition from state and management alike if collective goals were to be achieved. In view of the thoroughly politicized nature of the state, mandatory contact between trade unions and state administrators meant that the labor movement would be obliged to become political. The advocacy of a non-political stance meant ignoring the structural realities with which labor had to deal.

The nine countries examined in the present volume serve to illustrate the above generalizations about the state's role in seeking to control organized labor. What follows in this introductory chapter stresses the role of political parties as a possible mediating presence between the unions and the state. The discussion is organized into two time periods: (1) the years from the end of Anarchist predominance to the late 1950s/early 1960s and (2) the more contemporary years.[3] During the second period, countries can be divided into cases where (a) labor-oriented parties have been banned by an exclusionary military; (b) those in which they have been supplanted by a Marxist state; and (c) those where such parties exist within the confines of what had been populist regimes, but now increasingly subject to the pressures associated with economic austerity.

THE EARLY PERIOD:
PARTY LINAGES TO THE STATE

Over time, Anarchist (or similar leaning) union leaders who rejected partisan ties for labor as too compromising were increasingly replaced by those who argued that linkages with appropriate political parties were needed if labor was to survive the seemingly hostile attentions of the state.[4] The question was which party-affiliated group or groups would dominate. Typically, the pattern that emerged was one of a highly divisive partisan struggle between Communists and Socialists on the political left and a variety of more centrist populists, not to mention conflicts among themselves. Where populists could count on strong support from an anti-Marxist state, they were able to supplant their rivals, unifying most of the labor movement under their control. Such access to the state provided not only the coercion to intimidate opposing groups, but also the equally important economic largess upon which all populist leaders relied to solidify rank-and-file loyalty. Interestingly, cases of a state-Marxist alliance could also occur, although they were infrequent. Regardless of which party group gained official support, such labor leaders were aware that it was dependent on the continued good will of those dominating the state apparatus and on these benefactors being able to remain in power.

Cases of Exclusive Populist Party Control: Argentina, Brazil, and Mexico

In Argentina, the 1943–1945 period saw the populist supporters of military man Juan Perón use state power to oust Socialist and Communist unionists from control of the *Confederación General de Trabajo*, or CGT, the major labor organization since 1930. Subsequently, union support was a major factor in Perón's election victories in 1946 and 1952. After Perón's ouster during the 1955 coup, anti-Peronists alternated hostile acts like the intervention of the CGT, the arrest of its Peronist leaders, and support for non-Peronist unionists with efforts to win the cooperation of a new generation of Peronists through the return of the CGT and other kinds of official favoritism. Ultimately, neither repression nor cooptation would be able to seriously undermine the basic loyalty of the majority of workers to the Peronist cause.

The Brazilian case under populist leader Getulio Vargas is different due to his preference during the authoritarian *Estado Novo* period to use direct bureaucratic control over labor rather than work through a political party intermediary. Only with redemocratization in 1944–1945 and the emergence of the Brazilian Labor Party as one of the two pro-Vargas electoral vehicles would workers find a direct party link to the state. Nevertheless, with the exception of brief periods at the beginning and at the end of the 1946–1964 Republic when Marxist-influenced national labor confederations were allowed to coexist (although technically illegal), the state union structure set up under the old dictatorship prevented any real worker political input independent of official control.

In Mexico, the state has exercised a similar near monopoly over the unions through a sequence of alliances between major labor confederations and the official ruling party since the Revolution. The dominant labor body remains the *Confederación de Trabajadores de México*, or CTM, first organized by populist President Lázaro Cárdenas in 1936 and incorporated as the official labor sector in his 1938 party reorganization. Purged of dissident leftist elements in the years soon after World War II, the CTM leadership became a conservative bulwark of the regime.

Alternating or Shared Party Control:
Colombia, Cuba, Peru, and Venezuela

In Colombia, the competition between the two traditional parties for control of the state had major implications for organized labor. Under the Liberals, and especially during the two terms of reformist President Alfonso López (1934–1938 and 1942–1945), the Liberal and Communist-controlled *Confederación de Trabajadores de Colombia*, or CTC, held sway over a largely united labor movement. With the Conservatives in power after 1946 and with the increase of partisan violence, the new Church and Conservative-oriented *Unión de Trabajadores de Colombia* (UTC) gradually replaced the much more militant CTC. Only after the attempt by military populist Gustavo Rojas Pinilla (1953–1957) to rule independently of both Liberals and Conservatives – including the creation of his own labor group – would the two traditional parties agree to the 1958 National Front power-sharing agreement which was to run for 16 years. During this period the CTC and the UTC could also coexist, especially once the Liberals expelled the Communists from their more moderate confederation in 1960. The Communists formed their own separate labor group in 1964, the *Confederación Sindical de Trabajadores de Colombia*, or CSTC.

The Cuban case reflected the competition between civilian populist Ramón Grau and military man Fulgencio Batista to run the country. Having ousted Grau's 1933 provisional government, Batista eventually formed an alliance with the Communists, exchanging wage increases and legal recognition of the then Communist-dominated *Confederación de Trabajadores de Cuba* (CTC) for union votes and labor peace during his 1940–1944 presidency. With Grau's 1944 *Auténtico* Party election victory, the Communists sought to negotiate an alliance with the new president. But the Cold War and the 1946–1947 strife in the CTC between Communists and Auténticos led Grau to turn against the Communists, ousting them from the union leadership. Opportunistically, many of the new CTC leaders would end up supporting Batista after his 1952 coup and during his dictatorship.

Peruvian labor in the late 1920s was similarly divided between Communists and anti-Communists. The 1930 coup headed by Luis Sánchez Cerro and the outlawing of the Communist *Confederación General de Trabajadores del Perú* (CGTP), the disputed 1931 elections which anti-Communist populist Víctor Raúl Haya de la Torre of the newly organized *Aprista* Party supposedly lost to Sánchez Cerro, Aprista violence including the assassination of the president, and the outlawing of the Apristas all set the stage for the rest of the decade during which labor operated illegally. Although the Apristas and the Communists jointly founded a new labor group in 1944, the *Confederación de Trabajadores del Perú* (CTP), the Apristas took advantage of their links to the government of José Bustamante (elected in 1945) to seize full control a year later. The Aprista CTP was forced underground after the 1948 coup and the subsequent dictatorship of Manuel Odría. The CTP, however, was revived with the return to democracy in 1956. Though still dominant during the 1960s, the Aprista CTP encountered increasing competition from the Communists who benefited from worker dissatisfaction with Haya de la Torre's more visibly conservative politics. In 1968 the Communists revived the CGTP as a rival to the CTP.

In the case of Venezuelan labor, the initial advantage of the Communists (who had been actively involved since the 1936–1937 strikes) was negated by government repression. With the collapse of the 1944 Communist attempt to construct a national labor organization in cooperation with the populist *Acción Democratica* (AD) and the outlawing of the Communist unions, AD unionists gained a predominance that was to remain intact thereafter. AD monopolized the new *Confederación de Trabajadores de Venezuela* (CTV), founded in 1947, during the party's three-year rule during Venezuela's first democratic experience. Both AD and Communist labor leaders were persecuted by the 1948–1958 Marcos Pérez Jiménez dictatorship which set up its own labor confederation in 1954. As a result of a coalition effort involving Venezuela's major political parties, democracy was restored in 1958. Two formal pacts between the parties and labor and business placed limits on the social struggle that had undermined the previous democracy and guaranteed power sharing. With the expulsion of the Communists from the unions at the end of 1961 because of their participation in the Marxist insurrection, the remaining parties continued to share power in the CTV. Organized labor's unity was incomplete, however, owing to the simultaneous participation of Venezuela's second most important political party, the Social Christian COPEI, in a second labor confederation, the *Confederación de Sindicatos Autónomos de Venezuela* (CEDESA), it had founded in 1947.

Marxist-Dominated Labor: Chile and Uruguay

In Chile, the Marxists have always held majority control of the labor movement except when facing repression from conservative governments. The Communist-dominated *Federación Obrera de Chile* (FOCH) was the major labor organization from the time of its emergence as a radical group in 1917 and the imposition of the 1927–1931 Carlos Ibáñez populist dictatorship. Repressing the FOCH and other labor groups, as well as the Communist Party, in 1929 Ibáñez set up his own short-lived labor group. In the early 1930s, the FOCH reemerged and in 1936 joined with the Socialist Party's newly created confederation to form the Popular Front-inspired *Confederación de Trabajadores de Chile*, or CTCH. When the 1946–1952 Gabriel González Videla government turned sharply to the right during the Cold War, the CTCH split into separate Communist and Socialist wings. The organization was weakened further when the Communist part was suppressed as part of the 1948 Law for the Permanent Defense of Democracy. In 1953, a more broadly-based organization, the *Central Única de Trabajadores* or CUT was constituted, uniting the Socialists, the still illegal Communists, Catholic groups, and, for a time, even the Anarchists. Despite the efforts of conservative Christian Democrats to form a rival confederation to oppose the Marxist-controlled CUT, that ideologically divided body would remain the principal labor group for the next 20 years.

A similar case of Marxist hegemony existed in the Uruguayan labor movement. Because of the Russian Revolution, the then dominant Anarchists divided, with Anarcho-Syndicalists joining the Communists in 1923 in the *Unión Sindical del Uruguay* (USU). The Communists, in turn, broke off in 1928, forming the *Confederación General de Trabajadores del Uruguay* (CGTU) a year later. While there was some anti-union repression after the 1933 coup of Gabriel Terra, the existing labor organizations were allowed to continue. In the anti-Nazi atmosphere of World War II, a more broadly based body including Socialists, Anarcho-Syndicalists, and others joined with the Communists to form the *Unión General de Trabajadores*, or UGT. Resentful of Communist control, in 1946 the non-Communists formed a separate group within the UGT and in 1951 created a completely independent body, the Socialist-led *Confederación Sindical del Uruguay* (CSU). Benefiting from the prestige enjoyed by the Cuban Revolution, the Communists sought to reconstitute a single national labor confederation; their efforts were increasingly successful after 1964 with the creation and growth of the *Convención Nacional de Trabajadores*, or CNT.

RECENT CHANGES

In certain countries, the increasingly class conscious behavior of the labor movement and its political allies helped to precipitate the establishment of a new type of authoritarian order between 1964 and 1973. Unlike the earlier populist authoritarianism of men like Perón in Argentina, Vargas in Brazil, Ibáñez in Chile, Rojas Pinilla in Colombia, Batista in Cuba, and Cardénas in Mexico (or of a Juan Velasco still to come in

Peru), the new bureaucratic authoritarianism envisioned no political role for organized labor. The old politics of exchanging better worker income for political support now came to be a thing of the past. Instead, Marxist and populist political parties were suppressed or suspended, trade unions were placed under firm government control, and the right to strike was severely limited.[5] In the cases of bureaucratic authoritarianism discussed in the country chapters – Argentina from 1966 to 1973 and again from 1976 to 1983, Brazil between 1964 and 1985, Chile from 1973 to the present, and Uruguay between 1973 and 1985 – a negative income redistribution favoring the wealthy was used to lower inflation and to increase private investment. With the exception of Uruguay, the forceful state efforts to produce a non-political trade unionism acceptant of official economic policies eventually failed.

The State and the New Authoritarianism:
Argentina, Brazil, Chile, and Uruguay

In Argentina, the series of CGT-sponsored general strikes which followed the 1969 urban rioting in Córdoba and other interior cities helped to further undermine the 1966–1971 Onganía and Levingston military governments and to promote the 1973 elections which led to the return of Peronism after almost 18 years. With Perón's death in 1974, the widening divisions within Peronism led to new labor unrest and the suppression of the CGT at the time of the 1976 coup. While labor militancy from 1981 was a factor in hastening the end of the most recent military regime, domestic economic problems and the catastrophic Malvinas/Falklands adventure were more central. Under the current democracy, a reconstituted but internally divided CGT would lead Peronist opposition to the post-1983 Raúl Alfonsín Radical Party government.

In Brazil, the gradual political opening after 1974 made the emergence in 1978 of an independent union movement parallel to the official labor structure politically possible for the first time since the repression of the Marxist unions at the beginning of the military dictatorship. Having organized the strikes of the late 1970s as a means of regaining earlier wage losses and improving job stability, the metalworkers of the ABC industrial suburbs of São Paulo served as the base for the openly Marxist Workers Party and the 1983 national union confederation, the *Central Unica dos Trabalhadores*, or CUT. A rival national group founded shortly afterwards by more moderate workers took the name of the *Central Geral dos Trabalhadores* (CGT) in 1986. One of the areas of contention in the 1987–1988 Constitutional Convention has been how much of the repressive Estado Novo era labor laws would be retained under the more democratic New Republic introduced in 1985 to replace direct military rule.

In Chile, union opposition to the anti-Marxist military dictatorship of Augusto Pinochet became a serious factor only with the mass political protests of 1983–1986 following in the wake of the 1982 economic crisis. Responding to an initiative sponsored by the copper workers, rival Christian Democratic and leftist groups that had organized separately in the 1970s united in June 1983, forming a single umbrella organization, the *Comando Nacional de Trabajadores* (CNT), the first unitary labor body since the CUT was banned at the time of the 1973 coup. The new organization sponsored the general strikes of mid-1983 and end-1984 as well as coordinating labor participation in what began as monthly demonstrations against the Pinochet government.

With no national labor body after the suppression of the Uruguayan CNT in 1973, unions there had little political visibility prior to the beginning of the gradual return to democracy that followed the popular rejection of the military's proposed constitution in the 1980 plebiscite. Groups similar in ideology to those that had run the old CNT in 1982 organized the *Plenario Intersindical de Trabajadores*, or PIT, as a replacement. In 1984, the organization's name was amended to PIT-CNT. Efforts by the Communists to dominate the 1985 CNT congress led to a walkout of extreme leftists, almost splitting the organization. Given the prior low level of wages under the military regime, a high level of strike activity during the democratic government of Colorado President Julio Sanguinetti has been used to push wages up, especially in the public sector where wages have remained low.

The Marxist State and Organized Labor: Cuba

The 1959 triumph of the Cuban Revolution led to the subordination of the CTC to the new Marxist state. Union leaders that Fidel Castro judged to be non-supportive of the leftward course taken by the government were systematically purged. Throughout the 1960s, the role of organized labor was seen as encouraging worker economic production in return for the job security and extensive social services provided by the state. The high absenteeism and the low productivity evident by the latter part of the decade led to official efforts in the early 1970s to rejuvenate the decaying union structure by expanding labor's policy responsibilities. Workers have been encouraged to actively participate in production assemblies where they have the opportunity to critique local management; CTC leaders, in turn, were permitted to regularly attend meetings of the national government's ministerial and state committee management councils and are officially represented on the top-level Council of Ministers (and on its executive committee) which coordinates all Cuban economic activity. While not insignificant, labor's policy input is limited to what the major Communist Party leaders are willing to permit.

Labor and the Populist State Under Economic Stress:
Colombia, Mexico, Peru, and Venezuela

Recent economic difficulties in Colombia, Mexico, Peru, and Venezuela have produced noticeable tension in the relations between labor movements and states which in the past have been prone to populist styles of politics. The increasing economic constraints on government spending forced by austerity have meant that economic resources once directed to favored trade union leaders and their clientele are less available; instead, governments feel themselves compelled to call for sacrifices and patience from their supporters. Needless to say, such requests were not well received by trade unionists.

In Colombia, the initial links between the Liberals and Conservatives and the two major labor confederations, the CTC and the UTC respectively, began to weaken in the late 1960s under the National Front. By the 1970s, an increasing number of independent unions under leftist leadership were joining with the Communist CSTC and, to some extent, the UTC in strikes meant to provide wages commensurate with rising inflation. The joint participation (for the first time) of most of the labor movement in the 1977 *Paro Cívico*, or civic strike, caused great distress to the government and its conservative allies in business and the military.[6] With the high unemployment of the early 1980s, the now smaller labor movement witnessed both a surge in the number of the independent unions and their subsequent merger along with certain defectors from the UTC and CTC in late 1986 with the CSTC to form a single majoritarian labor group, the *Central Unitaria de Trabajadores* (CUT), controlled by the Marxists.

In Mexico, the semi-official CTM has continued its labor dominance, presiding over the 1966 creation of the *Congreso del Trabajo*, or CT, the umbrella group which now links the overwhelming majority of the labor movement made up by various pro-government union confederations. Unlike Colombia, the growth of a small number of leftist independent unions in Mexico during the 1970s was contained, leading to little direct challenge to state authority. The worsening economic crisis of the 1980s has seen the CTM join with the government in various solidarity pacts, exchanging severe wage controls for efforts to limit joblessness among the regularly employed workers from whom the unions draw their membership.

The Peruvian case has been one characterized by political confrontation. Under the populist government of General Velasco (1968–1975), the Communist CGTP rapidly outpaced a declining Aprista CTP in size. While innovative, the military's effort to defuse class conflict through the creation of profit-sharing worker communities and cooperatives led to relatively little increased popularity for the regime. Similarly, the 1972 creation of the official *Confederación de Trabajadores de la Revolución Peruana* (CTRP) generated little support and failed to supplant the various party-linked labor groups. The serious economic decline beginning in the mid-1970s led not only to Velasco's replacement by more traditional military officers, but also to record strike activity and, ultimately, the restoration of democracy in 1980. If sharply divided in the late 1970s owing to differing responses to the military, the various forces of the labor left joined together in the early 1980s to oppose Fernando Belaúnde's government which was blamed for heightened unemployment and rapidly sinking wages. By 1985, an expanded Marxist CGTP was once again contesting for control of the labor movement with an Aprista CTP strengthened by its ties to the successful presidential bid of Alan García.

The links of Venezuelan labor to the democratic regime have rested on the ability of the oil-based economy to generate the jobs, wages, and benefits to satisfy most of the work force. During the years of the oil bonanza, strikes were few in number. Alternating in control of the government, the centrist AD and COPEI parties used state resources to reinforce their partisans in the labor movement and in the dominant, AD-controlled CTV. With increased inflation from 1979, the weakening of world oil prices after 1981, and the emergence of a foreign debt crisis, wages began to deteriorate significantly. In response to worker discontent and anti-government protests organized by the weak labor left, the CTV has urged the government to strengthen the price regulatory commission set up in 1982 and to consider the state control of both prices and wages. Such steps mark the first hesitant efforts of organized labor to take a more directly political stand on issues where its interests diverge from existing government policy.

THE PRESENT VOLUME

The sketches provided here of labor relations in the nine countries under study are greatly amplified in the chapters making up the body of this volume. While reference is made to the initial period of populist and Marxist involvement in the unions, major stress is on the more contemporary time-frame. Focusing on the common theme of the struggle over labor autonomy, the contributing authors try to explain the resulting differences in terms of factors like the ability and willingness of state elites to use compelling force, the extent of ideological commitment and party linkages of the labor leadership, and the degree of structural unity achieved in any particular national labor movement. These same themes are again addressed in the conclusion where particular patterns of greater or lesser autonomy among the case countries are discussed in a comparative framework.

NOTES

1. Throughout these pages, the state is used as an analytic concept given that it adds the notion of control over the means of coercion to a general term for the institutions of government. See Max Weber, *The Theory of Social and Economic Organization* (New York: Free Press, 1964), p. 156.

2. Claudio Véliz, *The Centralist Tradition of Latin America* (Princeton: Princeton University Press, 1980), pp. 7–12.

3. Another reason was the gradual replacement in the working class of foreign-born immigrant workers who had picked up their Anarchist leanings in Europe by a native-born majority.

4. The summaries provided for each of the nine countries reflect to a considerable degree the individual accounts found in Gerald Greenfield and Sheldom Maram, eds., *Latin American Labor Organizations* (New York: Greenwood Press, 1987).

5. See Guillermo O'Donnell, *Modernization and Bureaucratic-Authoritarianism* (Berkeley: Institute of International Studies, University of California, 1973), as well as later writigs.

6. Also participating was the small *Confederación General de Trabajo*, or CGT, founded in 1971 by Social Christian unions as a fourth Colombian national labor group.

Chapter 2

Labor Populism and Hegemonic Crisis in Argentina

Edward C. Epstein

*J*uan Perón fundamentally changed Argentine politics by transforming the small, largely powerless existing trade unions into a highly politicized base for the mass movement that took his name.[1] Peronism (or *justicialismo*, after the Spanish word for justice) commanded more popular support than any other political force from the mid-1940s up through the early 1980s. This new version of Argentine populism articulated a serious alternative to the previous conservative model of ideological domination which had entered into crisis with the economic depression of 1930. In the time that followed Perón's initial coming to power with the 1943 military coup and the 1946 elections, such a populist vision of society competed for control with its elitist rival in what some observers have labeled a "hegemonic stalemate."[2] Politics over the next 40 years took the form of an alternation of populists based on electoral support and authoritarian conservatives relying on the military. Such regime instability can be seen as symptomatic of the lack of hegemonic control by any social class alliance.[3]

Labor's incorporation into the political system as a fundamental part of Peronism shaped its relations with the state. When the Peronists were in power during 1946–1955 and 1973–1976, most union leaders were united in support of major government policies. In return, the populist state offered the labor elite privileged economic and political consideration for themselves and their union members. After the military coups ousting Peronism, labor divided among those who sought accommodation with governments judged too dangerous to attack, those who urged strikes or other forms of collective action as the only means to preserve existing union gains, and those between the extremes who tried to negotiate for themselves a limited autonomy based on a combination of threats and potential cooperation.[4] The non-Peronists, in their turn, were equally varied as to the best strategy for dealing with potentially

13

hostile unions. Some governments pursued a largely cooptive approach, trying to induce those in control of the established national-level structure, Confederación General de Trabajo, to maintain rank-and-file acquiescence to official policy; some relied primarily on massive state coercion intended to destroy the unions' organizational ability to protest; and others fluctuated between sharp doses of repression and a subsequent willingness to negotiate on particular matters.[5]

Labor cooperation with or resistance to those running the state at any particular moment generally reflected the overall economic policies being pursued. With some simplification, one can talk of two distinct economic strategies reflecting the earlier mentioned alternation between populist and conservative rule.[6] The populist model emphasized the role of the state in achieving a more egalitarian income distribution, with the ensuing greater economic demand providing the domestic market necessary for the consumer goods stage of import substitution industrialization. At this point export agricultural earnings subsidized urban sector manufacturers and workers through cheap imports based on an overvalued exchange rate and low internal food prices. As long as they felt they were a privileged part of the populist coalition, the trade unions supported the state. In contrast with populism, the conservative project underlined the desirability of income reconcentration and low wages as necessary incentives for new investment. Depending on whether industry or agriculture was in the political ascendency, conservative policy stressed either additional industrialization using foreign investment and technology introduced by multinational corporations or the return to traditional raw material exports encouraged by an undervalued currency. Given that the urban workers made the largest sacrifice under either of these options, mass discontent was inevitable. The accumulated organizational experience of labor militants allowed for the ready conversion of such feelings into some kind of protest, to the extent political conditions permitted.

Trade union political behavior has paralleled that of most other organized interest groups in a polity characterized by a continual struggle over relative shares of national income. Each group has tended to see politics in largely zero-sum terms, that is, for anyone to gain, someone else must lose a corresponding amount. In this context, a change in political regime from populist to conservative, or the reverse, is likely to provide the means for dramatic shifts in income shares. Naturally, each group has a quite different perception of how such redistribution ought to be interpreted. Regained income occurring with a newly sympathetic government may seem merely a return to a just status quo ante to those benefiting, while those who feel such a change has occurred at their expense see it as an unacceptable action that must be reversed. Such divergent views reflect the lack of a single commonly shared notion of legitimacy in Argentine society, itself a reflection of the prevailing hegemonic crisis that has endured since the 1930s.

This chapter's account of the political role of organized labor in Argentina is broken down into three sections: (1) a recapitulation of the origins of the Peronist/anti-Peronist political cleavage that polarized the country's politics until the early 1980s; (2) a discussion of linkages between the state and trade unions in terms of the struggle over labor autonomy; and (3) some thoughts as to future developments given present structural changes in the labor market and a possible partisan realignment beginning with the Radical Party government elected in late 1983.

THE ROLE OF LABOR IN A POLITICALLY POLARIZED SOCIETY

Up until very recently at least, Argentine politics had been dominated by the rivalry between Peronism – based predominantly on the trade unions – and a variety of anti-Peronist forces. While various efforts were made to bridge the deep gap between the opposing sides, all collapsed because of the high level of distrust derived from the difficulties of sharing limited resources. In the end, only the increasing fragmentation of a Peronism deprived of the unifying presence of its now dead leader seems to have opened the possibility of constructing a new political power configuration.[7]

Much has been written about how Perón used his position as Secretary of Labor in the military governments of 1943–1945 to create a personal sense of loyalty from workers grateful for dramatic improvements in their standard of living.[8] By the time of Perón's ouster in 1955, the majority of the work force had developed a strong identification with Peronism that would be of major concern to all anti-Peronist governments that followed. The trade unions were seen as a possible threat not only because of their likely resistance to lower wages associated with conservative economic projects, but also owing to their potentially subversive identification with the ousted populist regime. The question of whether the workers could be won away from their Peronist loyalties was of critical importance in terms of creating a politically viable replacement.

The 1946 presidential elections, the first genuine expression of popular will at that level since 1928, captured the essence of the Peronist/anti-Peronist political cleavage that had been developing in Argentina since the 1943 coup.[9] Such a division can be mapped in terms of the positions taken by the various political parties, by the organized interests, and by various sectors of the electorate. Supporting Perón's candidacy was the newly formed Labor Party, representing key elements of the trade unions and dissident members of the previously dominant Radical Civic Union, the so-called *Junta Renovadora* group.[10] In the opposition stood nearly all the established political parties from the Socialists and Communists on the left to the Progressive Democrats on the right, but the dominant element in what was called the "Democratic Union" consisted of the centrist Radical Civic Union.[11] The various interest groups mirrored this polarization: among the anti-Perón forces was most of big business (the Buenos Aires Stock Exchange, the Rural Society, and the Industrial Union), most of the press, the navy and the more conservative parts of the army, and, especially, the United States Embassy; the pro-Peronists included most of the trade unions organized in the CGT, nationalist elements in the army, the hierarchy of the Catholic Church, and some of the smaller industrialists oriented toward the domestic market.[12] Such party and interest group support largely translated into a particular social class division of the electorate, with Perón gaining the votes of most of the urban and rural workers, plus – in the interior of the country – those of a large number of middle class individuals.[13]

In the years to come, the original Peronist populist coalition became fragmented. By 1955, the quarrel with the Catholic Church which had surfaced the year before offered a religious sense of grievance to already disaffected army officers. The contract signed with Standard Oil of California added a nationalist element to the various military conspiracies.[14] At the time of the coups of June and September – the latter of which led to Perón's ouster – the only interest group of any political weight that remained unequivocally loyal was the labor confederation, the CGT, which had become an official component of Peronism five years earlier.[15]

If in his initial two terms as President, Perón made various attempts to conciliate some of those who opposed him, such acts were inconsistent and achieved little. Those seen as threats to the consolidation of Peronist power were often treated harshly, be they dissident unionist Cipriano Reyes in 1947–1948 or Radical Civic Union leader Ricardo Balbín in 1949–1950.[16] In the elections of 1951, the Radicals again provided the principal opposition, unsuccessfully running the team of Balbín and Arturo Frondizi against Perón and what had been renamed the Peronist Party. Although the voting itself was reasonably honest, the campaign had been marred by acts of physical intimidation and the Peronist government's almost total domination of the mass media.[17] The 1951–1955 period saw an increasingly repressive atmosphere associated with various conservative military-civilian plots against the Peronist government and the latter's encouragement of mob violence against its so-called oligarchic rivals.[18]

The success of the anti-Peronists in September 1955 in ousting the man they called the "tyrant," led to an escalation of recrimination and a worsening of the existing political cleavage which divided Argentines. Once the conciliatory General Lonardi was replaced as president by the hardline General Aramburu, the Peronist Party was proscribed and the Peronist constitution of 1949 replaced by that of 1953.

As the major Peronist group, the unions were marked out for special discrimination. The CGT was "intervened" or placed under military jurisdiction. A purge of the old Peronists from leadership positions in individual unions, however, only led to the creation of a new generation of even more militant Peronist replacements.[19] In 1957, the government's attempt to turn a normalized CGT over to anti-Peronist "democratic" forces was frustrated, but the move led to the creation of what became the so-called "62 Peronist organizations" in the union movement.[20] The "62" would serve as the vehicle through which various Peronists and their allies dominated the unions and the CGT in the years to come.

The attempt of the anti-Peronist military in 1958–1966 to construct a democratic regime without Peronist participation proved unworkable. Someone less hostile to Perón like Radical Party leader Frondizi could be elected president in 1958 as part of a deal with the exiled caudillo, but he found his government undermined by the suspicions of the most virulently anti-Peronist military officers. Those unwilling to compromise with Perón would either be defeated like Balbín in that same year or, like Arturo Illia, who won in 1963 with only some 24.5 percent of the vote owing to Peronist mass abstention, find the legitimacy of his government always in doubt. The hopes that most Peronist voters had been absorbed into one of the branches of the Radical Party were crushed by the results of both the 1962 and 1965 provincial and congressional elections when Peronist candidates running as the Popular Union did embarrassingly well.[21] By the time of the 1966 coup, the military (led by General Onganía) had decided to rule directly without the pretense of democracy; the generals would remain until 1973.

What had seemed like a firmly entrenched military regime began to unravel in the face of protests launched by dissident trade unionists and radicalized university students. Preceded by labor demonstrations and strikes that had been occurring for over a year and by a wave of small-scale leftist guerrilla actions in April, the riots that took place in various interior cities in May 1969 – culminating with that in Córdoba, the *Córdobazo*, shocked the nation. Parts of the armed forces even began thinking of retreat from direct control.[22] If the initial ties of the protesters with Peronism were unclear, Perón took advantage of the regime's increasing vulnerability by encouraging, in turn, both Peronist union leaders and what he called his "special formations" among the student-based guerrillas to organize and participate in various national-level general strikes and armed probes against the government. A splintered military forced out Onganía in mid-1970 after the guerrilla murder of former President Aramburu. In early 1971 when Onganía's successor, General Levingston, proved unable to deal with the escalating violence of more assassinations and a renewal of the rioting in Córdoba, he was replaced by General Lanusse.[23] Unlike his military predecessors, Lanusse recognized the need to open negotiations with Perón in the interests of restoring domestic peace. Lanusse ended up committing the military to holding elections in 1973 despite the failure of his efforts to promote a Perónist abstention.

The Peronists regained political power only after making peace with their major civilian rivals, the Radicals. The first step in this direction occurred in November 1970 with the signing of the "Hour of the People" agreement, calling for the restoration of democracy without restrictions and promising to respect the rights of minority parties.[24] When Perón made a brief return to Argentina in late 1972, he met individually with most politicians, but lavished special attention on Radical leader Balbín. Finally, the Radicals and most other political parties joined with the Peronists to sign the detailed Common Program of December 7, 1972. The Peronists sought to portray themselves as part of a broad national movement calling for a return to democracy rather than as a narrow sectarian party; in contrast, the military seemed more and more isolated. When the March 1973 elections were held, the competition between Peronist and Radical candidates lacked the bitter divisiveness of former years.[25] With Perón's own candidacy for the presidency forbidden due to his refusal to return to Argentina and thus acknowledge the military's right to set the rules for the election, a loyal substitute, Héctor Cámpora, overwhelmed Balbín. Perón himself would have to wait until the September 1973 elections to win a third term in his own right, a term cut short by his death on July 1, 1974.[26]

With Perón's death, a Peronism divided into the political wing, the trade union bureaucracy, and the radical youth was unable to retain power.[27] If the new military regime which ousted Perón's wife and heir Isabel in March 1976 from the presidency manifested hostility to the party and, especially, to the Peronist-controlled CGT, its action seemed more of a repudiation of the entire political party establishment (in common with its military predecessors of a decade earlier).[28] When the post-1976 military regime itself collapsed in the face of an economic crisis and the humiliation of the 1982 Malvinas/Falklands War disaster, the same two political parties – Peronists and Radicals – once again contested a presidential election. In October 1983, however, with Perón now in his grave and his party discredited both by its previous performance in office and by rumors of a supposed trade union-military plot to pardon human rights violators, the new Radical Party leader, Raúl Alfonsín, was elected to a six year term.[29] His government would have to face a hostile, still highly Peronist labor movement.

LABOR, THE STATE, AND AUTONOMY

Control of the trade unions has been of great significance to all Argentine governments since Perón first made them a powerful political force in the mid-1940s. Given the traditional alliance between labor and Peronism, the unions could provide a Peronist government with an easily mobilizable source of popular support, as well as cooperation in economic policy. Over time, most workers had learned to identify their interests with their leader's dictates. To anti-Peronists in power, on the other hand, union autonomy often seemed a potential threat. Labor's ability to bring the economy of the country to a halt through strike activity could not be ignored; similarly, the strike weapon was seen as having a potentially dramatic effect on the level of wages and, ipso facto, on capital accumulation. Peronists sought to cement their relation with the typical worker; anti-Peronists viewed the same worker as dangerous unless he could be depoliticized.

The present discussion of state-union linkages falls into three parts: a survey of changes in the legal structure in which labor activity is regulated; an account of state efforts at cooptation and/or repression; and a description of union responses in the form of both negotiation with key governmental figures and strikes. While reference is made to earlier activity, the focus on each of these topics is the situation as it has developed after 1973.

The Law of Professional Associations
The Law of Professional Associations has been central to most efforts to unify and to regulate Argentine trade unions.[30] The 1945 version (Decree 23,582) passed by the Farrell military government and reflecting Perón's influence provided official recognition of the legal standing of only one union group in any enterprise or industry (*sindicato único*). Without such recognition, a union could not officially enter into collective bargaining, which was made industry-wide in 1953.[31] Interestingly, the granting of such legal status, or *personería gremial*, did not automatically go to the most representative group in a strictly quantitative sense, but rather to that one judged "sufficiently representative" by the government. Those in charge were obviously meant to have the power to exercise considerable discretion in awarding recognition.[32] One view expressed is that the legal ambiguity over recognition permitted the government to replace noncooperative unions with new parallel ones willing to accept official direction and, thus, to cement Peronist control

over the labor movement.[33] In 1950, the CGT Extraordinary Congress amended that organization's statutes so as to allow national-level union leaders to take over particular locals where necessary.[34]

In the years following Perón's overthrow in 1955, the Law of Professional Associations was altered repeatedly by various administrations in attempts to mold unions to their liking. The anti-Peronist Aramburu government used Decree-Law 9,270 of 1956 to reintroduce the possibility of a plurality of trade unions legally coexisting in any industry. This proposal was made in the hope of forcing the Peronists to share power with their non-Peronist rivals. For good measure, the same law prohibited all union involvement in politics. Law 14,455 of 1958, on the other hand, represented the newly elected Frondizi's desire to maintain his alliance with Perón.[35] This law restored single union representation (as in 1945), but with the added twist that such exclusive recognition should go to that group with the numerically largest number of dues payers.[36] Accordingly, the state lacked any legal room for maneuvering: if the Peronists were the largest, they had to be recognized. The government was forbidden from interfering in internal union affairs. In the absence of any specific ban on union political activity, the legal interpretation was that it was perfectly acceptable.[37] Trade union political involvement was once again outlawed in 1966 with Regulatory Decree 969 passed by a labor-harassed Illia Radical Party government, but first implemented by General Onganía in 1967. Strikes in protest of military policy were declared illegal on these political grounds, with the offending unions subject to attachment of their bank accounts and suspension or withdrawal of their official status. In 1966 the military government also introduced compulsory binding arbitration (Decree 16,936).[38]

Returning to power after 17 years, the Peronists modified the existing 1958 legislation with Law 20,615 of 1973, strengthening the power of national labor leaders at the expense of local ones, and of the latter over the rank-and-file.[39] The length of union office terms were extended and the convoking of a special assembly or congress made more difficult. The law reintroduced the possibility of a national-level federation "intervening" or taking over a local-level union. Under normal conditions, union leaders were given special protection against criminal charges.[40] Of special note was the authorization for unions to take political stands, including the endorsement of specific political parties or candidates.[41] In the hands of conservative CGT leaders willing to support the Peronist government's policies, the 1973 law was used to limit strike activity and to oust radical elements from particular unions.[42]

Although the military government that came to power as a result of the 1976 coup was clearly unhappy with existing Peronist labor legislation, it took well over three years to agree upon a new law. When enacted, law 22,105 of 1979 formally dissolved the intervened CGT, but left open the possibility of a replacement. The unions were deprived of control of their welfare services and were forbidden to engage in profit-making activities or to receive outside funds. As a means of ensuring central government control, the Ministry of Labor was given extensive powers to intervene in key aspects of internal union affairs. The constitutionally endowed right to strike which had been suspended by Law 21,261 of 1976 was never specifically mentioned. Finally, unions were categorically forbidden to engage in politics in any form.[43] The delay in the formulation of the law suggests that important differences of opinion existed within the military, especially concerning the future possibility of any nation-level confederation and minority representation within individual unions.[44] As one observer put it, the 1979 law sought to turn the unions into "organizations sufficiently strong to contain autonomous [worker] mobilization, but weak enough to avoid being an institutional political presence."[45] Despite the return to democracy in late 1983, the military law remained on the books until 1988 due to the inability of the Peronist unions and the Radical Government to reach agreement on the form of something more suitable.[46]

Government Labor Strategies
In all recent administrations, labor strategy has been an adjunct of the role given to wages amid the general economic program. As populists, the Peronists sought to combine the initial anti-inflationary price–wage freeze of the 1973 Social Pact with subsequent adjustments allowing the share of national income going to workers to gradually increase to the record level achieved in 1954.[47] Such a strategy used the increase in domestic demand to fuel rapid economic growth.[48] With the advent of conservative Peronists under Isabel Perón following her husband's death in 1974, the attempt to reverse the existing pro-labor bias of the government ultimately led to an open political confrontation with the unions and the collapse of price stabilization efforts. In the ensuing recession, wage levels began to drop.[49] Upon seizing power in 1976, the very conservative military imposed a major income reconcentration at the expense of the work force. An initial wage freeze accompanied by price decontrol greatly accelerated the drop in buying power begun at the end of the Peronist government. Thereafter, real wages were allowed to fluctuate, generally reflecting the level of inflation. They recovered somewhat from late 1978 through 1980, only to plummet again subsequently.[50] In addition to the changes in average wages, the military consciously increased wage differentials by job skill and between industries. While such action was justified in the name of increased productivity, it also had the effect of dividing the working class.[51] Under the Radicals, government policy has embodied a new populism tempered by

TABLE 2.1
Wages and Salaries as Percentage of National Income (1935–80)

Government	Years	%	%Δ
Various	1935–46	41.6	—
Perón	1947–49	47.6	+6.0
Perón	1950–55	49.2	+1.6
Aramburu (military)	1956–57	44.6	−4.6
Frondizi (UCRI)	1958–62	40.2	−4.4
Illia (UCRP)	1963–66	40.5	+0.3
Onganía (military)	1967–70	45.2	+4.7
Levingston (military)	1971	46.6	+0.6
Lanusse (military)	1972–73	45.6	−1.0
Various (Peronist)	1974–75	46.9	+1.3
Videla (military)	1976–80	35.6	−11.3

Sources: 1935–49 and 1972–80, Alvaro Orsatti, "La nueva distribución funcional del ingreso en la Argentina," *Desarrollo Económico* (October–December, 1983), pp. 316–317; 1950–71, Roberto Lavagna, "Distribución del ingreso e inversión," *Desarrollo Económico* (April–June, 1978), p. 141.

the exigencies of the debt crisis and inflationary pressures. The early priority given to improving real wages and reactivating the economy led to a huge inflationary surge. With the emergency Austral Plan of June 1985, Argentina returned to price-wage controls (as under the Peronists), but ones accompanied by more orthodox anti-inflationary tools. Later changes in the program led to erosion of real wages followed by protest and what appear to be temporary increases.[52]

The data on income and real wages provided in Tables 2.1 and 2.2, respectively, are arranged so that the impact of the significant political changes of recent years can be easily seen. If by 1974, wages and salaries recovered almost to the level of the previous Peronist regime, they would plummet to record lows under Videla.[53] Alfonsín, in turn, sought to compensate for the 1981–1982 collapse, but has had difficulty maintaining such earning power.

TABLE 2.2
Indices of Real Income, 1980–86 (1983 = 100)

Economic Activity	Military Government			Alfonsín Government			
	1980	1981	1982	1983	1984	1985	1986[a]
Private Manufacturing	107	97	83	100	126	110	116
Private Services	120	113	92	100	119	113	116
Private Construction	—	79	67	100	126	86	76
State Enterprises	120	112	85	100	113	103	117
Public Administration	106	104	83	100	122	94	95

Source: Ministerio de Trabajo, 1986.
[a] = January–March only.

The treatment of labor by each of the most recent Peronist, military, and Radical governments reflected the historic relationship these governments developed with the trade unions. While in office prior to 1955, Perón had thoroughly dominated the unions; during his lengthy exile, however, he found that labor leaders like Augusto Vandor used his absence to develop a considerable degree of independence. The Aramburu and Onganía military governments differed in their treatment of the unions. While the former alienated most of the work force by seeking to eradicate all aspects of Peronist influence, the latter showed some flexibility in supporting individual Peronist figures not openly challenging military authority so as to gain their aid in moderating workers' demands. The politically weak Illia Radicals used government supervision of trade union elections to harass the Peronists, but grudgingly accepted their domination of the labor movement.[54] Since the overall balance of power changed relatively little in the years to come, quite similar patterns of state-labor relations reappeared with each group's return to power.

With a new Peronist government in power, Perón was able to secure the support of a previously unreliable CGT leadership for the 1973 Social Pact. Aware that labor leaders would be subject to rank-and-file pressure to exceed government wage limits, he modified the Law of Professional Associations to strengthen the national leadership administratively vis-à-vis militant local groups of workers.[55] A provision for compulsory arbitration passed by the Onganía military in 1966 (Law 16,936) was retained as being useful for worker discipline, and the Internal Security Law was used to ban factory occupations. Labor was asked for temporary restraint on wages, patience that was rewarded with the 1974 Work Contract Law which provided for strengthened job security.[56] After Perón's death, the uneasy power equilibrium that emerged between conservative Peronist politicians led by presidential confident José López Rega and the "62"-controlled CGT soon broke down. The attempt by the former to force the unions to accept an orthodox price stabilization package in mid-1975 ended in a government crisis which a weak Isabel Perón was unable to control. Mrs. Perón's total loss of authority in the face of the unions' temporary triumph set the stage for a military takeover.[57]

After the 1976 coup, the new military government relied on coercion and fear to try to ensure labor's subordination to a new conservative order based upon sharply increased inequalities. The CGT and a number of the larger unions were immediately intervened, as in 1955. Many union leaders were arrested and hundreds of labor militants were murdered. In the same vein, the right to strike was indefinitely suspended (Law 21,161) and work slowdowns or economic sabotage were made punishable with lengthy jail sentences (Law 21,400). Additionally, the government used its authorization in Law 8,596 to reduce the public sector work force by some 200,000 people.[58] Clearly determined to crush all labor resistance, some of the officers led by Labor Minister General Horacio Liendo made discreet overtures to those union leaders willing to accept the new politics, seeking to coopt them with promises of relatively favorable treatment.[59] Until the military regime began to openly disintegrate in 1981–1982, it kept labor weak by depriving it of financial resources like the social welfare funds traditionally administered by the unions and by encouraging division of unions into rival blocs. With the decision after the Malvinas/Falklands War defeat to return power to the civilians, the military began to allow internal union elections and to prepare for the normalization of the CGT. At the same time, the ban on strikes, which by this point was only selectively enforced, was now formally overturned.[60]

Alfonsín's triumph over the Peronists in the October 1983 elections marked a reversal of previous fortune between the nation's two largest political parties. To Radicals like Germán López who remembered the labor hostility encountered in the earlier Illia government, the Peronist unions' unrestrained economic power seemed a dangerous threat to the new democracy. Following up on his politically effective criticism of labor in the 1983 election campaign, Alfonsín made an unsuccessful attempt to have the new Congress dilute Peronist control of the unions by allowing minority representation in union elections to be directly supervised by government appointees rather than the incumbents.[61] Although the president subsequently sought to make partial amends to the angry unions by replacing the anti-Peronist minister of labor with someone more conciliatory and, eventually, even a Peronist, his government found a residue of considerable union ill will and suspicion. Such feelings compounded Alfonsín's difficulty in persuading labor to cooperate with the Radical program of using wage restraint as an ingredient in fighting the serious inflation problem. Relations between the Radical government and the Peronist unions – whether at the tripartite Economic and Social Conference or prior to the threat of a new general strike – were often strained.[62] Each side seemed to be using the occasion to win public opinion rather than to resolve particular differences. Relations between the Radical Party controlled state and the trade unions seemed to have a built-in highly confrontational element, given the different interests each wished to maximize. Nevertheless, not all of the trade unions were equally militant in the face of a government willing to make amends to at least some of the Peronist incumbents in the interest of obtaining labor peace.

Trade Union Responses

The political behavior of organized labor has varied sharply depending on whether or not Peronism was in power. As part of the Peronist government in 1973–1974, a fairly united CGT leadership saw little alternative but to support official policy. Such leaders had the difficult task of mediating between the economic demands of the average worker for higher income and the needs of the administration to restrict inflation.[63] Given the existence of various leftist dissidents of a much more militant perspective, Peronist union leaders could ill afford to totally ignore rank-and-file wishes. Once unions became part of the opposition in 1976, the earlier unity rapidly disappeared. Repeating the experiences of the Onganía period, labor divided into militants fighting the new military regime, collaborators seeking to work with the generals at almost any price, and those taking intermediate positions.[64] With the return to democracy under the Radical Party government in late 1983, labor divisions continued, if slightly beneath the surface. This time divisions in the union movement corresponded principally to those found in Peronism as a whole, the reformers versus the old-line elements, with a middle group gathered around the figure of CGT General Secretary Saúl Ubaldini.[65] Each of the three experiences outlined here is discussed in more detail below.

The responsibilities of supporting a Peronist government in 1973 came hard for defensive-minded trade union leaders conditioned by almost 18 years in the opposition.[66] Faced by the wage restraints of the Social Pact signed in their name by CGT head José Rucci, they pressed continuously for modifications in the schedule of wage adjustments. The results of such changes were corresponding pressure for price hikes and, ultimately, the virtual collapse of the price-wage freeze in the face of increasingly widespread cheating.[67]

The behavior of the union leadership can be explained as the result of what was happening at the individual factory level. In the early months of the Peronist government, large numbers of workers mobilized to select more representative factory delegates who could seek ways around the official restrictions on wages. The pressure generated by strikes and sit-ins was enormous. Part of what was occurring was a challenge to the legitimacy of the national-level leaders who, under the previous military regime, had collaborated in government efforts to contain workers' demands.[68] Where such criticism of the existing labor leadership was made by militants of leftist political views, Peronist control of the unions was seen as potentially in danger. Upon Perón's return to the presidency, the CGT leadership focused its efforts on seeking to use the new administrative tools available to oust radical dissidents while simultaneously demonstrating concern for rank-and-file economic interests. Gaining results such as the large wage "catch-up" of March or the extra half *aguinaldo* of June (both 1974) could temporarily strengthen the position of the nation's labor bureaucracy.

Labor's conflict in 1975 with the López Rega-led Peronist right wing reflects similar origins. Coming on top of the dramatic increases in prices

TABLE 2.3
Strikes under Peronism, 1973–1976[a]

Year	Total	Total/Month
1973[b]	214	30.6
1974	330	27.5
1975[c]	300	25.0
1976[d]	65	21.7

Source: Adapted from Elizabeth Jelin, "Conflictos laborales en la Argentina, 1973–1976," *Estudios Sociales,* 9 (1977), p. 46.
[a]   Figures include only specific strikes, *not* mass street demonstrations. Figures provided by ILO (*Yearbook of Labour Statistics,* 1978, p. 622) were considerably higher where available – 1974 = 543, 1975 = 1266 – but may include at least some mass demonstrations.
[b]   July–December only.
[c]   Excludes first 9 days of July when entire country was virtually paralyzed by mass demonstrations. Even so, monthly average for July/August = 33.0.
[d]   Only up to March 24, the date of the coup.

for government services and gasoline imposed in June, Mrs. Perón's refusal to accept wage levels agreed to in the national labor-management negotiations set off a wave of spontaneous demonstrations and strikes. The strike figures found in Table 2.3 show a return in mid-1975 to the high-level activism of the first 12 months in office. The July decision to try to force the government's hand in the first general strike ever declared by labor against a Peronist government was merely a recognition by a hesitant CGT leadership of a rank-and-file fait accompli.[69]

The new ascendancy of the trade unions that came with the ouster of López Rega accomplished little, because of a fragmented government and a deteriorating economy. In the face of runaway inflation, the periodic wage increases conceded could only offer temporary relief. But the image of a weak government at the mercy of the trade unions did do one thing: it convinced the military of the need to act politically to end what to them was an unacceptable situation.

The smaller unions not intervened after the March 1976 coup sought unsuccessfully throughout the year to negotiate as a body with the military government over questions like salaries, the release of political prisoners, the return of control over social welfare funds, and new internal elections. Frustrated by the lack of response to their overtures, in the course of 1977 individual unions began to dare the harsh repression by challenging government policy. The principal vehicle for such criticism was the Commission of 25, formed in March of that year.[70] By April 1978 with the creation of the rival *Comisión de Gestión y Trabajo* (soon to be renamed the National Labor Commission, or CNT), organized labor had split. Based upon the intervened unions, the CNT represented those union leaders willing to cooperate with the military; the "25" would be

TABLE 2.4
Strikes under Videla Military, 1976–1980

Year	Total
1976[a]	89
1977	100
1978	40
1979[b]	188
1980	261

Source: Vencer, 8 (May–June 1981), pp. 6–7.
[a] April–December only.
[b] Does not include the general strike of April 27.

openly confrontational. After first unsuccessfully attempting to launch the political Peronist Labor Movement as a replacement for the banned "62 Peronist Organizations," the leaders of the "25" organized the first general strike against Videla since the protest immediately following the coup, on April 27, 1979. In addition to the usual complaints about low wages, a clear focus for resentment was the long delayed new version of the Law of Professional Associations. The strike was ruthlessly crushed with great use of force.[71] As is suggested in Table 2.4, the calling of the general strike marked the resurgence of a considerable level of worker resistance.

Continued labor militance under the direction of the "25" and its successor organizations (a renewed CGT, the CGT Brasil [an Argentine group named after the location of its offices on Calle Brasil], and the CGT of the Argentine Republic) only proved effective once the military regime began to unravel after the Malvinas/Falklands surrender in June 1982. Up until that point, the less militant union leaders of the CNT – later renamed the *intersectorial* – and the CGT Azopardo insisted on the possibility of negotiations with the government rather than supporting acts such as the general strike of July 22, 1981, or the street demonstrations of November 7, 1981, and March 30, 1982.[72] With General Galtieri's ouster as President, the days of the military in power were numbered. The weak Bignone transitional government that followed made major wage concessions to avoid a general strike called by the moderates for September 23. Labor pressure grew with the successful general strikes of December 6, 1982, March 28, 1983, and October 4, 1983, each jointly sponsored by the two major labor groups.[73] A consequence of the military's new political weakness was the increasing coalescence of the trade unions. Just prior to the October 1983 elections, the two major trade union groups announced plans for their unification in a single CGT, an action that took place in January 1984 after the civilian government was in place, and then with four separate General Secretaries sharing power.[74]

The leaders of the Peronist-dominated CGT reacted defensively to what they saw as the hostility of the new Alfonsín Radical government. A reason for the precarious CGT unity finally achieved was the need to effectively fight the new administration's proposed "democratic" union election law, a measure labor denounced as an effort by the Radical-dominated state to restrict its autonomy.[75] Relying on a legislative coalition dominated by Peronist votes in the Argentine Senate, CGT leaders were able to block what threatened their party's control of most unions.[76] In a subsequent compromise, labor and government negotiated a mutually acceptable election law (Law 23,071 of 1984), thus eventually permitting the completion of trade union normalization begun by the military.

In the months to come, worker income became a major issue for organized labor. In this context, Saúl Ubaldini, one of the four principal CGT leaders, became increasingly prominent. Having in the military period emerged as the head of the more confrontational unions, Ubaldini ended up as exclusive CGT general secretary. His militance reflected a heightened rank-and-file mobilization that seemed reminiscent of the early days of the last Peronist government.[77] He used the threat of national strike action to pressure the government into maintaining wages eroded by rapid inflation. Over the next several years, the number of general strikes called by the CGT rose, peaking in 1986 before a partial decline the following year (one in 1984, two in 1985, four in 1986, three in 1987).[78]

As is suggested by the figures on ordinary strikes for the period 1984–1987 found in Table 2.5, the rising militance of the CGT's leadership was not totally endorsed by the rank-and-file. The strike figures for both 1985 and 1987 represent a considerable decline from those in 1984 and 1986, respectively. One explanation for these drops relates to the economic recessions of late 1984/July 1985 and that beginning in the second half of 1987. In such instances, strike activity seemed related to the fear of unemployment as joblessness in 1985 and 1987 hit levels exceeding that of the recession of 1981.[79]

TABLE 2.5
Strikes under Alfonsín, 1984–1987[a]

Year	Total
1984	717
1985	344
1986	563
1987	398

Sources: 1984 from El Bimestre, 19 (January–February 1985), p. 15; 1985–1986, Héctor Palomino, "Los conflictos laborales de 1986," El Bimestre, 31 (January–February 1987), p. 11; 1987, "Los conflictos laborales de noviembre–diciembre de 1987," El Bimestre, 36 (November–December 1987), p. 20.
[a] Does not include general strikes.

The union leaders were divided over how to respond to Alfonsín's policy of strategic, limited concessions to wage demands. While Ubaldini's allies were supportive of his policy of continuing periodic general strikes to force across the board concessions, a number of the larger industrial unions led by metal worker leader Lorenzo Miguel, the head of the revived "62" and a major figure from the orthodox Peronism of the early 1970s, urged negotiation with the government. Not too surprisingly, these were the unions that had done reasonably well on their own in gaining wage increases. In between were many of the members of the "25", now largely associated with the reformers, or *renovadores*, in the Peronist Party.[80] Although the unions were formally united at the CGT "normalizing" congress of November 1986 where a joint slate of officers equally divided between the three major groups was presented, individual unions close to Miguel were content to undermine Ubaldini's bargaining position through their own direct negotiations with employers and with the government.[81]

In April 1987, many of those in the CGT unhappy with what they felt was Ubaldini's unnecessarily aggressive leadership created a new union faction, the "15". Supported by the Miguel-led "62" unions, the "15" signed a pact with the Alfonsín government, promising to forego confrontation in return for direct negotiations. In return, the Radicals committed themselves to the repeal of the 1979 Law of Professional Associations, free wage bargaining in *paritarias* from 1988, and union input into the management of the social welfare funds. With Carlos Alderete, a pro-"15" labor leader and an acknowledged Peronist, named as minister of labor, such an agreement was meant to seriously undercut the position of Ubaldini in the CGT.[82]

But such a government-labor pact raised more expectations than it could satisfy. In numerous internal cabinet disputes over wage levels, Alfonsín invariably ended up supporting the Economics Ministry's policy of strong wage restraints as part of efforts to contain inflation. As a result, real industrial wages in 1987 were allowed to erode, falling some 13.4 percent in the 12 months ending November 1987.[83] Efforts to replace the 1979 military-imposed Law of Professional Associations were repeatedly delayed due to strong differences of opinion between the CGT and the government and between labor and management on the contents of the new legislation.[84] While the government finally did agree (Decree 1,420 of August 1987) to restore free collective bargaining for the private sector, suspicions were common as to whether informal or formal maximums would be imposed when the *paritarias* finally met again in 1988.[85] If all of the above were not enough, the overwhelming Radical government electoral defeat in the September 1987 elections for the Chamber of Deputies and governorships knocked the final props out from under what remained of the labor-government pact agreed to seven months earlier.[86] From then on, organized labor began to look increasingly to Antonio Cafiero, the newly elected governor of Buenos Aires province and the then presumed Peronist presidential candidate in the 1989 elections when a successor to Alfonsín will be chosen.[87]

The Future

The Argentine labor movement has changed in terms of its makeup. Once based largely on the industrial sector, it has become considerably less so given the relative shift in employment away from manufacturing into services. In the same sense, the electoral loss suffered by Peronism in 1983 at the national level has been mirrored in an increased political fractionalization in the recent internal union elections. The effects of these changes will be felt in the immediate future.

The labor market in Argentina has changed dramatically in recent years. Between 1960 and 1980, the portion of the work force employed in manufacturing fell from 36 to 28 percent; in the same time period, the share of those with jobs in services rose from 44 to 59 percent.[88] While some of this shift in employment has been long-term in nature, some reflects the particular economic policies of the recent Videla government when the opening of the domestic market to foreign industrial goods accentuated the closure of many marginal firms in the manufacturing sector.

The changes in the relative availability of jobs has had the effect of altering the balance in the size and, hence, in the importance of individual trade unions. As is suggested in Table 2.6 which provides data on 20 of the largest unions, the period between 1973 and 1984 has seen an expansion of membership in service sector unions at the expense of those in manufacturing.[89] While the largest single union, the metalworkers – the union of Lorenzo Miguel and, before him, José Rucci and Augusto Vandor – did grow, other industrial blue collar unions like the auto and textile workers showed significant decline. Decline was even more pronounced for construction unions, although the fall in numbers was probably more temporary in nature due to the particular stagnant stage of the economic cycle in 1984. On the other hand, several service sector unions (banking, health, and sports, for example) made major gains in membership which presently appear to be permanent changes. Interestingly, these latter are all essentially white collar unions. Such middle class unions are likely to be less solidly Peronist in their political loyalties than those made up of the more committed working class trade unionists.

If labor remains heavily Peronist, it is less monolithically so than it once was. In late 1984 and early 1985, a series of internal union elections took place under compromise Law 23,071 worked out between the Peronist leaders and the government. What was unusual about these

TABLE 2.6
Changes in Size of Union Membership, 1973–1984
(in 1000's and as Percentage of 20 Largest Union Subsample)

	1973		1984		
	#	%	#	%	Δ%
A. Industrial Unions (N = 8)					
Metals (UOM)	270	(14.7%)	287	(16.4%)	+1.7
Construction (UOCRA)	260	(14.2%)	110	(06.3%)	−7.9
Autos (SMATA)	121	(06.6%)	54	(03.1%)	−3.5
Textiles (AOT)	110	(06.0%)	74	(04.2%)	−1.8
Meat	65	(03.5%)	70	(04.0%)	+0.5
Clothing (FONIVA)	60	(03.3%)	37	(02.1%)	−1.2
Petroleum (SUPE)	45	(02.5%)	45	(02.6%)	+0.1
Food	30	(01.6%)	40	(02.3%)	+0.7
TOTAL, Industrial		(52.4%)		(41.0%)	−11.4
B. Service Sector Unions (N = 12)					
State (UPCN)	180	(09.8%)	133	(07.6%)	−2.2
Railroads (UF)	168	(09.2%)	142	(08.1%)	−1.1
Banking (AB)	84	(04.6%)	186	(10.6%)	+6.0
State (ATE)	70	(03.8%)	80	(04.6%)	+0.8
Municipal (UOEM)[a]	70	(03.8%)	65	(03.7%)	−0.1
Transport (UTA)	60	(03.3%)	50	(02.9%)	−0.4
Restaurant	55	(03.0%)	80	(04.6%)	+1.6
Light & Power	53	(02.9%)	58	(03.3%)	+0.4
Health	42	(02.3%)	98	(05.6%)	+3.3
Telephones (FOETRA)	40	(02.2%)	40	(02.3%)	+0.1
Postal (FOECYT)	35	(01.9%)	40	(02.3%)	+0.4
Sports (UTEDYC)	16	(0.09%)	60	(03.4%)	+2.5
TOTAL, Services		(47.6%)		(59.0%)	+11.4

Source: 20 union subsample taken from sample of 42 unions found in Alvaro Abós, *Los sindicatos argentinos: Cuadro de situación, 1984* (Buenos Aires: Centro de Estudios para el Proyecto Nacional, 1985), p. 78.
[a] = Buenos Aires only.

elections, in contrast to those of the 1960s and the 1970s, was the relatively large number of cases with one or more opposition tickets competing and the frequent presence of electoral alliances between mainstream Peronists and leftist Peronists, Radicals, and/or Socialists. Victories of nonincumbent slates were much more frequent than in earlier years, although most of the top leaders elected were calling themselves Peronists.[90] This upsurge of challenges to existing leaders was seen as reflecting anti-bureaucratic feelings and resentment against individuals (in some instances last elected in 1974).[91]

The continuing control of the Argentine labor movement by various Peronist leaders reinforces the fundamental long-term ties between the unions and the party. The unions will continue to provide the major organizational component of what increasingly has become a labor party. Nevertheless, the party probably cannot count on the automatic total support of all such Peronists since experience suggests that the most important union leaders have always been quintessential power maximizers. Given their individual calculations of the realities of the short-term future, they will decide if their interests dictate a de facto accommodation with an incumbent Radical government, active support for a viable rival Peronist presidential ticket, or even a possible alliance with dissatisfied military officers in a situation of a weakening democratic regime. What such a conclusion implies is that in the absence of a strong Peronist government, individual union leaders will remain divided beneath the surface unity provided by their common Peronist label.

Whatever the strategy of individual leaders, the behavior of the past suggests that key elements of a divided Argentine union movement will continue to fight hard to maintain labor's traditionally strong autonomy from state control, an autonomy that has survived repeated efforts at cooptation or repression, and one which seems quite exceptional in the Latin American context. If Argentine labor leaders are realists who know when immediate resistance to state authority may be totally futile, they are aware that such a strong state has historically been evanescent; labor quiescence or pacts with the government have been traditional short-term survival tactics prior to the reemergence of a renewed labor-based Peronism facing a once again divided state.

NOTES

1. The term used by Perón to describe the trade unions was "the backbone" (*la columna vertebral*) of Peronism.

2. Torcuato Di Tella, "Stalemate or Coexistence in Argentina," pp. 249–263 in James Petras and Maurice Zeitlin eds., *Latin America, Reform or Revolution?* (Greenwich, CT: Fawcett, 1968); Juan Carlos Portantiero, "Clases dominantes y crisis política en la Argentina actual," pp. 73–117 in Oscar Braun ed., *El capitalismo argentino en crisis* (Buenos Aires: Siglo XXI, 1973); and "Economía y política en la crisis Argentina: 1958–1973," *Revista mexicana de sociología*, 39:2 (1977), pp. 531–565.

3. Guillermo O'Donnell, "State and Alliances in Argentina, 1956–1976," *The Journal of Development Studies*, 15:1 (1978), pp. 3–33.

4. Roberto Carri, *Sindicatos y poder en la Argentina* (Buenos Aires: Editorial Sudestada, 1967); "Sindicalismo de participación, sindicalismo de liberación," pp. 137–182 in Norberto Ceresole ed., *Argentina: estado y liberación nacional*

(Buenos Aires: Organización Editorial, 1971); Alberto Bialakowsky and Arturo Fernández, "Sindicatos y autoritarismo," *CIAS, Revista del Centro de Investigación y Acción Social*, 32:326 (1983), pp. 55–63.

5. Edward Epstein, "Control and Co-optation of the Argentine Labor Movement," *Economic Development and Cultural Change*, 27:3 (April 1979), pp. 445–465.

6. Marcelo Diamand, *El péndulo argentino: ¿Hasta cúando?* (Buenos Aires: CERES, 1983).

7. Edgardo Catterberg, "Las elecciones del 30 Octubre de 1983: El surgimiento de una nueva convergencia electoral," *Desarrollo económico*, 24:98 (1985), pp. 258–267.

8. Samuel Baily, *Labor, Nationalism, and Politics in Argentina* (New Brunswick: Rutgers University Press, 1967), pp. 71–84; Santiago Senén González, *El sindicalismo después de Perón* (Buenos Aires: Editorial Galerna, 1974), pp. 51–61; Joseph Page, *Perón, A Biography* (New York: Random House, 1983), pp. 63–72.

9. Page, p. 150; Eduardo Crawley, *A House Divided, Argentina 1880–1980* (New York: St. Martin's, 1984), p. 106; Robert Potash, *The Army & Politics in Argentina, 1945–1962* (Stanford: Stanford University Press, 1980), p. 45.

10. Other small pro-Peronist groups included the FORJA (Force of Radically-Oriented Argentine Youth, a group of middle class nationalist intellectuals associated with the Radical Civic Union) and the ultra-conservative Nationalist Liberation Alliance or ALN (Page, p. 139).

11. *Ibid.*, p. 139.

12. Crawley, pp. 102–105; Potash, 15–46; Eldon Kenworthy, "Did the 'New Industrialists' Play a Significant Role in the Formation of Perón's Coalition, 1943–1946?" in James Scobie ed., *New Perspectives on Modern Argentina* (Bloomington: Indiana University Press, 1972), pp. 21–22.

13. Manual Mora y Araujo and Ignacio Llorente eds., *El voto peronista* (Buenos Aires: Editorial Sudamericana, 1980), part 1.

14. Hugo Gambini, *El peronismo y la iglesia* (Buenos Aires: Centro Editor de América Latina, La Historia Popular 48, 1971); Potash, pp. 177–180.

15. Senén González, p. 71.

16. Page, pp. 214–216, 228–229.

17. Page, pp. 252–253; Crawley, p. 145.

18. Crawley, pp. 149, 158.

19. Juan Carlos Torre, *Los sindicatos en el gobierno, 1973–1976* (Buenos Aires: Centro Editor de América Latina, 1983), pp. 22–23.

20. Marcelo Cavarozzi, *Sindicatos y política en Argentina* (Buenos Aires: CEDES, 1984), pp. 81–83.

21. The 1962 election results precipitated Frondizi's ouster shortly afterwards. Those of 1965 probably played a similar role in inspiring Illia's overthrow the next year. See O'Donnell, *Modernization and Bureaucratic-Authoritarianism*, pp. 166–199.

22. Crawley, pp. 299–307; Francisco Delich, *Crisis y protesta social* (Buenos Aires: Siglo XXI, 1974); Beba Balvé, Miguel Murmis, Juan C. Martín, Lidia Aufgeng, Tómas J. Bar, Beatríz Balvé, and Roberto Jacoby, *Lucha de calles, Lucha de clases* (Buenos Aires: La Rosa Blindada, 1973).

23. Crawley, pp. 316–343.

24. O'Donnell, *1966–1973, El estado burocrático autoritario* (Buenos Aires: Editorial del Belgrano, 1982), p. 324.

25. Epstein, "Inflation and Public Policy in Argentina," *Boletín de estudios latinoamericanos y del caribe* [CEDLA, Amsterdam], 43 (December 1987), p. 84.

26. Crawley, pp. 371, 374, 395; Page, pp. 449, 475, 493.

27. Guido Di Tella, *Argentina Under Perón, 1973–1976* (London: Macmillan, 1983), pp. 68–83; Liliana De Riz, *Retorno y derrumbe* (México, D.F.: Folios Ediciones, 1981) pp. 113–144.

28. O'Donnell, "Las fuerzas armadas y el estado autoritario del cono sur de América Latina," in Norbert Lechner ed., *Estado y política en América Latina* (México, D.F.: Siglo XXI, 1981), pp. 211–215.

29. Crawley, p. 444.

30. Torre, p. 17.

31. See the establishment of equally divided labor-management national wage negotiation commissions, or *paritarias*, set up under Law 14,250 of 1953, but frequently suspended (Senén González, pp. 78–79).

32. Guillermo López, *Derecho de las asociaciones gremiales* (Buenos Aires: La Ley, 1980), p. 57.

33. Carri, p. 29; Rubén Zorrilla, *Estructura y dinámica del sindicalismo argentino* (Buenos Aires: La Pleyade, 1974), p. 103.

34. Zorrilla, p. 67.

35. Torre, p. 25.

36. For a discussion of non-Peronist union opposition to this point, see Cavarozzi, pp. 111–115.

37. López, pp. 57–58.

38. Carri, pp. 139, 149. Previously, there had been voluntary arbitration introduced by Frondizi in Law 14,786 of 1958. See Senén González, *Diez años de sindicalismo argentino de Perón al proceso* (Buenos Aires: Corregidor, 1984), p. 20, n. 10.

39. Elizabeth Jelin, "Conflictos laborales en la Argentina, 1973–1976," *Estudios Sociales*, 9 (1977), p. 17.

40. This special *fuero* would be declared unconstitutional in 1976 (López, p. 59).

41. For the text of all provisions, see Enrique Got ed., *Nueva ley de asociaciones profesionales* (Buenos Aires: Ed. Antorcha, 1975).

42. Bernardo Gallitelli and Andrés Thompson, "La situación laboral en la Argentina del 'proceso,' 1976–1981," p. 186 in their edited work, *Sindicalismo y regímenes militares en Argentina y Chile* (Amsterdam: CEDLA, 1982); Senén González, *Diez años de sindicalismo*, p. 32.

43. For a copy of the text and a commentary, see López.

44. Senén González, *Diez años de sindicalismo*, pp. 118, 122.

45. Delich, "Después del diluvio, la clase obrera," p. 143 in Alain Roquié ed., *Argentina, hoy* (México, D.F.: Siglo XXI, 1982).

46. A Law of Professional Associations (Ley 23,551) was finally passed in early 1988, replacing the one imposed in 1979 by the military. The new version represented compromises between the Radicals and Peronists which would limit national union intervention in locals to what was authorized in individual union statutes. It also allowed unions to administer their own welfare funds (*obras*

sociales) and, because it didn't specifically ban it, presumably permitted unions to participate in partisan politics. See Héctor Palomino, "Ley de asociaciones sindicales," *El Bimestre*, 38 (March–April 1988), pp. 14–16; *Review of the River Plate*, April 21, 1988, p. 305.

47. The Social Pact of 1973 was an official attempt to gain the formal support of both the CGT (representing labor) and the *Confederación General Económica*, representing domestic capital, to support a two-year wage-price freeze (Epstein, "Inflation and Public Policy," pp. 7–11).

48. Poder Ejecutivo Nacional, *Plan trienal para la reconstrucción y la liberación national* (Buenos Aires: República Argentina, 1973), pp. 13, 20–21.

49. Torre, pp. 131–136; Guido Di Tella, p. 76.

50. Roberto Frenkel, "Salarios industriales e inflación: El período 1976–1982," *Desarrollo Económico*, 23:95 (1984), pp. 13–14; Adolfo Canitrot, "Orden social y monetarismo," *Estudios CEDES*, 4:7 (1983), p. 28.

51. Delich, "Después del diluvio," p. 138; Ronaldo Munck, "Restructuración del capital y recomposición de la clase obrera en Argentina desde 1976," pp. 194–195 in Gallitelli and Thompson eds., *Sindicalismo y régimenes militares en Argentina y Chile*.

52. Frenkel and José María Fanelli, "Del ajuste caótico al Plan Austral: Las políticas de estabilización recientes en la Argentina" (Buenos Aires: CEDES, 1986), pp. 13, 30–34, 49.

53. But note the low unemployment maintained for almost all of the Videla years.

54. Epstein, "Control and Co-optation."

55. Torre, pp. 53, 74.

56. Senén González, *Diez años de sindicalismo*, pp. 18–20; Jelin, pp. 25–26.

57. Guido Di Tella, pp. 74–79.

58. Gallitelli and Thompson, pp. 145–157; Delich, "Después del diluvio," pp. 137, 142–143.

59. Canitrot, "Teoría y práctica del liberalismo: Política antiinflacionaria y apertura económica en la Argentina, 1976–1981," *Desarrollo Económico*, 21:82 (1981), p. 170; Alvaro Abós, *Las organizaciones sindicales y el poder military, 1976–1983* (Buenos Aires: Centro Editor de América Latina, 1984), pp. 8–9; Senén González, *Diez años del sindicalismo*, p. 60; Arturo Fernández, *Las prácticas sociales del sindicalismo, 1976–1982* (Buenos Aires: Centro Editor de América Latina, 1985), pp. 68–69.

60. Senén González, *Diez años del sindicalismo*, pp. 83–101, 188–195.

61. *El Bimestre*, 12 (November–December 1983), pp. 116–17; 14 (March–April, 1984), pp. 50–51; Ricardo Gaudio and Héctor Domeniconi, "Las primeras elecciones sindicales en la transición democrática," *Desarrollo Económico*, 23:88 (1986), pp. 424, 429.

62. The Economic and Social Conference was used by Alfonsín to assemble representatives of the government, organized labor, and big business to discuss national economic and social policy. The meetings were often quite conflictual, with CGT walkouts not infrequent as a protest of what were deemed government ultimata (*Review of the River Plate*, May 21, 1986, pp. 389–390).

63. Torre, pp. 53, 63–65.

64. Bialakowsky and Fernández, pp. 60–63.

65. *Somos*, November 12, 1986, pp. 8–9.

66. Torre, pp. 146–147.

67. Juan Carlos de Pablo, *Economía política del peronismo* (Buenos Aires: El Cid Editorial, 1980), pp. 80–83, 89; Torre, pp. 95–96.

68. Jelin, pp. 12–18.

69. Torre, pp. 134–135; Jelin, pp. 31–32.

70. Abós, *Los sindicatos argentinos: Cuadro de situación, 1984* (Buenos Aires: Centro de Estudios para el Proyecto Nacional, 1985), pp. 10, 34.

71. Bialakowsky and Fernández, p. 61; Senén González, *Diez años del sindicalismo*, pp. 116–117; Abós, *Las organizaciones sindicales*, pp. 46–56.

72. Senén González, *Diez años del sindicalismo*, pp. 155–164.

73. *Ibid.*, pp. 180–187; Abós, *Las organizaciones sindicales*, pp. 90–93.

74. Abós, pp. 93–106.

75. An earlier attempt to unify the unions in the short-lived Unified Leadership of the Argentine workers (CUTA) founded in September 1979 had had common origin in the desire to fight the military trade union law then about to be introduced (Bialakowsky and Fernández, p. 61).

76. Héctor Palomino, "El movimiento obrero y sindical en una larga transición," *El Bimestre*, 26 (May–June 1986), pp. 16–17.

77. *Latin America Regional Reports, Southern Cone*, June 29, 1984, p. 6.

78. *Latin America Weekly Report*, September 7, 1984, p. 8; Palomino, "La normalización de la CGT," *El Bimestre*, 31 (January–February 1987), p. 11; "Los conflictos laborales de noviembre–diciembre de 1987," *El Bimestre*, 36 (November–December 1987), p. 20.

79. Palomino, "Una imagen cualitativa de los conflictos laborales," *El Bimestre*, 27 (May–June 1986), pp. 19–21; *Review of the River Plate*, February 19, 1987, p. 109; Norberto González, "Balance preliminar de la economía latinoamericana en 1987," *Comercio exterior*, 38:2 (1988), pp. 112–113.

80. *Latin America Weekly Report*, October 2, 1986, p. 9.

81. Palomino, "Los conflictos laborales de 1986," *El Bimestre*, 31 (January–February 1987), pp. 5–10; *Latin America Weekly Report*, July 24, 1986, p. 5; August 14, 1986; p. 5; and March 12, 1987, p. 10.

82. *Latin America Weekly Report*, April 9, 1987, p. 4.

83. *Review of the River Plate*, December 9, 1987, p. 460, citing figures from the National Institute of Statistics and Census, INDEC.

84. *Review of the River Plate*, August 20, 1987, pp. 133, 134; *Latin America Weekly Report*, March 24, 1988, p. 5.

85. *Review of the River Plate*, September 10, 1987, p. 189.

86. *Clarín*, September 7, 1987, p. 1; *La Razón*, September 7, 1987, p. 1; *Buenos Aires Herald*, September 7, 1987, p. 1.

87. Labor would divide later in its support for Cafiero with non-"renovador" unions led by Lorenzo Miguel ultimately supporting Carlos Menem, the eventual Peronist candidate. See *Latin American Weekly Report*, 9 June 1988, p. 8.

88. Agricultural employment also dropped sharply, from 20 to 13 percent of the work force. For sectoral employment figures, see World Bank, *World Economic Report, 1984* (New York: Oxford University Press, 1984), p. 259.

89. Two very large service sector unions not included in the original source but which also grew tremendously in the period were those for commerce and for

teachers, both middle class unions. For figures for these unions circa 1970, see Juan Villarreal, "Los hilos sociales del poder," p. 279 in Eduardo Jozami, et al., *Crisis de la dictadura argentina: Política económica y cambio social, 1976–1983* (Buenos Aires: Siglo XXI, 1985); for ones circa 1985, see *El Economista*, August 17, 1986, p. 10.

89. In 96.4 percent of the cases in the 1984–1985 internal union elections, Peronists of some variety headed the winning list (Gaudio and Domeniconi, p. 449).

90. Palomino, "El movimiento de democratización sindical," in Elizabeth Jelin (ed.), *Los nuevos movimientos sociales*, Vol. 2 (Buenos Aires: Centro Editor de América Latina, 1985), pp. 45, 47; Gaudio and Domeniconi, pp. 428–429, 440–441.

Chapter 3 ————————————————————————

Trade Unions in Brazil: A Search for Autonomy and Organization

Maria Helena Moreira Alves

The history of the organized labor movement in Brazil is marked by the continuous attempts of different governments to regulate and bring the unions under the direct control of the state.[1] Laws were enacted to give the state the right to manage union finances, to regulate elections, and even to prohibit certain forms of organization, such as a single national-level labor confederation. The principal goals were to encourage the development of union collaboration with state economic plans while, at the same time, discouraging class-oriented trade unionism. The union response was a constantly renewed effort to create stronger organization and a permanent search for autonomy from state manipulation and control.

In this chapter, I will analyze the trade union movement in Brazil by focusing on four distinct time periods that have shaped the development of Brazilian working class organizations: (1) The period of the *Estado Novo* – whose influence continues to the present day – when the first laws were enacted to bring autonomous workers' organization under state control; (2) the period between the fall of Getúlio Vargas (and the subsequent enactment of the 1946 Constitution) and the military coup of 1964 when workers were organized both in the official state-controlled unions and in a parallel structure of independent working class organizations; (3) the period beginning with the 1964 military coup, characterized by worker resistance, state repression of working class organizations, and the eventual development of the New Trade Union Movement after 1976; and, finally, (4) the analysis of the union movement in the period of transition from military to the civilian government of the New Republic begun in 1985, with the state attempting to maintain its established control over the unions. In this latter period, the semi-legal organizations created by the New Unions have generated such pressure upon the state that significant modifications seem likely, granting unions greater autonomy from official control.

THE *ESTADO NOVO* AND THE UNION MOVEMENT

By the end of the 1920s, the trade unions were increasingly active, organized in confederations with a strong class base. The basic characteristic of the movement was its autonomy vis-à-vis the state, with organizations set up, financed, and run entirely by the workers themselves. The size, strength, and duration of strikes impaired both economic production and exports. The 1929 crash and the subsequent depression in the United States had serious repercussions for the Brazilian economy, particularly due to the sharp fall of agricultural prices in international markets. In Brazil, the severity of the economic crisis led to political upheaval and an armed rebellion. Getúlio Vargas, the officially declared loser in the 1930 presidential elections, took over the reins of government via a coup d'état.

The Vargas government sought to develop a new labor policy aimed at decreasing the autonomy and mobilizational ability of the trade unions. The first regulatory measure was the creation of the Ministry of Labor which, in 1939, decreed the Trade Union Law (*Lei de Sindicalização*) giving the Ministry the right to check union finances every three months and require ministerial delegates to be present at all union meetings. The Ministry of Labor also prohibited unions from engaging in politics, from supporting political parties, or from becoming affiliated with international union organizations. Perhaps the most important and long lasting in terms of its future influence on the unions was the requirement that a union be officially recognized by the Ministry. Only one union would be recognized for any specific territory. In this manner, the government was able to curb the free and autonomous development of trade unions, isolating the Communists and Anarchists who had previously predominated at the leadership level. Most unions recognized by the government were created with the Ministry's own encouragement. This process of recognition thus led to the formation of so-called ghost unions, led exclusively by hand-picked government men known at that time as *amarelos* (yellow dogs) and more recently as *pelegos* (after the wool that covers the saddle to cushion the horse's footsteps – an allusion to those union leaders who seek to soften the confrontation between labor and capital).

The 1937–1945 Estado Novo inaugurated in Brazil a new philosophy of labor-capital ties which governs industrial relations to this day. The policy of the state was to implement a concept of "social peace and harmony" based upon direct "state mediation." The Estado Novo explicitly rejected class struggle and sought to create a society which would bring about social harmony with workers collaborating with both capitalists and the state. The objective of achieving "social peace" and "cooperation between classes" was central to government policy during this period. Vargas controlled social relations through the signing of hundreds of decree laws that granted recognition for demands often already conceded at the bargaining table. Hence, if a demand of a particular professional group was granted by the employers, it would be later extended by official decree to all the different professional trades.[2] Eventually, so as to increase the efficiency of the social benefit regulations, the government unified all laws into the Consolidation of Labor Law, or CLT. The CLT was enacted on November 10, 1943 and is still in effect.

"Social harmony" was also pursued through strict governmental control of union activities. The CLT contained a specific section to deal with the organization of trade unions. Section v regulates all matters pertaining to unions, officially subordinating them to the Ministry of Labor. Translated from Mussolini's *Carta del Lavoro* of 1927, this section establishes a strictly pyramidal format of organization meant to implement a corporatist orientation. Due to its fundamental and historical importance in the formation of Brazilian unions, and because it is still in effect, it is important to describe its most important features.

First, the principle of *uniçidade sindical* (or exclusive union jurisdiction) is one of the most effective mechanisms for state control of the unions. The Ministry of Labor is allowed to decide not only the territorial jurisdiction of particular unions, but also which political/organizational groups will be allowed to legally form a trade union. The effect of such power upon union freedom of organization can be demonstrated by examining the power it gives any government. The policy of all governments since the time of Vargas's Estado Novo was always to actively create small unions throughout the country. Once a trade union was organized with state encouragement, then all other working class associations and groups which were also attempting to organize a union in that locality automatically were prevented from achieving legal recognition, from representing workers, or from bargaining collectively. Hence, by preventively forming "ghost unions," governments effectively stopped more politically radical groups from legal organizing.

Second, there are three different levels of organization specified in the law: local-level unions, federations, and confederations. Workers elect delegates, however, only in the local unions. Each union, in turn, has two representatives in the federation representing its category, but only one vote. In the same way, each federation has one vote to elect the leaders of the confederation for that specific trade. Unions are thus separated by trade: each individual trade forms a local union. The federation of that trade groups all local unions of that category in any Brazilian state. All state-level federations, in turn, form the national confederation. This indirect form of election ensures greater governmental control over the federations and confederations because the local unions, regardless of the number of members affiliated, all have the same vote. This is where the Ministry of Labor's power to recognize unions and form ghost unions becomes important for control. To make it clear how it works to impede union autonomy and to curb their combativeness, take the example of the metalworkers, one of the most important and militant trades in Brazil today. The Metalworkers Union of São Bernardo do Campo has a membership of 120,000 workers, but it has the same voting representation in the State of São Paulo Metalworkers Federation as the Metalworkers Union of Mauá which speaks for less than 10,000 workers and only has about 500 formal members.

Third, the Ministry of Labor has the right to recognize unions as well as to cancel such legal status. It also has the right of intervention on the board of recognized unions, federations and confederations. Simply by issuing a decree, the Ministry of Labor may remove from office one or all elected officials of a union. According to the regulations of section v of the CLT, once removed from office, a trade union official became ineligible or legally barred from participating in any other official position in unions at any level. The term used, *cassado* (deprived of political rights), became a description for the act of summarily eliminating legitimate working class leadership from any representative post in any union organization. Interventions in unions by the Ministry of Labor became systematic forms of interfering in the organization of workers.

A fourth important mechanism for union control elaborated during the Estado Novo period was the enforcement of the single Trade Union Law (*estatuto único*) which establishes that a "union must act in collaboration with the government and all other civil associations so as to increase social solidarity. Professional or economic interests must be subordinated to the national interest." Through the estatuto único, the internal form of union organization is directly established by the state and must be entirely complied with by all unions under penalty of cancellation of registration.[3]

Fifth, the Ministry of Labor also directly controls the finances of unions and has the legal right to gain access to bank accounts and to scrutinize them, as well as to approve or disapprove union budgets. All union accounts must be submitted every year to the Ministry of Labor. The justification for such a high degree of financial and budgetary control of unions comes from the fact that most funds are from the special union tax, the *impôsto sindical*, which is equivalent to one day's wages from every salaried person in the country, regardless of whether or not the worker is unionized. This tax is directly deducted from the paycheck and goes to the Bank of Brazil. The Ministry of Labor then distributes the money to confederations, federations and trade unions in the following manner: 60 percent goes to local unions, 15 percent to federations, 5 percent to confederations, and 20 percent stays in a special Account for Employment and Salary controlled by the Ministry itself.

The law establishes in detail how union funds may or may not be spent. They may be spent for medical, dental, and legal assistance to members, for schools and libraries, for vacation resorts, for sports activities, and other special activities. Funds cannot be spent for financing a strike or setting up a strike fund, may not be given as financial contributions to political parties or candidates, and may not be used to finance any activity the Ministry of Labor defines as "social agitation." These budgetary constraints have not only curbed the possibilities of a more combative trade union movement, but, perhaps more significantly, have transformed trade unions in Brazil into welfare organizations far removed from the day to day activities of defending workers' rights, wages, and working conditions, while liberating the state from many welfare obligations.

Last, during the Estado Novo period a special Labor Court was created. According to the Labor Code, all collective bargaining agreements had to be negotiated between unions of workers and unions of employers. This process is known as *dissídio coletivo*, with every trade having a different time for such collective negotiations. The collective agreement defines the working conditions for the specific trade or profession, the minimum salary level for that trade, and the basic benefits. They are negotiated at the local level, and only when no local union exists does the federation negotiate such collective agreements. When no agreement is reached between the union and the employers, the case automatically goes to the Labor Court; it is the Labor Court, then, which has the final say in all collective agreements. The Labor Courts have been, since their creation, extremely vulnerable to pressure from organized interest groups and particularly from the government. Sometimes, even clauses which were previously agreed to at the negotiating table are later denied by the Labor Court when the employer decides to break the agreement. The Labor Court may declare, for example, the legality or illegality of a strike, or the importance of a particular union demand.

The power of the Labor Court to determine the illegality of strikes has been effectively used to curb the mobilization of workers. Once a strike is declared illegal by the Labor Court, police repression may be employed in the company by the employer, with workers being fired without any right of appeal. The continuation of a strike after the Labor Court has declared it illegal may also become the excuse for a governmental intervention in the trade union.

The end of World War II made it impossible for a government inspired by Mussolini's fascist ideas to continue to exist. The growing pressure of the population for democracy resulted in Getúlio Vargas' fall from power; the Estado Novo was officially ended with the promulgation of a liberal Constitution in 1946. However, the legislation pertaining to trade unions was not modified, while the Consolidation of Labor Laws remained in effect throughout the entire period of more democratic government that followed.

THE PERIOD FROM 1946 TO 1964

With the fall of the Estado Novo, the unions created a coordinating body, the *Movimento de Unificação dos Trabalhadores*, or MUT. The idea of the MUT already existed and was discussed clandestinely, but as soon as Luis Carlos Prestes, Secretary General of the Brazilian Communist Party, was set free from prison, the MUT was formally established. Subsequently the MUT would fight for the complete union freedom of organization, and repudiation of all the restrictions and interference in the life of worker organizations. The MUT would also struggle for internal democracy in the trade unions.[4] The program of the MUT contained a series of goals meant to form a new and freely organized trade unionism outside of state control: the sovereignty of union assemblies, and the removal from union premises of representatives imposed by the Ministry of Labor; elections and the taking of office of those elected independently of prior approval by the Ministry of Labor; autonomy of administration and the elimination of state controls over union funds and budgets; and the end of the Ministry of Labor's single statute requirement. In essence, the MUT was born as the first movement parallel to the official union structure. At the same time, however, it did not question all of the regulations in the Labor code. For example, unionists then accepted the basic structural organization of trade unions and the existence of the union tax that would leave organized labor dependent on the state.

Stimulated by the economic program of the Juscelino Kubitscheck government, the industrial expansion of Brazil in the 1950s increased the size and influence of the industrial labor force. The trade union movement went through many years of rapid organization with a large number of victorious strikes organized both within the official trade union structure as well as parallel to it, utilizing a variety of coordinating bodies created so as to unify the actions of the different types of workers. Besides the numerous economic strikes, workers became more politically oriented, pressuring for governmental, economic, and social reforms. In 1962, workers organized the *Comando Geral dos Trabalhadores*, or CGT, and the *Confederação Nacional dos Trabalhadores Agrícolas*, or CONTAG. The latter marked the beginning of union organization in the countryside. The organization of rural workers increased in the 1960s, with the formation of the peasant leagues across the country.

During this populist period, the working class had a contradictory relationship with the state and the armed forces. During the government of João Goulart, the CGT worked closely with the state while, at the same time, organizing strikes of increasing intensity to create pressure for basic economic and social reforms. The CGT fought for a greater democratization of state power, for restrictions on foreign investment, for limits on the repatriation of profits abroad, for a deeper participation of the state in the economy itself (with the takeover of corporations to bring them under state control), and for an agrarian reform.

During the 1945–1964 period, unions organized in a climate of tolerated freedom, something which ought not to be confused with structurally-based autonomy. When it was in the interest of the state, different governments still made use of the mechanisms of control embedded in the CLT. For example, in 1949 during the government of Eurico Dutra, 234 unions were intervened by the Ministry of Labor. The populist governments which followed sought less intervention by the Ministry of Labor. Nonetheless, all of them continued to manage the finances and budgets of unions and coopt working class leadership to collaborate with the state. No government during this period made any efforts to modify section v of the CLT so as to grant autonomy and freedom of organization to working class trade unions.

In terms of the unions themselves, the basic contradiction of the CGT was that it existed as a parallel central organization outside of the official union structure; even though it was never legalized, it never questioned the Labor Code or fought for reforms which would truly grant labor the freedom of organization. The alliance of trade unionists with the reformist government of João Goulart in the early 1960s in support of a program of structural economic and social reforms was ephemeral, and insufficient to stop the growing rightist conspiracy which led to the 1964 military coup. The most important lesson from this populist period for the unions has been to avoid organizational arrangements which are limited to alliances between leadership at the top and disconnected from the vast base of workers inside the factories. Because the CGT was mostly concerned with such top-level interconnections and paid limited attention to organizing inside the plants, it did not have the mobilizational power which would have been necessary to stop the military coup. When the time came to call a general strike in support of democracy and the elected Goulart government, few localities were sufficiently organized in the factories to bring forth the necessary mass resistance.

THE PERIOD OF MILITARY RULE: REPRESSION, EXPLOITATION, AND THE BIRTH OF A NEW TRADE UNION MOVEMENT

Raising the Rate of Exploitation

During the more democratic period from 1945 to the 1964 military takeover, the most restrictive measures included in the CLT were not fully enforced. Working class organizations, both in urban and rural areas, were able to thrive on conditions of de facto autonomy in the parallel system outside of the official trade unions. They organized associations such as the peasant leagues and trade union centrals like the CGT which ignored the prohibitions of the Labor Code. The organization of workers during this period moved beyond strictly economic demands to more generally defined political struggle in support of fundamental economic and political change in Brazilian society. Although growing rapidly, the union movement was not sufficiently strong to survive the violent repression that followed the 1964 military coup.

As soon as the military came to power in 1964, they made full use of all the mechanisms for control and repression contained in the Labor Code as specified in section v of the CLT. Interventions became very frequent. During the first months of military rule, union offices were occupied by army troops, and hundreds of union leaders were arrested, tortured, or forced either underground or into exile. Interventions were established by executive decree, sometimes with the justification that the officials of the union had "disappeared" or were in "an unknown locality." Between 1964 and 1979, there was a total of 1,202 interventions in trade unions, 78 cases of legal removal from office (*destituição*), the cancellation of 31 different elections and the dissolution (that is, the cancellation of registration) of a total of 254 trade unions.[5]

In addition, the military made use of the Ministry of Labor's power to form unions, to recognize or cancel certain unions' official status, and to remove union officials from office. The estatuto único provided the military with a tool to directly control the form of union organization; those which refused to comply entirely were threatened with having their registration cancelled. In short, all of the mechanisms of control historically present in the CLT were utilized by the military governments after 1964 to weaken the existing unions, to create new obedient ones, and to control all labor activity.

This enforced silence enabled the successive military governments to pursue highly exploitative economic and social policies, thus ushering in a distinctly new period in the working class struggle and trade union organization. The civil-military coalition which took power in 1964 had the explicit goal of using mechanisms of control strong enough to ensure the full compliance of the working class. The economic model pursued extremely rapid rates of capital accumulation with a consequent high rate of labor exploitation. Wages were cut through a combination of three policies.

1.   A series of laws were enacted to control wages. At first, the controls were limited to state-owned companies, but soon the system was extended throughout the entire economy. Collective bargaining over salaries was prohibited, with wage increases to be determined by a simple executive decree. A complicated formula to calculate the index of salary increases was developed so as to tie percentual increases to the rate of inflation. Wages were pegged to the consumer price index (INCP) which was officially set monthly by the government statistics department. Since the INPC hardly ever reflected the actual level of inflation, real wages were constantly eroded across the board. A study conducted by the Inter-Union Statistical Department (DIEESE – *Departamento Inter-sindical de Estudos Estatísticos e Socio-Económicos*) calculated that during the period immediately following the implementation of these "belt-tightening laws," many workers suffered salary losses of more than 30 percent.[6] The salary loss was particularly severe during the "miracle" years of high economic growth in 1973 and 1974. At that time, the governmental statistical department manipulated the cost of living figures, causing an additional salary loss of up to 34.1 percent for some professional groups. The minimum salary has been decreed by the federal government in Brazil since 1959. Taking 1959 as the base year, DIEESE published a study analyzing the yearly loss of real purchasing power of the minimum salary; by 1976, the minimum salary had only 31 percent of the purchasing power it had in 1959.[7] Such practices had a tremendous impact upon trade union organization because unions were prohibited from negotiating wages, being forced, even more noticeably, into a purely welfare role.

2.   The military governments changed the regulations which established job security guarantees for those with more than ten years in a firm and which prevented indiscriminate firing of workers. The Time-in-Service Guarantee Fund (*Fundo de Garantia por Tempo de Serviço*, or FGTS) was established in 1966. Supposedly voluntary for workers who were free to choose the job loss indemnity plan to which they wished to belong, in reality there was not much choice. Those workers who did not choose the FGTS were simply not hired. This fund was available to all companies for indemnity payments when workers were fired. Hence, the actual new cash allocation which had to be disbursed by companies during periods of massive layoffs was insignificant given that such funds had already been collected. It became a matter of policy for corporations to fire hundreds of workers just prior to the yearly salary increase and hire others at the lower base-pay for those now with no seniority. Those workers fired by one company would often be hired by another to do the

TABLE 3.1
Brazilian Income Distribution Among the Economically Active Population,
1960–1980

| | | Years | |
Population Groups	1960	1970	1980
20% Poorest	3.9%	3.5%	2.8%
50% Poorest	17.4%	14.9%	12.6%
10% Richest	39.6%	46.7%	50.9%
5% Richest	28.3%	34.1%	37.9%
1% Richest	11.9%	14.7%	16.9%

Sources: Instituto Brasileiro de Geografia e Estatística (IBGE), Demographic Censuses of
1960, 1970 and 1980, as reprinted in *Boletim do DIESSE*, Edição Especial, April 1983, p. 3.

same job at a much reduced wage level. Therefore, the yearly indexed
wage increase decreed by the government was often applied upon a
lower base-salary than the worker had been receiving. The combination
of salary control laws and the high labor-force turnover allowed by the
FGTS program caused a progressive lowering of salary levels in all
trades. The salary policy was one of the principal reasons for the
increased level of exploitation that supported the high percentage
growth rate of the Brazilian economy, particularly during the so-called
economic miracle years.

The inequality in Brazilian income distribution is one of the most
pronounced in the world. Social inequality is not simply a result of
income distribution for it also results from the inequality in opportunities
in education, in access to public health systems, and social benefits
programs. Social inequality is also affected by the distribution of wealth
and the concentrated control of capital. Nonetheless, statistical data on
income distribution is an important indicator of the general pattern of
social inequality. The 1960–1980 period was marked by an extreme
process of personal income concentration, as seen in Table 3.1. Such
figures are indicative of the process of income distribution among the
working population where the poorest, with each decade of military rule,
received less of the total income, while the richest 10 percent increased
their percentage control of total income from 39.6 percent in 1960 to 50.9
percent in 1980. Income statistics in Brazil also measure the distribution
by taking as a base the minimum salary. Hence, the pattern of distribution can be measured by how many people among the economically
active population receive less than the minimum salary or, on the other
extreme, up to 20 times its value. In 1980, at the time of the last complete
census, the huge range among the salaried workforce was revealed by
the fact that 12.5 percent of the economically active population received
less than half a minimum salary; 20.8 percent received a monthly income

in between one-half and one full minimum salary (hence, were not paid even what the law establishes as the minimum for subsistence); and at the other extreme, 1.5 percent (largely executives and administrative personnel) received more than 20 times the value of the minimum salary set by the government at that time.[8]

In addition, the lack of job security guarantees also profoundly affected the possibility of trade union organization. Because of the FGTS plan, it was easier for corporations to periodically have massive layoffs because there were no penalties and no indemnity payments to be made. The FGTS plan freed companies to rotate the labor force so as to prevent salary increases. Massive firings would, of course, also eliminate the jobs of union leaders and corporations began to distribute "black lists" so they would not be rehired by other firms in the area. Particularly in areas where multinationals concentrated investment – such as in the automobile and the chemical industries – this process of labor force rotation became a powerful tool both for maintaining low wages and for "union busting." Often the threat of mass firings was enough to prevent workers from engaging in union activities. The lack of strong unions, in turn, tended to facilitate a situation of extremely high rates of labor exploitation.

3. Finally, the military governments were extremely careful to regulate the right to strike in such a manner as to make it practically impossible for workers to fulfill the requirements for a legal strike. Decree Law 4,330 of July 1, 1964 practically prohibited strikes altogether except in clear cases where workers had not been paid for more than three months. The law also established areas of the economy whose workers are considered "essential" such as garbage collectors, hospital and pharmacy workers, firemen, police, public employees, teachers, and even bankworkers. These sectors are strictly prohibited from striking under any circumstances, and are severely repressed if they disobey the law.

The Birth of the New Trade Union Movement:
A Fight for Autonomy
Organization from the Base. For many years, union activists debated which was the best strategy of organization to pursue. Even though many believed that it would be best to organize outside of the official trade union structure set up by the section v of the CLT in the period of the Estado Novo, the conditions of extreme repression under military rule made such a course now almost impossible. The unionists who organized outside of the official union structure basically kept to mobilizing clandestinely inside the work plants. They secretly formed the first factory committees. These forms of representation met with consistent resistance from employers and severe repression from the military government. In spite of this, these clandestine activities eventu-

ally reached such a level of underground growth that they became practically a parallel trade unionism. These groups, connected to union leaders in exile, also began to infiltrate the official trade unions, slowly developing union opposition groups that fought government-controlled officials in internal union elections. Hence they followed a two-part strategy, becoming – particularly after 1974 – a source of continuous rank-and-file mobilization and constantly emphasizing the need for union leaders to improve the quality of worker representation in the plants. Such activity was particularly common among the urban pro-letariat concentrated in the large multinational-run factories set up in Brazil in earlier decades.

The trade unionists organized the *Oposição Sindical* (Union Oppo-sition) movement and began to win elections in important trade unions. The group of new, combative, and politically active officials that emerged became known as the *Auténticos* or Authentic Unionists. Most of their effort was devoted to struggling to reverse state interventions, to win elections in unions, to form new associations, and to fight for recognition of those unions which were organized by more representative leader-ship. Though difficult and, at times, very limited in its accomplishment, such a strategy began a process of consciousness-building for workers which really began to show results after 1977 when the Union Opposition together with its auténtico leaders formed a sufficiently cohesive move-ment to become a major political actor.

The New Trade Union Movement began to act more openly in 1977. DIEESE, the technical services department of the unions, discovered and provided proof of the government's manipulation of official cost of living statistics. The military government eventually admitted this manipu-lation, particularly for the years of 1973 and 1974. Since salary raises were all calculated according to the inflation rate, this manipulation of cost-of-living statistics had led to a salary loss calculated by DIEESE at 34.1 percent. The Metalworkers Union of São Bernardo do Campo, now with a new auténtico President, Luis Inácio da Silva (or Lula as he was called), instituted a formal legal complaint against the federal government. The Union Opposition militants and the auténtico group of union officials mobilized their members in a series of demonstrations, rallies, and other actions meant to attract public attention. They demanded the immediate reimbursement for all workers in Brazil of the salary loss. The "Campaign of the 34.1 percent" was to develop into one of the first nationwide union activities to break the silence imposed by the violent repression in force after the enactment of Institutional Act 5 in 1969.[9] The actual percentage demands for each job category varied, but many different unions organized to demand a salary raise in compensation for the loss due to the manipulated statistics. The movement, however, went beyond economic salary demands to raise a series of questions about working conditions and trade union rights. The great mobilization of the metal-workers, in particular, publicized the problem of anti-worker repression inside the plants, including some cases of a police presence at the assembly line. Here the movement sought to join economic demands with the struggle for democratization in the workplace and an end to the military dictatorship.[10] The public action suit of the metalworkers of São Bernardo do Campo and the "Campaign of the 34.1 percent" showed the latent potential of organization of the working class and, hence, encouraged workers to adopt more aggressive positions in defense of their own interests. They were further encouraged by their ability to extract from the military government 10 percent as an anticipated salary raise.[11]

While the New Trade Union Movement erupted with the strikes of 1978, it is important to emphasize that its occurrence was the result of a long process of worker resistance inside the factories. Here the metal-workers of São Bernardo do Campo played a particularly important role since the 1970s, organizing in the multinationally-controlled automobile plants against the difficult working conditions, the lack of job security and the massive layoffs, and the repression inside the factories. In this process of resistance, workers of various categories made use of many, sometimes highly creative, forms of struggle. Each mode of resisting received a symbolic code name: "Operation Turtle" (slowdown); "Popcorn Strike" (stopping different sectors of the assembly line at different times); "Operation Lightning Bolt" (rapid strikes throughout the entire factory); "Silence Operation" (where workers would cross their arms in silence for a few minutes); or "Operation Sabotage" (where parts of the product would be left out). These actions meant to disrupt production without allowing management sufficient time to call in the police and/or appeal to the Labor Courts. These forms of resistance developed worker consciousness about the general process of production and brought them increasingly into direct conflict with capital. Hence, the strikes of 1978 were the end product of underground resistance inside the factories, coupled with the organizational work of the Union Opposition and the Authentic Unionists within the general historical context of a struggle for democracy.

Mass Strikes and the Struggle for Union Autonomy. The strikes of 1978 began in May when the metalworkers of São Bernardo do Campo walked off their jobs. Workers organized in all plants with the code name "Arms Crossed: Machines Stopped." One day, thousands of workers of Saab-Scania went into the plant, stood by their machines, and simply crossed their arms in silence. They were soon followed by workers at Ford and at Volkswagen. Within a week, there were 60,000 workers on strike.[12] The mobilization expanded throughout the country with amazing rapidity. Within a few days, workers were crossing their arms in all major plants of the industrial cities of São Paulo and Osasco (in São Paulo state) and, shortly after, in Belo Horizonte and Contagem (in Minas Gerais). Other professional groups soon followed the example and the strikes mushroomed in different industries for the rest of the year across the entire country.

Both the government and the auténtico union leaders themselves were surprised at the sudden strength of the strike movement. In most cases, the strikes were spontaneously organized by workers in the factories. Some of the more committed auténtico-led unions immediately took responsibility for the strike, as was the case, for example, with the Metalworkers Union of São Bernardo. This consolidated the leadership role of Lula who was often called upon to help organize the strikes in other states. When a specific local union refused to aid the strikers who were out on wildcat strikes, members of the Union Opposition often took over. This process greatly increased the legitimacy both of the rank-and-file militants of the oposição sindical and of their auténtico leaders allowing the two to work together to develop what would emerge as the New Trade Union Movement. The strikes of 1978 developed character-istics which were in marked contrast to traditional company-based strikes of short duration. Workers consistently utilized the tactics of "arms crossed: machines stopped." Thus, in each case, workers took over the factory, stood by their machines, and silently refused to work for as long as the strike lasted. The force of the movement pressured manage-ment to negotiate directly with workers, with different agreements being reached directly between union and management. Even though this was legally prohibited, in practice, the unions began to negotiate salary questions directly with management, without the interference of the national government or the Labor Courts. In terms of an overall struggle for autonomy, this was perhaps the most significant achievement of this strike period. The second most important result was to force owners of capital and the government to accept strikes as part of labor relations.[13] Furthermore, the New Trade Union Movement was greatly strengthened in the process of the struggle, learning to quicken its capacity to mobilize, to organize networks of support inside and outside the movement, and to tighten the ties between leadership and rank-and-file. The process of direct negotiation with capital taught unionists to bypass restrictive labor laws. In practice, a new kind of industrial labor relations was created within many companies. Slowly, the movement succeeded in imposing upon management more democratic labor relations, often breaking with the strict limitations sought by the government. One of the by-products of the strike was the increased space for trade union organizing inside the plants.

During the year 1979, the strike movement was considerably expanded, taking on a decentralized organization through its integration with other popular movements in society. The strikes of 1979 spread to all states in the country and mobilized other industrial workers as well as professional sectors such as bank workers, teachers, sugar cane workers, workers in commerce, and public employees. This was the year of greatest strike mobilization up to that point in Brazilian history with a total of 430 strikes involving 3,271,500 strikers.[14]

The 1979 strikes were characterized by vast assemblies of thousands of workers who gathered daily to discuss the ongoing movement and to make collective decisions in open voting. This was particularly true in São Bernardo, where the assemblies of metalworkers in the Vila Euclides Football Stadium often gathered 100,000 workers. In 1979, the government reacted with more severe repression, intervening directly in the local metalworkers unions in São Bernardo do Campo, Santo André, and São Caetano.[15] In spite of the repression, however, the movement was strong enough to demand, and obtain, the return of the cassado leaders (including Lula) to the union. For the first time since 1964, the military were forced to revoke an intervention and return the union to its legitimate leadership. This was a significant achievement for the New Trade Union Movement in its search for autonomy from the state.

In 1979, the differences between the auténticos and the conservative official trade unionists allied with the government became more pronounced as a result of two historic events. In November, the metalworkers of São Paulo went out on strike. The strikers could not count on the support of their union or its president, Joaquim dos Santos Andrade. Only those within the oposição sindical supported the strike movement. Weakened by lack of support from their own union, workers organized spontaneously in the factories of São Paulo. The federal government reacted with violence and repressed the picket line, a move resulting in the shooting death of Santo Dias da Silva, one of the most important Catholic union organizers. Santo Dias was a much loved member of the Union Opposition, and his death widened the gap between the new unionists and the more traditional sectors connected to Joaquim dos Santos Andrade and the official union structure. Another important event contributed to the ideological definition of the New Trade Union Movement in its resistance to the official bureaucracy: the increasing mobilization of the *Partido dos Trabalhadores* (PT), the Workers Party. Some of the most important union leaders of the country were directly involved in the process of building the PT. Lula became its president and worked to link unionists, progressive political leaders, and intellectuals in a political party that could channel the major demands of the New Trade Union Movement.

In 1980, another important strike occurred among the metalworkers of the ABC region. This strike turned into a veritable war between the workers and their union on one side, and the military government on the other. The strike began in Santo André, São Bernardo, and São Caetano, but received the support of metalworkers in the industrial districts of the interior of São Paulo as well. The major demands included the establishment of a 40 hour work week, a 100 percent raise in overtime payments, job tenure guarantees, and the formal recognition of the right to in-the-plant representation through shop stewards. The strike was carefully prepared by the Metalworkers Union of São Bernardo do Campo. There were over 300 meetings per factory to set up the basic organizational structure for the strike. Workers elected a mobilization committee made up of 400 representatives from all major business corporations which worked side by side with the leadership board and a union salary committee of 16 members in charge of running the strike. The salary committee was elected so as to replace the official union leadership board in case the government decided, once again, to intervene and remove the legitimate leaders from office. In the case of arrest of the leadership, these intermediate leaders were to take over the organization of the strike movement. The strike of 1980 attained two other important achievements for the overall union movement: workers set up a flexible structure of organization with direct representation of the rank-and-file, and strikers developed a vast network of strike support throughout the country. It was in 1980 that the New Trade Union Movement discovered its potential for unified mobilization with neighborhood committees in working class areas and with church-related organizations throughout Brazil. A strike fund was formally established and people organized in the different states to obtain political and material support for the strike in São Bernardo do Campo. Opposition politicians interceded with the federal governments to end repression of the picket lines. Money, food, and medical supplies were donated by workers in all states, which set up regional strike funds of support and shipped the goods to São Bernardo as a sign of the widespread support for the strike. Even rural day-laborers, perhaps the most impoverished of the working class in Brazil, participated in the strike fund to demonstrate their solidarity. The hierarchy of the Catholic Church openly supported the strike and turned the churches over to workers for assemblies and for the organization of the strike funds.

The solidarity achieved built a stronger base for the renewal of a union movement set on finding its own path to autonomy. It was not strong enough, however, to avoid a temporary setback after the violent intervention of the army and the military police finally ended the strike. The federal government employed close to 5,000 men to run the repressive operation aimed at breaking the back of the New Unions. The Metalworkers Union of São Bernardo do Campo was surrounded by troops and the leadership was removed from office. The union remained under intervention for almost one year until workers reorganized to win another election with a slate supported by Lula. All large corporations (except Termomecânica, a Brazilian-owned firm) maintained a united common front, refusing to negotiate the slightest union demand. They worked closely with the government during the repressive operation, supplying blacklists of leaders to be persecuted and arrested, sometimes taken from their homes or from inside churches. The strike was declared illegal. São Bernardo looked like a war zone, with armored vehicles parked in conspicuous places and heavily armed military police or army soldiers guarding the occupied union headquarters and surrounding the churches to prevent workers from assembling. Even helicopters were used to demobilize and crush the strike movement. Lula and 18 other top leaders were arrested and charged under the National Security Law with the crime of organizing an illegal strike. In spite of the violence of the repression, the strike continued, culminating with a huge demonstration of approximately 120,000 metalworkers in the Vila Euclides Stadium on May 1.

May 1, 1980 is an important moment in the history of the New Union Movement. The hierarchy of the Catholic Church, so as to demonstrate its total support for the strikers, celebrated a mass in the Cathedral of São Bernardo do Campo. Approximately 10,000 assembled around the Cathedral to follow the mass which was being broadcast through loudspeakers. Helicopters circled above and armored vehicles were parked in a ring just beyond the area. Suddenly, different groups of workers began to arrive from all streets and the crowd slowly grew to close to 100,000 people. The workers formed another ring around the military. They intended to break the circle and join those who were caught between the troops and the Cathedral. Tension increased as workers silently watched the troops and then began to shout slogans asking the soldiers not to obey their repressive orders.[16] The workers began to sing songs of the resistance while the Church hierarchy and opposition politicians negotiated with the army command. Finally, the troops began to withdraw from the square to the applause of the thousands of workers still gathered in the area. The crowd formed a long march of an estimated 120,000 people singing resistance songs and walked throughout the city until reaching the Villa Euclides Stadium. This was the first time that a direct order of the military government was disobeyed by those in the immediate command of the troops.

Nevertheless, ten days later, workers voted to go back to work. They had suffered a bitter defeat in economic terms because none of their demands had been met and the corporations deducted from salaries all the lost strike days. The union was under intervention and approximately 5,000 workers were laid off in reprisal for the strike. In spite of this setback, the 1980 strike became an important landmark because workers gained experience and tightened their organization among the rank-and-file.[17] As a union leader mentioned, "The strike was like a great school and served to convince us that if we do not take our own destiny into our hands no one is going to do it for us."[18] The defeat of the metalworkers in São Bernardo deeply undermined the union movement elsewhere, with the number of strikers in 1980 significantly decreasing in relationship to 1979.[19]

After 1981, Brazil went into a deep economic recession which seriously affected all workers. There were massive layoffs in all major corporations and unemployment grew rapidly throughout the country. This directly weakened the unions' capacity for mobilization and organizational maintenance. According to DIEESE, from April to June of 1981, there were approximately 800,000 workers unemployed, plus an estimated one million underemployed in the metropolitan region of São Paulo alone. These workers lived in a situation of extreme poverty since no unemployment compensation program existed.[20] The massive unemployment evidently had its repercussions in terms of workers' capacity to organize large scale mobilization as a public protest.

At this point, the union leadership began to evaluate the experiences of the recent past, reaching the conclusion that it was of utmost priority to expand union rights. The strategy change allowed unionists to devote more attention to organization inside the factories. During the period of economic crisis, unionists turned inward, worked more effectively in committees within the plants (such as on health and safety committees), and vigorously pursued every avenue to expand union representation. Most efforts were dedicated to forming elected factory committees and to reaching agreements with management in which shop stewards were given job protection.[21]

It should be pointed out here that the historical context favored a strategy to slowly expand the right of having autonomous union representation in the plant. The intense mobilization of society against the authoritarian government had had repercussions among employers who began to recognize that industrial relations in Brazil were too inflexible. Given that this total inflexibility was disruptive of production, many capitalists realized that a somewhat more democratic form of labor-management relations was needed. It should also be emphasized that although the workers suffered from the effects of the economic crisis, their power of mobilization, particularly in the industrialized ABC region, was by no means diminished. This point was made clear to employers through a variety of actions in protest against the massive layoffs in the wake of the important confrontation at Volkswagen. Workers had been on strike to demand a 40 hour week. Volkswagen decided to accept the reduction of the weekly workload but linked it to a 20 percent reduction in the salary of its São Bernardo employees. To support its proposal, the company presented a petition with 22,000 signatures. Alleging that these were obtained under pressure, the Metalworkers Union of São Bernardo suggested that a plebiscite be held to properly establish employee views. Somewhat surprisingly, the plebiscite was held, with the company's proposal losing by a large majority of votes. This was the first time in Brazilian history that a corporation agreed to hold secret elections to resolve a polemical labor issue. The events of Volkswagen were to open the door to many other gains in direct worker-management negotiations.

Increasingly after 1981 and 1982, the search for autonomous forms of organization led to the establishment of factory committees in industrial zones or committees for the representation of employees in other economic sectors. Numerous strikes were held to pressure management to recognize the right to union representation and the freedom to organize inside companies. In 1981, Ford recognized the union as a bargaining agent and formally accepted a factory committee. In 1982, workers elected a 28-man factory committee to handle grievances and to negotiate directly with the Human Relations Department of Ford.[22] This was the first case of union representation inside the plants. The recognition of shop stewards and of factory committees was formalized in legal agreements registered as civil contracts. In this manner, the New Union Movement began to build a de facto autonomous union structure for the organization of workers in their workplaces. These forms of rank-and-file organization, in turn, provided not only a direct contact between the unions and workers in the plants but, perhaps more importantly, became a crucial place for on-the-spot leadership training. Union activists gained experience while working in factory committees or on health and safety committees. Once a factory committee was established and an agreement legally registered in the courts, those elected to office were to benefit from job tenure for the period of their term in office and for up to one year thereafter. This job security, in turn, helped to increase the future number of workers who dared to become active in the union, as well as preventing actual leaders from being fired.

Because of these significant gains in organizing inside the plants, the New Union Movement grew rapidly throughout the years of 1982 and 1983. Different strike actions were held both inside the factories and, in a coordinated manner, with external professional unions. Perhaps the most significant of these was the strike of the petrochemical workers in Paulínia (São Paulo state) and Mataripe (Bahia) which led directly to the first general strike in Brazil since the military coup of 1964. Petrochemical workers organized a five-day strike to protest against the enactment of Decree Law 2,036 which had annulled many of the benefits they had achieved in previous years. The strike in both states was violently repressed, with the military government intervening in both unions. In solidarity, other workers went out on strike, including the chemical workers, bus drivers, glass workers, and the metalworkers of São Bernardo. In the ABC region alone, over 100,000 workers joined the solidarity movement which ended with another intervention in the metalworkers union of São Bernardo do Campo. These events culminated in a 24-hour strike in July 1983 against the economic policies of the government which involved over three million workers throughout the country.[23] This time, workers entirely ignored the interventions in the three unions, allowing their cassado director to organize strike actions thus creating an almost de facto parallel and autonomous union movement. It is interesting to note that the strength of this New Union Movement inside the plants became so significant that the multinational companies began to unofficially recognize its leaders and to negotiate directly with them for contracts which would later be ratified by the government-appointed administrators of the intervened unions. Thus, the multinationals were acknowledging that workers would respond only to agreements signed by their legitimate leadership. Therefore, as a result of their tight organization at the level of the rank-and-file inside the factories, workers were able to guarantee the de facto functioning of their union even during periods of official governmental intervention.

The Creation of Rival National-Level Union Centrals. By 1980, activists in the New Trade Union Movement already realized the importance of building an autonomous central organization to coordinate the activities of all trade unions. What stood in their way, as already mentioned, was the explicit prohibition in the CLT of any single national-level central labor organization which would directly undermine the corporative, purposely divisive, nature of the existing legal union structure. Hence, the building of such a central union had to be the result of organization activity outside the official union structure, in direct defiance of the wishes of the military government. Members of the New Trade Union Movement met secretly several times to discuss the founding of the Central Workers Union (*Central Unica dos Trabalhadores*, or CUT). Inter-union coordination grew with the strikes in different professional groupings throughout 1979 and 1980. Finally, a first national meeting was organized in August of 1981 in Praia Grande, São Paulo. This First National Conference of the Working Class (*Conferência Nacional das Classes Trabalhadoras*, or CONCLAT) was held in precarious conditions, under direct threat of repression by the military and with no funds or lodging for those attending. The conference took place in an empty building still under construction with delegates sleeping on the ground covered with newspapers. Over 5,000 delegates attended, representing 1,092 unions or associations from all regions in the country. All political tendencies were represented and a preliminary committee was selected to work towards founding a central union.[24]

During this first conference, the debate over the trade union structure revealed two deeply divided groups of opinion among unionists. Both tendencies favored a reform of the trade union legislation so as to guarantee freedom of organization and autonomy from the state. The combined authéntico and Union Opposition sectors defended some form of organization open to input from the rank-and-file, proposing to form a union central "from the base up." The structural makeup of the new unions, as well as the central, was to be highly decentralized and collegiate so that the rank-and-file could participate directly in decisions. They also proposed that members of the opposition within official unions be accepted as delegates representing their trade. With the development of a second current of opinion more closely linked to the existing official unions, a compromise agreement between these conservatives and members of the new union movement was discussed. Some of the latter had been state interventors and were now trying to re-establish some sort of legitimacy for themselves. Such was the case, for example, of Joaquim dos Santos Andrade, president of the Metalworkers of São Paulo and a highly controversial figure among workers. The Communist Party, during this first conference, formed an alliance with dos Santos Andrade, defending the notion that rank-and-file delegates of the Union Opposition not be allowed to represent their unions in future congresses or in the central. The two groups differed also in their proposals for the reform of labor legislation, with the group supported by the Communists defending a reform which would diminish, but not abolish the influence of the state. The auténticos leaders and the members of the Union Opposition, in turn, defended total autonomy from the state, going so far as to propose the elimination of the automatic union tax, which they maintained was an umbilical cord that linked the trade unions dependently to the Ministry of Labor.

The divisions among the two groups deepened in the course of the next few years. The Central Union of Workers or CUT was officially founded in the First National Congress of the Working Class, held in São Bernardo do Campo, São Paulo, between 26 and 29 August 1983. The end result of two years of organizational work by the pro-CUT Committee, this founding congress of the CUT had been called by delegates representing both major union groups. Nevertheless, at the last minute, agreement broke down as the allied sectors from the more traditional unionists and the Communist Party split. The reason the dissenting group gave for this formal split was that they felt that a union structure so openly challenging the wishes of the military might serve as a pretext which hardline officers could use to undermine the policy of President João Figueiredo of a gradual political liberalization. They proposed – and still argue – that a social pact should be negotiated between labor and the government to guarantee Brazil's peaceful transition from military rule.

In November 1983, the dissenting group held a separate congress in Praia Grande, São Paulo, to form a rival to the CUT, what became known as the National Coordination of the Working Class (*Coordenação Nacional da Classe Trabalhadora*, or CONCLAT). While the CONCLAT currently represents close to 9 million workers since it includes most of the official trade unions, it lacks a confederal structure as a union central in most states. The CONCLAT does not emphasize rank-and-file participation, so its deliberative congresses do not include representation from the base. Only recently, in March 1986, did CONCLAT apply for formal recognition. When it obtained legality, CONCLAT changed its name to the General Workers Central (*Central Geral dos Trabalhadores* or CGT).[25]

In contrast to the CGT, the CUT places great emphasis on guaranteeing internal democratic space for political debate. As a consequence, it has created a full gamut of organizations at every sub-national level, all of which have input into a national congress charged with all the major decisions on program and strategy. Leaders are elected at each level, with various political tendencies having a voice through a system of proportional representation. The CUT represents over 12 million workers and is organized in every Brazilian state.

The mobilization power of the CUT is particularly effective because of its format of organization which decentralizes activity to the local units, being particularly active in the workplace. This base-upward organizational format has enabled the CUT to exert mass political pressure for reforms of the union structure in its continued search for autonomy. This mass base has become particularly relevant in the period of transition from military rule in which the CUT plays a significant role as a political actor.

The year 1984 has become a part of Brazilian history characterized by the huge mobilization of the population in the "Campaign for Direct Elections for President." The political opposition to the military government – including prominent participation by both the CUT and CGT – organized a series of demonstrations in every major city of 100,000 people or more throughout the country. The theme, meant to emphasize the desire of the population to have a direct vote for the President of the Republic, mobilized a growing number of citizens which culminated in two huge rallies, one in Rio de Janeiro where 1 million people demonstrated in front of the Cathedral of Candelaria on April 1 and another in São Paulo, one week later, where close to 2 million people virtually occupied all the downtown area in the largest public demonstration ever held in Brazil. All in all, the campaign assembled over 11 million people in rallies to express the population's desire for the end of 21 years of military rule.

The two union centrals adopted opposite positions when part of the opposition formed the Democratic Alliance to negotiate a compromise solution with the military. Here direct elections for president would be avoided, but a civilian government elected by the old Electoral College would oversee a period of transition. The solution of negotiating with the military for an indirectly elected civilian President during such a transition, however, did not please everyone. The CUT, in particular, severely criticized the negotiations between such opposition groups and the military which ended up allowing a civilian President but avoided direct popular elections. The CUT asserted that without the legitimation of a direct popular vote a new government could not be truly democratic and would not have the necessary legitimacy to implement a real program of transformation capable of creating economic and social rights as well as formal political democracy in Brazil. The CONCLAT, on the other hand, supported the Democratic Alliance proposal for indirect elections, arguing that only such a gradualist transition would be permitted by the military government as a means of returning the country to democracy.

The CGT has differed from the CUT in terms of strategy for the unions to take in terms of organized labor's relations with the state. The CGT defends negotiations with the government to achieve gradual modification in the Labor Code. Although its program includes a search for autonomy and a criticism of the mechanisms which tie the unions to the state, the CGT, nonetheless, believes that some aspects should be retained. In particular, it defends the maintenance of the impôsto sindical with the argument that few unions would be able to financially survive a sudden withdrawal of the funds that come from the union tax. As an alternative, the CGT proposes that the tax money be placed in a special fund to be administered entirely by union officials.

The CGT also diverges from the CUT in regard to union organization. While the CUT defends the right of workers to freely organize associations and unions without any interference or regulatory action from the state, the CGT argues that the absence of a single union legal provision would encourage labor's fragmentation, with many rival unions being organized in any one plant. This outcome, according to the CGT, would vastly weaken the unions, allowing them to become divided along both professional and ideological lines. While the two centrals do not agree on all aspects of the relation between labor and government, the CGT does agree fully with the CUT when it comes to opposition to state intervention both in union elections and at the level of the leadership board.

The two major centrals also differ in terms of their political ties. The Workers Party has a predominant political influence in the CUT, followed by the Democratic Labor Party led by the ex-governor of Rio de Janeiro, Leonel Brizola. Other political influences in the CUT include a variety of Trotskyist groups, Socialists, dissenters ousted from the Brazilian Communist Party, and perhaps most numerous, militants of the progressive sectors of the Catholic Church. To accommodate the variety of political views in such a way that each has direct influence according to its representational strength, the CUT developed a system of election according to proportionality. This system of proportional representation encourages the variety of political tendencies and parties within the CUT to form alliances to run their own slates in elections to the general assembly of delegates. The makeup of the executive board of the CUT is then decided in a direct proportion to the percent support given to each different slate. For example, if Trotskyists receive 30 percent of the total vote they have the right to the same share of the posts on the executive board. This system was devised to allow flexibility of positions and to encourage as much as possible active participation by the rank-and-file. Although the CUT, by its statutes, is not directly tied to any political party, it does not shy away from recognizing the existence and influence of political party organization represented within the union movement.

The CGT, in its turn, is the product of a political alliance of the two main Communist Parties (the PCB and the PC do B) with such important center and right-of-center political parties as the *Partido do Movimento Democrático Brasileiro* (PMDB), the *Partido Trabalhista Brasileiro* (PTB), and the *Partido da Frente Liberal* (PFL). Given that the PMDB and the PFL together form the basic party support for the Sarney government which inaugurated the so-called New Republic in March 1985, the CGT has often been a supporter of Sarney policies. In contrast to the CUT, the CGT does not believe in a system of proportional representation. Its executive board is composed of the presidents of the most important and influential trade unions among its affiliates.

A third trade union central, the Independent Labor Union (*União Sindical Independente*, or USI), was created in 1986 by old-style trade unionists, with most connected to state-controlled unions. The USI is politically aligned with extremely conservative sectors and defends the integral maintenance of the Labor Code as well as the existing ties between unions and the state. The USI was formed to provide political coordination for those groups seeking to fight the growing movement to change labor regulations that control the unions. The name "independent" in the case of the USI refers not to a search for autonomous modes of organization, but to a position of distance from the left political parties which influence both the CUT and the CGT. It places itself squarely in opposition to the proposals set forth by the New Trade Union Movement. The USI, however, has achieved little support and remains very minor in the overall political and union scenario.

The New Trade Union Movement in the New Republic
The history of the Brazilian union movement cannot be understood outside of its political context. Workers have sought to gain the right to

organize at all levels in a constant struggle for autonomy from the state. By 1984, the growth and mobilizational power of the New Union Movement forced the recognition of organized workers as a major political actor. No longer was it possible for the state to simply repress the movement in order to silence the demands of workers. In 1985, with the advent of the New Republic – as the transition period from direct military rule is called – a new political line towards trade unions was developed.

The New Republic's labor policy is based on a two-part strategy: the state carefully conducts negotiations with sectors of the labor movement for gradual reform while, at the same time, it strictly enforces existing legislation which binds unions to the state, prevents rank-and-file organization at the workplace, prohibits strikes, and allows the government to set salaries by decree. Here it might be useful to show examples of specific events representative of the overall policy of the New Republic towards the union movement.

The initial policies of the New Republic encouraged dialogue and opening with the New Union Movement. Unions which were under state intervention were returned to the control of elected officials; union officials who had lost their union rights received an amnesty which allowed them, once again, to run for election and to participate in union activities; direct negotiation between workers and management was encouraged; the right of workers to organize centrals was recognized with the CUT and CGT being given legal recognition by the state. The policy of the New Republic, however, did not include negotiation of major reforms of the Labor Code which would grant autonomy to trade unions. It limited itself merely to palliatives, saying that major reforms were up to the Constituent Assembly elected in November 1985 for the purpose of writing a new constitution.

In reality, the labor policy of the New Republic has been characterized by a change of tactics. The growth of the trade union movement, particularly its ability to mobilize the rank-and-file, necessitated the development of a more sophisticated policy of labor control. The state began to encourage actions which would dismantle factory committees and other organized base-level activities occurring in the workplace. This policy became evident with the events at Ford Motor Company in July 1986.

From the time of its foundation in July 1981, the Ford committee was the first workers group to be legally recognized by a major corporation, with members regularly elected for a fixed period and with the right to negotiate directly with the company. It was considered an important victory of the New Union Movement because the pressure of the Ford workers enabled them to win guaranteed job security for the elected members of the factory committee. The board of directors of Ford initially negotiated with the factory committee, maintaining an open and respectful dialogue. With the policy changes introduced by the New Republic, this comity began to change; directors of Ford began to block every effort to meaningfully negotiate. They began to interfere with the work of the members of the factory committee, impeding their free access to workers, prohibiting publications being distributed in the plant, and refusing to negotiate any of the demands for better work conditions. Tensions grew when an elected member of the factory committee was summarily fired in clear violation of the contractual clause which granted him job tenure during the period of his mandate. Workers of Ford reacted with indignation: a retaliatory strike was called and the São Bernardo plant was totally paralyzed. After ten days of strike, Ford appealed for Ministry of Labor intervention. The Ford plant in São Bernardo do Campo was surrounded by a shock battalion of the military police and workers were physically forced to present their documentation and go back to work. The union leadership and the members of the factory committee were excluded from the plant; workers assemblies inside the plant were prohibited. All surrounding streets were blocked by the army – even the traffic had to be rerouted.

Only July 22, 1986, the Ford Motor Company sent a formal note to the Metalworkers Union of São Bernardo do Campo informing it of the summary dismissal, "for just cause" (that is, without compensation or legal rights of appeal), of the entire factory committee. In addition, Ford dismissed six members of the Internal Committee for the Prevention of Accidents who, by federal law, have complete job tenure during their legal mandate. The Ministry of Labor refused to put any pressure upon the corporation in spite of the fact that its action was clearly in violation of the law. Instead, the Ministry of Labor furnished Ford with a list of names of union militants employed there. Within a week Ford had fired a total of 204 workers, all of them union activists. Many of them were elected representatives and shop stewards in their work sections.[26]

Ford was only the first case. Since 1986, most multinational corporations have fired some or all of the members of their factory committees. The most recent one to follow this policy has been the Volvo plant in Curitiva, Paraná. Unionists bitterly remember that when the New Republic's Minister of Labor, Almir Pazzianotto, was a lawyer for the Metalworkers Union of São Bernardo, he used to openly comment that the military had a stupid labor policy: "If I was Minister of Labor, I would never intervene in the board of directors of a union. I would dismantle their structural organization, linking them to the rank-and-file inside the plants."

The policy of encouraging a centralized union bureaucracy without an active base has been at the heart of the New Republic's labor policy. This threat to union militants helps to explain why labor is fighting so fiercely in the Constituent Assembly to have provisions of job tenure guarantees included in the Constitutional text itself; as such, they cannot be undercut by ordinary legislation or simply disregarded in contractual clauses. In fact, many union leaders complain that organizing under the New Republic has been more difficult than during the period of *abertura* of military Presidents Ernesto Geisel and João Figueiredo.

The attack upon the rank-and-file organization has hurt the mobilizational power of unions and has served to discourage the formation of strongly representative mechanisms inside workplaces. Such change has weakened the overall ability of the unions to pressure for better working conditions and higher salaries. The complete lack of job security guarantees, coupled with massive dismissals of thousands of workers in all major industrial plants, threw the New Unions into great disarray by seriously weakening labor's organizational base. This, in turn, allowed the New Republic sufficient breathing time to enact a series of decree laws which cut deeply into the salaries of all workers.

The union movement, in regular negotiations carried out under the pressure of strikes, succeeded in gaining increasing benefits for workers during 1985; salary adjustments every three months allowed salaries to remain relatively at pace with the high rate of inflation.[27] With the salary policy of the Cruzado Plan implemented in March 1986, all this came to a grinding halt. Salaries were, by law, frozen at the level of the average salary of the previous six months, something which caused the greatest losses for workers who were reaching the end of a contractual period when their earnings were the most seriously undermined by the high inflation. At the same time, there was a general loss in salary due to the mechanism of conversion of the cruzeiro to the new monetary unit, the cruzado, again using as a base the average of the previous six months. After several months as inflation began to grow again, the salaries remained frozen, resulting in workers suffering a tremendous loss. The Cruzado Plan supposedly had a safeguard for workers in an "automatic trigger mechanism" which was to increase salaries by 20 percent every time inflation reached that minimal percentage. Even during the few months that the "automatic trigger" actually was in force, the salary increase granted was always smaller than an inflation then fluctuating between 22.5 and 24 percent per month.

Toward mid-1986, a more violent salary squeeze was imposed, again by a series of executive decree laws. The so-called Bresser Plan of July 1987 had specific provisions for a new salary policy of the New Republic: (1) it ended the "automatic trigger" mechanism of salary raises; (2) it spread over six months an adjustment for the gap between inflation and salary up until May; (3) it froze salaries during two months (July and August), except for those who had a new contract to negotiate in those months; (4) for the calculation of the percentage in salary raises – but not for any other adjustments in the economy – the plan simply ignored the

TABLE 3.2
Nominal vs. Necessary Minimum Salary, November 1985–November 1987 (in Cruzados)

Period	Nominal Minimum Salary[a]	Necessary Minimum Salary[b]
1985		
November	600.00	2,435.16
December	600.00	2,655.00
1986		
January	600.00	3,327.27
February	600.00	3,906.80
March	804.00	3,793.10
April	804.00	3,839.44
May	804.00	3,760.54
June	804.00	3,693.12
July	804.00	3,577.61
August	804.00	3,605.86
September	804.00	3,645.65
October	804.00	3,708.84
November	804.00	3,975.09
December	804.00	4,884.64
1987		
January	964.00	5,563.47
February	964.00	7,943.08
March	1,368.00	7,916.56
April	1,368.00	10,291.88
May	1,641.60	12,283.91
June	1,969.92	12,858.95
July	1,969.92	15,953.28
August	2,220.00	18,348.03
September	2,400.00	19,220.76
October	2,640.00	19,678.60
November	3,000.00	22,749.72

Source: Boletim do DIEESE, December 1987, p. 5.
[a] Nominal Minimum Salary = The legal minimum salary in effect.
[b] Necessary Minimum Salary = The minimum salary calculated in accordance with Article 165 of the Constitution which states that the minimum salary ought to be able to satisfy the normal basic value of basic foods in different areas researched. The family considered is composed of two adults and two children, with the children calculated to consume the equivalent of what one adult consumes. It includes the emergency raise of Cz$ 250.00 provided by Decree Law 2,325 of August 7, 1987.

26 percent inflation of June 1987, the month prior to the Plan's implementation; and (5) it established a new official index to be used for the calculation of salaries, the *Unidade de Referência Padrão* or URP.[28]

The correction of salaries using the URP has had a serious effect upon the buying power of salaries. Where the official rate of inflation for the month of December 1987, for example, was 14.14 percent, the URP was

TABLE 3.3
Number of Strikes[a] & Strikers,[b] 1986–1987 (by Month)

Month	Number of Strikes	Number of Strikers	Number of Strikes	Number of Strikers
	1986		1987	
January	37	92,484	67	219,671
February	34	96,736	129	416,599
March	49	239,180	147	1,491,491
April	88	260,960	107	822,382
May	99	635,706	93	1,335,798
June	98	657,415	52	905,260
July	229	500,588	44	943,322
August	147	330,801	46	328,811
September	86	1,631,558	73	804,152
October	82	971,717	107	535,953
November	80	198,138	147	763,729
December	53	141,820	89	443,215
Totals	993	5,747,193	1,122	9,010,383

Source: Compilation of DIEESE, December 1987.
[a] The strike totals are those reported by unions to DIEESE.
[b] The total number of strikers is calculated by totalling the membership in each striking union.

only 9.19 percent. Hence, salaries corrected by the second measurement rather than by the official rate of inflation, lost an average of 3 or 4 percent per month in real value. Taking the December results alone, the worker who had his salary readjusted 9.19 percent had his purchasing power adjusted at less than 70 percent of inflation. The Bresser Plan, when taken into account together with a rapidly accelerating inflation, has imposed the worst squeeze on workers salaries since the first year of the military government in 1964. The results can be seen in Table 3.2.

The squeeze in wages caused the largest period of strike activity in Brazilian history. In 1986, there was a total of 5,747,103 workers on strike. By 1987, this number grew to over 9 million workers. Table 3.3 provides strike figures broken down by month for the 1986–1987 period. This massive wave of strikes succeeded in pushing salaries up in excess of the government's official correction rates. In fact, DIESSE reports that "from September 1987, part of the union movement was able to obtain salary readjustments equivalent to the total inflation rate." Luiz Carlos Bresser Pereira, the Minister of Finance, complained that the salaries were destroying his anti-inflation plan and encouraged the Ministry of Labor to devise legislation to further regulate the right to strike.

As it now stands, the Brazilian law regulating the right to strike is so rigid that most strikes are declared illegal by the labor courts within a few days of their occurrence. However, as we have seen, labor's strategy has been to totally disregard such restrictive laws, seeking their replacement with a more realistic substitute reflecting the reality that strikes – legal or otherwise – will occur no matter what the government seeks to do. A general consensus now exists that the present restrictions on strike activity are ineffectual.

As an attempt to deal with organized labor's use of the strike, the Sarney government has drafted a law proposing the modification of the present basis of union organization and placing significant limitations on the right to strike. The Almir Pazzianotto Law proposal[29] will not be examined by the House of Representatives until after the Constituent Assembly is over. If the modifications proposed in the Assembly by the CUT are even in part approved, then the regulation by ordinary law of union organization and the right to strike shall be prohibited by the Constitution; the Almir Pazzianotto Law proposal would become a dead letter. On the other hand, if the Constitution provides for the regulation of unions and strikes by ordinary law, the government's project will be examined, discussed, and voted on by Congress.

As it now stands, the proposed Law Project 164/87 would maintain the Ministry of Labor's exclusive right to grant recognition to unions and would require that union statutes continue to be registered with the government. The proposal, in its enunciation of the principle of "union pluralism," encourages union fragmentation by permitting more than one union per company or workshop. While the project does prohibit direct state intervention in, suspension, or dissolution of unions – limits considered by union leaders as a step towards the attainment of labor autonomy – the project also provides for possible criminal and civil liability for union officers in cases of membership action, with implementation at the discretion of the Labor Ministry.

Both the CUT and the CGT have been actively against the proposed law. The CUT is against any kind of state interference, arguing that pluralism must be exclusively the consequence of independent unionism and of the political and ideological differences in the union movement itself. In the case of the Almir Pazzianotto Law Project, the CUT considers it an attempt of the government to limit strike activity while maintaining a degree of state control over union organization. The CGT is violently against the provision for a recognition of plural unionism within individual companies which would have the effect of fragmenting the organized workforce.

What is clear is that the union movement in Brazil now stands at the crossroads of major historical change. Either the state will revert to repressive policies (which, with the present level of mobilization will have to be enormously violent), or at least some of the demands for union autonomy will have to be accepted. If the Constituent Assembly approves the popular amendment proposal presented by the CUT which provides for autonomy while at the same time granting important guarantees to union representatives – even in the workplace – the union movement in Brazil will take an enormous step towards the attainment of more effective forms of organization emphasizing the local-level. The job security guarantees, in particular, are very important in keeping companies from dismantling working class organization through selective hiring and firing procedures. The format of organization from the base, which up to now has constituted the strength of the New Trade Union Movement is dependent upon legal guarantees of job tenure to ensure that leadership at the plant level cannot be simply fired whenever an impasse is reached in labor negotiations. A combination of the ratification of Conventions 87 and 151 of the International Labor Organization coupled with a similar set of guarantees for base-level leadership would provide an enormous boost to the union movement, providing the necessary conditions for a new growth period of union organization.

If, on the other hand, the Constituent Assembly rejects job tenure guarantees, approves institutionalized pluralism with state recognition of unions, and increases the policy of repression against workers in the plants, the union movement is likely to have enormous trouble in maintaining its present level of activism. If, in addition, the state implements a policy of direct physical repression against the unions – something that may well occur – then workers will have to search for alternative, perhaps more radical, forms of organization to those previously known in Brazil.

NOTES

1. I want to acknowledge with special thanks the help of Marcia de Paula Leite, who greatly assisted in the research and the writing of this chapter.

2. Cited in Astrogildo Pereira, *Ensaios históricos e políticos* (São Paulo: Ed. Alfa Omega, 1979), p. 29.

3. Important and extensive public opinion research on all parts of the CLT was conducted by the Centro de Estudos de Cultura Contemporânea (CEDEC) of São Paulo and the Instituto Brasileiro de Relações do Trabalho (IBRART) with the support of the International Labor Organization (ILO). The researchers interviewed trade union leaders, politicians involved in the Ministry of Labor, and leaders of the business sector. The opinions expressed by trade union leaders are unanimously critical of the estatuto único clause of the CLT which binds all trade unions to a single organization. See Roque Aparecido da Silva, *Os sindicatos e a transição democrática: O que pensam os interessados* (São Paulo: Instituto Brasileiro de Relações do Trabalho, 1986), chapter vi, pp. 93–106.

4. See CUT, *Historia do sindicalismo no Brasil* (São Paulo: Secretaria de Formação da CUT Estadual de São Paulo, Caderno de Formação, 1987), pp. 16–18.

5. See Maria Helena Moreira Alves, *State and Opposition in Military Brazil* (Austin, Texas: Texas University Press, 1986). The total number of interventions was probably much larger because the Ministry of Labor did not always follow the legal requirement of publishing the intervention decree in the *Diario Oficial da União*. Since only published information was used in this source, many interventions which were sometimes reported in the press but without any specific decree law being published were ignored. This was particularly true in the period immediately following the military coup of 1964 and in the aftermath of the issuance of Institutional Act No. 5 of 1969.

6. See DIESSE, *Dez anos de política salarial* (São Paulo: August 1975), pp. 64–65.

7. For a complete analysis of the minimum salary and its history in Brazil, see DIESSE, *Divulgação*, 1 (April 19, 1976).

8. These figures are taken from the *Boletim do DIESSE* of April 1983, p. 2, citing data from the official Instituto Brasileiro de Geografia e Estatística (IBGE) and the 1980 census. It is worthwhile to point out that according to the statistical department of the government, the bulk of the working population received between one and two minimum salaries (31.1 percent) or between two and five times the minimum salaries (23.6 percent). These were essentially the white collar or more skilled blue collar workers. It is also important to emphasize that a total of 43.3 percent of the working population received less than half, or between a half and one minimum salary. Since the law established the minimum salary at subsistence value, it is extraordinary how many employers simply disregard the law.

9. For more information, see José Moisés, "Current Issues in the Labor Movement in Brazil" and "Interview with Luis Ignácio da Silva ('Lula')," *Latin American Perspectives*, 6:4 (1979), pp. 51–70 and 90–100.

10. The overall climate of Brazilian politics at that time was marked by the growth of resistance to the military regime among all classes. Large demonstrations organized by workers, sectors of the middle class, and opposition politicians demanded the end of the repressive military Institutional Acts and a return to a legitimate democratic government. Even though the union movement, as such, did not participate in an integrated manner in these political events, the opposition struggle against the military, nonetheless, had profound repercussions among working class sectors, helping to break the fear, and creating an overall anti-authoritarian perspective which facilitated labor organization in the plants that eventually led to the large strikes after 1978. For more information on this point, see Marcia de Paula Leite, "Reivindicações Sociais dos Metalúrgicos," in Rosa Maria Fischer, Maria Fleury, and Teresa Leme, *Processo e relações de trabalho no Brasil* (São Paulo: Editora Atlas, 1985).

11. The anticipated salary raise is added to the salary but discounted from the next raise; it does not have cumulative value.

12. See Moreira Alves, *State and Opposition in Military Brazil*, for a detailed account of the 1978, 1979, and 1980 strikes.

13. Because of the widespread nature of the strike movement, the government was forced to accept them. However, in August of 1978, the federal government issued Decree Law 1,632 which regulated strikes, declaring illegal all strikes in essential sectors, including banks. This was an attempt to curb the expanding strike movement which, in 1979, mobilized over 3 million workers.

14. See "Balanço anual das greves de 1979" (DIEESE, 1979). The number of strikers was calculated according to the number of workers in each union that was on strike.

15. Santo André, São Bernardo do Campo, and São Caetano are three major industrial cities in the greater São Paulo region. Multinational corporations, particularly those connected to the automobile industry, have installed here what is probably the largest industrial park of the Third World. Together, these cities form what is known as the ABC region, the industrial heart of Brazil. It is an area characterized by modern industrial activity with an active urban proletariat organized in strong local-level unions.

16. The most often sung slogan went as follows: "Brother soldier, don't get into this" (Soldado, irmão, não entre nessa, não). Other slogans were all aimed at convincing the soldiers not to repress the demonstrators.

17. See Marcia de Paula Leite, *O movimento previsto no Brasil* (São Paulo: Editora Brasiliense, 1987).

18. Comment published in *Boletim do DIESSE*, March 1983, p. 14.

19. Throughout 1980, there was a total of 1,200,000 workers on strike as opposed to the 3,200,000 in the previous year. For more information on the 1980 strikes, see DIESSE, *Balanço Anual das Greves de 1980* (São Paulo: DIESSE, 1981).

20. "ABC Sociedade Cultural e Grupo de Educação Popular da URPLAN" (São Bernardo do Campo, 1980) and *Boletim do DIESSE*, March 1983. The URPLAN study mentioned that if both unemployed and underemployed were counted, then approximately 31 percent of the economically active population lived in precarious conditions. In 1981, the number of people employed in industrial production in Brazil was smaller than it had been in 1978. By 1982, there were less people employed in industrial production than in 1976.

21. See Leite, "Reivindicações Sociais dos Metalúrgicos," p. 32.

22. Some of these strikes were difficult, with workers facing direct police repression. One of the first legally recognized factory committees was the one established at Ford Motor Company. Management agreed only after workers had taken over the plant and staged a sit-down strike around the management building for several hours. For more information on this, see *A tomada da Ford: Nasce um novo sindicalismo* (Rio de Janeiro: Editora Vozes, 1985).

23. See *Boletim do DIESSE*, July 1983. There were 2 million workers on strike in the state of São Paulo alone, with the most industrialized state coming virtually to a standstill on the day of protest.

24. Comissão Nacional Pro-CUT (the National Committee for a Central Union) was formed by Lula and 16 other main leaders representing different trades. It was in charge of the basic work of organizing a Central Union that could be formally founded at the congress held in 1982.

25. This second central union became known as the CONCLAT because it inherited the name taken by the first two national working class congresses. Most official unions belonging to CONCLAT were in alliance with the Communist Party which is the strongest leftist group within CONCLAT. A third central organization, composed of very politically conservative unionists, was formed in 1986. In 1986, all three centrals were given legal recognition by the Sarney government.

26. For details on the Ford strike and the dismissal of the factory committees

see, Maria Helena Moreira Alves and Roque Aparecido da Silva, "Nas fabricas, a volta dos velhos tempos" in *Lua Nova*, 3:3 (January/March 1987), p. 49.

27. See Leite, *O movimento grevista no Brasil*; and her essay, "Tres anos de greve em São Paulo 1983/1985: Perfil de um processo," *São Paulo em perspectiva: Revista do fundação SEADE* (July/September, 1987), p. 36.

28. DIESSE, "Salarios e política salarial," *Revista da central unica dos trabalhadores*, 18 (January/February 1987), p. 15.

29. The Law Project is number 164/87, filed on June 22, 1987. It carries the name of the Minister of Labor of the New Republic, Almir Pazzianotto.

Chapter 4

Trade Unionism and the State under the Chilean Military Regime

Jaime Ruiz-Tagle

The state has played a central role in the makeup of Latin American nations, and especially in the Chilean case; the 1973 substitution of an authoritarian regime for a Democratic state constituted a fundamental change for all national institutions and, in particular, for trade unions. During the current military regime, Chilean unionism has not only suffered political repression and limitations imposed by a new juridical framework, but also the effects of the country's deindustrialization and the high levels of unemployment brought about by the relentless application of a neoliberal economic model.

Nevertheless, despite its structural and organic weakness, the union movement has had an important influence on national and international public opinion, and has been able to mobilize and solidify various social sectors behind massive protests. The Chilean unions have demonstrated that they have the capacity to represent the great majority of persons in the workforce, surpassing the mere representation of only unionized workers. The impact of the dictatorship and the changes that have occurred in the economic structure have led to new directions within the union movement such as the search for greater autonomy and the tendency to reinforce the union role as a sociopolitical actor in a democratic alternative.

The first part of this chapter provides historical antecedents which allow for the better understanding of the recent period. The second analyzes the changes that have occurred in the social and economic structure and its effects on unionism. The third is devoted to a characterization of the new legal framework established since 1979, within which all union action has had to develop. The fourth describes the recent development of unions, including those not legally recognized. The fifth analyzes the type of action carried out by labor at different levels in the last few years. The sixth and final section is dedicated to the deeper understanding of the relation between unions and the state in the context of the fight for the return of democracy.

HISTORICAL ANTECEDENTS

The origins of the Chilean labor movement can be traced to the end of the nineteenth century when organizations of a trade union nature, the mutuals or *mancomunales* that fought to defend the rights of the workers began to appear in the large nitrate mines situated in the north of the country. (At the beginning of the twentieth century, migrations from the north to central Chile caused by the international crisis in the nitrate trade implanted the idea of union struggle and the formation of class consciousness in the emerging industrial working class.) Because the state retained a part of the wealth extracted from the mining enclaves, union actions were directed at the government as well as the private owners. Consequently, the Chilean workers movement from its beginning sought to use the political system as a means to gain its objectives.[1]

When the economic crisis of 1930 took place, Chile was one of the countries most severely affected, with its exports falling rapidly. The state saw itself obliged to create and directly develop a policy of import substitution industrialization. In this manner, the growth of the industrial working class became directly tied to state policies and the growth of state enterprises. For these reasons, the social classes viewed the state and the political system as the principal places of confrontation in the social struggle. The greater part of the workers' achievements were obtained through laws, and the major social movements were directed not so much at the owners as at the state, especially since the 1930s. Periods in which social movements developed independently of all institutional contact were very few. Indeed, the mediation of the political parties and the labor union federations in state organs played a fundamental role.

Chilean unionism did not develop independently from, nor in opposition to the political parties. It was normally the parties that stimulated the development of union organizations and which contributed to legitimize union movements. Structurally weak, Chilean unionism found its strength in alliance with the parties which formed part of the political system and, as such, were considered the "backbone" of Chilean society. Because of their worker origins, the parties of the left (the Communists and the Socialists) were the principal creators of the union movement. But the parties of the center (the Radicals and Christian Democrats) also supported the development and actions of the unions, particularly in the modern state industries, the public services, and among the peasantry.[2]

The union movement was linked to the political parties through national-level organizations like the Chilean Workers Central (*Central de Trabajadores de Chile*, or CTCH) of 1936–1947, the Unitary Workers Central (*Central Unica de Trabajadores*, or CUT) of 1952–1973, and various federations and confederations. The local-level unions were generally small and weak, with an average of only 140 members each at the beginning of the 1970s, something which made national federations indispensable.

However, the alliance between the political parties and the unions was not totally beneficial. Frequently it also implied an excessive dependence, resulting in the superimposition and confusion of political and trade union functions. This blurring led to many internal conflicts within the union movement (such as the break up of the CTCH at the beginning of the Cold War) and was one of the causes of the violent repression against the union movement after the military coup of 1973.

Chilean unionism represented not only the interests of the salaried worker, but also defended the vast popular majority in such a way that its efforts transcended its members. By seeking to deepen economic and social democracy, it contributed to legitimizing representative democracy.

The Christian Democrats' coming to power in 1964 with a political project of economic and social reforms not only facilitated the growth of labor organizations – as we will see later – but also permitted the development of centrist tendencies within the unions. Such groups also reemphasized the importance of the autonomy of the labor movement from the state, as the CUT had done at its founding in 1952, insisting on the economic role of the unions. This meant that when the reformist plans of the Christian Democrats entered a relatively stagnant period (1967–1968), the center unionists united with those of the left to sponsor a broad and intense strike movement.

Although for the Christian Democrat unionists, economic actions basically constituted a means to promote the collective social mobility of the workers, for unionists of the left – and in particular far leftist leaders – these actions were also a form of weakening the capitalist system in order to facilitate the working class' taking of power. These two views were superimposed and frequently were not clearly differentiated. Nevertheless, faced with the risk of a rightist coup d'état (1969), the CUT established an agreement with the Christian Democrat government to defend democracy. This accord included a pact calling for the readjustment of earnings the following year and the formation of a permanent CUT/government commission to study the restructuring of renumerations in the public sector. This accord demonstrated the democratic will of the CUT as well as the limits of actions focusing on income as a means to promote revolutionary changes.

In 1970, Salvador Allende was elected President of Chile at the head of a predominantly Marxist coalition, Popular Unity, which proposed revolutionary changes and a path toward socialism. The basic consensus between the government and the unions permitted these changes to continue and accelerate. The CUT, for its part, assumed as its principal tasks the defense of democratic institutionality, the normal functioning of the productive processes, and the transfer of large enterprises to the Social Property Area (*Area de Propiedad Social*, or APS) of the economy. A pact between the CUT and the government was established to promote and organize the participation of workers in APS enterprises.

The unconditional support of the CUT for the government presented problems in terms of both the autonomy of the union movement from the state and the internal unity of the movement. Beginning in 1972, inflation accelerated, leading to a resurgence of actions to restore wages. In the first half of that year, the number of striking workers more than doubled that of the preceding year; it is estimated that strikes affected a third of the construction workers and half of the miners. The intensification of strikes was considered by sectors of the left as a positive sign in terms of the extension of the class struggle and the anti-capitalistic fight. Nevertheless, these wage oriented movements responded above all to a localist interest group mentality that had traditionally existed and was associated with the fact that the Popular Unity government had eliminated repression and had generated great expectations among the workers employed in private companies. The logic of seeking higher wages ended up conflicting with the national interest related to the need for the successful functioning of the economy and that related to the consolidation of new governmental structural reforms.

In this context, the Christian Democratic unions, as opponents of the government, strongly supported wage recovery actions, something which permitted them to gain new members. In the CUT elections of 1972, the Christian Democrats obtained 27 percent of the valid votes (compared to 31 percent for the Communists and 27 percent for the socialists), in spite of the fact that their peasant unions did not belong to that central. The strengthening of an oppositionist trade unionism while the CUT was directly tied to the regime strongly accentuated the problem of maintaining the internal unity of the unions.

The worsening of the economic crisis in 1973 accelerated wage pressures. With the occurrence of a long strike in the recently nationalized copper mines, the internal contradictions of the trade union movement became more visible. The dual logic of seeking the transformation of the system and focusing on income questions could not be adequately combined. The political polarization tearing at society penetrated the unions. Their appearance as a disunified body incapable of resisting the threat of a military coup contributed to the acceleration of the political crisis.

From 1973, a new scenario was imposed upon Chile, one in which social organizations and movements have had to act. Its most notable characteristic has been the authoritarian political regime which harshly repressed the union movement, especially the leftist leaders, silencing its organizations. Together with the emergence of an oppressive regime, the role of the state as an agent of economic and social development tended to disappear. The authoritarian regime used all its power to transfer responsibility for development to "market forces," by definition meaning large private national and multinational enterprises. The state and the political system were no longer relatively open spaces where workers could defend their interests and influence the direction of development.[3] The union leaders' intentions to make economic demands in the name of the working class for the benefit of the popular majority were disqualified as "political" diversions or as an intent to share in governing, both unacceptable to the authoritarian regime. On the other hand, with the political parties outlawed and their hands tied, they could not fulfill their mediating role between the working class and the state. Without such party mediation, Chilean trade unionism lost its principal means of action.

In the new scenario, the greater part of surviving unionism played an eminently defensive role. With the passage of time, certain leadership nuclei emerged that played an important role in the fight to regain democracy. Nevertheless, these nuclei filled a largely symbolic function, and were not able to speak for the whole working class. In this period (which extended to 1978), the union organizations — deprived of their natural mediators — resorted to the protection of the Catholic Church. Such ecclesiastical mediation substituted the language of human rights for that of union rights; the Catholic Church could not become a class-based party, nor could it seek to represent the working class as economic producer. While ecclesiastical support proved fundamental for the survival of the unions, it could not replace the mediation of the political parties.

In 1979, a second phase began within the new scenario: under the menace of an international boycott, the military regime, seeing itself obliged to make concessions on union matters, decreed a body of new laws known as the "Labor Plan." This legislation tended to consolidate the reduction of the state's role as mediator in social conflicts, reducing it to one of general support and to that of an "arbitrator" that would make sure that the rules of the game were respected. Nevertheless, the state continued intervening, even more decisively than before 1973, but with a difference: on one hand, it authoritatively delimited the field of action and the mark within which labor relations could be developed; on the other hand, it continued supplying the public force to maintain order and for repression in case the unions sought to escape the rigid limits that had been imposed on them.

The implementation of the Labor Plan and, in particular, the new possibility of collective bargaining, meant a reactivation of local unions and a legitimizing of their leaders. Nevertheless, the reactivation of local-level unionism and labor's formal reconstitution ran up against the limitations imposed by the authoritarian political system and the new labor code: they lacked the mediators necessary to obtain results for their demands at the society-wide level. In synthesis, this final phase of the new scenario witnessed a union movement in the process of reconstruction characterized by a dual tendency: (1) a reorientation toward local-level organizations to consolidate their internal structure and (2) socio-political action led by the union centrals and the largest confederations which sought to organize limited struggles, to generate pressure on the authoritarian state, and to accelerate the return to democracy.

STRUCTURAL CHANGES AND THEIR EFFECTS

During the four decades prior to the 1973 military coup, the Chilean economy was based upon an industrialization model, with the industrial sector growing much more rapidly than the overall economy. The industrial contribution to the gross domestic product grew from 13.4 percent in 1940 to 24.9 percent in 1970.[4] The state protected and stimulated national industry in such a way that industrial workers came to have an increasingly more important say in the economy and in national life.

Imposed after 1973, the neo-liberal economic model based on the opening of the economy to imported products provoked a serious crisis in the industrial sector.[5] Industrial production fell abruptly, dropping from an index figure of 117.6 in 1972 to 85.0 in 1975. Its subsequent recovery permitted it to surpass pre-coup figures, with the index rising to 129.3 in 1981. But renewed crisis touched off another fall in industrial production, lowering the index to 106.6 in 1982. The regime had to resort to successive devaluations and increases in tariffs, with the resulting import substitution permitting an industrial reactivation. Nevertheless, by mid-1986 the index was only at 134.2. Such changes meant that per capita industrial production in 1986 was 8.3 percent below that of 1972.[6]

In respect to industrial employment, its share of the work force decayed notably, falling from 19.1 percent in 1972 to 13.8 percent in 1985. On the other hand, those employed in commerce grew from 12.5 percent in 1972 to 18.4 percent in 1985.[7] This sharp growth in the service sector of the economy constituted a structural change that harshly affected the Chilean union movement. Industrial workers had made up the fundamental core of traditional unionism; workers in commerce, on the other hand, were largely isolated in small groups and frequently had behavioral patterns similar to the middle sectors.

It is critical to analyze the importance of these structural changes. Although it is certain that industrial workers do not have the same force as they held before 1973, they do continue to occupy a central role in production, above all in the largest businesses that were less affected by the crisis. Furthermore, their organizations have a tradition — and also at times experienced leaders and material goods — that permit them to maintain significant influence within trade unionism. On the other hand, some dynamic sectors within the new style externally oriented development (such as fruit and forestry), did not seem to offer a medium for the emergence of a new union nuclei of a weight equivalent to that of traditional centers like industry and mining. In addition, the state's production and service industries — despite their reduction in size — are still very important in Chile. The state controls large scale copper, petroleum, coal and steel production, the greater part of health and education, etc. This state sector maintains a certain autonomy from foreign capital and large national economic groups. As a result, and given its size, its workers can more easily see beyond their immediate problems and make demands which are national in scope.

Nevertheless, the structural change most influential for the unions has been the growth of under- and unemployment. In the 12 years between 1974 and 1985, the average figure for real unemployment (including those who only receive benefits in the government's special employment programs) has been 19.6 percent, more than tripling the historical rate.[8] With the increase of unemployment, the workers' power has diminished, especially since in the case of strikes they can rapidly be replaced by unemployed job seekers. The loss of work, or the fear of losing it, has tended to paralyze strike activity. High unemployment has not only been a means of excluding a part of the population from economic development; it has not only been a means of promoting income concentration; nor has it been only a means of maintaining a reserve labor force that answers the needs for workers in a capitalist expansion. Indeed, more than anything it has been a means to limit or repress organized workers. In fact, high unemployment has been the most effective means of repression against union activity because it has a more wide-reaching result than armed raids, jailing, and exile.

The high levels of under- and unemployment have also been causes for the reduction of remunerations. The real income index (1970 = 100.0) which had hit 126.6 in 1972, fell to 62.0 in 1975. It later recovered, reaching 96.4 in 1981, but in the following years it again began to fall, stopping at 82.2 in 1985. In other words, real income in 1985 was 17.8 percent lower than in 1970. If one considers the average of the 12 years between 1974 and 1985, real income then was 20.5 percent below 1970.[9]

TABLE 4.1
Percentage of Total Income Received by Population Groups

	Population		
Years	Poorest 40%	Next 40%	Wealthiest 20%
1971–1973	12.90	36.60	50.50
1973–1984	11.04	31.66	57.30
1984	9.33	29.74	60.94

Source: Francisco Labbé, Distribución del ingreso en la teoría económica: La visión neoclásica y la situación redistributiva de los ingresos en Chile (Santiago: CED, 1986).

The joint effect of high unemployment and low salaries has led to a negative redistribution of income, as can be seen in Table 4.1. The structural changes imposed by the military regime have been profoundly regressive, causing major impoverishment for the poor and extra-ordinary enrichment for the wealthiest.

It is also important to emphasize the growing inequality of remunerations between white collar employees and blue collar workers, as among diverse groups of those with regular employment. Wages of manual laborers deteriorated more than those of nonmanual workers; the legal minimum wage lost more buying power than other forms of remuneration; and the differences in income widened between that paid in large industries and that in small. In all, this was similar to what happened as disparities grew between dynamic industries producing for the foreign market and noncompetitive industries producing essential goods for the internal market.[10] In other words, the structural heterogeneity among salaried workers increased, affecting the base of the union movement and making unified action more difficult.

These structural changes require further analysis. First, in order to apply neo-liberal economic policy, the military regime ended the legal differences between blue collar workers (obreros) and white collar employees (empleados), with the latter losing many of their economic advantages in regard to social security (especially the higher old age pensions and family benefits). In the second place, some who enjoyed special benefits, like port and copper workers, have lost them as the neo-liberal norms have elimi-nated such differences through homogenization of workers rights.

In summary, the structural changes produced in the economy have harshly affected the conditions in which the Chilean labor movement is unfolding. Nevertheless, these changes have not been so radical as to permit the establishment of a new type of unionism, nor have they been so unidirectional as to always have the same influence on inequality and local level disunity. In short, workers from all sectors have experienced some type of exclusion from the authoritarian regime.[11]

THE LEGAL FRAMEWORK FOR UNION ACTION

Chilean labor legislation has developed since the 1920s, being in many aspects a pioneer effort in Latin America. Thanks to long battles fought by the unions, a "committed state" was established which contributed to a gradual economic and social democratization through the dictation of a body of norms that protected the workers and took into account the specific problems of diverse labor sectors. The authoritarian state – inspired by neo-liberal ideology – decided to radically change labor legislation and norms through the body of decrees and laws called the "Labor Plan" (1978–1981).

The norms referring to the work contract (Decree Law 2,200 and its regulations) authorize the employer to unilaterally modify the work contract (the nature of services, the work place, and work hours). Not only does this contradict the protective character that labor law ought to have, but also fails to respect the most elementary norms of civil rights which establish that contracts can only be modified by mutual consent. Accordingly, this gives the employers a means of pressure that can be used against union leaders and those who stand out in the defense of labor rights. In contrast, until 1973 the so-called job security law existed which established that workers could not be fired without just cause. The authoritarian regime, with the pretext of facilitating labor mobility, established the possibility of firing workers without giving cause by the simple wish of the employer. Moreover, the norms that limited mass dismissals were eliminated.

With respect to temporary, or limited-term contracts, their maximum duration was increased from six months to two years. The consequence has been (1) an increase in the number of workers that lack stable employment and (2) employers having more freedom to let go those employees that cause them problems. Moreover, as we will see later below, temporary workers cannot unionize or participate in collective bargaining. Therefore, the growth of workers in this category weakens the base of trade unionism.

One of the most important characteristics of the new legislation is the separation established between the unions and collective bargaining, contrary to Chilean historical tradition. There now exist unions that do not bargain collectively and there is collective bargaining without unions. Decree Laws 2,756 and 2,758 of 1979 (and some regulatory decrees) establish four types of unions: (a) the enterprise union that groups together workers from the same company; (b) the intercompany union that groups workers from at least three distinct companies; (c) unions for independent workers that group those who have no employer; and (d) unions for part-time, or transitory workers. The only group that has the right to participate in collective bargaining is enterprise unions. The next two groups are limited to representation, education and mutual help; and the last simply function as labor exchanges.

Under the legislation in force until 1973, once a majority of workers decided to form a union, all of the workers joined; there could not be more than one industrial union per company. Now, 10 percent of the workers are authorized to establish a union, with a minimum of 25 members. Moreover, if the company has less than 25 workers, 8 of them can establish a union as long as they represent over 50 percent of all workers within the company. These standards tend to fragment and atomize the unions consistent with the neo-liberal economic model.

The drift toward atomization also appears in secondary level organizations. Unions can affiliate with federations or confederations, but these cannot intervene in collective bargaining, being limited to functions of technical assistance, education, and mutual aid. The prohibition on bargaining through federations implies that the workers of small and medium-sized companies find themselves in a weak position vis-à-vis their employers. On the other hand, it is important to note that the law does not permit the creation of national centrals, so that organizations of a national character have only a de facto existence, and thus are easily the objects of repression.

With respect to collective bargaining, broad sectors of workers are excluded, such as those in state administrative institutions and services, in the judiciary, and in the universities. Moreover, the law has drastically restricted the subjects that can be the object of contracts or collective bargaining. Among the excluded materials are (a) those that limit the power of the employer to organize, direct, and administer the company; (b) those that imply the financing of union organizations; and (c) those that refer to workers who do not belong to the union (or to the negotiating group). Remunerations and working conditions are the only negotiable items rather than issues that relate to the rhythm of production, the system of promotions, the use of machinery, etc. The underlying logic of making the consolidation of the unions difficult and impeding active solidarity with those workers that do not participate in bargaining tends to safeguard the power of entrepreneurs. Since the benefits obtained by a union or negotiating group only apply to its affiliates or members, contracts are "collective" only in the narrowest sense of the word.

In addition to limitations on collective bargaining, the right to strike is subject to severe legal restrictions (as well as the constraints imposed by high unemployment). The right to declare a strike is excluded from areas of public utilities and from those industries whose paralyzation would damage the health or supply of provisions to the population, the national economy, or the national security. A fundamental restriction is that strikes can last a maximum of 60 days. At the end of that time, strikers must return to work, and if they do not, they are considered to have voluntarily resigned. Furthermore, after 30 days of strike, any striker is authorized to withdraw from negotiations and return to work. During the strike, an employer can hire any workers that he considers necessary. If the strike affects over 50 percent of the workers or means the paralyzation of activities indispensable to the company's ability to function, the employer can declare a 30-day partial or total closure of the company. With all these restrictions, it is understandable that strikes have been few in number and that their success has been very limited.

Finally, it is necessary to emphasize that special labor judges and courts were eliminated (Decree Law 3,648 of March 1981), so that labor disputes have had to be brought to civil tribunals. Five years after their dissolution, in 1986, a partial reconstitution of the labor tribunals was initiated in the face of proof that the neo-liberal policy of absorbing labor cases into the civil system had resulted in failure.

LABOR UNION ORGANIZATIONS

There is no precise information with respect to the real dimensions of Chilean labor organizations. The statistics released by the Labor Ministry are formal and union leaders consistently question them. Nevertheless, official statistics reveal the major trends in the evolution of union affiliation.

During the period preceeding the 1973 military coup, the creation of unions and the affiliation of new members underwent a rapid rise. After having suffered a strong reduction between 1957 and 1963 (−15.5 percent) — coinciding with conservative governments – the number of members rose from 268,035 in 1964 to 855,404 in 1972 — during Christian Democrat and Popular Unity governments.[12] In those same years, the number of unions rose from 1,875 to 6,118, and the percentage of unionization rose from 16.2 percent of the work force to 40.8 percent. It was, therefore, a period of great development for the trade unions.

At the beginning of the military regime, the *Central Unica de Trabaja-dores* was dissolved by decree, as occurred de facto with other important federations and confederations; together with the death, imprisonment, and exile of many leaders, these factors tended to paralyze union activities.[13] The regime prohibited collective bargaining and elections, union meetings were subject to extreme control, and the right of the leaders to be absent from work was annulled. Official statistics only partially reflect the blow suffered by labor organizations: union affiliation fell 2.4 percent between 1973 and 1977, and general union activity

TABLE 4.2
Union Membership, 1981–1985

Years	(1) Total Unionized Workers	(2) Total Number of Unions	(3) Federations and Confederations	(4) Union Organizations Affiliated to (3)	(5) Number of Workers in (4)
1981	395,951	3,977	92	770	115,641
1982	347,470	4,048	96	816	104,757
1983	320,903	4,401	111	1,059	124,491
1984	340,329	4,714	128	1,370	149,142
1985	360,963	4,994	147	1,603	173,570

Source: Reworking of statistics from the Ministry of Labor and Social Security at the Programa de Economía del Trabajo (PET), Academía Cristiana de Humanismo, Santiago, Chile.

dropped 25 percent. Moreover, industry and construction, which have been so fundamental in historical unionism, saw their membership shrink much more than average in the same years, 12 percent and 34 percent, respectively. As a result, the combined effect of political coercion and structural changes led to an important contraction in the bases of Chilean unionism.

Table 4.2 presents the most recent statistics provided by the Labor Ministry based on the new legislation established in the so-called Labor Plan.[14]

A number of observations can be made about union membership figures. First, the number of union members in recent years is far less than what existed in 1972, and by 1985 it equalled only 9.0 percent of the work force and 10.2 percent of the employed. Second, the average number of members per union in 1985 was 72 compared with 140 prior to 1973, which indicates a growth of small, local-level union organizations. Third, the local-level unions were severely affected by the crisis of 1982–1983, but significantly recovered thereafter. Last, there has been major growth in federations and confederations, and in their membership. The proportion of workers in federations went from 29.2 percent in 1981 to 48.1 percent in 1985, something which implies a better prospect for the national trade union movement.

It is also interesting to analyze the statistics by type of union, as is presented in Table 4.3. Those affiliated with company unions in 1985 represented only 69.5 percent of the total work force, and members of company unions, the only people who have rights of collective bargaining, in 1985 represented 7.1 percent of the employed workers. Members of intercompany unions represented 1.5 percent of all union members in 1985. The members of independent and transitory unions, whose only

TABLE 4.3
Union Affiliation by Union Type: 1981–1985 (Number of Unions and Members)

Types	1981	1982	1983	1984	1985
Company					
Unions	2,895	2,792	2,962	3,099	3,250
Workers	294,475	242,851	221,564	236,730	250,900
Inter-Company					
Unions	440	462	476	489	511
Workers	50,019	48,080	42,689	42,844	45,011
Independents					
Unions	565	661	784	926	1,017
Workers	43,497	44,061	42,525	50,135	51,422
Transitory					
Unions	77	133	179	200	216
Workers	7,960	12,478	14,125	13,616	13,630
Totals	3,977	4,048	4,401	4,714	4,994
	395,951	347,470	320,903	343,329	360,963

Source: Reworking of Labor Ministry statistics at the PET.

access to influence is by seeking to exercise pressure over the authorities and public opinion, in 1985 represented 1.8 percent of the employed population.

It is necessary to emphasize, nevertheless, that the impact of company unions is greater than indicated by the number of members, now that the effects of collective bargaining benefit workers who are not members. Moreover, the figures for the intercompany unions do not adequately reflect reality, since the number of declared members seems to be less than the actual figure in order to more easily fill the quorum that the law establishes in decisive union meetings. On the other side, affiliation figures in mining and industry are very much higher than average, above all in large companies, so that the union movement possesses greater force in those key strategic and historical sectors.

As has already been shown, official figures do not agree fully with the union structure, nor the radius of action and influence of the unions. As a result, to complete the picture it is necessary to analyze the informal organization of Chilean unionism.[15]

After 1977, national-level union groups involved in sociopolitical activity became consolidated as a replacement for the CUT. Among these, the *Coordinadora Nacional Sindical* (CNS), or National Union Coordinator, was particularly important. Given its internal composition, it was the most comparable to the old *Central Unica*. In the CNS sectors of the traditional and new left and the more open sectors of the Christian Democrats were grouped together. It drew support from workers in industry, mining (except those of copper and petroleum) and in construction, as well as from important groups of teachers and peasant trade unions.

Another important groups is the *Central Democrática de Trabajadores* (CDT), or Democratic Workers Central, whose principal bases are composed of union members from state sector companies, the attorney general's office, electro-metallurgical industries, and some peasant sectors. This group is formed by workers with centrist ideologies, especially Christian Democrats and Radicals.

Though much smaller than the others, a third group that has had national importance is the *Frente Unitario de Trabajadores* (FUT), or Unitary Workers' Front. Of Christian Social tendency, it has important support among the graphic and the transportation workers.

Alongside these groups or centrals – that together account for the major part of Chilean unionism – it is necessary to mention the *Confederación de Trabajadores de Cobre* (CTC) or Copper Workers Confederation. Upon taking control of the CTC in 1981, leaders in opposition to the regime have begun to act in coordination with the other groups. According to official statistics, this confederation has over 22,000 members, a figure greater than any other organization of its type. Moreover, its central position in the extraction of the principal Chilean export product gives it a weight greater than that indicated by the official number of members.

Finally, the *Confederación de Empleados Particulares* (CEPCH) or Private Employees Confederation, has also intervened nationally as an autonomous group. It has traditionally represented lower income private employees whose former relative advantages compared to blue collar workers has been affected by the neo-liberal economic policy.

These five union groups united in May 1983 in an organization of the national-level, *Comando Nacional de Trabajadores* (CNT), or National Workers Command, intended to coordinate actions in defense of union rights and to promote the return of democratic politics. Subsequent to the establishment of the CNT, some important confederations like the petroleum workers and bank employees joined. On the other hand, the CDT withdrew from the CNT in order to reaffirm its commitment to an autonomous central, unlike the old *Central Unica*.

The CNT has become the most representative organization in Chilean unionism. It broadened its council in 1986, with the latter directly made up by representatives of federations and confederations, something that gives it a greater weight than organizations of the second level. The CNT proposes to call a congress in 1988 to form a unified central that is both pluralist and democratic.

It is also necessary to mention a group founded in 1984 on a territorial basis, the *Movimiento Sindical Unitario* (MSU), or the Unitary Union

Movement, which is not affiliated with any of the national groups nor to the CNT. Its scope of action is limited.

The existence of groups or centrals that have a national influence clearly signifies the vitality of the Chilean union movement. This is especially clear if taken in the context of the authoritarian regime.

TYPES OF UNION ACTION

During the first six years of the military regime, union action was primarily defensive in nature. It centered on the legal defense of its members, the winning of joint contracts, and the denunciation of the repression imposed on the unions and their leaders.

The implementation of the "Labor Plan" marked a milestone in the recent evolution of the Chilean union movement. From a state of semi-paralyzation, the unions moved to a stage of defense and denunciation that united their forces for internal reconstruction and income recovery. After some vacillation – certain leaders were advocating that the new legislation was absolutely unacceptable – the union movement began to emerge as a force opposed to the new system of norms. This was a similar process to what had taken place in the 1930s when the unions adjusted to new social legislation despite the opposition of the anarcho-syndicalists. In this case, however, it seems that the emergence has been more conflictual now that the leaders have radically denounced the new legal code and have plans to demand its elimination with the return to democracy. In other words, they have taken advantage of the space opened by the authoritarian regime, but without accepting its functional logic.

One of the more relevant characteristics of the reconstruction and the new economic demands is that they have occurred in an atmosphere of increasing labor unity: no parallel unions have been created, in spite of the legal possibility, and frequently, even when various unions existed in the same company or firm, they have negotiated jointly. In the agrarian sector (particularly affected by the new legislation), communal unions have been reconstructed, converting themselves into multi-company unions; agrarian confederations of diverse ideological orientations have united in joint actions to the point of forming a single umbrella organization, the National Peasant Commission. Employers have appeared not only as adversaries who pressure through their economic power, but also as bosses who have at their service the military regime and the legal structures. As in other circumstances (in the mines controlled by foreign capital, for example), the visibility of an adversary has contributed to the formation of class consciousness and the unity in action of the rank-and-file.

The movement toward the reconstruction of local union organizations and collective bargaining at the company level has had as an effect the internal democratization of union life. Members perceived that their concrete interests were not ignored and they had more than just distant representation of the national unions. This involution of unionism in a period of economic recovery produced a certain distancing between the local unions and the centrals. To be sure, the fact that centrals did not have legal recognition and had difficulties in democratizing themselves raised questions with respect to their representivity. But it was not a new type of unionism that was centered and enclosed within the company, free from sociopolitical concerns, but rather one that proposed that the top pay attention to concrete problems and not limit itself to carrying out actions at the macrosocial level.

On the other hand, collective bargaining and strikes did not have the hoped for effects, instead producing a sense of frustration in most cases. The average of real salary readjustments obtained in collective bargaining in the 1979–1980 period reached approximately 7.5 percent, equivalent to the rate of growth of the economy during that period and to the increase registered in the index of wages and salaries (which includes the great majority who did not collectively bargain). In the 1980–1981 period, the average of real adjustments obtained in collective bargaining was approximately 3.5 percent, a figure below the increases in the wage and salary index. With respect to strikes (which were not very numerous, with only about 50 in each period), they permitted unions to obtain only very small increases over management's counteroffers. In many cases, they did not obtain anything.[16] As a result, workers – excluded for so long from the struggle for the companies' surplus – perceived themselves as a class repressed by economic and legal structures imposed by the authoritarian state. The hopes of recovering their power to negotiate, of getting better salaries and working conditions, and of gaining at least part of what they lost in the first years of the military regime were frequently frustrated. As a result, even the rank-and-file saw the need to obtain the workers' reinclusion in the economic and social system, a reinclusion that required a democratic reorganization of the political system.

When the Labor Plan was implemented, an important part of union action developed at the plant, or company level. The reorganization of the unions, elections, and collective bargaining absorbed the time and efforts of the leaders. Even more, in dealing with a period of economic recuperation, it became necessary to expand union action into new areas such as working conditions, culture, sports, etc. Indeed, economic recovery seemed to open the possibility of taking advantage of the favorable situation to broaden the field of union action and to consolidate the organizations, as had happened in other countries. Nevertheless, this tendency was never consolidated for various reasons, primary among which was the brief duration of the period of economic expansion and the penetration of "consumerism" in the labor rank-and-file. In fact, the possibility of gaining – even through expensive credit – goods that had been prohibited by simple economics (color televisions, refrigerators, or, at times, even automobiles) led many workers to value individual consumption over the advantages that collective action would bring. This "perverse" consumption – in terms of the cost and the addictive character of credit, rather than the goods acquired – frequently contributed to slowing the mobilizational capacity of the rank-and-file. In this manner, as well as through consumption, the neo-liberal model affected the unions, especially those which counted the highest income workers as members.

As the 1982–1983 economic crisis reduced gross national income per capita by 20 percent, the field of union action at the company level was reduced radically. Not only was it impossible to perform union activities, but collective bargaining lost much of its usefulness. The union ranks experienced a profound feeling of degradation, felt all the more as adjustments to deal with the recession consisted basically of a reduction in the buying power of wage earners. Between December 1981 and December 1983, the remunerations index fell 20.9 percent and the legal minimum wage 35.7 percent. The rate of unemployment rose from 16.0 percent to 28.2 percent during that same period. In these circumstances, union action at the company level assumed a totally defensive direction: the field of action was reduced and there was a shift from a consciousness oriented around income recovery to one of an oppressed class. Degradation was also felt in social sectors that had had relative advantages during the boom period (such as the workers in banking and those linked to the import business). Because of this, the crisis contributed to the homogenization of the Chilean worker class.

One of the principal objectives espoused by the military regime when it created the Labor Plan had been to avoid the "politicization" of the unions. To this end, unions had to confine their actions within the strict limits of productive units and they were not to concern themselves with global problems even when they affected a region or Chile as a whole. Nevertheless, faced with the impossibility of bringing forward effective collective bargaining, the unions demanded state intervention, pressuring for a radical change in the economic model and of the political system that sustained it. In this way, the politicization of union life occurred. The role of national labor leaders gained new importance, producing a greater closeness between them and local workers.

In more general terms, in this period as in other eras of Chilean union history, in years of expansion actions were centered in the area of organization and wage recovery. In the years of crisis, union action broadened, became politicized, and oriented itself to change the socio-economic system.

Until the beginning of the most recent crisis (1982–1983), the principal forms of political intervention by the national union organizations were declarations and public denunciations, letters directed to those responsible for national policy and, to a lesser degree, interviews with the authorities. These forms of action were aimed at defending and reaffirming the common interests of the workers, thus contributing to the formation and development of class consciousness. They constituted (limited) means of pressure on a very closed political system, and also permitted the maintenance of a union cultural presence in Chilean society. Although the national leaders who had access to public opinion had not been chosen by local level militants, the latter – and workers in general – felt represented. National labor leaders thus came to have a representational capacity that surpassed union organizational power.

The year 1983 marked a qualitative leap in the sociopolitical action of the union movement when the Copper Workers Confederation (CTC) called a national strike with the goal of showing the workers' rejection of the economic and political system on a massive scale. Despite a certain degree of volunteerism contained in this call – given the repressive capacity of the authoritarian regime – its mere announcement (reflecting the emergence of new leaders) constituted an unheard of action that shook the unions and evoked broad support. Faced with the regime's repressive efforts, the coordinating committee decided to replace the labor shutdown with a mass protest calling for the active support of slum dwellers, students, professionals, and even businessmen. Reaching even the middle sectors that at other times had been close to the dictatorship, the success of the protest showed the broad mobilizational capacity of the union movement and demonstrated its role as an actor to unleash a new social dynamic.

As noted earlier, in June 1983, the National Workers Command was established. One of its first actions was to call for a second protest. Because the call came from a unitary workers command (rather than from political parties) it had broad citizen response that conquered fear and extended the scope of the political awakening. The union movement thus became the cement binding different social forces that had been passive, or that had earlier acted in a disorganized way.

The repression unleashed by the regime against union leaders and, in particular, against those of the copper industry, aroused class solidarity. A general strike was declared in the large copper mines, the first one in ten years.[17] In this way, the decision to call an apparently unachievable, national stoppage incited an important strike in the principal export activity of the country. Once more this demonstrated that the direction of union action did not only respond to objective

conditions, but also depended on the nature of worker consciousness —
on subjective characteristics like the leadership ability of certain leaders
and on the combativeness of the rank-and-file.

The magnitude of the protests obliged the regime to make some
concessions in the area of public liberty and to recognize the political
parties. It was a very limited political opening, but one that permitted the
parties to initiate the reconstruction of their organizational structures at a
regional and national level. This partial reconstruction of the parties and
political coalitions provided reinforcement for the unions in a double
sense: it allowed them to count on emerging mediators in the "political
arena" and at the same time, on forces which contributed to the ideological and organizational development of their members. A dialectical
process of circular causality was present in which the union movement
and the political parties mutually reinforced each other. But the initiative
had come from the unions since political organizations – above all those
of the left – had been proscribed after the 1973 military coup.

The moderate political opening and the repression against the union
movement (particularly the massive firings in the large copper mines)
determined that the leadership of the protest would pass to the political
parties. This clearly indicates that the more closed the political system,
the more it tends to concentrate sociopolitical action in the union
movement.

The transfer of the leadership role in the movement for the return of
democracy to Chile to the political parties did not last very long.
Although the protests brought about revisions in the regime's neo-liberal
economic policy, it did not produce changes that directly favored the
workers. The massive demonstrations, even if partially tolerated by the
regime, did not lead to the modification of the state's anti-worker
orientation. As a result, the CNT decided to intervene in the area of
public decision, resorting to its traditional tactic, the national strike. The
new currency devaluation decreed at the end of 1984 which further
reduced the income of the salaried work force provided a favorable
environment. The climate for the work stoppage was reinforced by the
regime's inflexibility in its refusal to change the labor legislation, despite
repeated promises to do so. As a result, the return of the union
movement to the leadership of political protests was tied to two fundamental themes: the incapability of the political parties to force the regime
to make concessions, and the latter's lack of flexibility in responding (at
least in part) to the organized workers' demands.

The success of the national strike at the end of 1984, despite an almost
total lack of means of communication, was due to the close collaboration
between union organizations and the residents of Chile's poor districts.
A purely union strike would have been impossible, given the conditions
of strong repression and high unemployment; it was the intervention of

TABLE 4.4
Collective Bargaining by Economic Activity, 1984–1985

| | 1984 Negotiations | | | | 1985 Negotiations | | | |
	Total	Number of Unions	Number of Groups	Number of Workers	Total	Number of Unions	Number of Groups	Number of Workers
Agriculture	57	19	38	2,447	78	22	56	3,140
Mining	29	28	1	12,885	65	59	6	33,313
Industry	501	335	166	30,738	1,106	588	518	66,620
Electricity	22	13	9	4,007	11	6	5	1,854
Construction	3	2	1	118	15	11	4	873
Commerce	90	58	32	5,200	113	78	35	7,519
Transport	48	31	17	4,469	74	37	37	8,591
Finance	26	16	10	12,335	37	30	7	10,661
Services	120	77	43	8,636	180	123	57	15,602
Total	896	516	317	80,835	1,679	954	725	148,173

Source: Data calculated at PET on the basis of figures from the Dirección del Trabajo.

the poor urban areas, supported by the parties and political movements, that kept the employed from arriving for work. This meant that the unions had the capacity to bring out the workers, but could not openly assume the leadership of the process. Faced with an authoritarian regime, the basic role of the unions in the sociopolitical area seemed to be that of mobilizing, articulating their views, and unifying the various social forces. Unionism ends up informally representing all those who live by their labor, something which gives it a power which widely transcends its structural and organizational weakness.

Faced with the threat of a national strike, the military regime decided to reestablish a state of siege, restricting civil liberties even more than before. This caused trade unionism to reinforce its internal consolidation. We have already referred to the recovery of union membership after the 1982–1983 crisis. Collective bargaining also regained importance, as seen in Table 4.4.

Insofar as collective bargaining is concerned, the number of workers involved in 1985 was 4.2 percent of the employed labor force, and 59.1 percent of those unionized (that had the right to bargain). It should be noted that collective contracts normally last two years. The number of workers that bargained increased 83.0 percent between 1984 and 1985; and the average number of workers involved in each negotiation was 88.3. The number of bargaining groups increased notably, but there is no information with respect to the number of workers involved in such groups. The most important sectors and those that increased collective

TABLE 4.5
Strikes by Eonomic Activity, 1984–1985

| | 1984 | | | 1985 | | |
	Number	Number of Days	Number of Workers	Number	Number of Days	Number of Workers
Agriculture	1	2.0	259	1	55.0	28
Mining	—	—	—	3	12.3	5,159
Industry	32	12.8	3,088	26	22.8	2,179
Electricity	—	—	—	—	—	—
Construction	—	—	—	—	—	—
Commerce	1	17.0	11	6	16.2	605
Transportation	—	—	—	2	17.5	70
Finance	—	—	—	1	11.0	36
Services	4	7.25	237	3	12.0	455
Total	38	12.1[a]	3,595	42	20.5[a]	8,532

Source: Data calculated at PET on basis of figures from the Dirección del Trabajo.
[a] This is a weighted average.

bargaining the most were industry and mining, the traditional bastions of Chilean unionism.

There is no aggregate data with respect to the results of collective bargaining, but there is enough isolated information to suggest that 1985 was not as bad as 1984. In big companies (where the unions have more bargaining power) the salary adjustments obtained in collective bargaining were 93 percent of the consumer price index increase (compared to only 86 percent in 1984).

In reference to strikes, the most recent available data are those in Table 4.5.

The data provide the basis for some important observations. (1) The number of strikes was very low, so that the workers involved in 1985 corresponded to only 0.24 percent of the employed work force and 5.8 percent of those that collectively bargained.[18] (2) Between 1984 and 1985 the number of workers striking and the length of the strikes increased, an indicator of increased union activity. (3) Except for mining, the average number of workers involved was very low, an indicator of their scant power to pressure the total society. (4) In important sectors like construction and agriculture, strike activity was null or almost null because of the legal restrictions already mentioned.

The lifting of the state of siege in June of 1985 (due to international pressure) produced a reactivation of social and political organizations. In recent years, two opposition blocs had already been established: the Democratic Alliance, or *Alianza Democrática* (of the center left, led by the Christian Democrats), and the Popular Democratic Movement, or *Movi-*

miento Democrático Popular (of the left, led by the Communist Party). With the end of the state of siege, and under the stimulus of the influential Catholic Church, a new coalition appeared, The National Accord, or *Acuerdo Nacional*, that grouped together not only the center and sections of the left, but also diverse parties and sectors of the right. This shift by a part of the political right revealed the increase in the decomposition of the regime, and at the same time revealed the existence of a viable political alternative to the military regime.

The union movement, which already had had problems in not mirroring the divisions of the political blocs within its own ranks, found a new challenge in the National Accord due to the exclusion of the Marxist left from participating in the Accord. In addition, the unionists did not see their economic goals and projects plainly incorporated in it.[19] While the Central Democrática de Trabajadores enthusiastically joined the Accord, the Coordinadora Nacional Sindical and the Comando Nacional de Trabajadores valued above all its points referring to the support for labor organizations and reinforcement of labor rights. On the other hand, these central organizations perceived that the Accord – by incorporating groups from the right – could be converted into an element that would slow social mobilization. In other words, with the reactivation of political organizations and the establishment of blocs, the union movement perceived that it was not only ceding its leadership role in the Chilean struggle for the return to democracy, but that it could also lose a part of the relative autonomy that it had already won.

Precisely to reaffirm its autonomy of action, the union leaders fashioned a "workers petition" designed to express the demands of the rank-and-file and to bring about dialogue with other social sectors. To achieve the demands of its petition, the labor movement – together with students and organizations of the poor called for a new day of protest in September 1985, semi-paralyzing the country. But once again, the protest did not change the direction of the military regime; on the contrary, the regime began a violent repression, jailing the principal union leaders. As a result, today Chilean unionism finds itself in a critical place now that neither the broadest opposition political accords nor the most massive social demonstrations have been able to force the military regime to yield, in spite of that fact that the regime's exhaustion is more and more visible.

In 1986, the union movement outlined a new course of action that implied joint efforts not only with students and the poor, but also with other social groups. The *Asamblea de la Civilidad*, or Assembly of Civility, formed in April of that year fulfilled the requirements of a wide social coalition for the return of democracy that the CNT had been proposing for two years. In fact, the *Asamblea* – organized by the Federation of Professional Associations – included a broad spectrum of civil organizations, among which were found businessmen and truckers. As there was no form of exclusion, all ideological currents were represented. Incorporating particular claims, the "Demand of Chile" was formulated with the fundamental goal of restitution of popular sovereignty and the reestablishment of democracy. With the objective of supporting the "Demand," labor leaders called a national strike for the beginning of July, which notably reduced the country's productive activities for two days. It achieved significant participation from the middle sectors, especially from doctors and teachers. Even small and middle sized companies closed down out of an agreement between businessmen and workers. On this occasion the military regime again reverted to armed repression, and jailed the leaders who had originally called the strike; they gave no sign of acceding to the social and political pressures from the majority of the country.

This type of action implied new problems for Chilean unionism: first, how to participate in a broad social coalition without limiting itself to a subordinate role or losing its identity; second, how to break the linkage of mobilization and repression. After all, if no changes were obtained in the economic, social, and political system, the workers might become demobilized.

UNIONISM, THE STATE, AND DEMOCRACY

In all Latin America, the state has occupied a central place in labor relations. Conflict over redistribution of wealth has been more important in the area of the political system than in the area of labor relations; political bargaining has been more important than collective bargaining; and industrial and labor relations in general have been dependent on the political system.[20] Chile has not been an exception to this rule. In fact, according to theses proposed by various authors, the Chilean nation was shaped since its origins by the state, even more than other Latin American nations.[21] As a result, the state played a central role in the formation of the industrial working class and in the action of the unions.

During the military regime, the role of the state has tended to shrink – if not disappear – with respect to being a force for economic and social development and in being a mediator of social conflicts. In contrast, it assumed importance as an authoritarian, repressive force, inspired by "national security" ideology in combating "internal enemies" and their allies. Among those enemies (characterized as marxists, border line marxists, and those having ties to the marxists) one finds a good portion of Chilean unionism. The application of the neo-liberal economic model (which combats the big unions because it considers them to be "monopolies"), reinforces the repressive direction of the authoritarian state. A concentrated and exclusionary economic model that accepts high levels of unemployment allows the state to count on the support of big business in weakening the unions.

Nevertheless, as no state can maintain itself by force alone, after almost two decades, the Chilean authoritarian state – without abandoning repressive practices – presents itself as the guarantor of the functioning of the market economy. For that purpose it dictates legislation that permits certain areas of tolerance, but always within the context of a global strategy of excluding the organized working class: it seeks to eliminate labor conflict and to place very strict limits on collective bargaining.

The military regime has not sought to establish a highly centralized unionism, but has expounded its neo-liberal ideology according to which workers would obtain benefits to the extent that the market economy functions well. Nevertheless, this ideology has not penetrated the rank-and-file. The same unionists that for tactical motives have sought forms of bargaining with state organs have demanded the restitution of lost labor rights and the return to the institutional forms of recognition that existed before the dictatorship. The regime has only been successful in achieving very limited and conditional union support in some state enterprises by resorting to particularistic clientelism. The disposability of funds for leadership training activities, the selective assignment of social benefits, and resolving minor membership problems have permitted it to maintain this clientele. At the end of 1985, it was estimated that of a total of 147 federations and confederations, 10 were controlled by officialist unions. All the rest (93.2 percent) were controlled by the opposition.[22]

In spite of pressure by the state and the neo-liberal economic policy, there has been no surge of strictly wage-oriented company unions in Chile. The structural and organizational weakness of Chilean unionism, accentuated during the authoritarian regime, has reinforced the importance of the big national federations and confederations. This federalist unionism does not have pragmatic orientations other than to preserve its ideological options. In spite of official propaganda that tends to disparage the politicians as being guided by mean ambitions rather than defending labor interest, there has been no surge of apolitical, nor of anti-political or even anti-party trade unionism. Nevertheless, this does not mean that the orientation of Chilean unionism is exactly the same as it was prior to the emergence of the military regime. In the first place, there exists a clear tendency to obtain a greater autonomy with respect to the state. Even if there is a return to a democratic state, the experience of the dictatorship without doubt will result in unions avoiding being manipulated by government institutions. On the other hand, as we have already said, one of the limitations of historical unionism in Chile was its excessive dependence on the political parties. The repression exercised against political leaders and the impossibility of the parties exercising the mediating function that they had fulfilled at other times have brought the unions to seek greater relative autonomy with respect to the political parties. One is not dealing with the rise of a unionism of a corporatist or anarchist cut, but one with a greater relative weight for unions that have played a principal role while the parties were forced into recess. While it is possible that some union influence will be lost when the restrictions on political activities are lifted, it is unlikely that past levels of dependence will return.

The greater autonomy of the union movement can be attributed to the surge and development of a broad network of nongovernmental institutions that fulfill support functions in the areas of education, consultation, and extension. At other times, these functions were fulfilled first and foremost by institutions dependent on the political parties. The experience of the Latin American countries that have returned to democracy and in which nongovernmental institutions have continued functioning in a manner relatively autonomous of the political system leads one to believe that in Chile these institutions will also be able to continue fulfilling the functions that will make possible a greater degree of union independence.

Nevertheless, the increase in autonomy is conditioned by the unity of the labor movement. In order for Chilean unionism to become a national actor that decisively influences political life, it needs to act in a unitary way; divided labor is not considered a valid representative, especially if one considers the structural and organic weakness that has been accentuated in recent years. The internal unity of the Chilean labor movement has not been affected only by repression imposed by the state apparatus or by massive anti-Marxist propaganda. Internal labor unity has also been impacted as Chilean unions have had to resort much more than before to international solidarity, aid that seems to come linked to certain conditions. As a result, the ideological divisions that characterize the large international union organizations tend to be reproduced within the country.[23] For example, the exclusionary anti-marxism of the *Central Democrática de Trabajadores* is without doubt connected to the support that it receives from the *Organización Regional Internacional de Trabajadores* (ORIT).[24]

Notwithstanding, there are social conditions that push towards greater labor unity. One of these is the relationship with the Catholic Church, of great importance during the years of military repression. The union movement needs to act in solidarity if it wishes to maintain its support, now that the hierarchy of the Church tends to avoid interventions that could be interpreted as the taking of partisan political positions. As a result, the unity achieved among the peasant confederations – themselves of varied ideological direction – has been due in good part to the intervention of support institutions linked to the Church. On the other hand, owing to its own weakness, Chilean unionism has had to seek out multiple allies in various institutions, as much national as foreign, among which those that defend human rights stand out. This plurality of support not only contributes to a greater autonomy for the movement, but also stimulates its unity since these institutions normally favor unitary forms of action.

In summary, within Chilean unionism there exists a clear tendency towards greater autonomy with respect to the state and to political parties, but within that tendency there are social conditions that run in different directions. The second basic theme of Chilean unionism during the military regime – more fundamental even than the tendency for autonomy – is its demand for democracy.[25] The theme of democracy is present in every debate and action of the union movement, superimposing itself on the different ideologies. Prior to the military regime, the working class supported the democratic system with a double objective: (1) to obtain the collective advancement of the salaried workforce and (2) to achieve deep economic and social transformations. In other words, support for representative democracy was conditioned not only upon the latter respecting the rules of the game, but also on its making economic and social democratization possible.[26] In recent years, the democratic demands of the Chilean workers has also had the objective of the economic and social advancement of salaried workers, not so much to obtain new benefits, but, more basically, to win labor's reinclusion in society. Faced with exclusion by the authoritarian state, workers aspire to regain their lost rights and to have some decisional power in the distribution of sacrifices that the reestablishment of democracy will require.

During the military regime, Chilean unionism has redefined democracy as a system that guarantees the human rights of people and, in particular, labor rights. The position of those who defend the dictatorship of the proletariat as an alternative to the Pinochet regime are absolutely a minority within the union movement. The socialist option in some of its forms is present in debates, and is, without doubt, the majority view, but it is an option that does not question the fundamentals of representative democracy, instead proposing socialism as a means to deepen democracy, giving it a solid economic and social basis.

Finally, it is necessary to point out that the Chilean union movement has not renounced its objective of realizing profound economic and social transformation, but it now perceives with more clarity that these will not be possible nor stable if there is no agreement that can produce consensus among all of the social actors that have force and participate in some form in the wish for change. The active presence of labor in the *Asamblea de la Civilidad* is a clear indicator in this respect. The reduction in the importance that the industrial sector had at other times and the simultaneous growth by the tertiary sector (and, in particular, by informal urban activity) have forced Chilean unionism to redefine its role in the process of social change: it is now not limited to defending class interests, but also actively collaborates in the fashioning of a national project.[27] Unionism of a mainly worker cut tends to be displaced by a unionism that places emphasis on the defense and the promotion of labor rights through sociopolitical action within the democratic framework.

NOTES

This chapter has been translated from the Spanish original by Valerie Thurber and Edward Epstein.

1. Trade unionism of anarchist tendency which had some importance at the beginning of the century was losing force as the state legalized union action. See Jaime Ruiz-Tagle, *El movimiento obrero en Chile, 1850–1964* (Santiago: ILADES, 1974).

2. For all this section, see Ruiz-Tagle, *El sindicalismo chileano después del Plan Laboral* (Santiago: PET, 1985).

3. See Humberto Vega and Ruiz-Tagle, *Capitalismo autoritario y desarrollo económico: Chile, 1973–1981* (Santiago: Programa de Economía del Trabajo, or PET, 1982).

4. See Oscar Muñoz, *Industrialización y grupos de interés* (Santiago: CIEPLAN, 1977).

5. Tariffs were reduced abruptly, reaching 10 percent, and an artificially low exchange rate was maintained.

6. These figures are from the *Sociedad de Fomento Fabril* (SOFOFA), or the Society for Manufacturing Development.

7. Figures from the *Instituto Nacional de Estadistica* (INE).

8. In the decade 1964–1973, the average figure for unemployment had been 5.2 percent. Figures from INE.

9. Data from INE. See Berta Teitelboim, *Indicadores económicos y sociales* (Santiago: PET, 1985).

10. See Enrique Errázuriz, *La desigualdad de remuneraciones en la industria chilena* (Santiago: memorandum, Universidad de Chile, 1978); Ruiz-Tagle, *Situación salarial y modelo económico* (Santiago: VPO-PET, 1980); and Ruiz-Tagle, "El costo de la crisis": El poder de compra de las familias más pobres, 11, *Mensaje*, 344 (1985).

11. Guillermo Campero and René Cortázar, "Lógicas de acción sindical en Chile," *Estudios CIEPLAN*, 18 (1985).

12. *Estadísticas sindicales, 1956–1972* (Santiago: DERTO, Universidad de Chile, 1977).

13. See Campero and José Antonio Valenzuela, *El movimiento sindical en el régimen militar chileno, 1973–1981* (Santiago: Instituto Latinoamericano de Estudios Transnacionales, 1984).

14. Patricio Frías, *Prácticas y orientaciones del movimiento sindical en la lucha por la democracia* (Santiago: PET, 1986).

15. *Ibid.*

16. See *Informe de coyuntura económica* (Santiago: VECTOR, 1981).

17. In 1980 there was a legal strike at the "El Teniente" mine, one of the largest in the country, but this was a labor conflict limited in terms of its goals.

18. For a comparative point of reference, it is useful to mention that in 1967 there were 1,114 strikes in which 250,510 workers took part. See Ruiz-Tagle, *Dos enfoques metodológicos del sindicalismo en Chile* (Louvain: memorandum, Université Catholique de Louvain, 1971).

19. See Frías, *Prácticas.*

20. See Alberto Cuevas, *Sindicato e Potere nell'America Latina* (Rome: Edizioni Lavoro, 1985).

21. See, for example, Mario Góngora, *Ensayo histórico sobre la noción de Estado en Chile en los siglos XIX y XX* (Santiago: Ed. la Ciudad, 1981).

22. Cristián Riego and Gonzalo Rivas, *Evolución y perspectivas del sindicalismo oficialista* (Santiago: PET, 1986).

23. Campero, *El sindicalismo internacional y la redemocratización de Chile* (Santiago: CED, 1984).

24. ORIT (*Organización Regional Internacional de Trabajadores,* or the International Regional Workers Organization) follows the AFL-CIO line of the United States. The anti-marxism of the CDT also has as a basis old disputes before and during the Popular Unity period.

25. See Manuel Barrera, *La demanda democrática de los trabajadores chilenos* (Santiago: CED, 1984).

26. See Campero, "El tema de la democracia en las organizaciones empresariales y los sindicatos de trabajadores," *Opciones* (1984), special number.

27. See Alain Touraine, "El sindicalismo chileno frente al régimen militar," in Manuel Barrera, ed., *Sindicatos y Estado en el Chile actual* (Geneva: UNRISO-CES, 1985).

Chapter 5 —————————————————————————————

Trade Unions and Labor Policy in Colombia, 1974–1987

Rocío Londoño Botero

*F*rom its origins until the 1940s, Colombian trade unionism was associated with the Liberal Party and diverse Socialist groups. In 1936, the Confederation of Colombian Workers (*Confederación de Trabajadores de Colombia*, or CTC) was created, its leadership principally made up of Liberals and Communist Party workers. A small number of unions remained outside this confederation, with some of them receiving ideological counsel from the Catholic Church and the support of the Conservative Party. In 1946, the Union of Colombian workers (*Unión de Trabajadores de Colombia* or UTC) was founded as a project of labor organizing that was expressly Catholic, Conservative, anti-Liberal, and anti-Communist. From that date, the political schism of the union movement remained constant, its fragments corresponding to the divisions of the left and new centrist movements (like the Christian Democrats).

Colombian unionism has not been characterized by single party hegemony or by the control of one particular political leader. In some periods, Liberal influence predominated, the strong leadership of two political figures, President Alfonso López Pumarejo and popular spokesman Jorge Eliécer Gaitán, most noticeably. In spite of the immense support that movements with anti-oligarchical and populist characteristics like Gaitanism and Gustavo Rojas Pinilla's National Popular Alliance (*Alianza Nacional Popular*, or ANAPO) attracted, their efforts to form their own union movements did not achieve lasting results. The UTC was dominant between 1950 and 1970, but not because the Conservative Party had significant influence among the urban working class. The absence of party hegemony in the unions led to a diverse and complex process of alliances, the goal of which being the achievement of internal political balance and the attainment of the force required to confront official and management labor policies. While a detailed discussion of

101

earlier events would be interesting, the present chapter – for reasons of space – will focus on the union movement as it encountered recent economic change and the socio-political crisis that has emerged since 1974.

Since the mid-1970s, Colombia has experienced new economic problems as well as worsening of tendencies inherited from the previous decade. Import substitution, the heart of the Colombian economic model, ceased being a policy priority; in its place priority was given to the expansion of the export sector and the search for greater integration into the world market. Accordingly the national economy became more sensitive to the cycles and transformations of the world economy and, with recessions and the accumulation of internal problems, passed through particularly critical periods for industry and the financial sector. On the other hand, the parallel economy based on drug trafficking and contraband (which has enjoyed various channels of influence) has displaced some traditional economic sectors at the same time that inflationary problems have grown, both stimulating speculation in land and capital.[1]

In this new context, the union movement faces problems not previously encountered and more complex than those it has been accustomed to sort out by agile manipulation of labor laws and local-level bargaining skill. In the last two decades, the union movement has been socially transformed through the massive organization of white collar employees and the expansion of self-employment. From the political perspective, it is no longer possible to speak of Liberal and Conservative bipartisan union control in defining the CTC and UTC. The political spectrum has been diversified and inter-union conflict and alliances have varied substantially with the constitution of a new confederation, the Unitary Workers Central (*Central Unitaria de Trabajadores*, or CUT). The CUT groups between 60 and 65 percent of unionized workers and the majority of leftist unions, including the Colombian Workers Union Confederation (*Confederación Sindical de Trabajadores de Colombia*, or CSTC) and the 'independent union movement' and has merged with strong unions that left the UTC and the CTC.[2] In the face of these significant changes, no stable general structure has developed.

The principal factors of the new union dynamism can be examined through three key topics: (1) the effects of economic changes on labor; (2) the characteristics of union behavior in terms of strikes; and (3) the political crisis and the new pattern of union alliances. It is necessary to point out the tentative character of this analysis and the impossibility of reaching definitive conclusions given that the processes described are very recent and still unfinished.

THE EFFECTS OF ECONOMIC CHANGES ON LABOR

Although parts of the period under consideration were not marked by economic crisis, the two moments of recession – between 1975 and 1977, and between 1979 and 1985 – had a strong impact on national economic structure and the labor market, employment stability, and worker income. At the same time, the reorientation of economic development toward foreign commerce was accompanied by modifications of the exchange rate and fiscal policy, as well as sectoral policies that also affected labor's behavior. Inasmuch as the macroeconomic measures began to have a more direct impact on the welfare of workers, the usual union tactic of local-level bargaining began to lose its efficiency as the unions were progressively forced to concern themselves with general economic concerns and sectoral- and national-level bargaining with the state and major economic interest groups. The changes in labor policy and tactics led to the development of latent political conflicts and the redesign of the organizational and political structure of the labor movement.

The first years of the 1970s passed with signs of economic growth and prosperity expressed by such indicators as the availability of foreign exchange, the expansion of foreign trade, and the accumulation of international reserves. From 1976, the bonanza in the export sector linked to the exceptionally high price of coffee (lasting until 1980) and the boom in the drug trade produced considerable growth in reserves, sharpening the inflationary tendency begun in 1972. From an appreciable trade deficit at the beginning of the decade, the economy yielded a significant surplus at its end, and inflationary figures historically below 10 percent rose to the 20–27 percent range after 1972.[3]

In the opinion of economists, the change in the export sector had different effects on the economy. The agrarian sector experienced sustained growth until the end of the 1970s as well as important modernization in coffee production. The behavior of the industrial sector was, on the contrary, very uneven, with severe crises in 1975–1977 and in the first five years of the 1980s. The international recession of the mid-1970s drastically affected industry because of reduced demand for manufactured goods and greater competitiveness of imported goods in the internal market. The freeing of imports intended to open the domestic market for the purpose of controlling inflation especially weakened some portions of industry inasmuch as the greater productive specialization to which they aspired was slowed by the prolonged 1979 recession.[4] These fluctuations in economic development and the reorientation of macroeconomic policy negatively affected the basic interests of the salaried workforce, especially those of industrial workers.

The effect of inflation on the whole of the economy and on the population's standard of living occupied one of the central places in the economic debate and in the trade union opposition to official policies. In effect, the inflationary process produced a continuous deterioration of real urban salaries between 1971 and 1977 owing to the constant increase in the cost of living and a restrictive salary policy based on the view that the control of wage increases constituted an effective mechanism for the control of inflation. In this respect, the 1986 report of the Mission on Employment made the following evaluation:

> [U]rban salaries have been very sensitive to the acceleration of inflation. Between the beginning of the 1970s and 1977, the income of urban labor experienced a severe contraction which was particularly dramatic in the public sector. The rapid increment [of salaries] between 1977 and 1984 was above all a recuperation of the losses of real income during the years in which inflation accelerated.[5]

The unions did not accept the thesis that salary increases constituted one of the factors causing inflation or that, as a consequence, fixing of maximum limits was required in salary bargaining. Experience showed the disparity between the annually fixed salary increases and the continuous rises in cost of consumer goods, housing, and public services. Accordingly, salary restrictions faced very broad and diversified opposition. In contract negotiation, unions sought to exceed the general limits for salary increases fixed by the government and demanded improvements in the package of fringe benefits. In reality, these fringe benefits were an indirect form of salary increase. In contracts and national-level bargaining (some of which were preceded by strikes and demonstrations), the unions were shaping a broad economic program containing the following demands: an across-the-board increase of wages and salaries of some 50 percent; proper mechanisms for price control; a freeze or reduction of public service charges; and the freezing of rents and subsidies or low interest rates for the acquisition of housing. This double pressure for a general increase in salaries and against the elevation of the cost of living, inasmuch as it involved not just unions but very broad sectors of the population, stimulated the renovation of union tactics consistent with the search for sectional and national agreements among the diverse union groups. Agreements between these groups and popular organizations such as boards of Community Action, civic committees, associations of renters, and consumer cooperatives were also achieved. In this manner, a front against official policies and the high cost of living was organized. The traditional slogan of the general strike was replaced by "national civic strike," the first of which occurred on September 14, 1977. Finally, the unions displayed continuous pressure for annual increases and standardization of the minimum salary, utilizing their presence on the National Salary Council (NSC), the organization of government/interest group consultation with exclusive decision-making powers on minimum salary levels.[6] In earlier periods, increases in the minimum salary had been sporadic and utilized a scale differentiated by regions and categories, something which made bargaining very difficult. Not every increase was the result of mutual agreement and unions expressed continuous criticism of the NSC, but it is certain that the Council was one of the fronts where union struggle was most successful. From a code of 27 separate minimum rural and urban salaries, in 1983 the unions obtained the proviso for a single, national minimum salary and annual increases of its level close to the amount of inflation. Among the reasons for this advance was an agreement reached between union centrals and major employer groups made possible because the amount of the minimum wage was not seen to have much bearing on labor costs of large companies. In respect to the demands for a general salary increase in overall contract negotiation, the business groups maintained a hardline position of maximum limits on salary increases and aggressive support for the initial proposal of President Alfonso López Michelsen (1974–1978) of substituting a single "integral salary" for the separate salary and fringe benefit arrangements in existence.

A second group of problems and conflict has related to employment and labor stability. During the entire period under review these were obligatory themes for public debate, presidential programs, and union agitation, their salience associated with the second economic recession beginning in 1979–1980. In respect to the recent changes in the labor market, the structural limitations of the Colombian economy overlapped with the periods of recession and the policies to counteract them. To the average figure of structural unemployment (estimated at 8 percent), we can add the effects of the progressive dismantling of industrial protectionism, the general decline of economic activity, and business measures of personnel reduction, massive dismissals, and modifications in work contracts to reduce labor costs.

In quantitative terms, the figure for the increase in urban employment dropped from the 7 percent annual average of 1976–1980 to 3.6 percent after 1980. Between 1980 and 1985, manufacturing did not generate any new jobs. The urban unemployed who had been increasing by nearly 25,000 people per year increased by 100,000 annually during those years. In 1985, it was estimated that approximately 1.1 million citizens were without employment in major Colombian cities.[7]

For the unions, unemployment began to acquire new dimensions and characteristics. The volume of the unemployed numerically surpassed the unionized population, which was estimated at 873,000 workers.[8] This enormous reserve of skilled and semi-skilled workers during the 1979 recession allowed entrepreneurs to put into practice an aggressive policy of changing the disposition of personnel, massive dismissals and indemnizations, and the progressive substitution of temporary employees hired at lower salaries for permanent employees. As much for the unions as for businessmen, the question of labor stability and the terms of the labor contract became a key point of confrontation. While the first exhibited a tenacious resistance with appeals to the existing legal code, the second pressured for the realization of a labor code reform that would permit the unfreezing of the disposition of personnel, the abolition of indemnization for unjustified dismissal, and the implantation of an integral salary as a substitute for the regime of social and unemployment benefits.

Added to the growth of formal unemployment was expansion of informal employment – not subject to modern contractual relations – which today makes up over 50 percent of urban employment and, during the period in consideration, constituted the principal pool for the generation of new jobs.

This persistent phenomenon, of great importance in the development of the Latin American economies in the last two decades, has not only stimulated an intense debate among economists on the questioning of the validity of dualistic labor market theories, but has also attracted attention for dimensions previously unconsidered (like the quality of employment and the functioning of this activity in the maintenance of low salary levels).[9] On the other hand, Colombian governments have sought to rationalize informal job activity through the development of artisan production, small business, and mini-companies, with the view that this would be one type of solution for the problem of chronic unemployment. In spite of the economic and social importance of informal employment and of its diverse relations with the modern sectors of the economy, Colombian unionism only recently began to concern itself with this question. It has proposed the incorporation of self-employed workers into the social security system, denounced the precarious nature of the income and work conditions of this group, and admitted the necessity of fostering unionization in this area (which happens to be that where it has increased the most in recent years). It would not be logical to expect programs or solutions from the unions for a problem that economists and experts recognize as highly complex and in need of systematic investigation, the solution of which is related to structural proposals for economic and social development.

Similar to what has happened in respect to the inflationary process, the unions have been concerned on two levels with the problems of employment and labor stability: (1) in collective labor contracts defending present legislation dealing with labor stability[10] and in proposing a greater union participation in those organs linked with personnel hiring policies and the management of industrial relations, and (2) in the official consultation commissions where labor meets with government and major interests to demand the establishment of unemployment benefits, the reduction of the work day, the suppression by government decree of agencies and exchanges for temporary work, and official legal protection of labor stability. The historical experience of European and North American unionism in achieving unemployment benefits and reduction of the work week to 40 hours suggests that in the long term, these can turn out to be useful goals, but ones that require more practical formulations in accord both with the budgetary reality of the Colombian state and the bargaining power of the unions.

To conclude this point, it is worth briefly mentioning two themes closely related to the international dimensions of the economic crisis that are being felt in union policy and its implementation. In the first place, processes of business restructuring, renovation, and intensive use of technology – themselves rooted in the 1979 recession – began in certain industrial sectors like automobile and textile production, metalworking, etc. where their characteristics and effects on labor are only now beginning to be investigated. Studies indicate that these processes have been based in trend-setting companies where they are generating basic transformations in labor: (a) an important decrease of unskilled and semi-skilled workers, displacement of traditional artisan professions by technical personnel, and an increase of highly skilled workers and (b) modifications in the organization of work, especially in supervisory tasks where engineers and technicians have begun to displace foremen. A greater versatility in occupations has emerged that facilitates replacement of personnel and the contracting of temporary workers in both normal and peak production periods.[11]

Union behavior has varied from its initial defensive, conservative position. General attacks on the importation of technology and its consequences for the increase of unemployment has given way to a more realistic and rational position influenced to a certain degree by the experience and responses of European unions. The unions of the textile industry, for example, have had permanent advising from their international organization in the analysis of the effects of the textile crisis and union policies to deal with it. At the national level, the workers' centrals have demanded state intervention in the introduction of technology so that it does not affect employment levels and workers' labor conquests. Equally so, they demanded adequate retraining programs so that the job stability of workers can be assured. The reduction of work time from 48 to 40 hours per week, in their opinion, would permit new work shifts and positions. They maintain a critical attitude toward technology transfer without standing in the way of investigative studies and the creation of technology appropriate to Colombian conditions. Through collective contracts at the local and sectoral level, the unions have been proposing worker participation in decisions on committees selecting personnel and reevaluating jobs. They also have attempted to become involved in company implementation of retraining programs for workers.

Although anti-technological positions which idolize manual labor and the small company receive emphasis in union rhetoric, an advance of union consciousness is perceptible, but no conceptual elaboration or integrated policy has resulted. With respect to the changes in union organization and collective bargaining that these processes will demand in the near future, the confederations have done no more than push for the development of unions and union bargaining organized at the industrial level. Substantial progress has not yet been observed on this front.

In the second place, the magnitude the foreign debt of the Latin American countries has acquired in the last decade and the movement inspired by some governments to foster Latin American solidarity in renegotiating the terms of the debt, have stimulated strong support in a union movement already acquainted with anti-imperialist ideology. Although Colombia is one of the countries with the lowest level of indebtedness and the position of the government has been very moderate and diplomatic, the Colombian unions have adopted the radical slogans of "no payment on the foreign debt" and "break the pacts with international finance capital" as their own. Recently, the unions have proposed that Colombia adopt the position of the Peruvian government of only paying ten percent of its export earnings as service on the foreign debt.

The importance that the unions are giving to the country's relations with international financial entities has to do with two fundamental issues: ideological postulates such as national independence and sovereignty and opposition to imperialist domination being balanced against the economic and political interference that international credit agencies have had in the management of state investment and public utilities. In Colombia, for example, the restructuring of the tariff system and the indexing of public service charges were measures demanded by international agencies in return for the granting of credit. In summary, reasons of both an ideological order and pragmatic character, as well as political conditions required for Latin American solidarity, have led to this problem being given greater attention by the whole union movement rather than only by the union left, as had been usually the case.[12]

CHARACTERISTICS OF THE STRIKE MOVEMENT

In Colombia, as in most other countries, the type of legal norms and procedures related to the exercise of union rights constitutes one of the influential factors in the activity of labor organizations. In the Colombian case, the legal establishment still maintains restrictions that have been overcome in many other Latin American countries. In spite of having been questioned seriously by actual labor practices, the maintenance of this legal order by the state constitutes one of the central points for union challenge. It might be useful then to begin with a brief description of the most critical legal problems.

In the first place, the Substantive and Procedural Labor Codes (*Códigos Sustantivo y Procedimental del Trabajo*) issued between 1948 and 1950 have been partially modified by numerous laws and decrees without any new, coherent juridical corpus having been produced. Labor lawyers have indicated that in addition to the unstructured and anachronistic character of the Colombian labor code, the application of norms regulating union activity from the state of siege has restricted such activities and produced a legal parallelism which at times obscures a clear view of what the applicable norms are.

The dispersion and incoherence of labor and union law has in many cases led to the predominance of ad hoc interpretations of each law or decree so that the unions have become involved in unending debates and legal disputes.[13] Accordingly, the considerable weight of lawyers in the management of the unions and the figure of the traditional leader as a master in the interpretation of the Labor Code are not merely fortuitous characteristics.

In the second place, the norms applicable to union organization (originally established in Law 6 of 1945) permit diverse types of collective associations, but attribute to the local-level union (*sindicato de base*) priority in the representation of the members in most matters such as the presentation of worker demands, the naming of conciliators and arbitrators, and the signing of union contracts and collective agreements. From 1952, the coexistence of more than one union in the same company has been permitted, something which has intensified the atomization of the workers and made labor-management relations extremely difficult. These two aspects have had a definitive influence on the organizational structure and, together with other factors like the segmentation of the labor market and the diversity of bargaining and union competition, explain why in Colombia the dominant type of unions are local-level and craft unions, and that industry-wide organization has had a very precarious development (see Table 5.1).[14]

The legal prerequisite of a minimum of 25 members to create a union and the infinity of bureaucratic regulations for its legalization have acted as serious limits on unionization, especially since in Colombia 45.8 percent of urban industrial employment is found in companies of less than 10 workers and 55.5 percent of the jobs in the 10 principal cities are concentrated in the informal sector of the economy.[15]

TABLE 5.1
Number of Unionized Workers by Union Type and by Confederation, 1984 (in 1000s)

Union Type:	Company	Industrial	Craft	Various	Total[a]
TOTAL					
Number	399.0	143.0	330.0	1.0	873.0
Percent	45.7	16.4	37.3	0.2	100.0
Confederations:					
UTC					
Number	102.0	27.0	41.0	0.0	170.0
Percent	59.9	15.7	24.3	0.0	100.0
CTC					
Number	62.0	30.0	22.0	0.0	114.0
Percent	54.4	26.6	18.8	0.0	100.0
CSTC					
Number	44.0	34.0	16.0	0.0	94.0
Percent	46.9	36.3	16.6	0.0	100.0
CGT					
Number	23.0	8.0	18.0	0.0	49.0
Percent	46.0	17.1	36.6	0.0	100.0
"Independents"					
Number	170.0	44.0	233.0	1.0	445.0
Percent	37.7	9.8	52.3	0.2	100.0

[a] Fractional percentages have been rounded.
Source: Ministry of Labor, *Segundo censo nacional sindical,* 1985.

Third, the rights of collective bargaining and the strike, themselves crucial to any union, function under various restrictions in the private sector[16] and are expressly prohibited for state employees. This last point is one of the most serious legal problems facing the Colombian labor movement. In quantitative terms, it means that of the 915,307 workers employed in state entities, scarcely 17 percent have the right to sign collective contracts.[17] The remaining 83 percent are subject to whatever modifications in their contracts that the executive branch and Parliament determine, with the remaining work conditions being established in the particular statutes regulating each industry. The exclusion of the right to strike covers still greater numbers of workers given that this restriction also applies to "public service" (although not state-run) sectors of the economy. The definition of the "public sphere" has been widened as an indirect form of limiting strikes.

Finally, the crisis and fragility of legal labor practices present, among others, the following symptoms: the easiness and high frequency with which employers ignore contract provisions and omit the fulfilment of labor norms have been the cause of over half of the strikes of the last decade; in effect, of the inspection and supervisory activity carried out by the Labor Ministry in 12,452 companies between 1982 and 1985, reports conclude that scarcely 8.4 percent of these companies are totally obeying legal requirements relating to labor, and that the 91.6 percent in noncompliance are violating an average of 3.85 norms each. Faced with this anomalous situation, the capacity which the state has available to enforce industry compliance with labor norms through effectively sanctioning those in violation is largely nominal.[18]

In respect to the union rights of state workers, the final report of the Mission on Employment stated the following:

> [I]t is evident that legal and even constitutional standards have been widely exceeded. The strike is used regularly in the public services. On the other hand, despite the ban on collective bargaining by public employees, there exist multiple forms through which bargaining occurs on salary and fringe benefit agreements. Very diverse analysts have concurred in pointing out that the narrow legal mark in which the unions operate in the state sector has contributed to radicalizing labor conflicts, converting them into demands for broad union rights. . . .[19]

So far, we have noted the legal and economic elements that have affected union dynamics in recent years. We now move to examine one of its fundamental components, strikes and other forms of protest taken in worker confrontations.

Diverse factors are involved in the strike movement, and its various dimensions can be seen from different angles. In the interests of brevity and given the limitation of the information available, I will sketch those indicators and signs that suggest the strike movement's magnitude, its relation with economic and labor processes, and its connection to both the political climate of the country and the ideological currents within the unions.

In respect to the previous decade, that of 1974–1984 recorded a general increase in the average number of strikes and strikers. Nevertheless, in the last 25 years, the occurrence of an average of 70 strikes per year has remained constant except during moments of intense strike activity. A more precise, disaggregated examination of the data reveals that in Colombia the strike movement is markedly cyclical with differing particular characteristics. The moments of extensive strike intensity correspond to the years 1973–1975, 1977, and 1980–1982, while 1976, 1978–1980, and 1982–1984 saw less strike activity.

Although the general pattern of the strike movement corresponds to the strike cycles in the manufacturing and service sectors, the noticeably greater weight of services is perceptible, with particular periods of decline in strikes in the manufacturing sector (see, generally, that of 1981–1982) being related to the behavior of industrial activity. This tendency is even more evident upon examination of the number of

TABLE 5.2
Strikes, Strikers, and Strike Length by Economic Sector, 1964–1984 (Yearly Averages)

Sectors:	Years	Strikes	Strikers	Strikers/ Strike	Strike Days (1000s)	Strike Days/ Striker
Manufacturing	1964–70	21.4	11,629	543	291.3	25.0
	1971–80	25.7	15,326	596	567.0	37.0
	1981–84	27.8	21,476	774	753.6	35.1
Services,[a]	1964–70	13.0	7,993	615	121.6	15.2
Excluding Teaching	1971–80	19.0	48,392	2,547	516.4	10.7
	1981–84	41.5	149,726	3,608	556.2	3.7
Teaching	1964–70	20.7	58,852	2,841	727.7	12.4
	1971–80	12.3	94,355	7,671		
	1981–84	18.0	543,093	30,172	2,200.6	4.1
Transport	1964–70	5.9	14,622	2,496	68.0	4.7
	1971–80	4.6	8,621	1,874	45.1	5.2
	1981–84	12.8	47,528	3,728	425.4	8.9
Others[b]	1964–70	5.6	2,261	406	36.9	16.3
	1971–80	5.7	3,897	684	54.5	14.0
	1981–84	7.5	4,186	558	125.0	29.9
Total	1964–70	45.9	36,506	796	517.8	14.2
Excluding Teachers	1971–80	55.0	76,236	1,386	1,182.9	15.5
	1981–84[c]	89.5	222,916	2,491	1,860.2	8.3
Total	1964–70	66.6	95,358	1,432	1,245.5	13.1
	1971–80	67.3	170,590	2,534	2,486.9	14.5
	1981–84[c]	107.0	766,009	7,159	4,060.8	5.3

Source: Londoño, Grisales, and Delgado, "Empleo y sindicalismo."
[a] = Workers in state sector, finance, commerce, etc.
[b] = Workers in agriculture, mining, and construction.
[c] = There were 2 joint strikes of teachers and other state sector workers that were totalled separately under those sectors, but jointly in the total.

workers participating in strikes. For example, the increase in support was obviously greater between 1971 and 1980, and spectacularly so in the early 1980s (see Table 5.2). Although workers in services – especially in the state sector and teaching – represented the larger proportion of this increase, the increase was also noteworthy among industrial and transport workers. The increase in the number of strikers and work days lost denotes both the participation of the strongest unions and the notable economic and political impact of the strike movement.

The differences in strike behavior are evidently interrelated with the peculiarities of each economic sector, with the duality of labor law (the private sector versus the public sector), and with dissimilar strategies and influences of particular groups in the union movement.

A.   The strikes of industrial workers are closely related to collective bargaining on salaries and work conditions; the greater proportion (approximately one-fourth) occur in the process of negotiating demands because employers either fail to fulfill provisions of the collective contracts or violate labor norms. As is evident in table 5.3, the number of strikes due to such employer behavior increased significantly in 1980–1984 because of an important decrease in the number of collective contracts and the aggressive policy of reducing labor costs with which businessmen confronted the industrial recession. It is worth remembering that the nonfulfillment of labor norms has been a constant in Colombian business–labor relations given the very inefficient nature of state intervention at this level.

Despite the lesser statistical weight that industrial strikes have had, one cannot conclude that their importance has not been significant. Due to the structure of employment and because unionization occurs largely among the workers of the bigger establishments, the majority of strikes tends to take place in large-scale industry which accounts for 60 percent of the value added and 55 percent of industrial production, although it employs under 20 percent of the workers. In this sense, the economic and labor impact caused by this smaller number of strikes and strikers is probably greater than that produced by strikes in public services.[20] On the other hand, unlike what happens in services, industrial strikes develop within a process of bargaining structured and legally recognized, but suffering from restrictions such as the legal limit of 43 days duration, the use of arbitration tribunals, and the disposability or inflexibility of employers, all restrictions that have led to a relative politicization of working class strikes. Generally, these strikes are prolonged, with nearly half exceeding the legal limit, something which implies the existence among unions of a certain solidarity and resistance to legal and political restrictions: In short, these strikes create pressure for the widening of bargaining and strike rights.

There are other indices that point toward a greater politicization of the industrial strike, qualifying the widespread opinion in Colombia that industrial strikes have merely economistic orientations. A good part of industrial sector unions have actively participated in the repeated local and national actions against the economic and labor policy of recent governments; some workers, particularly those in the cement and textile industries, have established mechanisms for the coordination of demands and strikes with the goal of producing a greater economic and political impact. Since 1984, the labor and political protest strikes have increased as an answer to greater employer repression and the reoccuring murders of union and political activists by Colombian paramilitary groups.[21] In weighing this mode of protest, one has to take into account that workers run a great risk in that political protest strikes are not permitted by the Labor Code and businessmen are not as sensitive to political pressure as the state.

Finally, we have to point out that until the beginning of the 1980s, the *Unión de Trabajadores de Colombia* (UTC) controlled 40 percent of unionized workers in industry, followed in importance by the *Confederación Sindical de Trabajadores de Colombia* (CSTC) with 20 percent.[22] Control by UTC was, to a certain point, a limiting factor in strikes, given the tendency of this central to sign agreements and collective contracts, avoiding as much as possible the use of strikes. On the other end of the spectrum, the leftist CSTC unions demonstrated a much more marked inclination to use strikes in the process of collective bargaining and as a vehicle of political protest, of which more later.

B.   The magnitude of the strike movement in "public services" – particularly in those run by the state – constitutes without doubt, the most outstanding feature of the period considered.[23] As can be seen in table 5.2, in the years between 1971 and 1980, over 53 percent of the strikes and 88 percent of the strikers were found in such service industries (including teaching and transportation). Compared to the 1960s, the proportion of service sector strikers increased 86 percent. Although the recurrent strikes in teaching and the elevated numbers of participants overemphasize strike activity in this field, what is certain is that the volume of strikes and strikers in most other public services also experienced an obvious increase.

Among the factors which explain this phenomenon is the high proportion of unionized workers, the concentration of large groups of workers, and the persistent deterioration of salaries; on the other side, their exclusion from collective bargaining and strike rights (in the case of public employees) and of the right to strike (for the other workers in services) has led to greater radicalization. These circumstances have favored a large influence for leftist groups and the most radical union currents which, as has already been stated, take recourse to strikes with greater persistence.

In comparison to strikes in industry, those in the service sector present various peculiarities which require more discussion. Because of the legal prohibition against striking, and aided by an elevated concentration of workers, strikes in services are organized around the idea of massive participation, thus seeking a social impact that will protect workers from repression while simultaneously allowing them to bargain for their demands. To avoid the strike being declared illegal (and because the suspension of services, if prolonged, can have an adverse reaction on public opinion), the cessation of work tends to be of short duration and,

TABLE 5.3
Reasons for Strikes by Economic Sector, 1964–1984

Sector	Years	Changes in Contractual Demands (%)	Violations of Existing Labor Law or Contracts (%)	Solidarity or Protest Strikes (%)
Manufacturing	1964–70	80	19	1
	1971–80	82	18	1
	1981–84	67	31	3
Services,	1964–70	42	51	8
Excluding Teaching	1971–80	20	73	7
	1981–84	24	70	5
Teaching	1964–70	23	71	6
	1971–80	19	77	4
	1981–84	1	92	7
Transport	1964–70	22	51	27
	1971–80	17	80	2
	1981–84	6	80	14
Others	1964–70	54	44	3
	1971–80	33	65	2
	1981–84	37	63	0
Total	1964–70	47	46	6
	1971–80	44	52	3
	1981–84	31	64	5

Source: Londoño, Grisales and Delgado, "Empleo y sindicalismo."

on occasion, assumes distinct forms such as a slowdown strike (*operación tortuga*), a moving strike, and a permanent state of alert.

Since the majority of state employees nominally lack the right to sign collective contracts where work practices can be precisely defined, the strike is most commonly used to protest the frequent violations of labor norms (see Table 5.3).[24] The case of teachers presents a chronic situation: because of budgetary problems and fiscal disorder, delays in the payment of salaries and social benefits occur almost as frequently as prompt payment. On the other hand, typical promises rather than the legal obligations which typify most labor agreements in the state sector allow teachers' requests to be denied with greater ease once the political pressure which led to their adoption dissipates. There are many cases where managers or directors of public enterprises sign pacts with the unions without the necessary budgetary or legal support and are later forced to break them.

The greater proportion of strikes in this sector, as in industry, occur for economic and labor reasons; nevertheless, by challenging legal prohibitions and simultaneously pressuring the state to concede to them the right of a collective contract, the right to strike, and official union recognition, state workers give the strike a political character. In union activity, a broader consciousness of national problems such as the outline of reform proposals that exceed their own specific group interests is evident. The greater technical and political development of the unions for state workers has been stimulated not only by the circumstances which fall to their lot, but through their greater contact with the population, access to different sources of information, and the participation of an important number of professionals and experts on their leadership boards. [25]

C. From the political point of view, strike activity exhibits the increasing leadership of the leftist trade unions such as the CSTC and the "Independent Unions." It is also characterized by more or less periodic national and sectoral work stoppages and days of protest in opposition to government policies and to pressure for economic, social, and political reforms. Although guerrilla groups occupied the central place in political controversy at the start of the 1980s, the unions have also contributed to the movement for a "political opening and democratic reforms." [26] The rebirth of rural unions and the recognition that agrarian reform was not an anachronistic idea, as had been thought, but that it also constituted one of the axes of sociopolitical change has stimulated a considerable expansion of union agitation as much in terms of the type of participants as in the content and extension of the platform of struggle pushed by unions today. The obvious climate of social and political violence and the systematic murder of union and leftist leaders and activists, particularly of the Communist-led *Unión Patriótica*, has led to strikes and diverse forms of protest in the last two years. [27]

The greater influence of leftist unionism in the strike movement is not a recent phenomenon. In earlier periods when the UTC and CTC spoke for a sizable majority of the unions, the CSTC and the "Independent Unions" accounted for a far larger proportion of the strikes (see Table 5.4). Although this association between leftist unions and strikes has obvious ideological implications, the really new phenomenon has been the radicalization and rebellion of important individual UTC and CTC unions in respect to the conciliatory behavior of their national leadership. For the leftist unions faced with repression and violence, their response has necessarily become more consistently radical.

Of the strikes realized between 1971 and 1980, 74.4 percent were led by unions affiliated to the CSTC and the "Independent Unions." Of the 26.6 percent remaining (corresponding to the older UTC and CTC, and to the CGT founded in 1971), the role of the UTC was clearly the most

TABLE 5.4
Strikes by Confederation, 1971–1980

Year	Number[a]	% UTC	% CTC	% CGT	% CSTC	% "Independent"	% No Information
1971	37	16.2	08.1	—	27.0	48.7	—
1972	67	11.9	06.0	—	16.4	61.1	04.6
1973	53	11.3	09.4	01.9	22.6	52.8	07.5
1974	75	21.3	02.6	—	37.3	42.6	01.3
1975	109	14.7	04.6	04.6	28.4	42.2	08.2
1976	58	18.9	10.3	05.1	37.9	32.7	—
1977	93	24.7	09.6	01.0	40.0	35.5	—
1978	68	10.3	11.7	—	36.6	47.0	01.4
1979	60	21.6	15.0	—	26.6	38.3	—
1980	49	16.3	12.3	—	26.5	44.8	06.1
Total Avg.	669	17.0	08.5	01.5	30.7	43.7	01.4

Source: Alvaro Delgado, "El decenio huelguístico (1971–1980)," Estudios Marxistas, 23 (1982).
[a] In various cases, strikes had the joint union sponsorship of two or more centrals. Given this, the percentages totalled horizontally do not necessarily come to 100.

important.[28] In addition to the ideological aspects noted above, the high strike quota of the leftist bloc results from its almost hegemonic influence among the federations of state workers and teachers. Unfortunately, we do not have strike statistics by union affiliation for the 1981–1987 period, but a 1986 study by Alvaro Delgado shows that the participation of the UTC, CTC and CGT in the number of strikes of that year was reduced to 9.3 percent.[29] As we will see shortly, in 1986 a crisis broke out in those three labor centrals, with a significant part of their members supporting the creation of the new Unitary Workers Central (*Central Unitaria de Trabajadores*, or CUT) organized by the left.

Another politically significant phenomenon has been the realization of a general strike and a great number of regional and local civic strikes against each of the national governments in power since 1974. The political initiative for the national strikes was derived from union blocs created for that purpose whose alliance was based on (1) opposition to official salary and labor policies and to militant programs based on the economic and labor demands of the salaried workers; (2) petitions related to the increase in the standard of living of the whole population; and (3) broad proposals for social and political reform. The term "civic" has been used to indicate the link of these movements with strikes in neighborhoods, villages, and outlying areas that have occurred in Colombia for at least the last half century, and which involve popular associations and organizations other than trade unions. National-level civic strikes took place in September 1977, October 1981, and June 1985. The September 14, 1977 strike had the greatest political impact because sharp outbursts of urban violence recalled the surge of radical attitudes of the popular insurrection of April 9, 1948 in Bogotá, the "Bogotazo." Among the multiple characteristics and repercussions of these movements is that they generated processes of unity and inter-union alliances among traditionally hostile groups that later came together in an umbrella organization like the CUT.[30] On the other hand, the total opposition of the Liberal and Conservative Parties and the repressive responses of the various national governments contributed to broaden the weakening of union ties to the two traditional political parties.

THE POLITICAL CRISIS AND CHANGES IN UNION STRUCTURE

For any observer of the Colombian reality, the most obvious fact is that the country is now passing through a crisis of proportions similar to *la Violencia*, the period of violence between 1948 and 1957, but with different characteristics. In 1974, the constitutional period of the National Front nominally ended.[31] From then on, the country experienced new political processes such as the return of single party governments, the popular election of mayors, the dialogues and agreements of a cease fire and truce between the state and the guerrillas,[32] the various conflicts with drug traffickers, and an obvious increase in peasant and urban movements that have been modifying the sociopolitical scene. The shift from a relatively uniform and stable political system founded on the exclusive domination and shared control of the state by the Liberal–Conservative alliance to one based on political competition, the emergence of new social and political forces, and the maintenance of earlier coercive and repressive procedures (the State of Siege, the restrictive limits on union rights, and a considerable development of the military apparatus) occurred in the midst of an oppressive increase in political violence and crime.

The task of summarizing these processes and their connection with union dynamics is, at the very least, difficult. These are processes in mid-development, with roots in the political history of the country, and about which the first analyses and interpretations are only now emerging. This new crisis broke out when, at the intellectual level, the country had hardly begun assimilating the earlier *la Violencia* of 1948.

The union movement has been studied from its origins and first decades of its development; there exist more up-to-date studies, but these have a basically economic perspective. With the exception of the works of Miguel Urrutia and Daniel Pecaut that touch on some of the political aspects of the National Front, there are no specific studies on the relations among unions, the state, and political parties, and even less on

TABLE 5.5
Rates of Unionization, 1947–1948

Years	Number of Unionized (1000s)	Number of Employed (1000s)	Unionization (%)
1947	165.6	3,519	4.7
1959	250.0	4,511	5.5
1965	700.0	5,222	13.4
1974	835.2	6,656	12.5
1980	1,051.0	8,540	12.3
1984	873.4	9,370	9.3

Sources: (1) Number of unionized. 1947–1965: Miguel Urrutia, *Historia del sindicalismo en Colombia* (Bogotá, Universidad de los Andes, 1969), table 17. For 1959 and 1965, I have adopted the mid-point of Urrutia's range. 1974: Jaime Tenjo, "Aspectos cuantitativos del movimiento sindical colombiano," *Cuadernos Colombianos*, 5 (first quarter 1975), table 1, with adjustments: the number of unionized in the agricultural sector is reestimated, supposing a rate of unionization similar to that of 1980; in addition, the number of those unionized in industry is estimated supposing a figure of 64.4 percent of the workers in the manufacturing sector, as is used in Urrutia, Table 17, for 1965. 1980: Gómez, Londoño, and Perry, *Sindicalismo y política económica* (Bogotá: FEDESARROLLO-CEREC, 1986), with an adjustment: the rates of unionization in electricity, gas and water, the financial sector, and domestic services are presumed the same as in 1974. 1984: Ministry of Labor and Social Security, *Segundo censo nacional sindical*, 1985.

(2) Number employed. 1947: interpolated based on the population censuses of 1938 and 1951. In 1938, all data on domestic workers in the rural sector was excluded from the total of those employed. 1959–1984: Alvaro Reyes et al., "Tendencias del empleo y la distribución del ingreso," report prepared for the Mission on Employment, 1986.

the recent evolution of the unions as affected by internal changes and the general social crisis.

The Structural Weakness of the Unions and the Changes in their Social Composition

Among the researchers of the union question in Colombia, there is no consensus on the number of workers that presently belong to unions; the variation in the quantitative calculations is due to the lack of a systematic and reliable registry of the members and to conceptual and methodological differences in the determination of the economically active population. In spite of both mathematical differences and those of theoretical origin, the most commonly held opinion is that in historical and contemporary terms the unionized population is very small and the economic power of the unions quite limited.

Taking into account the statistical adjustments made by the Mission on Employment in 1986, it is possible to note that in the periods of greater organizational strength, the figure for unionization scarcely reached 13.4 percent of the active population (in 1965), a proportion that more or less remained constant until 1980 when a decline of the unionized population began (see Table 5.5). The low level of Colombian unionization can be

TABLE 5.6
Unionization by Economic Sector, 1974–1984[a]

Sectors	Rate of Unionization		
	1974 (%)	1980 (%)	1984 (%)
Agriculture[b]	1.5	1.5	1.8
Mining	31.8	19.6	12.9
Manufacturing	30.3	21.4	8.1
Construction	8.2	15.8	3.1
Commerce, Restaurants, and Hotels	8.9	3.2	3.0
Transport and Communications	42.2	39.4	50.8
Non-Domestic Services[c]	26.0	25.8	22.2
TOTAL	12.8	12.3	9.3
TOTAL, excluding Agriculture and Domestic Service	22.8	19.0	13.7

Source: Final Report of the Mission on Employment.
[a] Adjusted data as in Table 5.5
[b] Historically, the rate of unionization in agriculture has been very low, but in the 1980s there has been an intense union reorganization in the agricultural area that, possibly due to difficulties in data collection, is not depicted in the data of the 1984 union census.
[c] This includes services in finance, in the state sector, and in electricity, gas, and water. It is surmised that the number of unionized workers in domestic service is minimal.

attributed to economic and political reasons. In the first place, there is a considerable volume of under- and unemployed workers whose continuous pressure on the labor market has weakened the bargaining capacity of organized workers. In the second place, the continuous increase and the proportions reached by informal, scattered employment with dissimilar work conditions has noticeably diminished the possibilities for unionization. Third, the legal restrictions discussed above have made the creation of unions difficult and narrowed the margin of action for those already existing. Last, the state and management have created diverse obstacles that block the expansion and modernization of the union structure.

The decline of unions in recent years is principally related to the economic recession that affected the general level of employment, indicating business closures and failures, dismissals of large groups of unionized workers, and a progressive substitution of permanent workers by part-time workers for whom unionization is forbidden.[33] The examination by economic sector of unions shows the existence of very unequal development. Organization is particularly weak in agriculture, small industry, commerce, and construction, while the strongest unions are concentrated in the large factories, transportation, communications, state enterprises and institutes, and the financial sector. But perhaps the most obvious imbalance is found in the recent loss of power by manu-facturing unions and the new preponderance acquired by white collar unionism and workers in services (see Table 5.6). It is worth remember-ing that a sizable portion of transportation and communications workers belong to state enterprises. Two very recent processes not registered in the 1984 union census are the revitalization of agrarian unions stimu-lated by the political climate of the first years of the truce with the guerrillas and a continuous activity of forming unions by self-employed workers whose importance lies in smaller towns rather than in large cities.

These changes in union structure and the elevation of the edu-cational level of workers has led to a relative renovation of leadership ranks and to the ouster of bureaucratized leaders lacking the qualities required for a more technical and political union leadership style. The entrance of new leaders, many of them from the state sector, has been one of the causes of the accentuation of internal power struggles. In the case of the leftist unions, especially those of the CSTC, this generational change has assumed ideological connotations with the recrudescence of pro-worker positions on the part of sectors that have resisted accepting the new leadership of professionals and state functionaries. In addition, the dispersion of the union structure in company and craft unions and the poor development of unions organized by industrial branch has been reinforced by political polarization, the primacy of local leadership interests over more global ones, and internal struggles for power. Although the union left has had this sort of problem, they have been much more accentuated and widespread in the traditional confeder-ations.

The Crisis of the Confederations and the New Scheme of Union Alliances

In November 1986, the founding congress of the *Central Unitaria de Trabajadores* took place with the participation of 1,800 delegates repre-senting 45 federations and nearly 600 unions. Within one year of its founding, the CUT represented between 60 and 65 percent of the total of unionized workers in Colombia.[34] Only in 1936 when unionism was still in its early years had a similar level of organizational centralization existed. In short, the emergence of the CUT was a critical landmark in Colombia union history.

The decline of the UTC and CTC confederations and the stagnation of the CSTC can be seen in a quantitative sense in Table 5.7. The collapse of the CTC's influence gained momentum with the expulsion of Com-munist and Socialist unions in 1960. The disaffiliation of unions con-tinued because of internal struggles among factions and leaders for

TABLE 5.7
The Relative Size of the National Confederations, 1947–1984

| Confederation | Date of Origin | The Percentage of Unionized Workers | | | | |
		1947[a]	1965[b]	1974[c]	1980[d]	1984[e]
CTC	1936	66.1	34.4	25.0	20.3	13.1
UTC	1946	—	41.7	40.0	30.7	19.5
CSTC	1964	—	13.1	20.0	10.0	10.8
CGT	1970	—	—	—[f]	06.9	05.6
"Independents"		33.9[g]	10.8	15.0	32.1	51.0
TOTAL		100.0	100.0	100.0	100.0	100.0

[a] Contraloría General de la Republica, *Censo sindical nacional*, 1947.
[b] Miguel Urrutia, *Historia del sindicalismo colombiano*. Bogotá, Ed. La Careta, 3rd ed. of 1978.
[c] Jaime Tenjo, "Aspectos cuantitativos del movimiento sindical colombiano," *Cuadernos Colombianos*, 5 (First Quarter 1975).
[d] H. Gómez, R. Londoño, G. Perry, *Sindicalismo y política económica*. Bogotá, FEDESARROLLO & CEREC, 1986.
[e] Ministry of Labor and Social Security, *Segundo censo nacional sindical*, 1985.
[f] There are no figures for membership for the CGT in 1974: the CGT probably represented a minimum percentage included among the "Independents."
[g] Includes the Confederación Nacional de Empleados with 3,533 members.
Note: The data for 1965, 1974 and 1980 are estimates that present problems of interpretation. One commentary in this regard is found in Gómez, Londoño, and Perry.

control of the central, the markedly pro-government direction, and the corruption of some leaders. By 1984, the CTC had barely 13 percent of the unionized workforce and, after the creation of the CUT, it was reduced to minimum size when 5 of its federations and 1 national union disaffiliated.[35] What remains of the CTC is divided into two factions, the official CTC headed by Apécides Alviz, a union leader from the sugarcane mills, and the Committee to Reconstruct the CTC, led by Marco A. Córdoba of the metalworkers. During the National Front, this central lost its Liberal Party linkage; although a Liberal majority was maintained on its governing board, Manuel Felipe Hurtado presided over it until his death at the end of 1987. Hurtado, of Conservative Party identification and leader of the sugar workers, found himself discredited because of his personalist conduct of the central and his implication in fraudulent manipulations of union finances.

On two occasions, in 1980 and 1986, the CTC sponsored lists of candidates in the parliamentary elections, but they never even attained a thousand votes. Hurtado proposed that the CTC be incorporated into the CUT, provided that he was given the presidency of the new central. During this decade, the leadership of the CTC maintained an ambiguous and vacillating position toward the principal national political mobilizations; its involvement in the strike movement was minimal, with the exception of the Colombian Portworkers Union which for particular labor reasons sponsored various strikes. In March 1986, Pedro Julio Caro, president of the Del Valle Workers Federation, FITVA, and Silvio Parra, general secretary of the Santander Workers Union, USITRAS, were expelled: they were accused of having ties to the M-19 guerrilla group but, in reality, their expulsion was because they made serious denunciations of corruption against the CTC president and other members of the leadership and for CTC participation in joint activities with the CSTC and the "Independent Unions." The faction formed by FITVA and ISITRAS played an important role in the creation of the CUT.

The UTC maintained an ample majority of the unions as members until the beginning of the 1970s (see Table 5.7). With some important differences, the UTC faced problems that had similar characteristics to those plaguing the CTC. For two consecutive decades, its presidency was occupied by Tulio Cuevas, an active militant of the Conservative Party and, on various occasions, a deputy in parliament. In spite of Cuevas' leadership, internal factions developed and competition for control and internal differences occurred. When Cuevas retired from the presidency in 1982 due to his nomination as secretary of the regional labor organization, ORIT–CIOSL,[36] there was a limited revival of leadership which delayed the decay for the moment when Víctor Acosta, a Liberal, was elected president. However, two aspirants for that position remained who possessed different political positions on union leadership. The first was Jorge Carillo, a Liberal, who had been minister of labor in the last two years of the Betancur government. Unlike what might be expected, he stood for positions favorable to the interests of workers during his term as minister, thereby clashing with business; he also supported the President's peace policy. In a rapid and interesting political evolution that he labeled a process of "reeducation," he challenged the UTC leadership and was expelled, together with other members with solid UTC credentials. Toward the end of August 1986, Carillo reached an agreement with the CSTC and the "Independent Unions" on the creation of the CUT, and in November was elected president of the new union central.

The second figure was Alvaro Ramírez Pinilla, president of the Cundinamarca Workers Union (*Unión de Trabajadores de Cundinamarca*, or UTRACUN). In 1981, he favored an internal split because of his personal ambitions and disagreement with the UTC's participation in joint labor strikes and protests. He merged UTRACUN into the CGT, obtaining the presidency of this central. In July 1987, due to personal rivalries and accusations of dishonest use of union funds, Ramírez Pinilla was expelled from the CGT, with UTRACUN disaffiliating within a month. Through an agreement, the details of which are unknown, UTRACUN returned to the CGT without its traditional head, leaving the presidency of that group in the hands of Julio Roberto Gómez, leader of the state workers.

The UTC also encountered another problem in that it has been seriously affected by the loss of members during the industrial recession and by the disaffiliation of unions not sharing the conciliatory and ineffective positions of its national leadership against conditions strongly punishing workers. A typically illustrative case was that of the Antioquia textile workers unions.[37] Some of these groups were attracted by the more belligerent positions of the "Independent Unions" and later joined in the creation of the CUT. The discovery of embezzlement and improper expenditures of union funds by some leaders, together with ties to drug traffickers, has been a key factor in the loss of prestige of the UTC leadership and an important component in the labor union crisis. Appropriately, in November 1987, a group of UTC workers occupied the building of a cooperative linked to the central to demand a report on the withdrawal of 100 million pesos and the swindle committed at an auction of taxis belonging to the cooperative. Because of this protest, the *Unión de Trabajadores del Valle del Cauca*, the *Sindicato Nacional de Trabajadores del Dulce* and the *Sindicato Nacional de Trabajadores de Obras Públicas* all formally disaffiliated.

These recent disaffiliations and the number and size of the groups that entered the CUT (eight region federations, three industrial federations, and three national unions) give an idea of the level of dismemberment of the UTC.[38] It would be fitting to mention that the great depth of this confederation's crisis reflected its participation in strikes and protests in which leftist leadership was obvious. Those actions, as well as the drastic effects of official labor policy, stimulated radical attitudes in a rank-and-file which generally did not share the conciliatory attitudes, agree with the political maneuvers, or gain from the corruption of the union elite.

With an understanding that they faced crisis and as a reaction to the advance of leftist union committees (unified for the first time in the 1984 Committee on Behalf of a Unitary Central), the UTC, the CTC, and the CGT formed the Democratic Union Front (*Frente Sindical Democrático*, or FSD). The FSD launched a belligerent, anti-leftist campaign to form a "Unitary Democratic Central," counting on the support of the Liberal and Conservative political directorates, the Betancur government, and the major interest groups. Its principal initiative was the goal of forming a "social pact" with government and business based on a memorandum of requests sent to the government in May 1985. They presented the initiative as an alternative to the national civic strike organized by the other union group. The social pact never achieved anything concrete, instead causing internal friction within the FSD. Meanwhile in June 1985, the third national civic strike took place with relative success. In February 1986, as a plan was developing for unitary action to celebrate May Day, the FSD tried to revive the pact, something not possible because almost all of its requests had been denied by the executive branch. As the secretary general of the CTC, Ramón Márquez Iguarán stated, "The social pact was the great failure of the FSD. The government became very elusive in either responding to the formal requests or signing the 'famous' social pact."[39]

In August 1986, the Front, in association with independent unions not part of the CUT project, issued a communiqué rejecting the idea of forming a unitary central, thus hoping to impede new disaffiliations. Its effect, as already seen, was practically null. The collapse of the FSD's political initiative and its weak organizational base brought the Front to a rapid end. Although alliances persist between the three centrals that made up the FSD, sharp internal conflicts and rivalries among different leaders indicate that organizational unification is not possible in the short run. In addition, the CGT is, to a considerable extent, under the influence of Christian Democrats and radicalized Liberals who support a course of action independent of the FSD.

The evolution of leftist union groups has experienced different characteristics. From the 1960s, the division of the international Communist movement and the repercussions of the Cuban revolution have been felt in the union movement. To general ideological differences can be added dissimilar interpretations of the revolutionary process in Colombia. Faced with the constitution of the CSTC as an explicit project of the Colombian Communist Party, Maoist, Trotskyist, and pro-Cuban union groups were developing, with the greatest influence concentrated in unions in public education and state agencies. The sector entitled "Independent and Classist Unionism" emerged there, forming as a revolutionary union alternative to the "reactionary" and "reformist" centrals. With the exception of transitory alliances, the confrontation between this sector and the CSTC was characterized by extreme sectarianism.

At the beginning of the 1970s, a relaxation of relations between these two sectors occurred because of joint protest actions against the government and as a product of the electoral alliance between the Communist Party and the MOIR (*Movimiento Obrero Independiente y Revolucionario*, the Independent Revolutionary Worker Movement), then the principal Maoist group. In 1974, the National Opposition Union (*Unión Nacional de Oposición*, or UNO) was formed and, from that alliance, unions led by the MOIR (such as the Teachers Federation and the Telecom union) joined the CSTC. Their membership in the CSTC was ephemeral owing to the brevity of the electoral alliance, the differences within the new leadership in the management of labor conflicts and the distribution of leadership posts, and because of the CSTC which – having obtained legal recognition that year – unilaterally switched policy from support for a proposed new unitary union central to a strengthening of the CSTC.

After this disastrous attempt at unity, the "Independent Unions" undertook a search for agreements and a mechanism for joint action among the various non-Communist committees. The CSTC began a process of reconsidering its unitary project that basically consisted of the recognition that the formation of a single central was an impossible project, and that it was necessary to seek closer relations and joint actions not only with the left, but also with the traditional centrals. At its 1983 congress, the CSTC adopted the goal of forming a unitary central based on ideological and political pluralism.

During this entire period, the political and organizational work of the CSTC to a great degree was oriented toward stimulating the processes of unity and action and the coordination of union struggles with the diverse elements within the union movement. There was no shortage of internal political debate, nor of tenacious resistance from some leaders and unions. For its part, the "Independent Unions" maintained the formation of a "class-based central" as an objective, and through various committees where momentary alliances with the CSTC were established it attained the coordination and maintenance of a fragile political equilibrium among its diverse parts.

The national civic strike of September 14, 1977, confirmed a new direction and a distinctive dynamic on the process of unity. For the first time, the four union confederations and a part of the "Independent Unions" put aside their differences, succeeded in writing a single set of worker and popular demands, and realized the largest urban protest organized by unions acting autonomously. This event demonstrated the capacity for mobilization and pressure that the unions had been able to achieve through unity and a more political and independent leadership.

The response of the López Michelsen government was characterized by intransigence and the application of sanctions and military repression. It offered to talk with the UTC and the CTC with the warning that it would not negotiate any set of demands, describing the alliance of these centrals with the left as "subversion." The menacing and aggressive attitude assumed by the then minister of government, Rafael Pardo Buelvas, reinforced the anti-union image of the government and strengthened the ties of solidarity among the unions.

The Liberal and Conservative Parties, the large economic interest groups, and the Catholic hierarchy strongly opposed the strike. The Ospinista faction of the Conservatives expressed a certain sympathy with the movement in order to reinforce its opposition to President López. Political support then remained limited to the diverse groupings of the left – with the exception of the MOIR – the political leaders of Rojas Pinilla's ANAPO, and the Christian Democratic Party.

The 1977 civic strike was the first time that the official centrals participated in an action that constituted an open challenge to the government and to the traditional parties. The epoch in which the political directorates ordered or prohibited general strikes had become a thing of the past.

The leftist groups began questioning the position that saw unity and independence of the union movement as part of an ideological identification with Marxism, and that perceived the UTC and CTC as the conciliatory and corrupt expression of some of their leaders. The long and costly "project for unity" finally managed to take off on a more solid and realistic base. From the end of 1977 to 1980, the National Union Council (*Consejo Nacional Sindical*, or CNS) functioned as an organ of coordination among the four centrals. Its composition and its results were the object of a continuous polemic but it did manage to structure a common program of struggle and facilitated agreements and joint actions among region and local organizations.

Multiple actions and days of protest were simultaneously realized where the spectre of broad alliances did not always prevail, but where a sustained and uninterrupted rhythm of agitation and mobilization permitted the holding of a second national strike in 1981, and a third one in 1985.

At the beginning of 1986, the union movement had regrouped around two blocs: the *Frente Sindical Democrático* and the *Coordinadora Nacional de Unidad Sindical*. The second of these resulted from an initiative sponsored by the Colombian Federation of Teachers (*Federación Colombiana de Educadores*, or FECODE) with the participation of the CSTC and the majority of the unions and federations of the "independent" sector. The events of the second half of 1986 that ultimately led to the creation of the CUT are recorded in the documents of its inaugural congress:

> The crisis of the UTC and the CTC came to the surface in their respective plenums which took place in the city of Cali at the end of the month of June. Fifteen federations and 14 national unions representing approximately 65 percent of its groups disaffiliated from the UTC, and 7 federations and various national and regional unions left the CTC; the leaders of these organizations joined a unified union command and proposed the formation of a democratic and pluralist unitary central.[40]

The document affirms that the causes of this division "were not simple bureaucratic friction...," but profound reasons, among which it pointed to the following:

> They assumed a valuable critical position faced with the total economic and political dependence of the centrals in relation to the American Institute for Free Labor Development, a group financed by the United States Department of State. They denounced the collaborationist attitude of the leaders

who dared to propose that the policies of adjustment imposed by the IMF on our people be accepted.

They set down the discovery of moral corruption, the misapplication and theft of funds from the centrals, the blackmail, the lameness in the negotiation of demands, the ties to drug traffickers, and the proposals of silencing and maintaining immobilized their unions and federations. . . .

After successive meetings, on August 18, 1986, the representatives of these organizations and the Coordination of Union Unity signed a public declaration entitled the "solemn historic agreement for the unity of the workers," forming the Command in Favor of a Unified Central which would be in charge of the preparation for the founding congress of the CUT. At the same time, the CSTC made a decision to dissolve itself in order to make space for the new central. The CUT was finally constituted on November 15.

The CUT certainly appears to be a solid project and, to date, an alternative consistent with the union crisis. Nevertheless, it remains to be seen if it manages to establish itself as a really new confederation, structurally democratic in its decisions and pluralist in its leadership. For this, it requires not only the political will expressed by its founders, but also the minimal solution of three crucial problems. In the first place, the elaboration and practice of a coherent union policy that at the same time maintains the equilibrium between groups of very diverse political and union origins is required. In the second place, the replacement of national, regional, and local organizations – heirs to the previous union format – by a new, more centralized and functional structure must be made. Third, a reform of the present union legislation is needed. It is certain that the disposition for change and the force acquired by the CUT are decisive factors for the transformation of the organization, and its legal recognition is basic for the stability of the unions and for bargaining with the owners and the state.

While it was impossible here to systematically develop the problem of relations between the unions and the parties, the obvious modifications in the rigid arrangements between political parties and groups and the centrals and union factions that was predominant until the 1960s have been noted. Taking into account the events which characterize the present political crisis and the new union dynamics, it is possible to suggest that the tendencies toward greater union autonomy will continue without suggesting that this implies the rupture of ties with the parties. The formation of a labor party or movement with real perspectives for success does not seem likely. The tentative efforts, in this sense, have failed totally, given that union loyalties in Colombia do not necessarily correspond to political loyalties or vice versa. Today, for example, the great majority of workers electorally support the Liberal and Conservative Parties despite the widespread influence of leftist groups in unions. At the same time, political movements such as that led by Gaitán and Rojas Pinilla's ANAPO, movements that in their time obtained an extraordinary level of popular support, were not able to consolidate their own union organizations.

NOTES

This chapter has been translated from the original Spanish text by Edward Epstein.

1. For a discussion of the political and economic effects of drug trafficking, see various numbers of the newsweekly *Semana*; the Sunday supplement, "Por qué la economía va bien y el país va mal" of the daily newspaper *El Tiempo*, November 15, 1987; and Fabio Castillo, *Los jinetes de la cocaína* (Bogotá, Editorial Documentos Periodísticos, 1987).

2. The CSTC was organized in 1964 from the unions under Communist influence that had been expelled in 1960 from the CTC. See Hernando Gómez B., Rocío Londoño B., and Guillermo Perry R., *Sindicalismo y política económica* (Bogotá, FEDESARROLLO and CEREC, 1986), pp. 111–112.

3. *Ibid.*, chapter II.

4. Final report of the Mission on Employment, published as special number 10 of *Económica colombiana* (Bogotá, Contraloría General de la República, August–September 1986), chapter I.

5. *Ibid.*, p. 30.

6. The National Council on Salaries was created by Law 187 of 1959 with the powers to fix minimum salaries and to serve as a consultant for the government on salary policy. From its creation, it was made up of representatives of the government, the major interest groups ANDI, FENALCO, and SAC, the labor confederations UTC and CTC, and the Association of the Retired. In the Belisario Betancur government, the CSTC and CGT attended as specially invited groups. The administration of Virgilio Barco (1986–) eliminated the Salary and the Labor Councils (the latter created in 1968 by Decree 2210 with the same membership as the former), replacing them with the National Labor Council which combines their similar functions but lacks the power to make binding decisions. The CUT was included as part of the union representation.

7. Mission on Employment, chapter III.

8. Ministerio de Trabajo y Seguridad Social, Oficina de Planeación y Economía Laboral, *Segundo censo nacional sindical* (Bogotá, 1985). The first government labor census took place in 1947.

9. CEDE, Universidad de los Andes, *El empleo en las grandes ciudades colombianas* (Bogotá, 1981), Document 65.

10. Decree 2351 of 1965 remains in effect.

11. Eva Paus, "La dinámica de la acumulación y del empleo en la industria textil colombiana durante los 70s," *Coyuntura económica*, 12:4 (1982); Fernando Urrea, "Efectos de la tecnología en el movimiento obrero," *La investigación sobre el movimiento obrero en Colombia* (Medellín 1985); Gómez et al., chapter VII.

12. See *Documentos del congreso constitutivo de la CUT* (Bogotá, Ed. FECODE-CUT, 1987).

13. Gustavo Gallón, *15 años de estado de sitio en Colombia: 1958–1978* (Bogotá, Ed. América Latina, 1979); Jairo Villegas, *Derecho del trabajo* (Bogotá, Gráficas Pazgo, 1979); Diego Younes Moreno, *Derecho administrativo laboral* (Bogotá, Ed. Temis, 1978); Fabio Rodríguez V., *Elementos de derecho laboral* (Bogotá, Ed. CEIS, 1981); Francisco J. Triana, *Derechos humanos y garantías sindicales* (Bogotá, Gráficas Pazgo, 1978).

14. Articles 346 and 417 of the *Código Sustantivo del Trabajo* establish the following forms of labor organization:

> Colombian union structure is made up by three types of collective association, differentiated according to whether the member or affiliated is an individual, a union or a federation where these latter are labeled a union of the first grade, of the second grade or a federation, and of the third grade or a confederation. Organizations of the first and second grades at the same time can take the following forms:
>
> a. A local union (*sindicato de base*) formed by people working in the same company or establishment;
> b. A craft union (*sindicato gremial*) by people of the same profession, trade or specialty;
> c. A mixed union combining various trades (*sindicato de oficios varios*), by workers of diverse, dissimilar, or unconnected professions;
> d. An industrial union (*sindicato de industria*) by individuals who perform services in various companies of the same type of industry.

15. Gómez et al., p. 107.

16. In collective bargaining, the state has the role of arbitrator when there is no labor-management agreement in that stage of the process labeled as "direct bargaining" whose duration is 15 days from the presentation of the list of demands. The mediation of the Ministry of Labor and Social Security lasts ten days from the end of the former stage when, if there has been no agreement, private sector workers can declare a strike or ask for an arbitration tribunal; public sector workers must go to an arbitration tribunal because any strike is forbidden for them. Strikes have a legal limit of 40 days, at the end of which if there is no agreement between the disputants, the Ministry of Labor can unilaterally create an arbitration tribunal. A second way of bargaining is the anticipated collective agreement when workers are not unionized or the union represents less than a third of the workers. Generally, contracts or agreements are written for a two year duration.

17. Report of the Mission on Employment, tables 3–4, p. 56; Gómez et al., chapter IV.

18. Rocío Londoño, Orlando Grisales, and Alvaro Delgado, "Empleo y sindicalismo en Colombia," document prepared for the Mission on Employment, 1986.

19. Mission on Employment, chapter VI. The convening in the last two years of commissions to negotiate annual increases in salaries for the public sector has been unusual. Although they did not produce agreements and these commissions lack the ability to make binding decisions, they have constituted a

beginning of bargaining. At the same time, craft federations and unions have obtained modifications in fringe benefits and work conditions through informal agreements with management.

20. Ulpiano Ayala and Luz Amparo Fonseca, "El movimiento hulegüístico 1974–1981," *Desarrollo y sociedad* (published separately as *Estudios Laborales* 1), November 1981 (CEDE, Universidad de los Andes, Bogotá).

21. Alvaro Delgado, *Huelgas de trabajadores colombianos en 1986* (Bogotá, Instituto de Educación Obrera, INEDO, 1987).

22. Gómez et al., pp. 122, 146, 147.

23. In terms of the prohibition on the right to strike, the definition of "public services" includes all work realized in the public sector: transport, water and sewers, electric energy, telecommunications, health establishments, hospitals and clinics, charities, milk bottling and distribution, street cleaning and garbage collection, public markets; slaughterhouses, and the production and distribution of salt. Using this definition, one can estimate that over two–thirds of the strikes between 1981 and 1984 occurred in "public services." Of the total number of strikes manifested between 1975 and 1984, only nine percent were declared illegal by the Ministry of Labor (Report of the Mission on Employment, chapter VI).

24. State employees are allowed to present "respectful petitions" which their employers need not accept as a basis for negotiation.

25. Gómez et al., chapter III.

26. Although this slogan corresponded initially to the rhetoric of the Communist Party during the Betancur administration, its use became generalized by various social and political sectors including Liberal and Conservative Party groups.

27. From the month of November 1986 (when the CUT was constituted) to January 1988, approximately 70 members of that organization have been assassinated. Good documentation of this anti-CUT violence is found in Delgado, *Huelgas de trabajadores colombianos en 1986*.

28. The CGT was founded in 1971 based on the *Acción Sindical Antioqueña*, a 1961 Social Christian-influenced splinter from the UTC. It would absorb UTRACUN, the large Cundinamarca Workers Union, in 1981, thereafter being dominated by that group (Gómez et al., p. 112).

29. Delgado, *Huelgas de trabajadores colombianos en 1986*.

30. These movements have been examined in several interesting studies: Medófilo Medina, "Los paros cívicos en Colombia (1957–1977)," *Estudios Marxistas*, 14 (1977); Luz Amparo Fonseca, "Los paros cívicos en Colombia," *Desarrollo y Sociedad* (published separately as *Estudios Laborales* 3 (1982) pp. 17–30; Alvaro Delgado, "El paro cívico nacional," *Estudios Marxistas* 15 (1978) pp. 58–115; Victor M. Moncayo and Fernando Rojas, *Luchas obreras y política laboral en Colombia* (Bogotá, Ed. La Carreta, 1978).

31. The National Front consisted of an arrangement whereby the presidency would be alternated between the candidates of the Liberal and Conservative Parties in the period between 1958 and 1974, and all other offices would be divided equally between these two traditional parties. The goal was to reduce the interparty violence which had led to the brief loss of power by the traditional elite with the rise of the 1953–1957 military dictatorship of Gustavo Rojas Pinilla (Medófilo Medina, "Algunos factores de violencia en el sistema político colom-

biano, 1930–1986," *Anuario colombiano de historia social y de la cultura*. (Bogotá, Department of History, Universidad Nacional de Colombia) 13–14 (1985–1986).

32. This agreement was initially signed between the government and the FARC guerrilla group, going into effect May 28, 1984. A few months later, similar agreements were signed with the M-19, ELP, and ADO guerrillas. By 1988, the pact with the FARC was only partially in force. More detailed information can be found in Ricardo Santamaría and Gabriel Silva, *Proceso político en Colombia* (Bogotá, CEREC, 1984); and Olga Behar, *Las guerras de la paz* (Bogotá, Planeta, 1985).

33. Alvaro Delgado, *Anotaciones sobre el empleo temporal en Colombia* (Bogotá, Centro del Movimiento Obrero, Social y del Trabajo, Universidad INCCA de Colombia, 1987).

34. Through a rigorous examination of the unions affiliated with the CUT, Delgado considers that despite the clear majority represented by the new central, it does not represent the 80–85 percent of the unionized workers that its leaders have publicly claimed (Alvaro Delgado, "Bases para un debate sobre la lucha ideológica en la CUT," unpublished manuscript, 1987).

35. *Ibid*.

36. ORIT-CIOSL stands for the Interamerican Regional Workers Organization (*Organización Regional Interamericana de Trabajadores*), an affiliate of the International Conference of Free Union Organizations (*Conferencia Internacional de Organizaciones Sindicales Libres*), the anti-Communist world labor group with ties to the AFL-CIO of the United States.

37. Gómez et al., p. 138.

38. Delgado, "Bases para un debate,"

39. *Ibid*.

40. "Breve reseña histórica de la CUT," *Documentos del congreso constitutivo de la CUT* (Bogotá, Ed. FECODE-CUT, 1987).

Chapter 6

The State and the Unions in Cuba since 1959

Linda Fuller

*U*nions under socialism are often viewed as mere appendages of the state, lacking both the inclination and the ability to behave autonomously. Yet the opening paragraphs of the Statutes of the Cuban Union Confederation (CTC) declare that unions in Cuba are not part of the state (or party) apparatus, but mass organizations, independent of both.[1] Which description more accurately conveys the reality of the relationship between the unions and the state in post-revolutionary Cuba? This question does not lend itself to a simple or definitive answer. The reasons for this are threefold, and have to do with Cuban history, the concept of autonomy itself, and the status of knowledge about the socialist state. First, as shown in an examination of the organization and activities of the Cuban unions below, the degree of union autonomy from the state has undergone major changes in the post-revolutionary era. Thus, the answer to the question posed would differ depending on whether the historical referent were the first decade after the victory over Batista or a latter one.

Second, the concept of autonomy is multi-, not unidimensional, meaning the extent of union autonomy from the state can be gauged from various perspectives. Moreover, within each dimension there exists a whole range of empirical possibilities other than "total" dependence or "total" independence. As a result, though the focus of this chapter is limited to only two dimensions of autonomy (autonomy as *organizational independence* and autonomy as the *presence of conflict*), significant indications of both union autonomy from the state and dependence on it will be uncovered.

The third complicating factor in an investigation of union-state autonomy is related to the level of knowledge of one of the two partners in the relationship under study – the socialist state. Put simply, this

133

knowledge is as yet rudimentary, and so the temptation to presume an understanding of the socialist state based on our relatively far-advanced research on the state in capitalist settings is great. Yet even though the theoretical or empirical foundation on which to ground a satisfactory account of socialist state dynamics does not yet exist, this temptation should be resisted because there are strong indications that in many respects the socialist state is very different from its capitalist counterpart: the two types of states do not have identical functions; they derive their legitimacy from different sources and through different mechanisms; they bear a distinct relationship to classes, class struggle, and class interests in the wider society; and they do not have the same administrative or technological capacities and needs. A final difference between capitalist and socialist states is suggested by the content of the policies they execute, as will be shown below by means of an examination of some state policies that are of particular import to Cuban workers.[2]

With an understanding in mind of the difficulties to be encountered in gauging the degree of union autonomy from the state, this chapter begins to formulate an answer to the question of how much independence Cuban unions have through a look at the content of labor policies instituted by the Cuban state. These policies highlight one kind of difference between capitalist and socialist states, and form the backdrop against which unions and the state interact in Cuba. Changes in union organization and activities in the post-1959 period point up a general trend towards increased union autonomy from the Cuban state. An important question to address is why they occurred.

STATE LABOR POLICY

One indication of a way in which socialist and capitalist states differ emerges through an examination of types of policies implemented by the post-1959 Cuban state that determine the material position of labor. Though no systematic comparison with analogous policies of capitalist states can be attempted here, what cannot escape notice is that despite its small, underdeveloped, resource- and foreign-exchange-poor economy, Cuba has created a material environment for workers which in many respects is superior to that provided by capitalist states in many larger, richer, and more developed economies, not to mention the much poorer countries of the developing capitalist world.

By the mid-1960s, basic wages began to be set by the Cuban government through a system which classified jobs into general categories and specified numerous wage grades within each category. As Table 6.1 indicates, the basic monthly wage in Cuba rose until the mid-1960s, fell until the turn of the decade, and has continued to rise

TABLE 6.1
Average Monthly Wage in Cuba

Year	Amount
1962	130 pesos
1965	133 pesos
1970	115 pesos
1980	148 pesos
1981	168 pesos
1983	180 pesos

Sources: Claes Brundenius, "Measuring Income Distribution in Pre- and Post-Revolutionary Cuba," *Cuban Studies*, 9 (July 1979), p. 33; Carmelo Mesa-Lago, *The Economy of Socialist Cuba* (Albuquerque, NM: University of New Mexico Press, 1981), pp. 154, 193; Brundenius, *Revolutionary Cuba: The Challenge of Economic Growth with Equity* (Boulder, CO: Westview Press, 1984), pp. 109, 181–184; Medea Benjamin et al., *No Free Lunch: Food and Revolution in Cuba Today* (San Francisco: Institute for Food and Development Policy, 1984), p. 83. Mesa-Lago's figures are reported in current pesos. Other sources are not explicit.

since then. Basic wages were given a considerable boost in 1980 when General Wage Reform was instituted – the first time since the mid-1960s that remuneration for basic wage categories and grades had been revised. Over 2.5 million out of a workforce of 2.8 million benefitted, and an average wage hike of about 15 percent (22 pesos per worker per month) occurred.[3] Wage levels, which under capitalism are largely the outcome of the interplay of a myriad of market forces, just one of which is the activity of the unions, are determined in Cuba through bargaining within the highest levels of the state. Unfortunately, very little is known about state negotiations at this level, and so it is unclear what role, if any, unions play in this internal decision-making process. In the public forum, however, unions have not petitioned or pressured the state for overall increases in basic wages during most of the post-revolutionary era.

The total wage received by a Cuban worker, however, is affected by a variety of state policies besides those concerning basic wages, and in relation to this second kind of wage policy we have seen more debate both within the union and between the union and the state. Such policies have varied in their character and combination at different periods, but they have usually included ones dealing with overtime pay, rewards for especially hard or dangerous work, compensation to workers when production is interrupted for reasons beyond their control, and, very importantly, production norms.[4] Production norms began to receive special attention in the early 1970s as a way to solidify the connection between output and remuneration, neglected since 1966, and they have received ever-greater emphasis since then.[5] At present, the general policy is to set production norms in every job where it is feasible, and indeed the implementation of the 1980 General Wage Reform was made contingent on the institution of a number of measures aimed at improving productivity, including the expansion and improvement of these norms.[6] The overall result of this emphasis was that in 1982, 94 percent (1.1 million) of the country's workers whose work had been tied to production norms were actually being paid according to the norm system, and by 1984 the absolute number had surpassed 1.2 million.[7]

Production norms, the source of recurrent conflict between workers, unions, and owners under capitalism, have turned out to be controversial in socialist Cuba as well – this despite the fact that the unions have given their general approval to the state's attempts to expand and perfect their use. This was especially apparent in 1980 and 1981, the years when a massive country-wide campaign of production norm adjustment and implementation occurred in preparation for the implementation of the General Salary Reform. In 1980 alone, approximately 60 percent (about 1 million) of all production norms in the country were revised, and plans called for the readjustment of over 700,000 more in the next two years.[8] Problems centered on the state's contention that many production norms were too low, having been set that way in the 1970s or having gone unrevised despite technical or organizational improvements made in the work process, and that this negatively affected productivity and fueled inflation. Government figures for mid-1978 to the end of 1980 indicated that between 76 percent and 80 percent of workers were meeting or exceeding their production norms, between 33 percent and 38 percent of these by over 15 percent.[9]

However, workers and the unions did not always agree with the state's assessment, complaining that in some places production norms were being revised far too often, even when just a few workers were overfulfilling them. They argued that this threatened the stability of all workers' wages and encouraged them to restrict their work effort.[10] In two blunt speeches during this period, Roberto Veiga, secretary-general of the CTC, criticized the readjustment campaign for proceeding too quickly and without sensitivity, particularly in places where production norms had a long history of being overfulfilled and where revisions would certainly have a negative impact on workers' wages and create discontent. "One potato can upset a sack, and the big things always had a small beginning," remarked one Cuban leader in reference to this situation.[11] Despite state hopes to the contrary (and some union branches' overzealous support of the state's position), Veiga argued that in such cases the revision of production norms would have to slow down. There were even places, Veiga argued, where the whole idea ought to be scrapped for now in favor of some alternative system of remuneration.[12]

From the unions' and the workers' perspectives, a major part of the solution to the negative micro- and macro-political and economic ramifications of setting production norms too high, is increased workplace participation in establishing, revising, and implementing norms: When workers are involved in these processes they can counter tendencies to set production norms above what they find acceptable. "In every work center where the judgment of the workers and their leaders has been ignored with regard to the revision of production norms," commented Veiga, "we've confronted problems." Indeed, the Secretary-General has called workers' participation in setting production norms an "inviolate" principle of the union movement.[13] Apparently the state is convinced of the value of workers' involvement in establishing production norms as well, and it is built into the current resolution governing production norms and included in the instructions issued to officials who are responsible for setting them.[14] Moreover, there is evidence that workers' participation in setting production norms at their workplaces does occur: Zimbalist reported it "typical" for the official setting production norms, after making observations, to meet with concerned workers and the union to set the norm.[15] In a cigar factory I visited almost a decade later, the scenario described to me included consultation with workers before implementation of production norms that were based on average observations made by this official.[16]

It is very possible, however, that the "workers' participation prescription" for avoiding the political and economic ills resulting from production norms judged too high by producers might contribute to increased tension between workers, unions, and the state by creating a situation likely to result in the establishment of norms the state views as unacceptably low. Evidence from Cuba, and other socialist countries as well, suggests that worksite managers and workers, despite differing motivations, have a common interest in cooperating to keep production norms as low as possible, and they often appear to be quite successful in their efforts.[17] A key to success seems to be their ability to ensure that control of the process of setting production norms is retained at the worksite level, rather than being allowed to ascend into the hands of supra-worksite level political and economic managers. In other words, the more involved in setting norms actual producers become, though perhaps alleviating problems associated with high production norms, the greater the control over the process held at the point of production, and thus the greater the potential that exists for worker-management collusion against the desires of the state in depressing production norms.

Wage levels alone, however, are but crude indicators of workers' overall economic position. A more complete picture requires knowing, among other things, something about state policy affecting income distribution, unemployment, and living costs. A large and rapid redistribution of income in favor of the poorest segments of the Cuban population occurred in the first three years of the revolution. Scholars estimate that between 15 percent and 20 percent of the national income was transferred from the top to the bottom economic levels between 1959 and 1962, and that the lowest paid 40 percent increased its share of the national income from around 7 percent to 17 percent in those years.[18] Redistribution has continued since the early years, but at a far slower pace. Brundenius[19] estimates that in 1973 the poorest quarter of the population received the same share of national income it did in 1962 (10 percent); the poorest half increased its share 3 percent (to 30 percent), while the richest quarter's share declined 9 percent (to 43 percent). Estimated differentials between Cuba's highest and lowest paid workers since 1980 have hovered around 5:1 to 10:1, and differentials within occupational categories are estimated to have rarely exceeded 4:1 since 1962.[20]

Trends in the distribution of income across occupational sectors since 1959 has overall favored workers in agriculture as opposed to industry, though in absolute terms agricultural sector wages remain below those in the industrial sector.[21] Throughout the 1970s, the CTC publicly supported increased equality between these two sectors by calling for the elimination of the two lowest paid grades on the agricultural wage scale, something finally accomplished with the General Salary Reform of 1980.[22] The net effect of the 1980 Wage Reform on income distribution is, however, unclear: basic wage gaps within the agricultural and industrial categories were reduced; they were expanded in the service category; in the technical and executive categories minimum wages were increased, but ceilings were placed on the highest wages in these two generally highest-paid occupational categories; and the implementation of the entire reform was predicated on establishing a close linkage between effort and reward.[23] Nevertheless, compared to other countries in Latin America, Cuba's income distribution is probably the most egalitarian.[24] Brundenius has calculated a comparison with Peru and Brazil which is telling both in terms of percentages as well as trends over time (see Table 6.2).

A large share of the credit for Cuba's relatively equal income distribution can be attributed to the state's commitment to minimize unemployment. Precise data on this topic for all of the last 28 years is not available, but both Mesa-Lago and Brundenius have devised estimates which attest to the notable success the state has had in this area (see Table 6.3). The figures in Table 6.3 stand in contrast to those from many other countries in the region – e.g., Jamaica, 26 percent (1981); Colombia, 10 percent (1980); Chile, 20 percent (1982); and Guatemala, 31 percent (1978) – and have come as a result of a dramatic expansion of the education and social security systems, in addition to increases in employment opportunities.[25] Since 1959 the typical unemployed Cuban has

TABLE 6.2
Income Distribution by Strata: Peru, Brazil, and Cuba.

	share of per capita income of poorest 40%	share of per capita income of richest 5%
Peru		
1961	10%	26%
1972	9%	33%
1979	8%	37%
Brazil		
1960	12%	28%
1970	10%	35%
1980	10%	34%
Cuba		
1958[a]	7%	27%
1962	17%	13%
1973	20%	10%
1978	25%	11%

Source: Adopted from Claes Brundenius, *Revolutionary Cuba: The Challenge of Economic Growth with Equity* (Boulder, CO: Westview Press, 1984), p. 124
[a] based on the assumption there was no change in income distribution between 1953 and 1958.

TABLE 6.3
Unemployment in Cuba as Percent of Labor Force[a]

Year	Percent Unemployed
1957	12
1958	12
1959	14
1960–1965[b]	9
1966–1970	4
1971–1975	3
1976–1980	4

Source: Calculated from data taken from Carmelo Mesa-Lago, *The Economy of Socialist Cuba* (Albuquerque, NM: University of New Mexico Press, 1981), p. 122; and Claes Brundenius, *Revolutionary Cuba: The Challenge of Economic Growth with Equity* (Boulder, CO: Westview Press, 1984), p. 135.
[a] when authors' estimates for a year varied, the mean of both estimates was used.
[b] average of the rates for years indicated from 1960 to 1980.

been a male (though unemployment rates among women are much higher), 20–24 year old urban dweller, and very likely to be searching for a job for the first time.[26]

The incomes earned by Cuban workers provide the vast majority with adequate pesos to purchase those basic necessities not provided free or nearly free by the state. Principal among these necessities, and probably the largest out-of-pocket expenditure for most Cuban households, is food. One survey concluded that prior to the revolution, many poor families had to spend over two-thirds of their income to purchase a starchy diet, deficient in meat, vegetables, and dairy products.[27] Although the demand for a better quality and greater variety of food still outstrips supply, since 1959, this situation has improved immeasurably. Hunger and malnutrition have been virtually eliminated as per capita availability of food and beverages rose 50 percent between 1963 and 1980.[28] For this expanded and more nutritious market basket, informal surveys suggest households spend approximately 25 percent to 60 percent of their incomes, between 15 percent and 60 percent of their earnings being spent on highly subsidized, rationed foods.[29]

Cuban workers, however, receive only part of their "pay" in the form of wages. The state also provides numerous (and some very expensive) benefits to citizens. Some, such as free, universally available, and greatly expanded education and health care (there was no public health insurance available before the revolution) are well known. But Cuban workers receive other, less publicized benefits as well, including 18-week full pay maternity leaves, 1-month paid vacation each year, state-subsidized food amounting to 25 pesos per person per month in 1980,[30] rents capped at 10 percent of the income of the household's biggest earner, and expanding on-the-job training to diversify and upgrade skill levels.[31] In addition, workers are covered by social security (retirement), generally beginning at age 60 for men and 55 for women, at 50 percent salary for the first 25 years worked and 1–1.5 percent extra for each year beyond that. Workers are also eligible for a variety of social assistance programs if they are disabled, injured or sick either permanently or temporarily, or if their household income falls below 25 pesos per person per month.[32] The Cuban government's combined expenditures for social assistance and social security coverage have increased nearly every year since 1959. Totaling only around 106 million pesos in 1958, they rose to 441 million pesos in 1970, 755 million pesos in 1980, and 1 billion 15 million pesos by 1985.[33]

The foregoing discussion suggests that the Cuban state can be differentiated from many of its capitalist counterparts, especially developing countries, by the more egalitarian nature of its wage and benefit policies, and this fact, which shapes the context in which the state and unions interact, will have a bearing on the subsequent discussion of autonomy. Under capitalism, a major purpose of unions is to struggle to maintain and/or increase their members' share of the economic surplus. However, insofar as the outcome of socialist state policies – as compared to capitalist ones – establishes a relatively equal distribution of the surplus to begin with, we can anticipate that the content of conflicts between unions and the state will be somehow different in socialist societies. In particular, the predominance of antagonisms over economic or bread-and-butter issues will be muted under socialism. This is in no way to argue that grounds for dispute between unions and the state over economic matters will automatically disappear under socialism, as the earlier discussion of production norms in Cuba illustrates. In order to make sure not to overlook legitimate and important examples of union-state conflict in Cuba, we must remain alert to the fact that the state's wage and benefit policies contribute to a situation in which the substance of union/state conflicts will be likely to shift from those of a more to those of a less purely economic character.

CUBAN UNION ORGANIZATION

In terms of how they are organized, unions in Cuba have undergone a number of significant changes over the course of the post-revolutionary period. In general, these changes have contributed to a growing degree of union autonomy from the state. At the same time, however, especially if considered from the perspective of organizational independence, indications of some union dependence on the Cuban state persist.

Cuban unions are structured on the basis of two general principles: dual and sectoral unionism. Dual unionism refers to parallel sets of union structures – those of the CTC and those of the National Unions (*Sindicatos Nacionales*) in various economic sectors – which exist at the municipal, provincial, and national levels. Sectoral unionism means that, instead of organizing workers by trade, the national unions group together all workers in a particular branch of the economy, no matter what their specific job, and thus all workers at a given worksite are represented by one union. Though critics have implied that organization on the basis of economic sector instead of occupation weakens Cuban unions' ability to defend members' interests,[34] many Cuban workers who had been represented under both systems do not concur. They felt one union confronting management when disputes arose at the work center had strengthened, not diluted, workers' bargaining power.[35]

The full complement of dual and sectoral union structures has not been operative at all times during the last 28 years, however. In the latter half of the 1960s, the number of national unions was reduced from 25 to 15, and they were stripped of their provincial and municipal branches. Union sections, which group workers in the same department, area, brigade, and sometimes shift, and which pertain to the national unions rather than the CTC, were probably moribund in many work centers.[36] Moreover, the time span between union meetings and conferences, including the national CTC congresses, continued to increase.

By the last months of 1970, however, a campaign to revitalize union structures was begun. The number of national unions rose to 23, their municipal and provincial branches were reconstituted, and CTC congresses and other meetings began to be held on a regular basis. *Secciones* were reformed (37,000 by mid-1972; 41,000 by the beginning of the following year), and the minimum number of members per section was reduced from 15 to 10, allowing even workers in the smallest centers to form their own locals.[37]

Later in the decade, the union bureaus (*buros*) or second-tier national union structures, were strengthened and, in many cases, formed for the first time. The average buro encompasses around 850 workers, and is composed of all union sections within a given enterprise. The creation of the buros had important implications for union work because it meant the workers' organizations now had a structural counterpart to enterprise-level management, and could therefore participate more effectively in decision making at this level than the multiple, scattered union sections had previously been able to. With regard to the formulation of the annual enterprise plan, for instance, the buro was able to coordinate workers' input from all parts of the enterprise, making it more difficult for managers, using the familiar justification that they alone were in a position to judge the needs of the enterprise as a whole, to dismiss workers' ideas and criticisms as parochial.

A second aspect of union organization which also has important implications for union efficacy and has likewise shown variation in the post-revolutionary era, is the size of union membership. The 1959 victory provided a slight impetus for union growth. Civil servants, for example, were allowed to organize for the first time, and professionals were incorporated into unions. However, the remainder of the decade saw a stagnation, and possibly a decline in union membership: by the mid-1960s about 60 percent of the labor force was organized, up only slightly from before the revolution.[38]

After 1970, however, Cuban unions began a move to become mass organizations. Membership began to increase early in the decade and has continued to grow ever since: 88 percent of the Cuban workforce was affiliated by 1974; 94 percent belonged by 1978; and, in 1984, Veiga reported over 99 percent affiliation in the country.[39] Affiliation figures as high as these have raised questions about how voluntary membership really is. Undoubtedly, some workers, for personal, political, or social reasons, join reluctantly. However, just as in other places, one important thing reflected in high membership figures is the steady and determined efforts of union organizers and supporters. One man, who had been in charge of organizing in his section, explained that some people need to feel as if the union wants them, as individuals, to join, and thus need to be approached and convinced on a very personal level. Then too, he added, there are the *medio gusanos* who take much more work and who sometimes will never become union members.[40]

The financing of unions in Cuba is a third organizational area of interest. Immediately prior to the victory, unions were financed through automatic pay deductions. Workers resented this compulsory contribution, however, and it was repealed 21 days after Batista was overthrown. Since then it has been the joint responsibility of members and the section treasurer to make sure that dues – which amount to 1 percent of a worker's wages – are paid each month. Many workers said that in-person dues collection discourages the growth of barriers between union leaders and rank-and-file, and that the percentage of workers who pay on time each month was one of the best indications of how good a job members felt the union was doing.[41] Despite its advantages, this method of collection is not without problems. The unions' financial base, at least in the short run, is less secure, and the process of periodically collecting dues from fellow workers, besides being time consuming, can be an unpopular and delicate task that union officers would sometimes just as soon avoid. "You always have to stay on top of the few that don't pay each month," reported one woman who had once been the treasurer of her section. In her case, this had meant seeking out each individual who didn't pay to try to find out what was wrong and what could be done about the situation.[42]

Once collected, union dues are first sent to a superordinate union body and then divided up according to budgets submitted by the national unions and the CTC. Eventually each union section receives 10 percent of the total dues it collected for the month.[43] Dues retained at each level are allocated among a host of union activities which include, among other things, periodic congresses and other meetings, the publication of a daily union newspaper (*Trabajadores*), the operation of a nation-wide system of union-run schools, and the sponsorship of a variety of sports, recreation, and cultural programs for members. Members' dues also cover the salaries of all union officials and employees above the level of the bureau. Section and bureau leaders are not paid. Beginning in the 1970s, unions have been required to operate their multi-levelled structures and perform their many functions, while balancing their budgets. Whereas prior to this time, unions could and did draw on state funds whenever necessary, "We are self-financing now," explained a national official of the CTC. "The unions receive nothing from the state."[44]

A fourth important aspect of Cuban union organization is the process through which leaders are selected, and here again we find significant contrasts between earlier and later post-revolutionary periods. Not surprisingly, in light of the support most of the Cuban labor leadership had given Batista in his fight against the July 26th movement, the first years after the victory saw a rapid turnover in union leaders under less than optimally democratic circumstances. Within a month after the victory, the new government passed a law suspending all union officials that were in office on December 31, 1958, and establishing a provisional committee to head the CTC. Elections were held in ensuing months for section officers, positions in the national unions, and delegates to the upcoming 10th national CTC congress. Candidates aligned with the July 26th movement registered strong victories in all these contests. However, by the time the 10th congress was held in November 1959, the Cuban labor movement revealed itself as badly split between the right, consisting of reform elements (including many July 26th unionists) and some sympathizers of the pre-revolutionary pro-Batista union leadership, and the left, composed of mostly Communist unionists and those who supported the radical changes then being instituted by the new government. After many tumultuous hours and the personal intervention of Castro, a compromise leadership was accepted by the congressional delegates. But as the polarization of Cuban society into opponents and supporters of the revolution assumed a rapid pace in the months following the congress, many union leaders who could not work under this leadership, or who opposed the nationalizations and other measures being enacted by the state, either quit or were summarily removed from their posts.[45]

In sum, the process of leadership selection in the early years cannot be described as democratic, and from what little information is available on the selection of union leadership from 1961 to the end of the decade, it would not be far off the mark to conclude that the spirit of Castro's 1959 promise to bring real democracy into the selection of union leaders was not being fulfilled.[46] Government interventions were common and decisive. Winners of "elections" for important posts, for example the CTC Executive Committee, often had no opponents. Nor were there many pretensions that the membership had been consulted before the dismissal of many union leaders. As a result, union officers tended to be more responsive to outside authorities than to the members of the organization they were supposed to be leading: hence Gilly's mid-decade observation of strong worker support for the revolution and its leadership, yet equally vehement opposition to the union and its leaders.[47]

One of the facets of union revitalization receiving the most attention after 1970 was election procedures. Since that date, union members have elected their section leaders in direct and secret votes every two and a half years. Candidates are nominated in general assemblies at which each one's qualification are discussed. In 1977, regulations stipulated that these assemblies had to be attended by at least 75 percent of the section's members. Workers I spoke with said they usually knew the candidates' qualifications pretty well before the assembly anyway, since they are in all cases fellow workers, and the average union section is not a large body. Anyone can be nominated for section office as political restrictions earlier in force have been eliminated. Workers vote for as many candidates as there are openings (between 3 and 13 depending on the size of the section), putting two checks beside the name of the person they want to be executive officer. In 1977, the number of candidates per post was not specified, but it was suggested that members be presented with a ballot containing more names than section positions, but no more than two nominees per post. In all, 233,724 section officers were elected in 1977, an average of about five per section. Fifty-four percent of these were elected to office for the first time. Final figures indicated 87 percent of the Cuban union membership participated in the electoral process that year – up 37 percent from 1970.

Above the section level, however, union officers are not elected directly by the rank-and-file. In 1977, bureau officers were elected by union section officers and by the candidates for delegates to the national congresses of the sectoral unions. These electors were presented with a list of candidates for bureau office by a superordinate union body, but the electors themselves could also make nominations. Voting is secret, and no candidate can be elected to a bureau post if he or she does not receive at least half the votes cast plus one. The newly elected bureau officers, who like the section officers serve two and one half year terms, elect their own secretary-general in an open vote.

Cuban workers also participate, in an indirect fashion, in the selection of both their intermediate level (municipal and provincial) and national leaders in both the national unions and the CTC.[48] The procedures in all these cases are somewhat similar, so only the elections for the national leadership of the CTC will be described here.[49] National leaders of the CTC are elected every five years by delegates to the national CTC congress. These delegates elect a National Council by secret ballot, and they determine its size, which in 1978 numbered 143.[50] Published accounts reveal few specifics about the process of electing the National Council, thus we do not know, for example, how competitive elections are at this level or where nominations originate. A portion of Castro's closing speech to the 1978 Congress, however, conveys some notion of what takes place:

> Some of our most outstanding and worthy union leaders received a few opposition votes. I remember some murmurs as the vote tally was read and I said, "Very good, very good!" ... because the right to cast a vote against someone is one of the most sacred rights of any delegate.[51]

The National Council, in turn, elects among its members the National Committee, its secretary-general and second secretary, the secretariat, and other national officers. According to the 1978 CTC statutes, the National Council also establishes the procedure whereby delegates to the national CTC congress are chosen. Prior to the 1978 national congress, 45,000 candidate-delegates were selected in workcenter general assemblies at which the issues of the upcoming congress were also discussed. Of these 45,000 candidates, 2,104 were eventually elected as delegates in meetings at the municipal and provincial levels. Sixty-eight percent of the delegates at both the 1978 and 1984 national congresses came from the grass-roots level of union organization – 20 percent more than the corresponding figures for the 1973 congress.[52]

The flip side of the leadership selection coin – how a leader can be removed from office during his/her term – is also very important. The 1978 CTC statutes stipulate that an officer can be recalled at any time by a majority vote of whichever body elected him or her in the first place. In cases where a leader was elected by a council, conference, or congress which may not convene again for some time, the person can be removed by whatever body is charged with running the union in the interim, so long as the action is ratified at the next meeting of the appropriate council, conference, or congress. Any union leader who is removed has the right to appeal, up to the national CTC congress if necessary. A vacancy in any of the offices in the union section, except executive secretary, can be filled by a nominee who received votes in the last election but did not get elected to a post. New elections must be called if no such alternates are available, or if the position of the executive secretary becomes vacant.[53]

Summing up this review of changing union organization in post-revolutionary Cuba, we find that overall, if gauged from the perspective of organizational independence, union autonomy has increased in Cuba. The fact that unions now operate without financial assistance from the state, and since 1976 have registered growing budgetary surpluses making it unlikely they will need to accept state monies in the future, bodes well for union autonomy in Cuba.[54] Likewise, the very high percentage of workers who are organized provides a necessary, though not sufficient, foundation for independent action. In Cuba, as elsewhere, the ability of union opponents to dictate its positions and priorities is more certain to the extent that workers are unorganized, divided, and thus less powerful politically. Finally, the post-1970 conduct of union elections offers an additional indication of organizational independence. Officers at the base level are selected in elections that are frequent, direct, and secret. Nominations originate from below, the rank-and-file are presented with meaningful choices, and there are no restrictions on who is eligible to run, aside from the prohibition (which applies not only in the secciones, but at all higher levels of the union as well) against administrators holding any union office.[55]

At the same time, by uncovering indications of union dependence on the state, our review of changing union organization underscores a point made earlier: neither "complete" autonomy nor "complete" subservience can adequately characterize the union/state relationship in Cuba. Thus we find that *everyone* who works in Cuba is eligible to join a union, including managers, who under socialism, are state representatives. Even though managerial personnel are unlikely to total more than 8 percent of the unions' members, their role in the unions demands close scrutiny in terms of the possible effect on the autonomy of labor organizations.[56] In addition, there are aspects of union electoral procedure that seem likely to set important limits on their ability to maintain organizational independence from the state. Thus, above the section level, all union officers, though still elected, are elected indirectly, albeit in processes which incorporate safeguards against the circumvention of mass influence. Moreover, both the extent to which these higher-level union elections are contested and exactly where nominations originate is not clear.

CUBAN UNION ACTIVITIES

Changes in the activities of Cuban unions over the last 28 years have accompanied the organizational changes discussed previously, and in the main they follow a like pattern: when viewed from the perspective of the presence of conflict, they point to growing union autonomy from the state. Yet at the same time, this review of changing union activities will reveal that the general trend towards increased autonomy does not mean unions act completely independent of the Cuban state.

During the first decade after the ouster of Fulgencio Batista, the unions' principal function was to support state efforts to develop the economy. As one of Cuba's most prominent Communists explained it in 1962, "If previously, the fundamental function of the unions was to fight for the partial and immediate demands of each labor sector . . . today the fundamental task of the unions is to fight for an increase in production and productivity."[57]

The major methods the union used to encourage workers to produce more goods, better and faster, included programs, such as socialist emulation and voluntary labor, both designed to mobilize the workforce to support and to implement decisions made by the nation's political leaders. In other words, the unions tried to ensure cooperation by fostering a passion and an enthusiasm among workers for the production tasks placed before them. Something of this cheerleading approach is captured by a worker's recollections of planning discussions during this period: "What is sought now is no longer the patriotic appeal, the revolutionary sloganeering after a figure . . . In those days it was *Patria o Muerte!* as we used to say. Now this stage of *Patria o Muerte!* is being left behind."[58]

Encouraging workers' involvement in actually making decisions about production as an alternative way of securing their cooperation and support in the fulfilment of production goals was only a minor concern of unions during this early period. Production meetings were apparently sometimes held by the unions, but according to Gilly, attendance was very poor, and in 1966 the secretary-general of the CTC described them as gatherings "where cold figures are released by officials without any participation or lively discussion among the workers."[59] "The union didn't have a very important role in these assemblies, which were much more informal then," a CTC official explained in 1982. "Generally, we didn't insist that they even be held at all."[60]

There can be absolutely no doubt that maintaining and increasing production continue to be primary tasks of the Cuban unions. No Cuban I spoke with in 1982 or 1983 failed to mention these as central union functions. Nevertheless, since 1970 there has been an important shift in the focus of the unions' production-related activities. Projects and campaigns designed to mobilize the rank-and-file behind the implementation of production decisions made by the state no longer exhaust the extent of union work in this area. In addition, the workers' organizations have begun to organize workers to participate in decision-making about production.[61] This occurs in a variety of forums at the micro level: production and service assemblies, planning assemblies, management councils, and finally, in grievance councils. I will discuss only union activities with relation to the first of these micro forums before turning to union involvement in supra-worksite decision making about production, another new task they have assumed since the beginning of the 1970s.[62]

Production and service assemblies are held on a monthly basis at all Cuban worksites. They generally last between 45 minutes and an hour, although many workers I spoke with said when their assemblies were "heavy," they might go as long as two or three hours.[63] Unions take primary responsibility for preparation of the production and service assemblies, and workers said it was up to their local unions to make sure they are meaningful. Good preparation by the union includes developing and posting an agenda in advance, attending training seminars offered by the CTC, inviting people pertinent to the discussion to attend, and working with management to make sure its reports are neither excessively detailed nor lacking in substance. The unions also chair the assemblies, and how well they handle this job has a great deal to do with workers' satisfaction with the meetings.

The agenda of the assemblies appears fairly standard. First come reports, always from worksite administrators, sometimes from various workers, and on occasion from the party as well.[64] After these reports, the union opens the floor to discussion. Any topic related to production and service delivery might be broached, including plan execution (workers' input into the *formulation* of the plan occurs in the annual planning assemblies), workers' dining rooms, lighting, uniforms, fulfillment of inter-enterprise contracts, discipline, and raw materials and supply procurement. Several workers mentioned the value of the assembly discussions in terms of grasping how individual producers contribute to the larger picture of the production or delivery of a certain good or service. As a tobacco worker near retirement explained:

> The assemblies help build our understanding of production and work in the factory. Before 1959, many things were done to try to lessen each individual worker's knowledge of what went on in the rest of the factory. For example, the *patrón's* machines were kept in a separate part of the factory and no workers aside from the few who tended them were allowed to go into that room.[65]

A most popular topic of assembly discussion is the administration's performance: "The production assembly is your chance to throw mud at the administration. When I get up and complain, the administration gets real nervous," explained one worker, somewhat gleefully.[66] It is not easy for workers to criticize managers and managerial matters in the public forum of the assembly. Yet, the majority of workers I spoke with reported high levels of participation in their assemblies, and this is corroborated by the findings of Herrera and Rosenkranz.[67] However, it is clear that there are exceptions, worksites where workers' interventions are minimal and perfunctory, for example. Here the unions can be an important force for improvement. First, union officers can take advantage of their status as legitimate workers' leaders to set an example of critical intervention in the assemblies. A vocal and combative local union leadership encourages other workers to speak up, but if union leaders hang back, the rank-and-file might consider it wise to follow suit. This is why, explained a CTC official, "a good union leader has to be ready to speak up without thinking about personal considerations."[68] Second, the union as an organization must be ready and willing to close ranks behind workers who stand up to managers, as the following comment on the difference between production and service assemblies in the 1960s and in later decades reveals. "Workers always had the right to confront managers in the production assemblies, but as individuals. The important difference now is that they do it with the support of the unions. They can do it better now."[69]

Because workers' input into production and service assemblies is technically only advisory, the unions' most important work does not occur until after the meeting has concluded. The most commonly voiced complaint I heard about the assemblies is that managers are not inclined to take workers' suggestions seriously or to act on them regularly. Thus, as one disgruntled worker noted:

> We call the production and service assemblies *"las asambleas de no se puede"* [It can't be done assemblies] since we bring up suggestions and issues over and over again and this is often the answer. This is the main thing that discourages workers from participating in the assemblies. Over and over again they speak up, but nothing is ever done.[70]

The union's role is crucial in correcting this kind of deficiency because it is the body that must bring pressure on management to consider and implement workers' proposals originating in the assemblies. It does this on an informal basis through direct discussions with workplace management. Beginning in 1981, however, the unions instituted a new procedure aimed at improving managers' response to workers' assembly proposals. According to this plan, workers' proposals collected by the union are forwarded directly to the national office of the CTC, which brings them up with the appropriate ministry, state committee, national union, or party organ at the same time local union officers are discussing them with worksite managers.[71]

The unions' post-1970 activities in the area of organizing workers to participate in decision-making about production are not limited to their involvement in decision-making forums at the worksite level, such as the production and service and planning assemblies. Beginning in the 1970s, Cuban workers, through their unions, have also been represented in some important supra-worksite bodies which make macro-level production decisions for the entire economy. Preliminary ideas for union participation in these high-level decision making organs were suggested by the unions at the time of the 13th national CTC congress in 1973. In his main report to that congress, Lázaro Peña, the secretary general at the time, called for more direct union participation in determining social security policy, setting prices, and distributing goods, and the Theses of the Congress specifically added to the list union participation in planning, investment, the determination of wages, hours, norms, and workers' rights and obligations.

Since the 13th congress, some important steps have been taken to formalize union involvement in decision-making above the worksite level. One of the first and most widely publicized of these was the inclusion of the secretary-general of the CTC on the Council of Ministers and its executive committee, a move that was subsequently written into the Cuban Constitution. The Council of Ministers is the top administrative *and* executive organ of the Cuban state. It is made up of about 45 people, including high-ranking political figures and the heads of all the state committees and ministries. Its executive committee is much smaller, and exhibits a great deal of overlap with top party organs.[72] Union participation, however, has been interpreted to mean having an active voice but no formal vote in the proceedings of the two bodies.[73]

Nevertheless, by virtue of union attendance at the meetings of the Council of Ministers and its executive committee, unions are now present at discussions of issues of major, though sometimes indirect, importance to producers. The Council of Ministers develops the country's budget, directs its economic activities, oversees foreign trade, and regulates and coordinates the activities of all the ministries and state committees. The Council also approves decrees relevant to production at the micro-level, such as the one governing the conduct of production and service assemblies in 1979.[74] Yet as the sole worker representative on the Council, it is not likely the secretary-general of the CTC is able to secure decisions opposed by many other Council members. The secretary-general of the CTC is also the only union representative on the executive committee, though this body has only 14 members, and not even the president of the Central Planning Board, the National Bank, or the heads of the state committees or ministries belong. The executive committee can render decisions on any issue the Council can. A recent example of a decision made by the Executive Committee that has had important ramifications for workers was a decree transferring responsibility for employing redundant workers from central state organs to local government bodies.

Also starting in the mid-1970s, the unions began to participate in decision-making in other supra-worksite forums. Thus, in a 1976 law, the secretaries-general of Cuba's national unions were granted the right to participate at any meeting of the management councils of the ministries and state committees which dealt with workers' issues. Though technically union officials are not considered regular members of these management councils, Veiga noted in 1978 that they had been attending regularly.[75] It would be a mistake, however, to assume that formal participation in such high-level management sessions is the unions' only opportunity to influence activities of the ministries and analogous government organs. There is also a great deal of informal interaction between the unions and these bodies, as an official of the Education and Science Workers' Union suggested in 1983:

> The relationship between the national union and the Ministry of Education is close and amply developed. We have tight relationships with those in charge of every sphere of education activity at the ministry. Every time there's a problem or a certain matter needs to be attended to, we're in contact with them and we discuss the best way to deal with the situation.[76]

Through their involvement in the formal and informal decision-making activities of the ministries and certain state committees, Cuban unions participate in deliberations which sometimes have immediate and direct relevance to production and service units and individual workers in them. For example, the ministries and state committees direct and coordinate all economic activities in their particular spheres, one of the most crucial of which is planning. Planning at this mid-rung (intermediate between the top level of the Central Planning Board and the Council of Ministers and the bottom level of the enterprises) involves elaborating and overseeing the execution of the general plan for the sector on the basis of guidelines, proposals, and suggestions coming from above and from below. The presence of the unions in management sessions of state administrative bodies, as well as their informal contacts there, also helps insure regular union involvement in commissions set up to implement resolutions and decrees affecting work and the economy. Recent important examples in this area include: (a) participation of the top provincial officers of the CTC on provincial committees in charge of implementing the General Wage Reform of 1980,[77] (b) cooperation between the national unions and organs of state administration in determining the rules governing the distribution of enterprise reward funds in each sector of the economy, and (c) joint participation of the national office of the CTC and the National Sugar Workers' Union with the State Committee of Labor and Social Security and the Sugar Ministry on a National Commission of Health and Safety in the Sugar Industry.[78]

Besides organizing workers to participate in decision-making at both the micro- and macrolevels, since 1970, Cuban unions have become heavily involved in a second major activity considered the essence of union functioning under capitalism: the defense of workers' rights. Though before that time unions were very hesitant to actively and publicly stand up for the rights and perceived interests of workers,[79] in the early 1970s, they began to demonstrate a concern for protecting their members from abuses they suffered in the process of fulfilling their productive obligations. After such a long period of inactivity in the realm of defending workers' rights, the unions were at first badly prepared to take on such a task. Thus, as late as 1975, Pérez-Stable found that only 18 percent of the workers she interviewed mentioned the defense of workers' interests as a task of the local union.[80]

Yet by the early 1980s, every worker I interviewed mentioned the defense of workers' rights as an important union task. As a tobacco worker noted, "Any worker *must* be able to call on his/her union leaders when his/her rights are being violated and the union leaders *must* help them. The union has to protest if, in the course of doing its work, the administration breaks a law protecting workers."[81] Another worker commented, "The union has to watch out for the workers' welfare. It has to confront management when workers are being shafted."[82] These comments suggest it is no longer acceptable for union officers to sit quietly by – as they often did in the 1960s – when a worker is "being shafted." Nor, as these comments also suggest, would workers consider it enough for the union to act as a neutral intermediary in a conflict over workers' rights. The unions nowadays are supposed to do more: they are expected to act as workers' representatives and advocates, to aggressively defend their members' rights and interests whenever there is occasion to do so, which nearly always demands confrontation – of varying degrees of acrimony – with state representatives, as well as with union leaders whose relationship with state managers remains untainted by cronyism.

Cuban unions go about performing their advocacy function in a variety of ways. Most workers said their union leaders would nearly always take an informal approach initially, this being a swifter, more circumspect, and more amicable method of dealing with disputes over workers' rights. Workers I interviewed offered numerous examples of cases at their worksites where the union, via this informal method of discussion with the administration, had been able to resolve disagreements in favor of either individual workers or groups of workers. One worker recalled three instances at her worksite where the union had successfully used this approach. The first was when an administrator tried to introduce an unpopular work schedule change in several departments for what she described as "arbitrary" reasons. The second was when a position, which by law must first be opened to internal applicants even if they require further training, was filled without due consideration of the qualifications of people already employed at the work center. The third was when the discretionary powers of the personnel director were cut after many workers expressed dissatisfaction over how he treated them. "We complain to the union here when our rights are overlooked because they fight a good fight. They have influence up there," this particular worker explained.[83] Another worker, the executive officer of her section, recalled a recent example where she had successfully bargained with management and gotten a woman's vacation rescheduled so it coincided with that of her son, who was studying in the countryside. "I stood up for the worker even though the administration and the party were against me!" she exclaimed.[84]

It appears unions at the base-level regularly resort to, and have at least a fair degree of success, employing informal tactics in defending workers' rights. Yet there are other means whereby unions perform this function, for example in the production and service assemblies and the other microforums mentioned above. Unions also engage in the defense of workers' rights in ways that rely less heavily on the capabilities and initiative of individual union leaders, and more on the organizational capacity and power of the union as an institution. A good example is the union's role in the area of health and safety rights, as detailed in Law 13, passed in December 1977. What is interesting about this legislation is the variety of ways in which it mandates union involvement in the defense of workers' health and safety rights. For example, the union is to participate in making up the health and safety plan for each enterprise, and to ensure that new workers receive safety training and disabled workers are retrained and suitably placed. The union must also conduct on-site health, safety, and accident investigations, and inform the workers of their results. For this last task, the CTC hoped to train 50,000 workers as inspectors by 1985.[85] Moreover, union health and safety technicians can order the shut-down of a worksite for unhealthy or unsafe working conditions. Finally, if management disagrees with any worker's decision to refuse potentially life-threatening work, it is the union that is called on to determine whether the workers' decision is justified.

Focusing on the presence of conflict as one indicator of autonomy, what can this review of changing union activities in Cuba tell us about the evolution of the union–state relationship? Strikes, the ultimate example of antagonism between management and unions under capitalism, do not occur in Cuba, though there is no legal prohibition against them, and both wildcat and CTC-sanctioned work stoppages, though rare, have taken place.[86] Yet the absence of strikes alone does not mean there is never overt disagreement between unions and the Cuban state. Indeed over the years union–state conflict has increased, in part because unions have assumed responsibility for the defense of workers' rights, and pursuit of this activity has greatly expanded the possibilities for union–state confrontation compared to earlier times when workers' organizations were mostly limited to mobilizing members to implement production decisions made by others. This and other situations in which disagreements between the union or union members and the Cuban state occur were discussed previously; there are others as well, two of which are presented below.

The first example concerns the Council of State's 1980 passage of Law 32, ending workers' long-held authority to review and reverse disciplinary actions taken against them by managers. The unions initially lent quick approval to the new law, yet once implementation began the law sparked a great deal of debate and controversy both within the union and between the union and the state. The principal point of contention was the upsurge of disciplinary actions initiated against workers, and the comparative infrequency with which managers themselves were being disciplined for misconduct. After verifying this imbalance through a union-conducted study, the workers' organizations began to engage in frequent public criticisms of the situation, and as a result, by mid-decade, they had succeeded in tempering management abuse of Law 32, in part by increasing managers' own vulnerability to sanctions when they proved overzealous in punishing workers.[87]

A second situation where union–state conflict can be observed in Cuba is when unions have tried to oust managers who have been targets of repeated worker complaints. While unions do not have final authority to remove unpopular managers, from cases described to me it is clear they have played a major role in such situations, which by their very nature involve confrontation with the state. Thus, unions have collected written and oral complaints against some managers and have accused them publicly or privately. Unions have also been involved in the investigation of charges against managers made by their members and in the presentation of the results of their inquiries to the disputed administrators' superior. How successful the unions have been in cases of this sort is unknown. What is certain is that they have been willing, on at least some occasions, to actively work to oust administrators, and that most workers I spoke with felt that if the workers' charges against a manager were serious and could be supported, "the workers, with the union, can move the manager out!"[88]

However, despite various examples of union–state conflict in Cuba, it would be inaccurate to characterize the relationship as essentially adversarial. This is suggested by the nature of the second main union activity in Cuba – organizing workers to participate, along with state managers, in making decisions about production. As noted earlier, this activity is carried out at different levels, in different forums, and by different means. But in all cases, even though co-management is not totally devoid of conflict, performance of this task demands cooperation with the state. Thus, insofar as one indication of autonomy is the unions' ability and willingness to assume an oppositional stance towards management, their involvement as management's co-partner in directing production introduces the possibility of dependence into their relationship with the state. When, for instance, do the unions' activities in planning, organizing and conducting production and service assemblies, and encouraging and preparing workers to participate in them become more a device for fostering worker docility vis-à-vis the state than a means for ensuring that members' interests are protected and their points of view taken seriously? When does the union's presence on such powerful supraworksite bodies as the Council of Ministers and ministry management councils smack more of corporatism than a genuine effort to empower Cuban workers? To pose such questions is to recognize that by becoming involved along with state managers in making decisions about production, unions in Cuba risk some dilution of their own independence.

ACCOUNTING FOR CHANGES IN CUBAN UNIONS

In the previous two sections, we have seen that over the course of the last 28 years Cuban unions have gained in autonomy from the state, even though gauging their degree of autonomy either in terms of organizational independence or the presence of conflict, their relationship with the state continues to exhibit some elements of dependency. The obvious next question is *why* did this change take place?

An immediate, if oversimplified, response to this question might be: union autonomy from the state increased as a result of decisions taken by high-level state leaders in Cuba. This response is true, as far as it goes, but we need to probe further and ask both why the leadership decided to make these particular kinds of changes, and why it decided to make them when it did.[89]

A large part of the explanation for why Cuban unions were so closely identified with the state in the early years must be sought in the relationships between the unions and the July 26th Movement before the victory over Batista, and between powerful sectors of the union and state leadership after Batista's defeat. Though numerically strong since the late 1940s, the Cuban labor movement had been under the control of the notorious Eusebio Mujal, who presided over an era of economism, reformism, corruption, and bureaucratism unprecedented in the annals of Cuban unionism. During Mujal's tenure, union leadership collaborated closely with whomever held state power, regardless of their politics, the result being that the unions came to be widely regarded as appendages of the state rather than independent representatives or spokesmen of the workers. As the war to overthrow Batista intensified in the 1950s, the CTC organization proved the dictator's most faithful, and in the end, almost exclusive political ally. CTC leaders denounced labor sympathizers of the July 26th movement as Marxist, actually applauded government repression of anti-Batista dissidents within the ranks of organized labor, mobilized workers for pro-government demonstrations, and in response to a 1957 call by Castro's forces for a general strike declared, "People who treat labor well deserve well of labor, and President Batista has done more for labor than any other president Cuba ever had."[90] Not surprisingly, Mujal and his chief lieutenants followed Batista into exile in January 1959.

Given this pre-revolutionary history, it is not difficult to imagine the apprehension with which the victorious July 26th movement viewed organized labor on the morning of the revolution, a mistrust not belied by its actions. We have seen how, only 20 days into office, the new government rid the unions of top-level *mujalistas* with one sweeping decree. However, given the length of Mujal's reign, and the fact that the July 26th Movement had few people to spare for union work, replacing mid- and low-level *mujalista* union officers and completely eradicating *mujalista* (and pro-Batista) sympathies within the unions was more complicated. The difficulties stemmed from the fact that the political loyalties of the people who filled the union leadership vacuum created by the departure and ouster of many *mujalistas* were divided and uncertain. A visible number opposed some actions the new state leaders strongly considered to be both necessary and desirable, such as the agrarian reform and nationalizations, and some even supported the external and internal counter-revolutionary challenges, which reached troublesome proportions between 1959 and 1961.

The events which transpired during the first two years after the victory could not but have reinforced the preexisting proclivity of the Cuban state leadership to look askance on the possibility of autonomous and active unions, since it was very likely at the time that the leaders of these unions would have opposed the direction the revolution was taking.[91] By 1962, however, the state was fairly secure on all social fronts, and the leadership of the unions had come out solidly for the construction of socialism. Yet for the remainder of the decade, the unions demonstrated little autonomy from the state. How can this be explained? Part of the reason lies in the dearth of good models of autonomous unions in other socialist countries which Cuba could emulate. Moreover, the development of autonomous unions was further inhibited by the fact that during the struggles over leadership of the unions in 1959 and 1960, the state was forced to throw its support behind the Communist unionists, who thereby gained a great deal of influence within the labor organizations which they might have capitalized on had union autonomy expanded. However, the Communists' relationship with the July 26th movement had been and continued throughout the 1960s to be characterized by considerable tension as a result of both the party's late and tepid support of the armed struggle against Batista and its numerous post-1959 disagreements with the state over policies and tactics including agrarian reform, nationalizations, and planning. Given this unsavory history, independent unions, heavily influenced by Communists, were surely not viewed as desirable by the leaders of the new Cuban state.[92]

The turnaround in the union–state relationship began in 1970, as the negative results of a number of policies pursued in the 1960s started to assume distressing proportions. During the 1960s, economic and political decision-making had become increasingly centralized. Overcentralization was partially responsible for the adoption of widely unpopular policies, such as the decision to restrict individual consumption to spartan levels in order to pursue a massive program of capital investment.[93] It resulted in a host of operating inefficiencies as well – improper allocation of inputs, unrealistic and constantly revised plans, and excessive waste, to name only a few. And it produced contradictions that fed an undercurrent of declining morale, disquiet, and cynicism within the population. Principal among these was the heavy emphasis placed on egalitarian wage distribution, particularly in the late 1960s. This policy, aside from depressing output, rendered ever more obvious the growing inequality in the distribution of political power in the country, which contrasted sharply with the ideology of the socialist state.

The inconsistencies, injustices, and inefficiencies that were the product of 1960s' overcentralization did not go unfelt or unnoticed in Cuba. This was especially apparent at the workplace: absenteeism swelled, and declining productivity plagued the nation. For example, at the peak of the 1970 harvest, the absentee rate for the whole country was 29 percent, and between 1966 and 1969 the number of hours worked per day averaged only four or five.[94] Yet while the symptoms of discontent may have been most evident in the economic arena, they had very important political dimensions as well. For one thing, the spreading inclination of some producers to slack-off, which was fueled by managerial inefficiencies, the scarcity of consumer goods, and workers' lack of input into decision-making processes, strained the unity of the working class that was held to be of such importance to the strength and stability of the Cuban state. Second, absenteeism and reduced work effort were also indications of political crisis in the sense that their root causes could be easily traced to and identified with the country's political processes, institutions, and leaders.

The political threat to the Cuban state was probably not imminent in the late 1960s, though a number of observers have suggested that if the growing problems had not been rectified, the revolution would have been in for some tumultuous times.[95] A strong political challenge to the state was averted, however, because the implications of disappointment and discontent among the population were perceived by the state's leadership and, as a consequence, they made a number of major changes, most important (given the focus here) being those that directly or indirectly increased union autonomy.[96] But, despite the Cuban political leadership's oft-demonstrated concern for the plight of Cuban workers, the changes that occurred in Cuba after 1970 should not be seen as originating in the largess, benevolence, or democratic inclination of the powerful. Rather, they were prompted by the actions of Cuban workers, actions though of a more negative or passive rather than positive or active kind, to which the state leadership was compelled to respond.

But why this kind of response? After all, history is replete with examples of repression and militarization as antidotes for disquiet among society's producers. Barring or coupled with this, a further narrowing of the already small circle of citizens who made major decisions in Cuba might have been attempted, and such an attempt might more logically have been accompanied by abolition of the unions than by an expansion of their autonomy. In fact, for a short time in the late 1960s and early 1970s, some moves were made that could be interpreted as an indication that the state leadership might be turning in this direction. An anti-loafing law, for instance, was passed in 1971, and in late 1969 another law decreed that updated and detailed labor records must be kept at each worker's place of employment and that workers carry a labor card on their person which summarized this information. That actions such as these took place at almost the same time as calls were being made for the revitalization of the unions indicates there may have been some disagreement within the state's top leadership over exactly how to respond to the urgent situation before them. We know little of the character of what may have been such a split. We only know that a defining feature of the post-1970 period in Cuba has been a systematic devolution of political and economic authority to groups in society who had previously had much less. Changes in the degree of union autonomy from the state are but one example.

To understand why certain choices were made at this juncture, we must look to the history of the institution and consolidation of socialism in Cuba. The differences in this regard between Cuba and much of Eastern Europe are suggestive, though there remains a great deal of systematic and comparative historical work to be done before their importance is fully understood. To begin with, the seizure of power by the July 26th Movement was a purely indigenous affair. It involved far greater participation of the Cuban population than was true in many parts of Eastern Europe where socialism had comparatively weak internal roots, being imposed, in large measure, from the outside.[97] In Cuba, by way of contrast, the success of the Rebel Army was only possible because of the daily activities of the Oriente peasants, who served as its rearguard for years. Moreover, urban and rural workers conducted paralyzing strikes, disrupted harvests, engaged in sabotage, and sent material aid to the front. Naval officers arose in Cienfuegos, and some church, professional, and student groups lent financial and moral support to the anti-Batista efforts.

In the years of planning and conducting all these activities, strong connections were forged and mutual commitments were made between the minority who led the opposition to Batista and a large number of Cuban people, very unlike the kind of relationship between the Communists and the citizenry which developed during the institution of socialism in most of Eastern Europe. And while the links and the trust that grew up between leaders and masses in the struggle against Batista do not, by themselves, explain the direction change took after 1970, they helped create a reservoir of goodwill on which the Cuban leaders could draw in the ensuing years as they attempted to consolidate socialism for the first time in the Americas.

In the consolidation of socialism – even more than in its institution – there was a marked contrast between Cuba and much of Eastern Europe in terms of mass participation and involvement. At various junctures from the very beginning, socialism in Cuba was either kept alive or considerably strengthened through the widespread participation of great numbers of Cubans. Examples of large-scale popular participation in the consolidation of the new society are numerous, but three in particular stand out: the National Revolutionary Militias, voluntary labor, and the literacy campaign.

The call for the creation of the National Revolutionary Militia, which as far as I know has no analog in Eastern Europe, was first put out in October 1959 after an aerial bombing raid which killed 40 Cubans. This made the militias the first political organization to be formed in post-revolutionary Cuba.[98] Estimates of the number of people incorporated in the early 1960s range from 183,000 to 500,000. A cross-section of the population signed up to serve in these volunteer forces, including women, young and old, workers and peasants, blacks, mulattos, and whites. Being a *miliciano* demanded a considerable commitment in terms of training, which Zeitlin observed to be "grueling and thorough."[99] Members of the National Revolutionary Militia were exposed to considerable physical danger as part of their service, and were instrumental in repelling the U.S.-sponsored invasion at Playa Giron in 1961.[100]

Voluntary labor was important to the accomplishment of many economic tasks in agriculture and elsewhere throughout the 1960s. Voluntary labor programs began on a small scale in 1959, expanded from 1960 to 1962, and then mushroomed in the latter half of the decade. It is difficult to measure the number of Cubans who participated in voluntary labor, but in terms of the sugar harvest alone, it has been estimated that 86,000 were involved in 1966, 93,000 in 1967, 142,000 in 1968, and 1.2 million in 1970.[101] These volunteers included workers on leave from regular jobs, as well as weekend and holiday volunteers and some unemployed, who were provided room and board and social security benefits. The willingness of these hundreds of thousands of Cubans to give up a portion of their free time, away from family, friends, work-mates, and the comforts of home on repeated occasions stands as testimony to their considerable political commitment to and involvement in the social revolution then under consolidation on the island.

A final example of mass participation in the consolidation of Cuban socialism can be seen in the literacy campaign, which got fully under way in 1961. Altogether well over 1 million Cubans participated in the campaign: over 900,000 as students, between 260,000 and 300,000 as teachers, and 60,000 who helped build schools. The teachers included the *brigadistas*, mostly high school and primary students who went to remote rural areas to teach, and the *alfabetizadores populares*, adults who held classes an average of two hours a week, mostly in more urbanized areas. The 1961 literacy campaign, however, was merely the initial phase of an ongoing educational drive which has involved many additional Cubans as students and as teachers, and has helped stamp the consolidation of socialism in Cuba with its particular participatory character.[102]

The preceding paragraphs suggest that the institution, but particularly, the consolidation of socialism depended on the involvement of a great number of Cuban citizens. This extensive popular participation helps explain the post-1970 decentralization and democratization, of which growth in union autonomy is one small part. For more than a decade *before* state leaders turned in the direction they did in the early 1970s, they had had a history of calling for base-level participation and involvement, and very significantly, of receiving an enthusiastic and widespread response to those calls each and every time they were put out. But more than this, the state's leaders were aware that the depth and staunchness of citizen response had been a critical factor (Cuban leaders often refer to it as *the* critical factor) in the arduous process of consolidation. This history is not one Cuba shares with many countries of Eastern Europe. And perhaps it can help us understand why increasing union autonomy from the state became an important pillar of the state's reaction to the crisis of the late-1960s, even though such a course would have been inconceivable and unworkable elsewhere, given the very different processes though which socialism was instituted and consolidated.

CONCLUSION

An issue that deserves further attention in subsequent studies of autonomy in the union–state relationship under socialism is the fundamental contradiction or tension that appears to exist between the unions' role as workers' defenders and advocates before state managers, and their role as collaborators with this same stratum in making decisions about production and the economy. Unions in Cuba, and quite possibly in other socialist countries as well, are carrying out these two divergent kinds of activities at once, and the more energetically they perform both tasks, the more acute the tension between them can become. After all, diligent union work in one area can hinder success in the other. Thus, defending one worker's or a group of workers' rights and managing efficiently can demand opposing types of union action. Effectively involving workers in enterprise management or forcefully representing them in supra-worksite decision making is likely to carry a cost in terms of the neglect or infringement of certain workers' rights. How should the unions decide in any given instance whether urging and improving workers' participation in decision-making forum or protecting workers' rights should take precedence? Dilemmas such as these are not exclusive to unions operating under socialism. But due to the distinctive "class" character and ideology of socialist societies, the unique potential they harbor for workers' participation in management,[103] and the structure and wide-ranging activities of the socialist state, how such dilemmas are resolved becomes central to understanding the union movement.

The dynamics of this tension or contradiction in union activities has a potentially great impact on union autonomy from the state, if measured by the presence of conflict, because there are many reasons to suspect that concerted union activity in the defense of workers' rights will induce greater union autonomy from the state, while emphasizing the unions' role as co-manager will diminish it. The impact on workers both of how this tension is resolved or managed and what results this has on union autonomy from the socialist state is an open question. Would workers benefit if the unions suspended their co-management activities altogether and concentrated on defending workers' rights, thereby adopting a more adversarial stance vis-à-vis the state – in one sense bolstering their autonomy, but in another, perhaps, cutting themselves out of the action? Or would the multiple interests of workers really be better served if unions pushed for more involvement in management, in the process sacrificing some of their power to successfully defend workers' rights along with some of their independence from the state? Perhaps under socialism producers really need two (or more) separate kinds of workers' organizations, each handling different tasks. Or perhaps the unions must try, as they appear to be doing at present in Cuba, to act both as the state's adversary *and* its partner, despite the unavoidable tensions and the dangers to union autonomy that accompany such a course.

NOTES

The author would like to thank Michael Burawoy, many Cubans in official and unofficial capacities, and Carlos Forment, along with the Center for Latin American Studies at the University of California, Berkeley, the University of Southern California Faculty Research and Innovation Fund, and the Joint Committee on Latin American Studies of the Social Science Research Council for advice and assistance in the preparation of this study. Many thanks also go to Ed Epstein for his valuable critique of the first draft of this chapter.

1. Central de Trabajadores de Cuba [CTC], *XV congreso de la CTC, Memorias* (Havana: Ed. de la Ciencias Sociales, 1984), pp. 183–184. Though they are both involved in economic decision making, in theory and in practice, there is a greater distinction in Cuba between the state and the Communist Party than is sometimes recognized. The role of the party is to ensure production runs smoothly and efficiently according to the overall social, economic, and political guidelines set

forth in the development program it formulates for the country. The party is to guide the sectors of the State involved in production, not by issuing orders, but by discussion and persuasion. In contrast, the state is the implementor, the detail person. At the macro-level, it devises policies aimed at fulfilling party goals; at the micro-level, it administers the production of goods and services in accordance with the worksite's plan. Thus, though the functions of state and party are connected, they are not identical. Each has distinct institutional structures and lines of authority within them. Moreover, most state personnel with responsibility for economic decision making are not party members, nor are most party members state functionaries. Though interesting and important, the relation of the unions to the party is thus a separate topic from the one treated in this chapter. For discussion of the complex aspects of state–party interaction in Cuba, see Jorge Domínguez, *Cuba: Order and Revolution* (Cambridge, MA: Belknap, 1978), especially chapter 8; Rhoda Rabkin, "Cuban Political Structure: Vanguard Party and the Masses," pp. 251–269 in Sandor Halebsky and John Kirk, eds., *Cuba: Twenty-Five Years of Revolution, 1959–1984* (New York: Praeger, 1985); William LeoGrande, "The Communist Party of Cuba Since the First Congress," *Journal of Latin American Studies*, 12 (1980), pp. 397–419; Marta Harnecker, *Cuba: Dictatorship or Democracy?* (Westport, CT: Lawrence Hill, 1980), especially the introduction; Partido Comunista de Cuba, *Tesis y resoluciones: Primer congreso del Partido Comunista de Cuba* (Havana: Ed. de las Ciencias Sociales, 1978), especially pp. 45–46 and 57–99; and Raúl Castro, "Discurso pronunciado ante los cuadros y funcionarios del Comité Central el 4 de mayo de 1973," in Fidel and Raúl Castro, eds., *Selección de discursos acerca del Partido* (Havana: Ed. de las Ciencias Sociales, 1975), pp. 55–88.

2. Works that have made a contribution to our understanding of the capitalist state in terms of these dimensions include James O'Connor, *The Fiscal Crisis of the State* (New York: St. Martin's, 1973); Nicos Poulantzas, *Political Power and Social Classes* (London: New Left Books, 1975); Claus Offe, *Contradictions of the Welfare State* (Cambridge, MA: MIT Press, 1984); Ralph Miliband, *The State in Capitalist Society* (London: Weidenfield and Nicholson, 1969); Theda Skocpol, "Strategies of Analysis in Current Research," pp. 3–43 in Skocpol, Peter Evans, and Dietrich Rueschemeyer, eds., *Bringing the State Back In* (Cambridge: Cambridge University Press, 1985); Jurgen Habermas, *Legitimation Crisis* (Boston: Beacon Press, 1975); Seymour Lipset, *Political Man* (Garden City, NY: Doubleday, 1963); and Goran Therborn, *What Does the Ruling Class Do When It Rules?* (London: Verso, 1980). On the socialist state, see Alex Nove, *The Economics of Feasible Socialism* (Boston: Allen & Unwin, 1983); Rudolf Bahro, *The Alternative in Eastern Europe* (London: Verso, 1981); Wlodzimierz Brus, *Socialist Ownership and Political Systems* (London: Routledge and Kegan Paul, 1975); Ferenc Feher, Agnes Heller, and Gyorgy Markus, *Dictatorship Over Needs* (Oxford: Basil Blackwell, 1983); Neil Harding, ed., *The State in Socialist Society* (Albany, NY: State University of New York Press, 1984); Janos Kornai, *Overcentralization in Economic Administration* (London: Oxford, 1959); and Ivan Szelenyi, "Whose Alternative?" *New German Critique*, 20 (1980), pp. 117–134.

3. Roberto Veiga, *Report Presented to the 15th Congress of the CTC* (Havana: 1984), p. 23; Medea Benjamin, Joseph Collins, and Michael Scott, *No Free Lunch: Food and Revolution in Cuba Today* (San Francisco: Institute for Food and Development Policy, 1984), p. 83; CTC, pp. 27, 215.

4. At the 13th national CTC congress in 1973, the union supported the institution of overtime pay and extra pay for hard or dangerous work, for which workers can now receive additional pay increments of between 25 percent and 30 percent of their basic wage. Over 300,000 workers received such supplements in 1984. Before 1973, workers received 100 percent of their wages when production was interrupted. This percentage was subsequently reduced to 70 percent, and now is being debated publicly: a resolution taken in 1984 by the 15th national CTC congress called for new legislation allowing reimbursement to vary by branch of the economy and facilitating the relocation of workers affected by interruptions. On these matters, see Carmelo Mesa-Lago, *The Economy of Socialist Cuba* (Albuquerque, NM: University of New Mexico Press, 1981); p. 149; Veiga, p. 23; CTC, pp. 142, 216–218; Marifeli Pérez-Stable, "Class, Organization, and Conciencia: The Cuban Working Class After 1970," in Halebsky and Kirk eds., p. 299; and Elaine Fuller, "Unions Debate Productivity, Wage Policy, Women's Demands," *The Guardian*, May 9, 1984, p. 15.

5. Norms work in the following fashion in Cuba. Workers fulfilling their quota by 100 percent receive 100 percent of their basic wage. With each percentage of overfulfillment, workers' wages are increased by an equal percentage. If the quota is underfulfilled, wages are reduced in a like manner.

6. For a summary of these measures, see *Trabajadores*, July 16, 1982, p. 2.

7. *Trabajadores*, October 25, 1982, p. 3 and CTC, 1984, p. 94. In 1982, 93 percent (1,165,900) of the workers considered normable were actually normed. The total occupied labor force (state and private sectors) numbered 3,381,000 in 1980. See Claes Brundenius, *Revolutionary Cuba: The Challenge of Economic Growth With Equity* (Boulder, CO: Westview Press, 1984), p. 134.

8. *Trabajadores*, March 25, 1981, p. 2; October 25, 1982, p. 3; March 14, 1981, p. 3.

9. *Trabajadores*, March 25, 1981, p. 2.

10. See, for example, *Trabajadores*, May 24, 1980, p. 2 and September 28, 1981, p. 2. A normer's guide published in 1983 indicated that norms should be revised every one to three years or when average fulfillment was above 115 percent to 130 percent or below 95 percent. See Brundenius, p. 134.

11. *Trabajadores*, December 2, 1980, p. 2.

12. *Trabajadores*, December 2, 1980, p. 2; March 24, 1981, p. 2.

13. *Trabajadores*, December 2, 1980, p. 2; March 14, 1981, p. 3.

14. Comité Estatal de Trabajo y Seguridad Social (CETSS), *Indicaciones para el trabajo de los normadores* (Havana: CETSS, 1983), p. 11; *Trabajadores*, June 24, 1982, p. 2.

15. Andrew Zimbalist, "Worker Participation in Cuba," *Challenge*, 18 (1975), p. 51.

16. Interview with members of the Tobacco Workers' Union, Havana, September 30, 1982.

17. On this issue, see Frank Fitzgerald, "Politics and Social Structure in Revolutionary Cuba," unpublished Ph.D. dissertation, SUNY, Binghamton, 1985, pp. 294 ff.; and Charles Sabel and David Stark, "Planning, Politics, and Shop-Floor Power: Hidden Forms of Bargaining in Soviet-Imposed State-Socialist Societies," *Politics and Society*, 11:42 (1982), pp. 454–457.

18. Brundenius, p. 104; Mesa-Lago, p. 103. Scholars working in this area are

always careful to warn of the methodological difficulties that attend the estimation of income distribution.

19. Brundenius, "Measuring Income Distribution in Pre- and Post-Revolutionary Cuba," *Cuban Studies*, 9 (1979), pp. 34–35.

20. Fuller, p. 15; Pérez-Stable, p. 298; *Trabajadores*, June 10, 1980, p. 2; Eugenio Balari, *Cuba–USA: Palabras cruzadas* (Havana: Ed. de la Ciencias Sociales, 1985), p. 208; and Brundenius, "Measuring Income Distribution," p. 34. See also Mesa-Lago's computations (p. 153) of change in ratios of highest and lowest wage means from 1962 to 1975. For estimates at other periods, see Pérez-Stable, 1985, p. 298; Mesa-Lago, p. 155; Fitzgerald, "A Critique of the 'Sovietization of Cuba' Thesis," *Science and Society*, 42 (1978), p. 24; Zimbalist, p. 48; Maurice Zeitlin, *Revolutionary Politics and the Cuban Working Class* (New York: Harper and Row, 1970), p. xix; and Robert Hernández and Mesa-Lago, "Labor Organization and Wages," in Mesa-Lago, ed., *Revolutionary Change in Cuba* (Pittsburgh: University of Pittsburgh Press, 1971), pp. 230–231.

21. For information on inter-sectoral wage differences, see Domínguez, pp. 228, 243, 390; Brundenius, "Cuba: Redistribution and Growth with Equity," in Halebsky and Kirk, eds., p. 202; and Brundenius, *Revolutionary Cuba*, p. 20.

22. Veiga, "Informe central presentado al XIV Congreso Nacional de la CTC," *Trabajadores*, special supplement, November 29, 1978, p. 13. Likewise Jerry Hough, "Policy Making and the Worker," in Arcadius Kahan and Blair Ruble, ed., *Industrial Labor in the U.S.S.R.* (New York: Pergamon Press, 1979), p. 376, has uncovered some official union sentiment for decreasing wage inequality in the Soviet Union.

23. Brundenius, *Revolutionary Cuba*, p. 115.

24. Mesa-Lago, *The Economy of Socialist Cuba*, p. 144.

25. Tom Barry, Beth Wood, and Deb Preush, *Dollars and Dictators* (Albuquerque, NM: The Resource Center, 1982), p. 124; James Wilkie, ed., *Statistical Abstract of Latin America*, UCLA Latin American Studies, 24 (1985), chapter 13; International Labour Organization (ILO), *Yearbook of Labour Statistics*, 1984, chapter 3. Mesa-Lago has characterized the increase in jobs as "in large measure achieved by transforming open unemployment into underemployment" (*The Economy of Socialist Cuba*, p. 188). However, it is important to recognize that the term unemployment, as Mesa-Lago uses it here, does not imply the temporary, erratic, low paid, informal sector work that it usually does elsewhere in the developing world. Rather, it refers to underutilized and thus "unproductive" labor. Migration has also had a negative effect on the number of unemployed in Cuba.

26. Mesa-Lago, *The Economy of Socialist Cuba*, p. 123; Brundenius, *Revolutionary Cuba*, p. 135.

27. Benjamin et al., p. 3.

28. Benjamin et al., pp. 90, 181; Brundenius, *Revolutionary Cuba*, p. 84.

29. Benjamin et al., pp. 37–38; Brundenius, *Revolutionary Cuba*, pp. 111–112. Food prices in Cuba remained unchanged from the early 1960s to the early 1980s, when, one year after the General Wage Reform, they were raised an average of 10–12 percent. Benjamin et al.'s budget calculations require updating. Mesa-Lago "The Economy: Caution, Frugality, and Resilient Ideology," in Jorge Domínguez, ed., *Cuba: Internal and International Affairs* (Beverly

Hills, CA: Sage, 1982), pp. 157–159 and Pérez-Stable (p. 298) give much higher estimates of food price increases.

30. Brundenius, *Revolutionary Cuba*, p. 112.

31. CTC, pp. 219–220.

32. Social assistance beneficiaries receive benefits in cash, services, and in kind. For more information on social security and social assistance programs, see Ken Schulman, "Social Security: More Than a Safety Net," *Cubatimes*, 2 (1982), pp. 21–24; and Gil Green, *Cuba at 25* (New York: International Publishers, 1983), especially chapter 8.

33. Mesa-Lago, *The Economy of Socialist Cuba*, p. 171; Schulman, p. 21; and Fidel Castro, "Fidel's Main Report to the 3rd Congress," *Granma Weekly Review*, February 16, 1986, p. 4. The 1980 expenditure equalled 8 percent of Cuba's national budget of approximately 9.5 billion pesos. Between 1958 and 1985, Cuban government expenditures for social assistance and social security increased over nine-fold. During the same period of time, the size of the labor force did not even double.

34. Hernández and Mesa-Lago, p. 214.

35. Indeed, this view was expressed to me by workers themselves. An analogous point can be made regarding the pursuit of workers' interests *above* the level of the work center. Since much of the administration of the Cuban economy is in the hands of sectorally organized bodies (e.g., the Ministries of Agriculture, Construction, Education, Sugar, etc.), if unions are structured in a parallel fashion, and workers in one particular economic sector are all represented *above* the workplace by one instead of several different unions, the opportunity to play one group of workers off against another at the supra-worksite level is minimized.

36. Pérez-Stable, "Wither the Working Class?," *Latin American Perspectives*, 2 (1975), pp. 66, 69; Hernández and Mesa-Lago, pp. 215–217.

37. Pérez-Stable, "Wither the Working Class?" p. 69; *Trabajadores*, February 1973, second half; Hernández and Mesa-Lago, p. 25.

38. Hernández and Mesa-Lago, p. 215; Cuban Economic Research Project (CERP), *Labor Conditions in Communist Cuba* (Coral Gables, FL: University of Miami, 1963), pp. 93–94; Arthur MacEwan, *Revolution and Economic Development in Cuba* (London: Macmillan, 1981), p. 25. This percentage represented 1.5 million workers.

39. CTC, p. 57. 99.2 percent affiliation would equal approximately 2,777,600 union members in the country.

40. Interview with a member of the Public Administration Workers Union, Havana, October 13, 1983. *Gusano* (literally "worm") is the Cuban term for those who don't support the revolution, most of whom now reside outside the country. *Medio* means "half" or "medium," so a *medio gusano* is someone who only half-heartedly or halfway supports the revolution.

41. Figures published at the beginning of 1979 indicated that the previous year the national unions were able to collect between 80 percent and 100 percent of their dues. The average for all national unions was 93 percent (*Trabajadores*, January 27, 1979, p. 5).

42. Interview with a member of the Commerce and Restaurant Workers Union, Havana, October 5, 1982.

43. CTC, *Estatutos de la Central de Trabajadores de Cuba* (Havana: CTC, 1978), VIII, pp. 82–86.

44. Interview with an official in the national office of the CTC, Havana, September 29, 1982.

45. According to Baran's account, "The trade unions reproduced on a small scale the tensions and differentiations besetting the nation as a whole," Paul Baran, *Reflections on the Cuban Revolution* (New York: Monthly Review Press, 1961), p. 17. For more details of this period, see the often widely diverging accounts of Hobart Spalding, "The Workers' Struggle: 1850–1961," *Cuba Review*, 4 (1974), pp. 23–30; and *Organized Labor in Latin America* (New York: NYU Press, 1977); CERP; Hernández and Mesa-Lago; Lionel Martin, "Reestructuración sindical en Cuba," *Cuba Internacional*, April 1974; Andrés Vilariño Ruiz, "Surgimiento del sistema de dirección de la economía socialista en Cuba y sus particularidades," *Cuestiones de la Economia Planificada*, 3:3 (1980); pp. 60–94, and Pérez-Stable, "Wither the Cuban Working Class?"

46. Donald Bray and Timothy Harding, "Cuba," in Ronald Chilcote and Joel Edelstein, eds., *Latin America: The Struggle with Dependency and Beyond* (New York: Wiley, 1974), p. 686.

47. Adolfo Gilly, *Cuba: Coexistencia o revolución* (Buenos Aires: Ed. Monthly Review, 1965), p. 18.

48. Surely it would be unduly cumbersome to require a direct vote for every one of the many union offices above the section level, and no worker I spoke with seemed troubled by indirect union elections. Some, in fact, argued that direct election of higher offices was a poor idea, since workers would not know who they were voting for, whereas the people chosen as electors realize that it is their job, have greater interest, and therefore make the effort to get information on the candidate running for office. Despite this, further democratization of Cuban workers might result if more officers came to be elected directly by the membership.

49. For information on elections for intermediate and national officers of the national unions and the intermediate officers of the CTC, see Linda Fuller, "The Politics of Workers' Control in Cuba, 1959–1983: The Work Center and the National Arena," unpublished Ph.D. dissertation, University of California, Berkeley, 1985, pp. 176–181.

50. *Trabajadores*, February 20, 1979, p. 1.

51. *Trabajadores*, December 4, 1978, p. 3.

52. Veiga, "Informe central," p. 7; and CTC, *XV Congreso*, p. 114.

53. CTC, *XV Congreso*, sec. III, p. 9 and sec. IX, pp. 89–90.

54. After a deficit of 6.5 million pesos in 1975, the unions registered a surplus of 400,000 pesos in 1976 and 1977. Between 1979 and 1983, the average annual surplus totaled nearly 880,000 pesos (CTC, *XV Congreso*, p. 165).

55. Party members are also encouraged to minimize their candidacy in local union elections. Green (p. 62) reported that 16 percent of local union leaders were Party members.

56. In 1980, the labor force was divided as follows: production workers (54 percent), administrative and service workers (20 percent), professional and technical workers (18 percent), and managers and political workers (8 percent). Pérez-Stable, "Class, Organization and *Conciencia*," p. 295.

57. Blas Roca, quoted in Hernández and Mesa-Lago, p. 212.

58. Harnecker, p. 11.

59. Gilly, pp. 40, 42; Hernández and Mesa-Lago, p. 239.

60. Interview with a CTC official, Havana, September 29, 1982.

61. An important aspect of organizing workers to participate in decision making about production is preparing them to take part. Although not discussed here, this is also an important activity of Cuban unions, and involves substantial efforts in the area of technical, economic, and general education.

62. For information on the planning assemblies, management councils, and grievance councils, see Linda Fuller, pp. 98–101, and chapters 7 and 8.

63. Zimbalist (p. 51) reported that attendance at the assemblies ranged from 80 percent to 100 percent in the mid-1970s.

64. Worker reports include those from union section officers and from workers elected to represent their department or work group during the representative assemblies (asambleas de representantes) which are held on a trimestral basis at the enterprise level.

65. Interview with a member of the Tobacco Workers Union, Havana, September 30, 1982.

66. Interview with a member of the Public Administration Workers Union, Havana, September 13, 1982.

67. José Herrera and Hernán Rosenkranz, "Political Consciousness in Cuba," in John and Peter Griffiths, eds., Cuba: The Second Decade (London: Writers and Readers Publishing Cooperative, 1979), p. 48.

68. Interview with a national CTC official, Havana, September 29, 1982. Also see Trabajadores, September 22, 1981, p. 2.

69. Interview with a member of the Health Workers Union, Havana, September 27, 1982.

70. Interview with a member of the Light Industry Workers Union, Havana, October 9, 1983.

71. These new procedures were reported in Trabajadores, December 9, 1980, p. 1; January 31, 1981, p. 1; February 21, 1981, p. 1; and March 21, 1981, p. 2.

72. Domínguez, "Revolutionary Politics: The Demands for Orderliness," in his edited work, Cuba: Internal and International Affairs, p. 27; Fernando Álvarez Tabío, 1981, pp. 301–313.

73. Fernando Álvarez Tabío, Comentarios a la constitución socialista (Havana: Ed. de Ciencias Sociales, 1981), pp. 313–315.

74. The draft was sent to the national council of the CTC for review before it was finally approved by the Council of Ministers (Trabajadores, October 9, 1979, p. 1).

75. Enrique Hernández González, "Participación de los trabajadores en la dirección de la producción socialista," Cuestiones de la economía planificada, 3:5 (1980), pp. 18–19; Veiga, "Informe central," p. 16.

76. Interview conducted by Sheryl Lutgens, Havana, March 31, 1983.

77. Before the General Wage Reform was implemented, it was, according to Green (p. 61), "first discussed throughout the labor movement."

78. For additional examples, see Trabajadores, October 4, 1979, p. 4; CTC, XV Congreso, IV.4.1; p. 13; and Manuel Gómez, Cuban Occupational Health and Safety Law (Havana: 1965), p. 8. Aside from direct union participation at these two

highest levels of decision making, the 1976 Constitution also specifically mentions the right of the national committee of the CTC to initiate legislation before the supreme political organ of the country, the National Assembly of People's Power. I am unaware whether the union has yet proposed any piece of legislation to the National Assembly. Workers I spoke with generally knew that the unions had the right to do so, though they were unable to provide any details concerning the unions' exercise of this right.

79. Their reluctance is well illustrated by Reckord's description of a workplace assembly he attended in the late 1960s, and by Gilly's observations from a stay on the island in the early part of the decade. See Gilly, pp. 20, 22; Barry Reckord, *Does Fidel Eat More than Your Father?* (London: Andre Deutsch, 1971), pp. 101–106.

80. Pérez-Stable, "Institutionalization and Workers' Response," *Cuban Studies*, 6 (1976), p. 44. At the same time, however, 72 percent of Pérez-Stable's sample said they would go to the union if they had a problem, while 11 percent had no clear idea what the unions' role was. Pérez-Stable suggests that these somewhat contradictory responses reflected the fact that the people she interviewed "were living in a period of rapid change, a period during which the consequences of the disarray of the late 1960s were still fresh, but one in which the first evidence of the order of things to come was everywhere apparent" (p. 38).

81. Interview with a member of the Tobacco Workers Union, Havana, September 30, 1982.

82. Interview with a member of the Health Workers Union, Havana, September 27, 1982.

83. Interview with a member of the Cultural Workers Union, Havana, September 25, 1982.

84. Interview with a member of the Health Workers Union, Havana, October 10, 1983.

85. Green, p. 62. The 15th national CTC congress in 1984 engaged in detailed self-criticism of the unions' involvement in the health and safety area (CTC, *XV Congreso*, pp. 32–34, 145–148).

86. Information from Paul Bigman, May 9, 1985. The dearth of such actions might be partially, though not totally explained, by the fact that mechanisms for resolving disputes that are unavailable elsewhere (e.g., production and service assemblies, planning assemblies, management councils, representation on the Council of State, etc.), have been instituted throughout Cuba, and because the state, through its wage and benefit policies, has provided things that unions must often strike to obtain in other places.

87. Linda Fuller, "Power at the Workplace: The Resolution of Worker-Management Conflict in Cuba," *World Development*, 15:1 (1987), pp. 139–152.

88. Interview with a member of the Education and Science Workers Union, Havana, October 3, 1982.

89. In considering these questions, I will emphasize "internal" rather than "external" explanatory factors. However, a more complete answer would also have to examine "external" factors in some detail, especially the relationship between Cuba and other socialist nations and the fact that Cuba, a developing socialist country, must exist within the context of a pervasive capitalist world market.

90. Spalding, *Organized Labor in Latin America*, p. 237. For accounts of the Cuban labor movement during the years of *mujalismo*, see Spalding, pp. 231–233, and "The Workers' Struggle," p. 6; Bray and Harding, p. 601; Ramón Ruiz, *Cuba: The Making of a Revolution* (Amherst, MA: University of Massachusetts Press, 1968), pp. 133–134; MacEwan, p. 25; Baran, p. 17; Martin, p. 29; Domínguez, *Cuba: Order and Revolution*, pp. 96–97; Vilariño, Ruiz, pp. 85–86; and Pérez-Stable, "Wither the Cuban Working Class?" pp. 64–65.

91. For more information on this period, see Spalding, *Organized Labor in Latin America*; Ruiz; Martin; Pérez-Stable, 'Wither the Cuban Working Class?'; CERP; Grupo Cubano de Investigaciones, *Un estudio sobre Cuba* (Coral Gables, FL: University of Miami Press, 1963); O'Connor, *The Origins of Socialism in Cuba* (Ithaca, NY: Cornell University Press, 1970); J. P. Morray, *The Second Revolution in Cuba* (New York: Monthly Review Press, 1962); and Ralph Woodward, "Union Labor and Communism: Cuba," *Caribbean Studies*, 3:3 (1963), pp. 17–50.

92. For further information on the relationship between the Communists and Cuba's political leaders during the 1960s, see LeoGrande, "Continuity and Change in the Cuban Political Elite," *Cuban Studies*, 8 (1978), pp. 1–31; Hans Enzensberger, "Portrait of a Party: Prehistory, Structure, and Ideology of the PCC," in Ronald Radosh, ed., *The New Cuba: Paradoxes and Potentials* (New York: William Morrow, 1976); Andrés Suárez, *Cuba: Castroism and Communism, 1959–1960* (Cambridge: MIT Press, 1967); Morray, especially pp. 170 ff.; Domínguez, *Cuba: Order and Revolution*, especially, pp. 210 ff.; and Samuel Farber, "The Cuban Communists in the Early Stages of the Cuban Revolution: Revolutionaries or Reformists?" *Latin American Research Review*, 18:1 (1983), pp. 59–83.

93. The percentage of Cuba's GMP destined for gross capital formation rose from approximately 16 percent in 1962 to 20 percent in 1965, 27 percent in 1967, and 31 percent in 1968.

94. For information on absenteeism, see MacEwan, p. 145; Fitzgerald, "A Critique," p. 11; Domínguez, *Cuba: Order and Revolution*, pp. 275–276; Archibald Ritter, *The Economic Development of Revolutionary Cuba* (New York: Praeger, 1974), p. 282; and Rolando Bonachea and Nelson Valdés, "Labor and Revolution: Introduction," in their edited work, *Cuba in Revolution* (Garden City, New York: 1972), p. 375. For discussions of productivity, see Mesa-Lago, *The Economy of Socialist Cuba*, p. 134; and Ritter, pp. 283–286.

95. For example, see Pérez-Stable, "Wither the Cuban Working Class?" p. 62; Mesa-Lago, *Cuba in the 1970s: Pragmatism and Institutionalization* (Albuquerque, NM: University of New Mexico Press, 1978), p. 156; Leo Huberman and Paul Sweezy, *Socialism in Cuba* (New York: Monthly Review Press, 1969), pp. 217–218; and Lourdes Casal, "The Cuban Communist Party: The Best among the Good," *Cuba Review*, 6 (1976), p. 24.

96. Besides the kinds of changes which bolstered union autonomy, other important ones were also a part of the leadership's response to the crisis of the late 1960s: a new governmental system was introduced (the Organizations of Popular Power), the mass organizations were revamped, material incentives received more emphasis, income differentials were increased, the investment rate was lowered, more consumer goods were produced, and some prices went up.

97. Doménico Nuti, "The Contradictions of Socialist Economies: A Marxian

Interpretation," in Ralph Miliband and John Saville, eds., *The Socialist Register* (London: Merlin Press, 1979), pp. 252–253; Brus, p. 61.

98. Domínguez, *Cuba: Order and Revolution*, pp. 207–208.

99. Zeitlin, p. 39.

100. For more information on the militias, see Zeitlin, p. 39; Richard Fagen, "Mass Mobilization in Cuba: The Symbols of Struggle," in Bonachea and Valdés, eds., p. 208; O'Connor, *The Origins of Socialism in Cuba*, p. 305; and Boris Goldenberg, *The Cuban Revolution and Latin America* (New York: Praeger, 1965), pp. 208, 237.

101. MacEwan, p.115. See also Mesa-Lago, "Economic Significance of Unpaid Labor in Socialist Cuba," in Bonachea and Valdés, eds.

102. On the literacy campaign, see Valdés, "The Radical Transformation of Cuban Education," in Bonachea and Valdés, eds.; Huberman and Sweezy; and Fitzgerald, "Politics and Social Structure."

103. On this point, see Linda Fuller, "The Politics of Workers' Control in Cuba," chapter 3 and Conclusion.

Chapter 7 ——————————————————————————————

Labor and Politics: The Mexican Paradox

Francisco Zapata

Within the Latin American context, the relationship between labor and the Mexican state is quite exceptional. Both actors have created a complex and durable relationship which, at least since the 1940s, can be characterized as mutually beneficial.[1] Such has not been the case in most other countries where labor and the state have tended to interact conflictually and without having a common ground upon which to pursue their respective interests. Even in the recent period since 1970 when Mexico has begun to experience the economic problems which typify other Latin American countries in terms of inflation, monetary devaluation, and instability in its development process, one may note that the appearance of relatively autonomous labor organizations — so-called "independent unionism" — has not changed the fundamental relationship between organized labor and the political system.

Having posed the stability of this relationship as a given within the present analysis, the body of this chapter focuses on two general themes: (1) an attempt to explain the relation between labor and politics in both historical and structural terms, and (2) an analysis of the way this compact has operated in the post-war period, the time of most interest in a comparative sense.

THE HISTORICAL ORIGINS OF THE RELATIONSHIP
BETWEEN LABOR AND THE MEXICAN STATE

When the *Casa del Obrero Mundial* (the House of the World Worker) was created in 1912, Mexican labor acquired representation within the revolutionary process, achieving an identity it did not previously possess.[2] During the struggle against General Victoriano Huerta, the *Casa* became an active supporter of the Constitutionalist forces and of General Obregón, one of its leaders. This support eventually led to the agreement

173

signed in 1915 whereby the *Casa* committed its support to the Consti-
tutionalists in exchange for economic and social benefits for workers. This
instance was the first indication of an alliance that was to be pursued when
the *Confederación Regional Obrera Mexicana*, CROM, or the Mexican
Regional Workers Confederation, was created in 1918. In many ways, the
CROM was the prototypical modern Mexican labor organization in that it
represented an explicit commitment of labor to the objectives of the
Mexican state. Two political leaders closely associated with the CROM,
Luis Morones and Vicente Lombardo Toledano, were instrumental in the
passage of a series of labor laws, with the 1931 Labor Code being the most
important. As a result of such political gains, the CROM saw its membership grow from less than 10,000 workers in 1918 to over 500,000 by
1926–1927. Labor's official political ties strengthened as the revolutionary
regime became more and more institutionalized, culminating in the 1934–
1940 Lázaro Cárdenas presidency with the creation of the *Confederación de
Trabajadores de México* (CTM), or the Mexican Workers Confederation, in
1936. Lombardo Toledano was central in the creation of this new labor
confederation not only in organizational but also in ideological terms.
Indeed, his position as both a labor, political, and intellectual personality
contributed to the emergence of a series of CTM commitments which have
remained important up to the present in shaping the identity of the
relationship between organized labor and the Mexican political system.

It is important to mention here that throughout the 1912–1936 period,
Mexico's social structure did not change as rapidly as did the political
sphere. Agricultural employment continued to represent more than
two-thirds of the total economically active population, while jobs in the
industrial and service sectors increased very little in relative terms. After
1940, however, both total employment and its distribution would change
dramatically.

TABLE 7.1
Change in Sectoral Distribution of the Mexican Labor Force, 1950–1980

Economic Sector:	1950		1960		1970		1980	
	%	Δ	%	Δ	%	Δ	%	Δ
Agriculture	61.2	(—)	54.2	(− 7.0)	39.5	(−14.7)	26.0	(−13.5)
Industry	16.7	(—)	18.9	(+ 2.2)	22.9	(+ 4.0)	20.4	(− 2.5)
Services	22.1	(—)	26.9	(+ 4.8)	37.5	(+10.6)	53.7	(+16.2)
EAP (in 1000s)[a]	8,272		11,332 (+37%)		12,995 (+14.7%)		21,941 (+68.8%)	

Source: International Labor Office, *Yearbook of Labor Statistics* (Geneva: 1955, 1965, 1975, 1984).
[a] EAP = Economically Active Population.

TABLE 7.2
Sectoral Distribution of the Economically Active Population and Strikers,
1964–1969

Economic Sector[a]	EAP	Strikers
Agriculture	39.5%	7.7%
Industry	22.9%	51.4%
Services	37.5%	40.8%

Source: International Labor Office, Yearbook of Labor Statistics (Geneva: 1955–1975).
[a] Definitions: Industrial sector includes mining, manufacturing, and construction; Service sector includes health, education, and personal services.

But, in political terms, the 1930s marked a deepening of the Revolution. Serious agrarian reform and the constitution of the *Partido Nacionalista Revolucionario* or The Revolutionary Nationalist Party, institutionalized social change at the national level. From 1936 onwards, Mexico began to industrialize within the political structure that had been consolidated during the Cárdenas presidency.

During this time, the CTM was ideologically on the left, despite its explicit commitment in support of the Mexican state. The presence of Lombardo Toledano, the existence of many high level political leaders in the Cárdenas government who adhered to a Marxist perspective, and the then radical nature of the regime contributed to the development of a special type of relationship between the unions and the state where each coexisted and supported mutual projects. A good example of this alliance is the oil nationalization controversy of 1938 which began as a labor conflict between the foreign oil companies and the various unions representing the workers.[3] The refusal of the companies to negotiate forced the government to intervene and, eventually, to decree the nationalization of the oil industry. At this point, Cárdenas explicitly gave his support to the petroleum unions, thus ratifying the alliance that had emerged two years before with the creation of the CTM. As was true throughout the 1912–1940 period, this alliance between the state and the labor movement permitted a certain ideological commitment by the unions to revolutionary nationalism.[4]

The turning point for this relationship came during World War II when Mexico intensified its industrialization as a response to difficulties in importing manufactured goods from the United States.[5] Private and public investment increased markedly, as did output in electricity, steel, cement, communications, oil, and housing. With the resulting growth of the industrial labor force, the national industrial unions consolidated their power in the area of railroads, mining and metallurgy, oil, and electricity. Labor conflict also increased, especially in 1944.

But such conflict was not allowed to continue. In 1945, the CTM signed the *Pacto Obrero Industrial*, or the Worker Industrial Pact, in which the labor movement committed itself to support the official strategy of national industrial development.[6] At the same time, divisions began to appear within labor leadership. The role of Lombardo Toledano was increasingly questioned by a new generation of leaders headed by Fidel Velásquez. Ultimately, in 1950, Velásquez succeeded in winning the elections for the head of the CTM executive committee, a post he has since held.

The Velásquez election should be seen as one consequence of President Alemán's offensive against labor radicalism. This offensive resulted in the state's consolidation of control of the national industrial unions where some supporters of Lombardo Toledano still remained. The Alemán government's intervention to exclude leaders of leftist tendencies in the railroad workers (1948) and the petroleum workers unions (1951) demonstrated that the state would not allow the existence of an autonomous labor leadership.[7] What is usually referred to as *"charrismo,"* or rule through cooperative labor bosses, began at this time. Although allowing the continued presence of the labor movement within the government alliance, the state sought to subordinate the unions to the interests of its bourgeois faction, a bourgeoisie increasingly in command of a clearly defined project of capital accumulation.[8]

This structure for controlling politics within the national industrial unions, as well as the demands of rank-and-file workers, paid off in terms of the resulting high rates of economic growth. The gross domestic product in Mexico grew at a rate of 6.1 percent in the 1941–1946 period, at 5.7 percent in that of 1947–1952, and at 6.4 percent in 1953–1958. But if per capita distribution was slower, it permitted reinvestment in productive facilities. Real salaries actually decreased: the rural minimum salary fell 46 percent in the 1939–1950 period, and the average salary in 35 industries declined some 26 percent over the same time span. Real salaries surpassed prewar figures only after 1958–1959, doing so only up to 1971 when they once again resumed a downward trend.

Such income data demonstrate that the existing relationship between organized labor and the state was highly beneficial to the process of capital accumulation. For the sake of completeness, however, one ought to mention that despite the decline in real salary, worker benefits in housing, education, health, and social security experienced substantial improvements in the same period. What labor did not obtain in salaries it obtained collectively through benefits provided directly by the state rather than by entrepreneurs. Such improvements help to explain why the alliance has persisted instead of the intensification of labor conflict which otherwise might have been expected.

I argue in favor of what could be called a "trade-off hypothesis," where Mexican labor maintained a relationship with the state that relied not only on the satisfaction of economic demands, but also on the satisfaction of the collective needs of the country's workers. Such an alliance appears as a mediating structure which promotes the general welfare of the working class through intervention at the political level. The Mexican labor movement and its bureaucratized leadership has succeeded in linking itself with the overall dynamic of the political system in a way which guarantees the latter's efficient operation. The high rates of growth, in part, have been the result of union quiescence. The considerable decline in the intensity of strike activity — to be discussed below — and the practice of trade-offs of economic and political demands between labor and the state have given considerable reinforcement to the process of capital accumulation.

This brief historical overview of the period from the Revolution to the early 1950s captures the image of the process whereby the unions integrated themselves with the Mexican political process. What it does not provide, however, is a structural explanation of how that system functions in regard to organized labor. The next section addresses this question focusing in particular on three basic aspects: the legal provisions governing union activity, the national union structure itself, and an analysis of strike activity.

LINKAGES BETWEEN THE STATE AND LABOR

A. Legal Provisions

Article 123 of the 1917 Constitution, the basic statement regarding what labor can and cannot do in the Mexican context, distinguishes two major categories of unions.[9] In Section A, it refers to unions of "industrial workers, agricultural day laborers, domestic employees, artisans, and in general to all [covered by private] labor contracts." Such private sector unions are, in turn, subdivided, depending on whether they fall into federal or local-level jurisdiction. Section B pertains to all public sector workers employed by the national government, the various Mexican states, and all municipalities. Each type has a separate specified type of bargaining procedure. Defining labor unions as "associations formed for the study, betterment, and defense of the interests of workers and their employers," the law recognizes five distinct types which, with the exception of the final category, must group a minimum of 20 workers: (1) *gremiales*, or those of the same profession, (2) *de empresa*, or those of a single company, (3) *industriales*, or those in two or more companies located in the same industry, (4) *nacionales de industria*, or those in one or more companies of the same industry located in two or more states, and (5) *oficios varios*, or those including less than 20 workers of the same profession, but located in the same municipality. It is also necessary to distinguish between national industrial unions — the fourth category above — where the various sections share a common charter, and the more decentralized national federations where each section has its own separate charter.

B. The National Union Structure

Mexican labor, through the CTM, is one of the three official components of the present dominant political party, the *Partido Revolucionario Institucional*, or PRI, along with the *Confederación Nacional Campesina*, or CNC, and the *Confederación Nacional de Organizaciones Populares*, or CNOP.[10] The CTM is a part of the *Congreso del Trabajo*, or CT, an umbrella organization that groups all major labor confederations, including those not affiliated with the PRI, national industrial unions not part of the CTM, and the confederation of unions representing government workers (the *Federación de Sindicatos de Trabajadores al Servicio del Estado*, or FSTSE) regulated by Section B of Article 123 of the Constitution. The CT is a kind of forum where labor organizations present common positions to the state, going beyond the bounds of what strict PRI membership might allow. The CT is the heir to a number of earlier similar groupings, many of which also reflected CTM sponsorship. Indeed, Fidel Velásquez encouraged the formation of such a broad-based grouping so as to be able to widen the scope of his organization and, thus, to allow for some diversity of opinion within the official labor movement. In the 1960s, the *Bloque de Unidad Obrera*, or BUO, played a similar role.

The decision-making process in organizations like the CTM, the CT, and the national industrial unions is cloaked in secrecy. While it is not clear how election procedures for the higher posts actually function, reelection is typical. The case of the secretary general of the CTM, Fidel Velásquez, is indicative: he has occupied the post continuously for more than 30 years after being first elected in 1950. If CTM organizations like its National Congress and National Council have clear-cut formal functions, much of their power appears to exist largely on paper. At lower organizational levels, action is taken to persuade or force those unions departing from the CTM line to conform.

In general, the CTM fulfills a fundamental role in the capital accumulation process through the maintenance of wages at levels acceptable to capital, its support for the government in any critical situation, and its control of what happens at the rank-and-file level through clientelistic means and with the aid of corrupt union officials. Until now, the CTM has been successful in making it possible for the political system to rely upon it to provide a relatively quiescent labor force. This pattern was consolidated at the end of the 1940s and has been in operation ever since. Very few unions have questioned such control, and those that have, have done so only in the very recent period.

FIGURE 7.1
Organization of the Labor Movement in Mexico

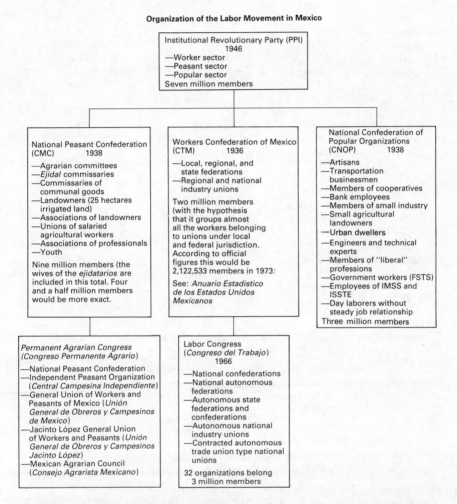

Organization of the Labor Movement in Mexico

Institutional Revolutionary Party (PPI)
1946
—Worker sector
—Peasant sector
—Popular sector
Seven million members

National Peasant Confederation
(CMC)   1938
—Agrarian committees
—*Ejidal* commissaries
—Commissaries of
 communal goods
—Landowners (25 hectares
 irrigated land)
—Associations of landowners
—Unions of salaried
 agricultural workers
—Associations of professionals
—Youth
Nine million members (the
wives of the *ejidatarios* are
included in this total. Four
and a half million members
would be more exact.

Workers Confederation of Mexico
(CTM)   1936
—Local, regional, and
 state federations
—Regional and national
 industry unions
Two million members
(with the hypothesis
that it groups almost
all the workers belonging
to unions under local
and federal jurisdiction.
According to official
figures this would be
2,122,533 members in 1973:
See: *Anuario Estadistico
de los Estados Unidos
Mexicanos*

National Confederation of
Popular Organizations
(CNOP)   1938
—Artisans
—Transportation
 businessmen
—Members of cooperatives
—Bank employees
—Members of small industry
—Small agricultural
 landowners
—Urban dwellers
—Engineers and technical
 experts
—Members of "liberal"
 professions
—Government workers (FSTS)
—Employees of IMSS and
 ISSTE
—Day laborers without
 steady job relationship
Three million members

*Permanent Agrarian Congress
(Congreso Permanente Agrario)*
—National Peasant Confederation
—Independent Peasant Organization
 (*Central Campesina Independiente*)
—General Union of Workers and
 Peasants of Mexico (*Unión
 General de Obreros y Campesinos
 de Mexico*)
—Jacinto López General Union
 of Workers and Peasants (*Unión
 General de Obreros y Campesinos
 Jacinto López*)
—Mexican Agrarian Council
 (*Consejo Agrarista Mexicano*)

*Labor Congress
(Congreso del Trabajo)*
1966
—National confederations
—National autonomous
 federations
—Autonomous state
 federations and
 confederations
—Autonomous national
 industry unions
—Contracted autonomous
 trade union type national
 unions
32 organizations belong
3 million members

Source: Francisco Zapata, "Afiliación y organización sindical en México," in José Luis Reyna, Francisco Zapata, Marcelo Miquet Fleury, and Sylvia Gómez-Tagle, *Tres estudios sobre el movimiento obrero en México* (Mexico City: El Colegio de México, Jornades 80, 1976), p. 100.

What is most significant is the high degree of integration between the labor movement and the government. For each type of worker, be he blue collar, white collar, or peasant, there is a specific organization said to represent his interests in the larger political world. These labor organizations are incorporated into other broader entities for the purpose of reconciling conflicting group interests. Thus, the PRI interacts with

TABLE 7.3
Membership of Various Mexican Union Organizations, 1975

Name	Membership
1. *National Confederations*:	
Confederation of Mexican Workers (CTM)	1,400,000
Revolutionary Confederation of Workers	
and Peasants (CROC)	700,000
Federation of Government Workers Unions at the	
Service of the State (FSTSE)	680,000
Revolutionary Workers Confederation (COR)	225,000
Regional Confederation of Mexican Workers (CROM)	200,000
General Confederation of Workers (CGT)	165,000
Others	60,000
2. *National Industrial Unions*:	
Mexican Railroad Workers Union	100,000
National Union of Mining, Metallurgy, and Similar	
Workers of Mexico	67,900
Union of Electrical Workers of Mexico	5,828
Mexican Electricians Union	8,056
Telephone Operators Union	9,000
Aviators Union Association	800
Various Others	
3. *Others*:	
Federation of Independent Unions of Nuevo Leon	25,000
TOTAL:	3,646,584

Sources: Renate Rott, *Die Mexicanische Gewerksschaftbevegung* (Federal Germany: Scriptor Verlag, 1975), p.257; Carlos Sirvent, "La burocracia en México, El caso de la FSTSE," *Estudios Políticos* 1 (April–June, 1975).

business and with government officials to discuss labor demands. The active presence of many public officials at labor congresses and, reciprocally, the presence of the CTM secretary general at many government functions, illustrates the close relationship that exists among these actors. Such multi-group integration through the political system permits a high degree of flexibility in the negotiation of mutual demands. No possibility exists for a breakdown of inter-group communication or the denial of formal meetings. Of necessity, labor officials, political leaders, and government office holders must maintain steady contact in their efforts to reconcile the wishes of various groups. The presence of federal deputies in Parliament recruited from the labor sector and their increasing relative weight among the PRI delegation is one indication of the importance of labor representation in the governing coalition.

In any overall evaluation of how the highly centralized Mexican political system functions, it is undoubtedly necessary to emphasize the importance of the PRI's role in overseeing the interaction of the various union groups (as in the case of the *Congreso del Trabajo*) as well as the reality of the interplay of interests of its worker, peasant, and popular sectors. One might even assume from this depiction that the political system is not so much a place where control is imposed — as is usually affirmed — as the source of important political benefits for those groups so incorporated.

The usefulness of the labor movement to the political system, and vice versa, is only one aspect of their mutual relationship. At other levels such as in collective bargaining negotiation, the importance of the state is critical. The collective contracts signed reflect the political wishes of the state leadership as much as the economic realities of particular businesses. Salary increases, for example, relate directly to general development strategies defined by the government rather than to the profitability of particular companies. In recent years, the so-called *tope salarial*, or maximum salary limit set by the government, fixes the absolute level which unions cannot exceed. In cases where a union has gained what is deemed an excessive concession from management, the Labor or Budget Ministry has intervened to stop its implementation. The consequence is that official salary policy has resulted in negotiations where salary increases are not the central point of contention; instead, discussions have centered on the extent of fringe benefits, or *prestaciones*, where state control is not exerted to the same degree. One important result of the government decision to fix limits on salary hikes has been the serious undermining of union capacity to bargain at the plant level; as a result, the real negotiations are transferred to the highest political level within the government itself.

C. Strike Activity

An important indicator of the way the state–labor relationship functions in Mexico is the overall tendency for a decrease in the average number of strikers from the 1940s to the present, something surprising given the rising share of industrial workers in the work force and the intensification of industrialization and urbanization in that same time span.[11] The general decline in strikers is evidence in support of the thesis of increased state control over labor demands in recent years. More detail on such control can be provided through the examination of strike figures presented in Table 7.4 which are grouped by each six-year presidential term beginning with that of Cárdenas.

During the Cárdenas presidency, but especially in its first three years, strike activity was intense. The average number of strikers in the entire period was the highest of any moment in recent Mexican history. Such labor activism took place in an economic context of little inflationary pressure; strikes seemed more a response to political mobilization than to economic problems.

TABLE 7.4
Averages of Strikes, Strikers, and Strikers/Strike by Six-Year Presidential term, 1934–1982[a]

Presidential Period	Number of Strikes	Number of Strikers	Number of Strikers/Strike
Cárdenas (1934–1940)	479	61,422	128
Avila Camacho (1941–1946)	387	53,658	139
Alemán (1947–1952)	108	16,200	150
Ruiz Cortines (1953–1958)	248	25,057	101
López Mateos (1959–1964)	488	47,175	97
Díaz Ordaz (1965–1970)	223	7,714	35
Echeverría (1971–1976)	359	11,934	33
López Portillo (1977–1982)	886	51,909	59

Source: Dirección General de Estadística, Anuario Estadístico de los Estados Mexicanos, various years.
[a] Data do not include strikes located at the federal level (see text for the distinction between local and federal jurisdiction in Mexican labor law).

In the Avila Camacho *sexenio* of 1940–1946, strike activity did not intensify but, on the contrary, tended to decrease. It was during this time that the CTM signed two agreements with the administration in which it committed itself to support government economic policy. As a result, labor peace tended to prevail during the war years, while import substitution industrialization was intensifying. So-called "national unity" was the ideological message that Avila Camacho directed toward all social organizations in his attempt to reverse the confrontational politics that had prevailed under Cárdenas. The central government concern focused on ways to stimulate private investment and to conciliate the divergent interests that participated in power.

At the end of the war, when Alemán took power, the more repressive stance adopted by the government toward labor resulted in an actual overall decrease in strike activity and in the specific efforts to gain control over the railroad and oil national industrial unions where dissidents had begun to appear. On the basis of the average number of strikers per strike, one can infer from the data that strikes took place more in large enterprises than in small and medium-sized factories. Such figures statistically reflect the influence of the very large oil and railroad workers unions. The pro-business views of Alemán's minister of labor were reflected in his hostile attitudes toward worker demands. While the basic parameters of the relationship were not broken, it was clear that the state consolidated the subordination of labor it had been seeking to attain from 1940 on. The process of control was represented by the election of Fidel Velásquez as CTM secretary general and the rise to prominence of such leaders as Francisco Pérez Rios and Napoleón Gómez Sada in the electrical workers and mining unions, respectively. The phenomenon of *charrismo* had become institutionalized. After 1952, labor relations would be part of a structure where labor was still strong, but where it could not challenge state decrees.

Under Ruiz Cortines (1952–1958), strike activity increased slightly in relation to the level attained under Alemán.[12] The frequency of conflict increased, reaching an average of 24 strikes per year, though the average number of strikers increased a little less; the average number of strikers per strike resulting decreased in relation to the earlier period. Such an exclusive focus on aggregate data, however, overlooks important events like the large-scale mobilization of railroad workers that occurred at the end of the Ruiz Cortines administration.

In 1957, labor-management disagreement resulted in a long and bitter rail strike.[13] The overlapping of the strike with the PRI nomination process may have been influential in the choice of Adolfo López Mateos as the PRI's candidate for the presidency. As the Minister of Labor in the Ruiz Cortines government, López Mateos had had a lot to do with the development of the railroad conflict. Once President in December 1958, he decided to resolve the strike through the temporary militarization of the railroads. The resulting government repression against the strike leadership succeeded in finally consolidating state power in a union which had sought to challenge official authority.

After its initial show of force, the López Mateos government moved away from anti-union repression for the rest of its time in office.[14] In the entire 1958–1964 period, the average number of strikers and strikes sharply increased to levels not seen since the Cárdenas years. One explanation for this subsequent toleration of strikes may be found in an effort by López Mateos to seek to relegitimize his government with labor after the confrontation of 1958–1959. Another relates to the sharp improvement in economic conditions as inflation decreased, nominal and real salaries reversed their previous decline, and the country experienced general economic growth. The combination of a greater official toleration and better material conditions, in turn, seemed to have led to a noticeable worker mobilization marked by new strikes, an increase in union membership, and a renewed union presence in the political sphere.[15]

The events of the López Mateos years are indicative of the particular characteristics of state-labor relations in Mexico. Here one can argue that the assumption of control by the CTM over worker demands could transform such petitions in the eyes of the state, making them more acceptable for presentation at a later time when economic conditions were more opportune. The resulting strike activity which followed ought to be seen as a safety valve for accumulated worker pressures, the release of which is facilitated by the political linkage of organized labor and the state. The overall labor process is oriented toward containing worker demands within official structures like the CTM rather than allowing them to be spontaneously released in the economy at large. The political opening represented by reduced repression permitted an increase in demands from accepted labor leaders operating within the official ruling coalition. Responding to such labor pressure, the state provided material benefits like salary hikes and the creation of a social security system for government workers in the *Instituto de Servicios y Seguridad Social de los Trabajadores al Servicio del Estado*, or ISSSTE. Such benefits help to explain why strike activity declined in the next presidential period.

Indeed, for the entire six years of the Díaz Ordaz government, strike activity decreased to very low levels.[16] Such a decline is especially apparent in terms of the number of strikers, which averaged less than 8,000, or not even one-sixth of that of the López Mateos period. If one assumes that good economic conditions facilitate strike activity given low unemployment and high employer profits, the decrease observed in strikes during the continued economic expansion of the Díaz Ordaz years is likely to be more a response to political than to strictly economic conditions. Under such a political interpretation, the labor leadership is seen as capable of mobilizing or not mobilizing the union rank-and-file according to the momentary needs of the political system.

From the election of Echeverría in 1970 to the present, a new labor situation has appeared characterized by continued deterioration of the national economy and the appearance of the so-called "independent unions" in the automobile industry and elsewhere.[17] Both factors help explain the intensification of strike activity in this recent period, as measured by the number of strikes and of strikers. Worsening inflation, the promotion of "real prices" with the elimination of government subsidies, and the establishment of salary limits led to increased pressure for salary hikes. For the first time since Cárdenas, the demands of the labor movement were now responding to economic causes as workers sought to recover losses in their standard of living.

The same kind of economic motivation clearly continued as the cause of strikes in the López Portillo period of 1977–1982.[18] The number of strikes averaged 886, and the number of strikers rose above 50,000, both much higher figures than those experienced under Echeverría. Such militancy was the result of the kind of economic deterioration that had long been the case in many other Latin American countries. Indeed, with price increases of 98.8 percent in 1982 and 80.8 percent in 1983, the limited salary hikes permitted by the state led to consecutive drops in real salary of 4.3 percent and 23 percent in those years. During this period, the relationship between labor and the state experienced considerable tension due to the unyielding stand taken by the latter. The sexenio ended with a dramatic rise in strikes and in *emplazamientos a huelga*, the official notice given by unions to employers that a strike will occur unless worker petitions are accepted.

The events of the Echeverría and López Portillo presidencies suggested how much the special relationship between labor and the state suffered as a result of the worsening in inflation, unemployment, and the standard of living. The state, in turn, sought to moderate some of these effects with new food subsidies, permission to grant fringe benefits not directly affecting salaries, and policies geared to the maintenance of existing employment levels. Additional measures included low interest loans from the social security system to ease the short-term financial needs of workers and government employees, and loans for house construction and car purchases for middle-level technicians and professionals linked to the state sector. While not fully compensating for real salary losses, such official responses permitted at least part of aggregate economic demand to continue to rise. It is worth noting that these measures were implemented through agreements between the unions and the state where the political commitment of both to Mexico's development was always publicly emphasized. These agreements took place within the political alliance between labor and the state, and were perceived as such by Mexican workers.

Legal provisions, labor union structure, and strike activity reveal the way in which the Mexican system of labor incorporation within the state functions.[19] Such a relationship is dynamic where both actors interact with each other in a variety of ways, reflecting the influence of other factors (like economic forces). Given the difficulty of presenting its nature abstractly, we have chosen to illuminate it by reference to the way each of these components has influenced the development of the relationship. The concluding section of this chapter extends the earlier analysis into the period of the De la Madrid government.

LABOR AND THE STATE UNDER DE LA MADRID (1982–1985)

Relations between organized labor and the De la Madrid government have elements of continuity with what occurred under Echeverría and López Portillo.[20] The increase in inflation from 1974 forced labor to seek

TABLE 7.5
Percentage Changes in Prices and Salaries in Mexico, 1977–1983

Year	Variation in Consumer Prices (Dec-Dec)	Increases in Minimum Salary	Limits on Contractual Negotiation[a]	Variations in Real Salaries (Annual Average)
1977	20.7	27.9	10.0	−1.0
1978	16.2	13.5	12.0	−3.4
1979	20.0	16.8	13.5	−1.3
1980	29.8	17.8	20.0	−6.7
1981	28.7	30.9	29.0	−2.4
1982	98.8	52.1	25.0	−4.3
1983	80.8	55.4	30.0	−23.0

Source: Comisión Económica para América Latina, Notas para el estudio económico de América Latina (Mexico), 1979, 1981, 1983.
[a] The notion of limits to contractual negotiations refers to the maximum percent which salaries above the minimum level can rise in federally regulated industries. It is frequent for these limits to be considered a base for other negotiations. Since 1976, there have been no increases that exceeded these limits. Frequently, however, increases are added to fringe benefits to circumvent this restriction.

measures to protect the standard of living of the Mexican worker. Debate on this problem took place in the Comisión Nacional de Salarios Mínimos, or Minimum Salary Commission, where representatives of the unions, business, and the government meet at least once a year to discuss the level of such minimum salaries. In the 1979–1983 period, negotiations were contentious, with national labor leaders having to maintain pressure to obtain any increase in existing levels. One result was the creation of the new concept of "emergency salaries" that partly broke with the normal yearly ritual. From then on, the combination of political pressures from the CTM, the increase in emplazamientos a huelga, and intense campaigns in the national press (through whole page ads placed by the national-level industrial unions) resulted in making it clear to the state that labor would not passively accept further falls in real salary such as those depicted in Table 7.5.

One labor initiative consisted of efforts to limit unemployment in contract negotiations. Guarantees of employment stability frequently were accepted in lieu of salary increases. In a similar vein, the unions sought a decrease in the number of hours normally worked per week, the creation of some type of unemployment compensation, price controls, and retraining schemes for the unemployed.

During these critical years, salary policy could not be separated from employment concerns and social measures to reduce the impact of the economic crisis on the lives of workers. Although workers accepted salary increases equal to one-half of inflation in 1982, 1983, and 1984, the level of open unemployment was kept at the existing level of approximately 2.2 million people. If hidden unemployment did increase much more, to a level of at least 10 million, or some 40 percent of the labor force, the unions seemed less concerned; their membership was drawn primarily from those with stable jobs who typically earned salaries above the minimum wage. The unions focused their attention on those workers who might be fired from jobs in the formal sector of the economy.

The present account would be incomplete if it did not mention other factors contributing to limiting the effects of the economic crisis on the labor sector. One effort has been the attempt by the state to maintain social cohesion among workers by explaining to them the problems the country faces. In emphasizing the supposedly central role of labor in the management of the economic crisis, such official ideology seeks to lessen the possibility that the unions would question state legitimacy. The absence of any alternative characterization by the unions helps the state maintain its influence on the workers. While various leftist parties have had more representation in Congress since 1977, they have had little success in recruiting labor support for their positions.[21] The official labor organizations retain a virtual monopoly over worker ideological views, with no other message able to supplant it. As a result, animosity toward the state is kept at a minimum, with that which exists being directed instead toward national or multinational private enterprise. The privileged position of the CTM and the CT in negotiating with the government reinforces their joint role as the exclusive representative of workers and as a major advocate of state economic policies. These groups have become a central element in the ruling coalition where their hegemonic position — rather than a resort to outright repression as has been erroneously asserted by some analysts — has allowed them to limit worker economic demands.

The general predominance of labor peace, however, does not preclude the presence of some labor conflict. The present political system allows for the coexistence of tension and flexibility in the relation between labor and the state, something that can be easily illustrated by the analysis of evolution of recent conflict in particular sectors of Mexican labor.

A. The Situation in Official Unions

1. The Private Sector. In 1983, the CTM and the government operated in the context of a "solidarity pact," where each of them committed to sacrifices in order to limit the effects of the crisis on the workers. As its part, the state proposed the relocation of some of the unemployed, price controls, and the creation of new jobs in the public sector. It would also facilitate the creation of stores where low priced goods were sold and would extend lines of credit for the small and medium-sized enterprise (traditionally flexible in matters of employment). In exchange for these concessions, organized labor promised to limit its salary demands.

Nevertheless, in some economic sectors like automobiles, steel, and metalworking, conflict erupted. Discontent among workers in these sectors was not only economic; it also derived from rank-and-file refusal to accept proposals that the labor leadership frequently had accepted without a fight. In their desire for a union democracy that associated demands for the renovation of the leadership with those for increased worker participation in union life, reformers never really questioned the entirety of the established union structure.[22] Conscious of the risks entailed in such an extreme position, most limited themselves to issues relating to the particularities of their individual companies. Union democracy, as an issue, was raised within the framework of official labor law, thus making it more difficult for the state to reject it out of hand.[23] Reformers were merely seeking to put into practice rights that existed on paper, but which had never been implemented.

   2. The Public Sector.   Ironically, where relations should have been running smoothly (as in unions representing government workers, especially the *Federación de Sindicatos de Trabajadores al Servicio del Estado*, or FSTSE), important manifestations of unrest surfaced in 1983–1984 linked to the particularly strong effects of the economic crisis felt there.[24] State sector salary increases fell far behind inflation, while many fringe benefits — worker health care, for example — deteriorated in quality, bringing strong criticism from recipients. The ISSSTE, the public sector's social security system, particularly experienced such worsening service. State sector workers, accustomed to special yearly salary increases announced in the annual presidential state of the union message of September 1, found this form of favoritism discontinued as salary policy for the bureaucracy became assimilated into that experienced by the rest of the working class. Another area of discontent was among school teachers belonging to the *Sindicato Nacional de Trabajadores de la Educación*, or SNTE. Unhappy with the way the national SNTE leadership was dealing with membership problems, dissident locals organized the *Coordinadora Nacional de Trabajadores de la Educación*, or CNTE, which became quite active in challenging the official union.[25] Given the sheer size of the 650,000 teachers involved, such a conflict would have major national ramifications.

B. The Situation in the Independent Unions
   1. The Private Sector.   Unions not part of the official labor sector account for some 420,000 workers, found principally in the automobile, aviation, and metalworking industries. Rather than seeking to promote a

radical ideology seeking fundamental changes in Mexican society, these unions have restricted their activities to local-level concerns like improved salaries or the reform of internal union affairs both of which they have militantly pursued. In contrast to the general passivity of the official unions in relation to salary increases, the independent unions have asked for amounts exceeding the maximum limits set by the state. Within the automobile industry, Volkswagen, Nissan, and General Motors have had to deal with such demands, as well as those for more democratically run union locals. In the course of much of the 1970s, the *Unidad Obrera Independiente*, or UOI, played a major role in channeling demands by automobile workers for higher wages and in elaborating proposals for union democracy.[26] Having learned from the violently repressed strikes of 1947–1948 and 1958–1959 that the state could not be challenged frontally, the UOI concluded that independent unionism in Mexico had to act within the limits of an official labor law which the state already accepted as legitimate. The state was faced with labor mobilization not seeking radical political ends, but limiting itself to questions of worker salary and local union democracy. The independent unions almost never questioned the political system itself; when they were initially so inclined as in issues related to worker lay-offs at the factory of Diesel Nacional (DINA), they almost immediately reconsidered.

2. *The Public Sector.* In addition to the state workers organized in FSTSE, public employment in Mexico includes university faculty and administrative personnel. A new type of independent unionism similar to the UOI appeared at various institutions of higher learning like the National University (*Universidad Nacional Autónima de México*, or UNAM).[27] The salary demands made in excess of the state-imposed limits benefited from the high visibility of union members who were both columnists in newspapers as well as university instructors. Strikes were frequent, especially in the 1974–1978 period. Usually headed by unofficial leaders, these unions could go beyond what those in the private sector sought, not confining themselves to economic matters, but directly challenging the state ideologically. On balance, they were not particularly successful in either regard, something which eventually led to a serious internal crisis in the 1984–1985 period.

Independent unionism has been a new force in the Mexican labor movement, contributing to the renovation of labor-state relations by both challenging the subordinate behavior of the official union leadership and making demands for internal union democracy. The leaders of the official unions have responded to this external competition by becoming more active in the promotion of worker interests and, at times, attempting to coopt some of their rivals with offers of positions in the mainline union hierarchy. One case of the latter was that of the telephone workers leader, Francisco Hernández Juárez, who is now an official in the national-level *Congreso del Trabaja*.

CONCLUSION

In summary, three important differences stand out between the Mexican labor movement and those of most other Latin American unions. First, we have observed that a series of historical, legal, and structural factors have contributed to the integration of Mexican labor into the political system of the country. Blue and white collar workers in both the private and public sectors belong to the CTM and, through it, to the ruling political party, the PRI. As such, their leaders participate in some important political discussions at the national-level. With the partial exception of the Venezuelan case, such closeness to the state is rather unusual. Indeed, most Latin American unions seek to actively defend their autonomy from such state influence. Even in cases such as those of Argentina and Brazil, which at specific times seemed similar to Mexico, labor was always closer to the rank-and-file than to ministers and bureaucrats. In other countries, such as Chile, Bolivia, or Peru, the labor movement has normally been associated with the political opposition, ideologically offering an alternative type of society. The close link of Mexican labor to the structure of domination seems unlike the situation found most commonly in the region.

Second, the general decline in strike activity in the 1934–1970 period suggests a major way in which the relationship between labor and the state has operated. By controlling worker demands, the labor movement has contributed decisively to the industrialization and capital accumulation processes in years when the country experienced growth rates which averaged in excess of six percent per year for almost three decades. At the behest of the state, organized labor was willing to sign agreements with capital to suppress radical leadership in important unions like the railroad workers, the oil workers, and the miners. Most of the 1940s, 1950s, and 1960s saw labor peace as a predominant feature. Events like the railroad strike of 1958–1959 were exceptions which really did little to undermine this image of general labor tranquility. This situation, however, changed in the 1970s and, even more so, in the early 1980s, as strikes increased in response to the weakening of the economy undermined by inflation, devaluation, and the foreign debt crisis. Official labor organizations have had to become more militant in their pursuit of worker demands as a result of pressure from the new independent labor movement developing in the automobile, electrical, and metals industries. As a result, Mexican labor in the most recent period has become more like its counterparts elsewhere. Nevertheless, the direct ties to the state and the subordination to the latter's economic policies have not substantially changed. The state has reacted to the deterioration of economic conditions by trying to limit the effects of inflation on the standard of living with more adequate social services in health care, education, and housing. Many workers have been incorporated into the social security system (*Instituto Mexicano del Seguro Social*), have received low interest housing loans through the *Instituto del Fondo Nacional de la Vivienda para los Trabajadores* (INFONAVIT), and have received scholarships. These new benefits are meant to reinforce the state-labor alliance and to discourage the temptation from the independent labor movement from directly challenging government policy. As a result, Mexico has been able to limit the effects of the economic crisis on the unions and, thus, to strengthen the country's political institutions.

Third, it is impossible believe that the present situation can continue indefinitely. Indeed, as real salary decreases recur in the face of labor's incapacity to limit this process, and as the state progressively distances itself from group support for its policies and becomes immeshed in defining the country's problems in a strictly technical fashion, the political structure will begin to encounter serious challenges to the way it has been operating. In the future, it will not be as easy as it has been to maintain labor's allegiance to the political system if significant benefits are no longer forthcoming to the union rank-and-file. As the official unions encounter more difficulty in limiting worker demands, the independent unions will gain greater worker support; these official unions, in turn, will be under greater pressure to support more radical positions in their efforts to maintain their support. Ultimately, the official unions may be forced to seriously question their alliance with the state if they are to retain their legitimacy. Any change of this nature would fundamentally alter one of the basic conditions under which the Mexican political system has been operating up until now. Such a change would contribute to the elimination of the Mexican paradox of mobilization without conflict and conflict without mobilization.

NOTES

1. Pablo González Casanova has edited a collection entitled *La clase obrera en la historia de México* (hereinafter referred to as COHM) (Mexico City: Siglo XXI, various years), where numerous authors have reconstructed the history of the Mexican working class from the last decades of the nineteenth century to the Echeverría presidency. It is by far the most recent and best historical account of this topic. For an analysis of the interconnection of the political system with civil society, see Luis Javier Garrido, *El partido de la revolución institucionalizada: La formación del nuevo estado en México, 1928–1945* (Mexico City: Siglo XXI, 1982).

2. For the historical background, see Marcelo Miquet and José Luis Reyna,

"Introduccion a la historia de las organizaciones obreras en México: 1912–1966," in José L. Reyna, Francisco Zapata, Marcelo Miquet Fleury, and Silvia Gómez-Tagle, *Tres estudios sobre el movimiento obrero en México* (Mexico City: Jornadas 80, El Colegio de México, 1976); on the CROM, see Barry Carr, "El movimiento obrero y la política en México: 1910–1929," *Setentas*, 256 (1976); on Vicente Lombardo Toledano, see Francie R. Chassen de López, *Lombardo Toledano y el movimiento obrero mexicano: 1917–1940* (Mexico City: Ed. Extemporáneos, 1977); the political process which gave rise to the CTM is well described in Adolfo Gilly, "50 años después: La fundación de la CTM," *El Cotidiano*, 10 (1986).

3. See Lorenzo Meyer, *México y los Estados Unidos en el conflicto petrolero: 1917–1942* (Mexico City: El Colegio de México, 1972).

4. Revolutionary nationalism can be considered ideologically as a product of the Mexican Revolution of 1910. It is identified both with nationalism in regard to the ownership of natural resources, public education, and state enterprise, and with an anti-imperialism in regard to foreign investment and foreign political intervention. Ideologies such as Vicente Lombardo Toledano (1894–1970) and Víctor Raúl Haya de la Torre, a Peruvian influenced by the Mexican Revolution, were its most prominent practitioners.

5. See Blanca Torres, *México en la Segunda Guerra Mundial* (Mexico City: El Colegio de México, 1980); Luis Medina, *Civilismo y modernización del autoritarismo* (Mexico City: El Colegio de México, 1978); and Gilly.

6. See Miquet and Reyna.

7. See Medina.

8. *Ibid*.

9. For an overview, see Francisco Zapata, "Estructura y representatividad del sindicalismo en México," in Reyna, et al.

10. See César Zazueta, *El Congreso del Trabajo: Sindicatos, federaciones, y confederaciones obreros en México* (Mexico City: Fondo de Cultura Ecomómica, 1982); and Richard Miller, "The Role of Labor Organizations in a Developing Country: The Case of Mexico," Ph.D. Dissertation, Cornell University, 1966. On the CTM, see Sergio L. Yañez Reyes, *Génesis de la burocracia sindical cetemista* (Mexico City: El Caballito, 1984).

11. See Francisco Zapata, "Les conflits du travail al Mexique: 1934–1980," *Problemes d'Amerique Latine*, 69 (1983).

12. See José Luis Reyna, "El movimiento obrero en el ruizcortinismo: La redefinición del systema económico y la consolidación política," in Reyna and Raúl Trejo Delarbre, *De Adolfo Ruiz Cortines a Adolfo López Mateos: 1952–1964* (Mexico City: Siglo XXI, vol. 12 of COHM, 1981).

13. See Raúl Trejo Delarbre, "Los trabajadores y el gobierno de Adolfo López Mateos," in Reyna and Trejo Delarbre.

14. Trejo Delarbre.

15. See Octavio Rodríguez Araujo, *En el sexenio de Tlatelolco: 1964–1970* (Mexico City: Siglo XXI, vol. 13 of COHM, 1983).

16. Rodríguez Araujo.

17. See Jorge Basurto, *En el régimen de Echeverría: Rebelión e independencia* (Mexico City: Siglo XXI, vol. 14 of COHM, 1983).

18. See Ilán Bizberg, "Política laboral y acción sindical: 1976–1982," *Foro Internacional*, 100 (1985).

19. See Raúl Trejo Delarbre, "El movimiento obrero," in Pablo González Casanova and Enrique Florescano, eds., *Mexico, Hoy* (Mexico City: Siglo XXI, 1980).

20. See Francisco Zapata, "El sistema político mexicano y el conflicto sindical," paper presented at meetings of the Programa Regional de Empleo en América Latina y el Caribe (PREALC), Santiago de Chile, May 1985.

21. The total number of Deputies representing labor in the Congresses since 1964 on is as follows: XLVI (1964–1967): 34; XLVII (1967–1970): 54; XLVIII (1970–1973): 27; XLIX (1973–1976): 30; L (1976–1979): 41; LI (1979–1982): 86. The decrease in the XLVIII session can be explained totally by the decrease in the representation of the FSTSE, the government workers union, in that period. The CTM increased its delegation consistently all through the 1964–1982 period from 17 Deputies in 1964 to 43 in 1979.

22. A good case study of a local union where this issue is central is that by Ilán Bisberg, *La acción obrera en Las Truchas* (Mexico City: El Colegio de México, 1982), which refers to events in a new steel plant to the north of Zihuatanejo on the coast of Michoacán, which employed 7,000 workers.

23. Mark Thompson and Ian Roxborough address this problem in their "Union Elections and Democracy in Mexico," *British Journal of Industrial Relations*, 20: 2 (1982). Contrary to superficial analysis, this article shows there is much more democracy in Mexican unions than the usual discussion allows for. Union executive committees, even in those controlled by the CTM, turn over their leadership much more frequently than some analysts have suggested (Francisco Zapata and Ian Roxborough, "Algunos mitos acerca de la CTM," *Diálogos*, March 1978).

24. Unpublished paper by Patricia Ravelo, "Movimientos de los trabaja-dores al servicio del estado ante la crisis," Centro de Investigaciones Superiores en Antrología Social (CIESAS), December 1983.

25. Unpublished paper by Luz Elena Galván, "Movimiento magisterial en la zona metropolitana," (CIESAS), October 1983; María de la Luz Arriaga, "El magisterio en lucha," *Cuadernos Políticos*, 27 (1981); and Rogelio Luna Jurado, "Los maestros y la democracia sindical," *Cuadernos Políticos*, 14 (1977).

26. Although the Unión Obrera Independiente has not yet been studied, research has been done on some of its constituent parts, as in the automobile industry. See, for example, Ian Roxborough, *Unions and Politics in Mexico: The Case of the Automobile Industry* (London: Cambridge University Press, 1984). The UOI can be characterized as an organization centered on economistic demands and very careful not to exceed the political limits fixed by the state.

27. Administrative and academic employees at universities only began to organize around 1970, as a result of the events of 1968. In 1972 when Pablo González Casanova was Rector of UNAM, he was confronted by the University Workers Union (*Sindicato de Trabajadores Universitarios*, or STUNAM). He ulti-mately was forced to resign his post after a long strike which paralyzed activities for several months in the most important university in the country. New confrontations would occur in 1974 and 1977, but these times the state inter-vened, reopening the university by force. In spite of STUNAM being strong enough since then to maintain its control of administrative workers, it has been unable to represent academics, who negotiate apart from the STUNAM.

Chapter 8

Political Transition and the Peruvian Labor Movement, 1968–1985

Nigel Haworth

The period between 1968 and Belaúnde's second fall in 1985 saw the Peruvian labor movement finally consolidate its position as a key actor on Peru's political stage. Prior to this period, the formally constituted labor movement — unions, worker-based parties, and associated pressure groups — achieved only transient significance in political events, generally taking a secondary role to those in political power as a more broadly-based mass urban and rural opposition. Yet this coming of age brought mixed blessings to a maturing movement. A consolidated political presence was qualified by internal clashes, aggressive state opposition, declining economic fortunes, and the relatively small fraction of the population encompassed by the formal labor movement. The advent of García's APRA (the American Popular Revolutionary Alliance) government has done little to change this picture of qualified success.

THE LABOR MOVEMENT BEFORE 1968

Two labor movement-related aspects of the pre-1968 period warrant close attention — the structural, demographic, and economic contexts which defined the growth of the labor movement, and the political framework in which the incipient labor movement emerged. Commencing with demographic factors, Fitzgerald has applied the concept of dualism in his analysis of the Peruvian economy, pointing to the one-third of the population located in the "modern" sector and the other two-thirds in the relatively unintegrated "traditional" rural and marginal sectors.[1] Bearing this distinction out are data on the level of urbanization. In 1940, for example, only 18 percent of the population was located in urban centers of 2,500 or more. Even after the dramatic urbanization of the 1940s and the 1950s when this figure rose (by 1961) to 39 percent,

TABLE 8.1
Sectoral Composition of the Labor Force, 1950, 1961, 1970 and 1972 (%)

	1950	1961[a]	1961[a]	1970	1972
Agriculture	58.8	52.8	49.8	44.5	42.0
Mining	2.2	2.2	2.2	1.9	1.4
Manufacturing	13.0	13.5	13.2	14.5	12.8
Factory	—	—	4.5	5.4	8
Artisan	—	—	8.7	9.1	—
Construction	2.7	3.4	3.3	3.0	4.2
Commerce	6.6	8.6	8.9	10.9	10.5
Electricity	0.2	0.3			
Transport	2.7	3.1			
Banking	0.4	0.6	18.9	21.3	23.9
Government	4.0	5.5			
Other services	9.3	10.1			
Not specified	—	—	2.6	2.2	4.2
Aspirants	—	—	1.1	1.1	—

Source: for 1950, 1961 and 1970, Rosemary Thorp and Geoffrey Bertram, *Peru 1890–1977: Growth and Policy in an Open Economy* (London: Macmillan, 1978), p. 259; for 1972, Denis Sulmont, *Historia del movimiento obrero en el Perú* (Lima: Ediciones Tarea, 1977).
[a]Estimates of the Central Reserve Bank and Ministry of Labor, respectively.

substantial numbers of the population remained in the rural setting in circumstances inimical to either union or party activity. Table 8.1 indicates the implications of this demographic pattern for the sectoral composition of the labor force. Agricultural employment, though declining, continued to be the major source of work, while manufacturing maintained a relatively constant percentage of total employment since the Second World War.

Two other areas of employment merit comment. First, one should note the continuing, even increasing, importance of artesanal production, a sector notoriously difficult for the traditional union movement to encompass. Second, hidden in the figures is a dramatic rise in white-collar employment since the War, again a sector often difficult to organize, and in this case, offering many women new opportunities of employment. If, therefore, the potential base for unionization and labor movement political action was historically relatively small, the corollary was that unbalanced urbanization into a handful of major cities (Lima and Callao especially, Arequipa, Trujillo, Chiclayo, and Cuzco) was paralleled by the development of centers of primary product production — for example, the sugar estates of the North, the mining regions of the Center and the South, cotton production in the Coastal Center — wherein the forces of proletarianization gave birth to small, localized but increasingly effective union and party organizations.

Molding and, in some contexts, debilitating labor movement dynamism were both macro- and microeconomic factors. At the macro level, I have argued elsewhere that the failure of an indigenous economic development model, traced consummately by Thorp and Bertram,[2] and the consequent subordinate integration of the Peruvian economy into the world economy resulted in a labor movement constrained and directed by enclave, export-orientated, and foreign-owned production.[3] One crucial consequence of this world market integration was the weak industrialization experienced throughout this century. Between 1950 and 1975, manufacturing, as a contribution to GDP, increased from 16.7 percent to 26.2 percent, as, over the same period, the contribution of agriculture dropped from 20.4 percent to 12.7 percent. Yet the 1975 figure, barely over a quarter of GDP, and "of some moment" in Fitzgerald's eyes, must be seen in the light of the preceding post-war period (especially between 1955 and 1965) which saw one of the most dramatic increases in manufacturing investment in Peruvian history, fueled in great part by direct foreign investment. Despite this activity, the percentage increase over the 1950–1975 period of less than 10 percent indicates a lacklustre growth performance, described by Fitzgerald as:

> [a] particular manner of industrialising [involving] a dominant role for foreign firms and foreign technology, with capital-intensive output geared to the needs of a relatively narrow market. In consequence, even though manufacturing emerged as the largest single production sector in the economy it remained concentrated on Lima producing relatively-sophisticated goods for a minority of the population without being integrated into the rest of the economic structure and heavily reliant on imports for its input requirements, while providing little employment.[4]

Despite substantial growth in the construction and services sectors over the same period, in which employment and unionization opportunities expanded, and the continuing importance of wage employment in both export-oriented agriculture and the mining industry, the relatively low-key performance of the manufacturing sector constrained the opportunities for labor movement expansion.

At the micro level, the failed indigenous model resulted in a numerical predominance of small productive units. Thus, for example, in 1973 the 200 largest firms produced 52.3 percent of the gross value of manufacturing production with only 12.5 percent of the manufacturing workforce. At the other extreme, in 1973, 45 percent of Lima's manufacturing workforce were in plants employing less than 5 workers; 20 percent in plants of 5–99 workers; and only 30 percent in plants of 100 workers or more. Though it would be wrong to draw directly from these figures any conclusions about the political power of organized labor, they do suggest a fragmentation of the potential organizational base of the union movement.

Previous to the 1960s, the Peruvian labor movement's political experiences were torpid. Small in size, it emerged onto the political scene as an early anarcho-syndicalist manifestation around the Eight-Hour Day struggle in the period up to 1919. Anarcho-syndicalism lost its appeal in the early 1920s, to be replaced by the transcendent opposition of Haya de la Torre's APRA populism and Mariátegui's adherence to the Communist Third International. However, the manner in which the crisis of the Depression was resolved in Peru involved the eclipse of the urban labor movement as a significant political force, simultaneously as the Communist tradition in mass politics was forcefully usurped by APRA's presence. Indeed, the Communist tradition was not to emerge as a major force again until the 1960s. The defeats of the early 1930s, coupled with the small numbers of organized urban and rural workers, defined the political muscle of the labor movement until the late 1960s. Even in the liberal era of the Bustamante y Rivero government (1945–1948) organized labor failed to assert itself and thus consolidate its status in civil society. Thereafter, during the repressive regime of Odría, the labor movement played a minor role to that of APRA, the new parties of the middle classes, and the traditional power brokers of the oligarchy.[5]

The marginal political role of a coherent labor movement before the 1960s underpins the movement's role post-1968. It must be understood that the labor movement did not constitute an autonomous political force in the major political events during the previous decades. It lacked the institutional, ideological, and numerical strengths necessary to play such a role, particularly in a society in which challenges to the dominant power base were relatively ineffective, and where regional political orientations were inordinately important. Consequently, for much of the post-war period, the labor movement's national organization — the *Confederación de Trabajadores Peruanos*, or CTP (the Confederation of Peruvian Workers) — was subservient to APRA, leading Payne to his perhaps overdrawn analysis of "political bargaining" in the later *convivencia* period.[6] The hold of APRA over the labor movement via the CTP was to be broken finally in 1967, with the move towards the formation of the Peruvian Communist Party (PCP) led *Confederación General de Trabajadores Peruanos* (CGTP).

However, the image of the labor movement as secondary to wider-based political organization must be complemented by a further argument which maintains its relevance to the present day. One cannot presume that there existed, or exists today, a clear identity between individual employee attitudes and expectations, union policies and political affiliations, and political party action. Indeed, some may argue that the term "labor movement" is too homogeneous a description to use in the fragmented circumstances of Peru's urban masses. I have argued elsewhere that an individual worker may well find him/herself represented by three different political perspectives in plant union, regional, and/or national union confederation, and party affiliation.[7] And, of course, this leaves to one side the wider question of community-based political action and related affiliation, a factor of great significance in the post-1968 period of popular mobilization. Yet, despite this general proviso, the 1960s saw the consolidation of a sufficiently-defined socio-political space in which individual, union, and party mutually interact to warrant the use of the term "labor movement," providing it is understood as a term denoting sets of changing institutional, ideological, and action-based characteristics rather than in its more traditional, narrow, institutional usage.

LABOR AND STATE POLICY 1968–1980

On the eve of the 1968 coup, major changes were in train in the institutional structure of the labor movement.[8] Throughout the 1960s, opposition to the dominant APRA line grew within the CTP, principally organized around the burgeoning PCP.[9] After 1965, the need for a new central beyond the control of APRA was recognized by some CTP members, many of whom were recent arrivals in urban centers and recent recruits to the union movement. At a famous congress in Callao in 1967, the *Comité de Defensa y Unificación Sindical*, or CDUS (the Committee for Union Defense and Unification) set in motion the formation of the CGTP, named after its Mariátegui-inspired predecessor of 1930. The new CGTP united some 140,000 workers from a broad range of industries, including construction, engineering, steel, brewing, chemicals, and fishing. However, numbers of workers in textiles, construction, engineering, printing, and agricultural production, remained loyal to the CTP, creating the basis for heated inter-confederation struggle at national, regional, and industrial levels. Furthermore, within the new CGTP and also on its margins ebbed and flowed what may be called the "New Left." Maoist, Castroite, Trotskyite, and independent revolutionary traditions, vanquished in the guerrilla campaigns of the early 1960s, maintained their presence in student circles and sought to extend their impact into the organized labor movement. The upheaval created by the 1968 coup was to give those erstwhile marginal traditions greater visibility in the 1970s.

The Velasco Reforms
The political trajectory of the labor movement after the coup should be understood against the background of the reforms of individual and collective employment conditions and the enterprise introduced in Velasco's "First Phase of the Peruvian Revolution." Between 1968 and

1975, the Velasco regime sought to create a degree of autonomy for Peru within the world market, a policy at odds with that adopted after 1948. As the agricultural sector was modernized and transformed through agrarian reform, the industrial sector was to be impelled into a dynamic leadership role within the economy. The key to industrial expansion was seen to be closer involvement of the workforce in the enterprise by means of radical new forms of participation and self-management. Greater worker involvement, it was argued, would result in greater productivity, consequent increased efficiency and profitability, and the eventual creation of an integrated and coherent nationally-controlled industrial base. Uniquely in Peruvian economic thinking, the Velasco regime's rhetoric entrusted to the wage workforce in both urban and rural settings the crucial responsibility for the experiment's success. Indeed, some of the earlier statements of Velasco's ministers echoed the preeminence given to labor in marxist economic analysis.

The reforms must also be understood against the background of traditional bargaining practices in the industrial sector.[10] Peruvian industrial relations has never been codified in the Chilean manner. Based primarily on plant-level bargaining and closely patrolled by an interventionist Ministry of Labor, the IR system consisted of piecemeal custom and practice processes appropriate to local circumstances. The relative scope of the measures discussed below was consequently substantial, particularly in respect of the participation legislation. However, despite these measures, traditional patterns of collective bargaining continued, varying juridically only to the extent that ministry intervention chose to increase or decrease its intensity.

Two particular policies highlighted the changed fortunes of organized labor in the post-1968 industrial relations model. First, in 1970, *estabilidad laboral*, or labor stability, was decreed. Under its provisions, no worker could be dismissed unless it was shown that a serious misdemeanor had been committed, or that economic or technical restructuring demanded redundancy. Unfair dismissal could result in various forms of compensation for the ill-treated employee. Notwithstanding the exception of state employees from the effects of this measure, or the likelihood that high financial costs might deter workers from raising an action against unfair dismissal, or even that perhaps only 15 percent of the economically active population benefitted from the measure, the legal enforcement of *estabilidad laboral* came to be seen as a significant advance for employees. It placed employee rights firmly on the agenda, and spoke to many commentators of the state's intention to consolidate a pluralist industrial relations tradition in Peru. Furthermore, it could be seen by these same commentators, and by managers in particular, as an overt attack on managerial prerogatives within the enterprise. Already perturbed by the radical, populist rhetoric employed by the Velasco

TABLE 8.2
Patterns of Trade Union Recognition

(a) Recognitions by period

	All Unions	Industrial sector
Unions recognized before 1968	2,152	776
Unions recognized 1968–75	2,020	931
Total	4,172	1,707

(b) Unions recognized 1979–84 by sector	Number of Unions
Agriculture	172
Mining	88
Manufacturing	776
Construction	28
Energy	7
Commerce	250
Transport	88
Services	177
Total	1,586

Sources: (a) Alan Angell, "Peruvian Labour and the Military Government since 1968" (Institute of Latin American Studies, Working Paper No. 3, 1980) p. 9, citing Evelyn Stephens, "'The Politics of Workers' Participation: the Peruvian Approach in Comparative Perspective" (Yale University, Ph.D. thesis, 1977); (b) Denis Sulmont, "El Desarrollo de la Clase Obrera en el Perú" (Lima: Pontifícia Universidad Católica, Departamento de Ciencias Sociales, mimeo, 1974).

Unions recognized 1974–1984

Year	Number of Unions recognized
1974	344
1975	234
1976	126
1977	30
1978	54
1979	28
1980	61
1981	60
1982	42
1983	22
1984	6

Source: Adapted from Isabel Yepez del Castillo and Jorge Bernedo, *La sindicalización en el Perú* (Lima: Pontifícia Universidad Católica, 1986).

regime, employers saw increased rights for employees as justification for their fears. It should be noted, however, that managerial power in the workplace and its accompanying ability to mobilize legal and financial resources, often led to the negating of the measure's effects, though this in turn led to little diminution of the critical outcry from managers.

The second policy concerns the growth of union organization during the early Velasco years. As Table 8.2 shows, unionization was given a great boost after 1968, with the increase in recognized unions particularly evident in the 1970–1973 period. It is notable that unionization in the manufacturing sector contributes most to the overall total of new unions. It is clear that in the early part of the "First Phase," the state was prepared to permit the increased organization of waged labor despite the potential threat this might pose. After 1972, some of the increase may be explained by the expansion of the state's own union organization, the *Confederación de Trabajadores de la Revolucíon Peruana*, or CTRP (the Confederation of Workers of the Peruvian Revolution), yet the growth period commenced well before the creation of the CTRP and most significantly enhanced the power of the resurgent PCP-led CGTP, officially recognized by the Ministry of Labor in 1971. Even though the PCP adopted a broadly pro-regime, pro-reform line until after the fall of Velasco in 1975, this is not sufficient to explain the state's willingness to accept increased employee organization. It might be explained simply in terms of the inability of the state to counteract the impetus given to worker mobilization by the creation of the new CGTP in the context of growth in key economic sectors. It has also been suggested that organized labor might have provided a constituency in which the Velasco model could seek support against attack from the traditional oligarchy or industrial bourgeoisie. This argument gives credence to the rhetorical commitment to a pluralist society found in government commentaries. However, a further argument interpreted the willingness to concede greater levels of unionization as a short-term measure to be tolerated while the radical enterprise reform was carried through. Once successful, this reform might obviate the need for unions at plant level and, consequently, undermine any politicization of the workforce by either APRA or the PCP. It was felt also in some governmental circles that the formation of the CTRP in 1972 might also help to undermine the strength of independent, radical parties within the labor movement.

Elsewhere I have discussed the enterprise reforms, presaged in the 1970 *Ley General de Industrias*, and consolidated in specific legislation in the manufacturing, fishing, telecommunications, and mining industries, in terms of their intent to incorporate the workforce into a unitarist company framework through the agency of profit and capital-sharing.[11] The *comunidades industriales* (CI) introduced into the manufacturing sector were by far the most significant of the enterprise reforms, coming to effect over 200,000 workers in 3,500 plants throughout Peru. Throughout the 4 industries, 288,000 employees in nearly 4,000 enterprises were affected — only 6 percent of the national labor force, but approximately 21 percent of GNP. The mechanisms for participation contained in the CI proposals were radical. Apart from a cash pay out dependent on profit margins achieved in the enterprise, it was proposed that the collective workforce should hold an increasing percentage of the enterprise's capital, commensurate with which would be appointed worker directors to the board. The aim was to apportion 50 percent of the enterprise's capital to the CI with worker directors consequently taking up an equivalent number of seats on the board.

The expectations vested in the CI by the regime were made quite explicit. Productivity was expected to increase, industrial conflict was to decline, the rationale behind independent labor organization was to be invalidated, and traditional employee values were to be redefined through the effects of increased material returns to work and direct representation in company decision-making. Undoubtedly, the reforms meant different things to different elements within the state apparatus over the period 1970–1976. Some proponents of the reforms were clearly committed to a radical restructuring of production relations, and were willing to offend traditional managers and owners in the process. However, the more pragmatic position emanating from the relatively conservative Ministry of Industry and Tourism (MIT) focused on the issue of increased productivity and growth at the expense of the reforming aspect of the proposals. Growing economic crisis from 1973 onwards reinforced the MIT perspective, particularly as there is little evidence that productivity was greatly affected by increased levels of participation, or that levels of a "disruptive" industrial action were falling as a result of a new employee consciousness. Between 1970 and 1975, the number of strikes increased from 345 annually to 779, with workers affected increasing from 111,000 to 617,100 and man-hours lost from 5.8 million to 20.3 million (see Table 8.3). This constituted a substantial increase in strike activity over the previous decade.

The political terrain on which the enterprise reform battle was fought was defined by the employers who were vehemently united in their opposition to (a) the theory and the practice of the enterprise reform; (b) the labor movement — to which I shall turn shortly; and (c) the competing state agencies charged with responsibility for the reform's implementation. The key clash was between the *Sistema Nacional de Apoyo a la Movilisación Social*, or SINAMOS (the National System of Support for Social Mobilization), and the *Oficina de Comunidades Laborales*, or OCLA (the Office of Labor Communities), of the MIT over which agency should control the development of industrial participation, and what form the ideology governing such development should take. The outcome of this clash, fought against the backdrop of the 1973 first national congress of the *Confederación Nacional de Comunidades Industriales* (the National Confederation of Industrial Communities), was a pyrrhic victory for the more populist SINAMOS line: the future of SINAMOS was already under threat from more pragmatic, less activist government quarters, and, more importantly, the clash between the two state agencies gave rise to a radical *autonomista* tradition opposed to government direction. In this

TABLE 8.3
Strike Figures 1968–1984

Year	Strikes	Workers Involved (1000s)	Hours/Person Lost
1968	364	107.8	3.4
1969	372	91.5	3.9
1970	345	111.0	5.8
1971	377	161.4	10.9
1972	409	130.6	6.3
1973	788	416.3	15.7
1974	570	362.7	13.4
1975	779	617.1	20.3
1976	440	258.1	6.8
1977	234	406.5	6.5
1978	364	1398.4	36.1
1979	637	841.1	13.4
1980	739	481.5	17.9
1981	871	856.9	20.0
1982	809	548.8	22.5
1983	843	785.0	20.0
1984	247	452.0	8.0

Source: Adapted from Isabel Yepez del Castillo and Jorge Bernedo, *La sindicalización en el Perú* (Lima: Pontifícia Universidad Católica, 1986).

way the attempt to institute a unitarist company-based industrial relations framework paradoxically provided scope for the increased politicization of the workplace, and complemented the growth of the CGTP.

The creation of the CTRP in 1972 backfired similarly. It was intended
to undermine the CGTP, CTP and the CNT (*Confederación Nacional de
Trabajadores*) — the centrist, Christian union confederation — and simultaneously provide an institutional framework in which pro-government
workers could offer support to the "revolution." Enjoying substantial
state patronage, the CTRP grew rapidly in the fishing industry and
traditionally less-organized sectors of the economy. However, as an
institution of the labor movement, it failed to transcend its artificial
beginnings and did little to weaken the CGTP. Moreover, when Velasco
fell and was replaced by Morales Bermúdez in the so-called "Second
Phase" of the revolution (1975–1980), sections of the CTRP moved into a
position of outright and active opposition to the "betrayal" of the Velasco
model.

Challenges to the CGTP

Throughout the 1970s, the CGTP took center stage within the
organized labor movement. The CTP appeared a shadow of its former
self, dependent on a resilient core of pro-APRA union organizations.

APRA itself faced internal dissension as the 1968 coup removed electoral politics from the agenda and brought to power a military steeped in antipathy towards Haya de la Torre and his party.

However, the PCP-CGTP unity was not unassailed. Notwithstanding the PCP's substantially positive line on the Velasco regime, ministers consistently pointed to the disruptive effects of the CGTP as it "politicized" industrial relations, and they counterposed the positive aspects of the CTRP against the negative of the CGTP. Equally, community-based activities around issues such as housing in which government agencies were active became the focus of clashes between PCP activists and the state. The offer of support to the government by the PCP-CGTP also helped to confirm the beliefs of both *aprista* and leftist *clasista* critics in their attacks on the CGTP.

In 1974, leftist dissatisfaction led to the creation of the *Comité de Coordinación y Unificación Sindical Clasista*, or CCUSC (the Committee for Class-Based Union Coordination and Unification), opposed to the "collaborationist" policies of the CGTP. Though CCUSC was never strong numerically (and by 1976 was in decline), it gained some success in organizing militants in many key industrial centers, and indicated the extent to which a pro-*velasquista* line could be squeezed between the regime on the one hand and its vocal critics on the other.

The clash between government, parties, and union traditions was fought out across all industrial sectors, but three groups of workers merit particular mention. Miners were militant, well-organized with a history of union and party activity, and, markedly, a critical approach to foreign investment in the sector. Despite the nationalization of the Cerro de Pasco operation in 1974, industrial disputes and confrontations, often violent, dogged the mining sector during the early 1970s. Miners in the *Federación Nacional de Trabajadores Mineros y Metalúrgicos del Perú* (National Confederation of Mine and Metalworkers of Peru) turned against the "collaborationist" policies of the CGTP and withdrew from membership, and, together with CENTROMIN unionists, were represented at the founding conference of CCUSC. Moves to reaffiliate with the CGTP under the title of the *Federación de Trabajadores Mineros y Metalúrgicos del Perú* were partially successful, but the independent traditions of miners' organizations were clearly asserted in the early 1970s.

A second group was state employees. Teachers came together in 1972 in the *Sindicato Único de la Educación del Perú*, SUTEP (the Union for Peruvian Education), a radical union partially under the influence of the Maoist *Patria Roja*, *Vanguardia Revolucionaria*, and other revolutionary tendencies. Bearing in mind the proviso made at the beginning of this account, one should not assume that Peruvian teachers adhered to revolutionary doctrines to a person, or that membership of SUTEP constituted active support for those groups with some influence in

SUTEP. However, poor salaries, politicization of teacher training, and government intervention into education created a climate of tension within the profession which promoted simultaneously organization and militancy. Other state sector workers were equally militant as they perceived private-sector workers receiving better treatment in legislation, material returns to effort, and workplace conditions. For example, in 1976 a *Frente de Trabajadores de Empresas Estatales* (the State Enterprises Workers Front) brought together the unions in CENTROMIN and SIDERPERU (steel workers from Chimbote) with the hope that other state sector workers might be drawn into a national representative body. Meanwhile, in the same year, PESCAPERU workers in the fishing industry entered into a bitter dispute with the regime over the proposed return of the anchovy fleet to private ownership. The potential power of state workers was enhanced dramatically by the expansion of state involvement in the economy, doubling from 11 percent of GDP in 1968 to 21 percent in 1975,[12] with a parallel increase in the numbers of wage employees falling under the aegis of the state.

Finally, the enterprise reforms, combined with economic crisis after 1973 and increased levels of union organization, engendered increased confrontation in the urban manufacturing sector. In this context, the manufacturing primacy of Lima-Callao (74 percent of reporting industrial plants in the economy in 1973) led to a particular density of industrial union organization and confrontation in the conurbation. Equally, the CGTP found itself under threat from the left in key unions such as the engineering workers' FETIMP.

A Growing Crisis

Between 1968 and 1973, the Peruvian economy presented a picture of reasonable stability. Despite a depressed level of aggregate demand, there was relatively low inflation and a healthy balance of payments. As Fitzgerald points out, between 1969 and 1972, aggregate output growth averaged 6 percent and inflation was kept down to 5 percent.[13] However, in 1973, crises in fishing, mining, and agriculture compounded very low levels of private investment, causing rapidly rising inflation, an increasing fiscal deficit, and pressure on the balance of payments. Effective countermeasures were compromised by the need to maintain the public investment program, while pressure to maintain purchasing power led to increased wage demands. The Velasco model had met its economic Waterloo.

In 1975, Velasco, plagued by debilitating illness, factional infighting in the military, and popular unrest leading to riots in Lima in early 1975, fell and was replaced by Morales Bermúdez, ending the "First Phase" and introducing more pragmatic, less radical strategic thinking into government. Foreign funds were borrowed to tide the government over the immediate economic circumstances, but by 1977 Peru was forced into the arms of the IMF and its traditional stabilization policy. 1976 had already seen the introduction of substantial deflationary measures including cuts in public investment, lower food subsidies, and a wage freeze, each resulting in the costs of the crisis being passed on primarily to the urban masses in terms of falling employment and lower incomes. For example, the cost of living increase in 1976 was 44 percent, in 1977, 32 percent, and in 1978, 73 percent. Wages declined 21 percent in real terms in 1977 and 18 percent in 1978.

The effect of falling real wages was compounded by industrial relations measures introduced by the new regime. The populism of the previous era was rejected as was the stress on participative mechanisms in the workplace. In February 1977, the CI was reduced in scope to a simple profit-sharing exercise with considerably fewer rights to challenge traditional management prerogatives. Perhaps more provocatively, in March 1978, the provisions concerning *estabilidad laboral* were replaced by new measures which dramatically reduced employee protection. The argument for this change was couched in terms of the need to reduce constraints on the enterprise and its managers, presaging calls for greater flexibility in the labor market in the post-1980 period. The interventions by the Ministry of Labor into collective bargaining, never particularly pro-union, reinforced the sense of increasing strictures on the labor force.

Reduced wages, less employment protection, and reduced rights in the enterprise combined with a strong sense of betrayal felt by many who had invested commitment and energy into the "First Phase." The ideological success of Velasco's revolution was uneven, winning great commitment in some quarters, but facing much opposition from others. However, among the urban masses, the period 1968 to 1975 was seen by many to be "space" in which organizations could flourish, debates could develop, and policies for change could prosper. The advent of Morales Bermúdez seemed to end this period of openness, returning Peru to a situation of oligarchic control in economic crisis. The expectations kindled in the earlier phase were too deep-rooted to fade away innocuously. Rather, they were components of the power behind the popular reaction to the "Second Phase" and, in 1980–1985, the remarkable return to political preeminence of APRA.

Moving towards Democracy

The labor movement found itself constrained when it moved to challenge the pragmatism of Morales Bermúdez. The regime imposed a year-long state of emergency in July 1976, designed to curb popular opposition to the consequences of deflation. Intimidation on the streets and dismissal of activists in the plant were potent weapons. Furthermore, the PCP-CGTP, having offered support to the regime until 1976, took some time to reorientate itself into a position of outright opposition. Alternative leaderships, such as CCUSC, proved to be ineffectual and faded from the picture.

However, in mid-1977, the regime imposed further substantial price increases without comparable wage adjustments. The CGTP, in alliance with sectors of the CTRP and the CNT, reacted by creating the *Comando Unitario de Lucha*, or CUL (United Struggle Command), which organized what many have seen as the first truly national general strike in Peruvian history. Concessions were won over prices and wages, the end to the state of emergency was achieved, and an acceleration of the democratization process promised. The unifying power of the CUL was not maintained easily after this success. For example, SUTEP and CENTRO-MIN members had not supported its activities from the left, whilst APRA and the CTP were opposed by the right. Political divisions were reinforced when the CGTP failed to support a general strike called by SUTEP and other leftist unions in September 1978, and the CNT was riven by faction fights (see table 8.3).

Popular political action received a boost as the June 1978 Constituent Assembly elections approached. On the one hand, there were successful general strike calls in February, April, and May, reflecting a reasserted coherence within the organized labor movement. There were also protracted and important disputes with teachers and miners during 1978–1979. On the other hand, the formation of two leftist electoral fronts (FOCEP and UDP) to compete in the elections represented a remarkable achievement in the context of a highly sectional and combative party tradition. April saw these two dimensions of popular politics united against the changed *estabilidad laboral* regulations. The CUL, the *Frente Unitario de Trabajadores* (FUT), the UDP, FOCEP, much of the recently-split PCP, and the radical *velasquistas* in the *Partido Socialista Revolucionario* (PSR) came together to denounce the regime's measures.

The period between 1978 and 1980 was a highwater mark for popular political organization and the labor movement. Democratization went ahead rapidly as the economy began to show signs of improvement. Union organization took on the Morales Bermúdez regime effectively as it attempted to introduce further deflationary measures — particularly in May 1978. The left won a surprising 30 percent of the vote in the Constituent Assembly elections, behind APRA's 35 percent and the right-wing Popular Christian Party's 24 percent. The boycott of these elections by Belaúnde's *Accion Popular* (AP) appeared to many to have been a strategic mistake. Yet this period of upturn in union and leftist party fortunes was shortlived. In the 1980 elections for control of the new democratic process, Belaúnde stepped in to sweep to power with 45 percent of the vote. APRA was split by internal squabbling following the death of Haya de la Torre in 1979, and had to bide its time until García consolidated his power for the 1985 elections. The hopes built around the successes of 1978 foundered on political sectarianism. The ARI front, based on the UDP, *Patria Roja*, small trotskyite elements, and others, burst asunder as dramatically as a parallel attempt to unite around the PCP, PSR, and elements of FOCEP. Tactical voting appears to have led many who might have supported a more united leftist campaign to opt for Belaúnde as President.

1968–1980: An Overview

In many ways, this period saw the emergence of the labor movement as a national force, first, in terms of an agenda laid down by the military's reforms, and, second, as the reform process ebbed and went into crisis, in terms of both plant-based and community-based political action channeled against the regime. The political space provided by the reforms was used to establish worker organizations which rarely succumbed in the long-term to the incorporationist strategy upon which the military based its development model. Repression, redundancy, and economic crisis debilitated the growing movement to some extent, but as democratization provided a goal around which unity could be forged, positive developments outweighed the effects of these adverse factors. Though the FOCEP and UDP campaigns in 1980 fragmented badly, the basis for future united action had been laid.

BELAÚNDE'S SECOND COMING

Belaúnde returned to power amidst the political flux of democratization. With APRA and the left in disarray, and bolstered by a solid electoral performance, the AP government believed itself to command an unchallengeable mandate within Peru. It was undoubtedly in a strong position. First, the return to democracy was seen by the majority of the population as a victory over the discredited Morales Bermúdez regime. Popular sentiment tolerated opposition to AP, but was wary of any moves which might threaten the new order. Though a coup was unlikely, it being generally believed that the previous 12 years had deterred the military from further adventures in the foreseeable future, instability which might undermine the democratization process was a significant popular fear upon which AP could play.

Second, and most important, was the upturn in the economy at the turn of the decade. The AP government can take little credit for the upturn: its origins lay in the export-led growth model introduced in 1978 despite IMF strictures, which was supported by favorable movements in the market price of Peru's primary exports. Blue-collar wages in Lima, which by 1979 had fallen to nearly half their 1973 value, began to regain some lost ground, moving from 54 (1979) to 66 in early 1982 against a 1973 index of 100. White-collar salaries showed a smaller gain from a 1979 level of 67 to an early 1982 rating of 73 on the same index.[14] However, these wage improvements were not uniformly distributed across sectors or across the blue-collar/white-collar division. Blue-collar workers with a stronger tradition of organization tended to perform well, while many white-collar workers performed poorly. However, the benefits of the upturn were short-lived. Despite an expansion in nontraditional exports, neither these nor the traditional manufacturing sector were sufficiently strengthened to withstand future downturns. Dependence upon primary exports, often still in foreign hands, was a further constraint on the effective consolidation of the upturn. Yet these factors paled in comparison with AP's handling of the economy.

Monetarism, Peru-style

In 1980 the AP rejected much of the reformist orthodoxy which had marked its first period in government. Gone was the faith in state-led investment coupled to central planning, aggregate demand management, and a protected productive base. Instead, under the guidance of Prime Minister Ulloa, there emerged a Peruvian version of the "New Orthodoxy," then in full force in Chile, the United States, and the United Kingdom. Stressing the importance of the private sector at the expense of the greatly-expanded state sector, Ulloa and his team (collectively known as "The Dynamo") looked to increased competition and international comparative advantage as the way forward for the Peruvian economy. Emphasis on commodity exports was supported by the steady devaluation of the currency; private sector investment was reinforced at the expense of the public sector; and protective tariffs on manufactured goods were eroded. The freedom of foreign firms in the economy was increased in direct contradiction of both the Andean Pact and pre-1980 policy.

The disaster which ensued was of historic proportions. Commodity prices slumped in 1981–1982; the balance of payments plunged into deficit; reduced tariffs caused imports to decimate manufacturing, which fell by more than 20 percent between 1981 and 1983; by 1984 industry was operating at 40 percent capacity;[15] and inflation began to rise inexorably as credit became short and foreign banks thought twice about lending to Peru. Ulloa resigned in late 1982 before the full effects of the crisis had been felt, but his successors continued with deflationary policies which hit at both prices and wages. Peru was in the arms of the IMF again by mid-1982, but the poor economic performance of the following years resulted in increasing difficulty in the servicing of IMF and other debts. As the 1985 elections approached, the AP government found itself discredited by its economic policy and unable to adopt alternative policies which might have given Belaúnde crucial political maneuverability.

The labor movement reeled under the effects of this economic reverse. Manufacturing employment suffered, falling in Lima from a 1982 third quarter index of 101 to 85 in 1984 against a 1979 score of 100. Overall, unemployment in Lima rose from 6 to 9 percent between 1982 and 1983, but this seemingly small annual rise is to be understood against estimates of increased underemployment which show a rise from 28 percent to 45 percent over the same period. In 1984 national figures show unemployment reaching 11 percent and underemployment 57 percent. Incomes were similarly affected as inflation took its toll. In Lima they fell by 15 percent in 1983, and by a further 20 percent in 1984. These general figures hide a major feature of the crisis as it affected the labor force. In the manufacturing sector, engineering, vehicle assembly, textiles, and animal products all suffered disproportionately from the opening-up of the economy by the Dynamo. Their products were displaced most rapidly in the national market by imports, and their workforces faced more immediate threats to employment and wage levels. The boom in primary product prices in the early years of the AP government gave a degree of protection to workers in those areas, but when prices fell on the international market in 1981–1982, they too suffered. Parodi suggests that one way out of this crisis for members of the urban population was to take up employment in the informal sector, becoming part of the army of street-sellers, petty traders, and sellers of services which rapid urbanization threw up after the Second War.[16] However, there is evidence to suggest that the intensity of the crisis resulted in a contraction in the opportunities available in this sector also. Such was the extent of downturn that many who might have made use of informal sector services were themselves in straitened economic circumstances.

AP and Labor Relations

The adoption of the "New Orthodoxy" by AP might have given rise to a coherent alternative approach to the Peruvian labor relations system. For example, in Chile, where the "Chicago Boys" guided the pioneering turn to monetarism, a comprehensive restructuring of the traditional IR system was attempted in order to bring collective bargaining in line with the new economic order.[17] In Chile, it was argued that many of the ills which the new economic model had to cure were a consequence of the traditional collective bargaining structure which had fostered inflation, politicized labor relations, and an interventionist state. However, a root and branch rethink of the labor relations system was not undertaken by AP. Because little research has as yet been carried out on this question, only speculation may be offered to explain this omission. First, the

Peruvian IR system was substantially less formalized in law or in practice than the Chilean model. It was also in place in a less industrially-dependent economy. Perhaps, therefore, AP did not perceive the IR system to be the root cause of economic crisis in the economy, and therefore felt that a root-and-branch reform on Chilean lines was unnecessary. Second, the context in which the Chilean reform was introduced was qualitatively different from that reigning in post-1980 Peru. Peru was in a process of democratization in which pluralist interests were at least formally guaranteed by the state and the constitution. Government did not have a free hand with which it could reform social practices at will. In Chile, under a military dictatorship, these constraints were unimportant. Finally, as we shall see, the labor movement was not quiescent during the AP government, and, standing as a major political force in the way of IR reform, capitalized on the organizational growth achieved under military rule.

Whatever the reasons, Belaúnde's IR policy was initially placatory. The Ministry of Labor sought to create a "Social Contract" between the main participants in production. To be overseen by a tripartite commission, employers, unions and the state would seek to increase productivity and wage levels, while simultaneously controlling the rate of inflation. An essentially pluralist model of industrial relations with strong corporatist overtones, it is not surprising that it failed as the crisis took hold. Simply, it could offer little to each partner in the contract. Its pluralist format was in stark contrast to the economic rationale of the Dynamo, particularly as it committed that most "heinous" of crimes — the politicization of labor relations at the cost of a rational economic bargaining model. Employers felt themselves under attack in many sectors as the cold winds of international competition, debt, and inflation took their toll. If possible, employers wished to pass the costs of the crisis on to labor, in line with the Dynamo's own thinking, and in a context where protective labor legislation could do little to prevent such a disposition. The union movement comprehended this to be the likely outcome of the contract, as the control of inflation and an increase in productivity rapidly became the primary goals of labor relations policy. Labor's demands could only take second place to those of employer and state, and conflict was inevitable. Furthermore, the labor movement took the offensive on the issues of jobs, wages, and labor legislation as the crisis deepened, action bound to break asunder a contract which from its inception had not included the independent and more radical union organizations.

There ensued a piecemeal attempt to weaken the legislated status of the labor movement within the industrial relations system. The ministerial force behind the "Social Contract" capitulated in mid-1983, resigning from office and intimating that a cooperative model of labor relations was impossible in the contemporary context of inflation and reduced living standards. Although attempts to remove *estabilidad laboral* and to abolish the *comunidad laboral* were beaten off in the first two years of AP rule, other legislation which amended the law on strikes, social security provision, rights of state employees, and statutory impositions on new enterprises were enacted. The battle lines between employers and the state on the one hand, and the labor movement on the other, were drawn up.

Labor Mobilizations after 1980

In early 1985, the potential base of the labor movement was estimated by Yepez and Bernedo to include 1.3 million in plants of 20 or more workers, out of an economically active population of approximately 6 million.[18] Of this 1.3 million, nearly 900,000 were unionized (360,000 in the private sector and 500,000 in the public). The growth of unionization in the 1970s, and the expansion of state participation in the economy is evident in these figures. As Sulmont points out, the unionization rate is about 15 percent of the EAP, a figure which compares favorably with the U.S. figure of about 18 percent. Furthermore, the economic expansion of the 1970s further established unionized workers in the key centers of economic activy — manufacturing, export crop production, mining, and the expanded services in both private and state sectors.

General strikes were called on six occasions between 1980 and the end of 1984 (January 1981, September 1981, March 1983, September 1983, March 1984, November 1984). All involved the CGTP, with the CTP involved in the January 1981 and the March 1984 actions. Unity in the labor movement was consolidated in the *Comando Nacional Unitario de Lucha*, or CNUL (National Unitary Struggle Command) in 1983, and, later, in the March 1984 *Asamblea Sindical Popular* (the Popular Union Assembly). Sectoral campaigns were waged, particularly in steel, mining, fishing, and power industries, wherein *Frentes de Defensa* became the umbrella bodies in which different union traditions united. Certain sectors, such as water supply, came to create their own union federations for the first time, particularly in the state sector where the Dynamo wished to make cuts or introduce private capital. Equally, and importantly, there emerged regional fronts in which community, union, and party organizations united around regional opposition to governmental programs. Table 8.3 again offers an overview of strike statistics for this period.

The reaction to the "New Orthodoxy" unleashed by the labor movement raises a number of issues. It has been noted frequently that new generations of activists politicized under the military regime were at the fore in the clashes post-1980. Also, a greater unity was possible between contending union bases when confronting AP than when confronting

Morales Bermúdez. No union central owed allegiance to AP, and the party could not mobilize a worker base easily. Existing union bodies, perhaps adopting contrary positions vis-à-vis Morales Bermúdez, could sink their differences in a common rejection of the AP economic strategy. As the government's reaction to union militancy grew more violent, and as the impact of the recession called forth more dramatic reactions from redundant workers, such as the miners' marches and the descent on Lima in 1983, the basis for united action across traditional union boundaries increased. Evidence of this may be found in the entry of SUTEP and independent miners' unions into the CGTP, an act unthinkable in the days of Morales Bermúdez.

A view which has gained ground in recent years stresses the interaction of the union tradition with the wider community, as the crisis unfolded. The clear organizational and spatial distinction between economistic union action and community responses to state policy which marks, say, the British political tradition, does not hold for Peru. The emergence of union organizations has always been closely integrated into regional issues in Peru, not only because regional politics are a crucial and often contradictory component of the national scene, but also because the growth of unions has played an equally contradictory role in the context of regional power bases. Worker organization has often been one aspect of a wider community assertion of regional identity and opposition to the power of a local oligarchy. Arguably, any study of the Peruvian labor movement involves an implicit acceptance of some aspects of the current "social movement" analysis, without perhaps taking on board all the model's baggage. If so, then the 1980–1985 period saw the integration of sectional union demands into wider campaigns against the government, which consequently found itself increasingly isolated at national, regional, and community levels. The image of remoteness from reality attributed to Belaúnde by Reid bears out this point admirably as it also captures the distance between the abstract monetarist model and the real world consequences and reactions it engenders.[19]

The Changing Political Context

Organized union action took place against a background of changing political orientations in the wider popular movement. The campaigns of 1978 onwards established organized labor in the renewed electoral process which under AP focussed on the municipal elections of 1982 and the national elections of 1985. Parties seeking to eject AP from power looked to union affiliations as a means of extending their influence within the enfranchised population. Thus, in 1982, when García emerged as APRA's dominant leader, the CTP worked closely with the party apparatus to mobilize both the existing membership and potential new supporters in the CGTP and independent union camps. This expansionist strategy implied a willingness to consider a more open political style in order to attract a new constituency. Simultaneously, as the membership of the CGTP was increased by the inclusion of independent unions such as SUTEP, the control over the CGTP imposed by the PCP was qualified accordingly. The left, in disarray in 1980, sought to overcome dissension and defeat by creating a broad unity in the *Izquierda Unida* (IU) for the 1980 municipal elections, which was revamped for the 1983 municipal elections. In the latter, APRA asserted its new-found vitality and unity by gaining 33 percent of the vote against IU's 29 percent and AP's disastrous 17 percent.

The 1985 national elections saw unions and their national federations firmly allied to one or another party structure. The CGTP and the majority of the independent union centrals were for IU, while APRA counted on the CTP and allied transport, printing, fishing, and service sector union organizations. However, this seemingly coherent integration of union with party masked a continuing contradiction. As electoral politics became the focus of political activity, and as the defense of the democratic process reinforced this commitment to the constitutional way, regional and national political organization increasingly absorbed the energies of party activists at the expense of the link to organized labor. Sulmont talks of a "divorce" of union activity from party political activity as the 1985 elections approached, which created resentment within the neglected union movement.[20] Of course, the contradiction between sectional interests on the one hand, and wider, pluralist responsibilities on the other, is a hallmark of union-party links in the liberal democratic order. The crisis after 1983, and the growing belief that AP must be replaced reflected in the 1983 municipal election results, would inevitably focus opposition group attention upon the wider political context, in the process subordinating union demands to electoral programs. Yet this was a labor movement which had suffered dramatically under the effects of the Dynamo's policies, and such a subordination was not accepted easily. Consequently, the 1985 APRA victory neither cheered those unions which had supported the IU, nor did it resolve the broader question of union leverage on party policy and orientation. The labor movement may well have come of age between 1968 and 1985, but the future role of unions in the democratic process was still to be determined.

A Difficult Future

Any overview of the 1980–1985 period must take into account the interpretation of changing union and bargaining circumstances offered by Parodi.[21] He offers a textured, if pessimistic, view of the effects of the post-1980 bargaining process on union activity which adds depth to our understanding of the labor movement. Parodi is overly pessimistic in his argument, and there is some question as to the universality 'of the material he presents. However, his focus on the bargaining process and its fragmenting effects is important, for it reminds us that the coming of age noted above, and the status of the organized labor movement on the political stage, rests upon a labor relations system which tends frequently to disunite rather than unite sectional interests. Particularly where recession reinforces this effect, the potential noncoincidence of plant-based and central-based material and political orientations emerges as a continuing bugbear within the Peruvian labor movement. Compounding this problem are the many logistical and ideological difficulties which unions continue to face, including the consolidation of union bodies, the effective resourcing of union activity, the building of a committed union consciousness and the establishment of bargaining practices as the first choice strategy for workers confronting mnagement. Of course, it should be recognized that these have been the adverse circumstances which have dogged the labor movement throughout this century, and, given a political context which permits labor organization a degree of latitude, we can at least expect the labor movement to tackle these problems with determination.

NOTES

1. See E. V. K. Fitzgerald, *The Political Economy of Peru, 1956–78: Economic Development and the Restructuring of Capital* (Cambridge: Cambridge University Press, 1979), for a detailed and sophisticated analysis of economic dualism applied to Peru.

2. Rosemary Thorp and Geoffrey Bertram, *Peru, 1890–1977: Growth and Policy in an Open Economy* (London: Macmillan, 1978), offer a detailed account of the Peruvian economy up to 1977 — that is, until the beginning of the "second phase" — as part of their interpretation of the Peruvian economy since the end of the last century.

3. See Nigel Haworth, "Proletarianisation in the World Order: The Case of Peru," in B. Munslow and Henry Finch, eds., *Proletarianisation in the World Economy* (London: Croom Helm, 1984), for an analysis of proletarianization in Peru seen as an effect of integration into the world economy.

4. Fitzgerald, p. 75.

5. I provide an interpretation of the historical crisis of the Peruvian labor movement in my two works, "Reordering Disorder: Problems in the Analysis of Peruvian Industrial relations," in R. Miller, ed., *Region and Class in Modern Peruvian History* (Liverpool: University of Liverpool Institute of Latin American Studies Monograph No. 14, 1987); and *Labor and Politics in Peru Revisited* (Glasgow: University of Glasgow Institute of Latin American Studies Monograph, 1987).

6. See James Payne, *Labor and Politics in Peru* (New Haven: Yale University

Press, 1965); and the two 1987 works cited by Haworth for a commentary on Payne's work.

7. See Haworth, "Proletarianisation in the World Order."

8. I provide a more detailed account of the period 1968–1979 in "The Peruvian Working Class, 1968–1979," in David Booth and Bernardo Sorj, eds., *Military Reformism and Social Classes: The Peruvian Experience, 1968–1980* (London: Macmillan, 1983).

9. Throughout this account, I use acronym PCP to denote the pro-Moscow Peruvian Communist Party. In recent years, due to splits and divisions, the pro-Moscow party has been denoted as the PC-U (*Partido Communista-Unidad*) after its newspaper in order to ensure clarity. I have remained with the original usage because it was the form in use at the beginning of the period addressed in this account.

10. It should be noted that the governments in power between 1968 and 1980 were not tempted to engage in wholesale or even significant reforms of the collective bargaining process, beyond the effects of the industrial community, Labor Stability Law, and unionization policies. Thus restrictions on collective bargaining during this period were much as those discussed in Payne and in David Chaplin, *The Peruvian Industrial Labor Force* (Princeton: Princeton University Press, 1967). Similarly, the piecemeal nature of the bargaining process resulted in similarly piecemeal attempts of the Belaúnde government to limit the effectiveness of collective bargaining by, for example, limiting strike action without engaging in a comprehensive restructuring of the enduring ad-hocery.

11. See, for example, Haworth, "The Industrial Community in Arequipa: The Failure of Two Unitarisms," unpublished Ph.D. dissertation, University of Liverpool, 1982; DESCO, *Dinámica de la comunidad industrial* (Lima: DESCO, 1974); Hugo Cabieses, *Comunidad laboral y capitalismo* (Lima: DESCO, 1976); Peter Knight, "New Forms of Economic Organization in Peru: Towards Workers' Self-Management," in Abraham Lowenthal, ed., *The Peruvian Experiment: Continuity and Change under Military Rule* (Princeton: Princeton University Press, 1975); Evelyn Huber Stephens, "The Politics of Workers' Participation: The Peruvian Approach in Comparative Perspective," unpublished Ph.D. dissertation, Yale University, 1977; and Giorgio Alberti, Jorge Santistevan, and Luis Pásara, *Estado y clase: La comunidad Industrial en el Perú* (Lima: Instituto de Estudios Peruanos, 1977).

12. Fitzgerald, p. 183.

13. Fitzgerald, p. 228.

14. Jorge Parodi, "La desmobilización del sindicalismo industrial peruano en el segundo belaundismo," in E. Ballón, ed., *Movimientos sociales y crisis: El caso peruano* (Lima: DESCO, 1986), p. 50.

15. M. Reid, *Peru: Paths to Poverty* (London: Latin American Bureau, 1985), p. 85.

16. Parodi, *Ser obrero es algo relativo* (Lima: Instituto de Estudios Peruanos, 1984).

17. See Jackie Roddick and Haworth, *Chile, 1924 and 1979: Labour Policy and Industrial Relations through Two Revolutions* (Glasgow: University of Glasgow Institute of Latin American Studies Monograph, 1983), for a lengthy account of the origins of the Chilean industrial relations system and the reforms introduced in 1979 by the military regime.

18. See Isabel Yepez del Castillo and Jorge Bernedo, *La sindicalización en el Perú* (Lima: Pontifícia Universidad Católica, 1986) for an informative account of unionization in Peru which breaks new ground with the information gathered.

19. Reid (*Peru: Paths to Poverty*) has written the most accessible study of contemporary Peru for the specialist and nonspecialist alike. Unfortunately, it draws to a close towards the end of the Belaúnde government and, therefore, says little about the APRA vistory in 1985.

20. This is drawn from a short piece by Denis Sulmont, "Resistencia sindical y alternativas politícas," *Cuadernos Laborales*, 26–27 (February 1985). The point is borne out thereafter in the conduct of the 1985 national elections.

21. Parodi, "La desmobilización del sindicalismo industrial peruano."

Chapter 9 ————————————————————————————

The Uruguayan Labor Movement in the Post-Authoritarian Period

Martín Gargiulo

————————————————————————————

*T*he aim of this chapter is to provide an overview of the Uruguayan labor movement in the second half of the 1980s, the period that follows Uruguay's return to democratic rule. Although my analysis will primarily focus on this period, a proper understanding of the subject requires a reference to the historical legacy of labor prior to the authoritarian experience. Such reference becomes more important given the strong similarity between the unions that reappeared during the transition to democracy and those existing at the beginning of the 1970s.

THE HISTORICAL LEGACY OF URUGUAYAN LABOR

Uruguayan labor politics has been largely a neglected topic of research, both inside and outside the country.[1] In one of the few systematic explorations of the field, Errandonea and Costábile argued that the relation between labor and society proceeded along two different lines.[2] On one hand, the unions acted as a pressure group in order to defend the working conditions of their members. On the other, labor was a key component of an "opposition subsystem" operating through the identification of its leadership with parties and groups of the political left. This situation was related to the "dual" pattern that characterized Uruguayan unionism. In this pattern, two different views of the labor movement's goals were combined. In the leaders' "long-run" perspective, the unions were conceived as an instrument of the working class in its struggle for the revolutionary transformation of society. For the "short-run" view that predominates among the rank-and-file, the unions were merely instruments enhancing workers' capacity to obtain favorable salary and working conditions. Given this "dual" purpose, a potential for tensions between leaders' strategic options and rank-and-file economic demands existed, as well as conflicts opposing alternative strategic orientations for political action within the leadership.

This particular structuring of the labor movement can also be examined from the point of view of the relationship between unions and political parties. Available evidence suggests that the effective support received by leftist labor leaders within the unions did not yield major working class electoral endorsement of leftist parties, although the latter enjoyed full legal participation in periodic nation-wide elections. Instead, working class ballots were more likely to favor one of the two traditional "catch-all" political forces, the Colorado Party and the Blanco (or National) Party, which account for nearly 90 percent of the votes.[3] Thus, the parties that had a real chance to form governments lacked organizational links with the labor movement, whereas leftist parties failed to reflect in the elections their overwhelming influence within organized labor. Although the unions were indeed an arena of recruitment and political socialization for the left, this phenomenon was mostly limited to the militant strata, and did not reach the vast majority of its members.

This particular arrangement within the polity allowed the channeling of workers' economic demands without jeopardizing the traditional internal power mechanisms and electoral strength of the major parties. At the same time, it defused the threat of a potentially "anti-system" left by tacitly giving it a place in the polity, albeit a secondary one.[4] Institutionalized procedures of collective bargaining ensued after 1943,[5] and the growing income redistribution that characterized Uruguayan society until the 1960s favored the economic role of the unions against the political mission postulated in the ideology of their leaders. Moreover, labor rank-and-file seems to have had a moderating effect on elite ideology.

The origins of this arrangement can be traced back to the economic and political transformations that took place in Uruguay during the first decades of the century. The changes in the economy during the 1930s and 1940s shaped a process of industrial growth through import substitution that provided for the emergence of big factories and a new urban proletariat.[6] These new workers brought along expectations and a political culture which were fairly different from those of European immigrants strongly influenced by Anarchist ideologies, the dominant component of the Uruguayan proletariat in the previous decades. As has been stressed by Errandonea and Costábile,[7] the new situation undercut the role of unionism as a radical opposition force characterized by a close relationship between leaders and the rank-and-file and by a predominance of active militants among the membership. The new context favored a differentiated leadership function and a massive affiliation of passive rank-and-file, thus promoting "dual" unionism. In ideological terms, this process corresponded to the increasing dominance of Communist over Anarchist leadership.

Political factors were also extremely important. The industrial transformation occurred after the initial incorporation of organized labor into the political system. This process took place in the first two decades of the century on the initiative of the influential Colorado Party leader, José Batlle y Ordóñez.[8] Uruguay underwent the earliest Latin American experience of initial incorporation of organized labor. According to Collier and Collier,[9] the incorporation of Uruguayan labor was completed during the period 1906–1915 and resembled the Colombian process of 1930–1945.[10] However, a significant difference between these two countries was the lack of bureaucratic links between the labor movement and the governmental elites that characterized the Uruguayan case. This difference is crucial to understanding the peculiar incorporation of organized labor in the Uruguayan political system, as well as the links of the unions with the left.

Batlle's strategy focused on the creation of legal conditions for an effective expansion of the political and economic citizenship of the working class, thus disabling two crucial forces in the development of revolutionary movements.[11] Universal male enfranchisement, the guarantee of strike rights, and the enactment of social legislation, most notably the 1915 law limiting the length of the working day to eight hours, made working class claims effective through indirect political mediations rather than through the direct action preached by anarcho-syndicalists. These reforms contributed to shape the *obrerista* profile of *Batllismo* and defused revolutionary hostility against a "bourgeois" order that, in fact, conceded more than what was ever expected.

Under these conditions, a popular Batlle could have tried to step into union politics with the purpose of coopting its leaders or, at least, of developing ties between his party and organized labor, as was successfully attempted by López in Colombia.[12] However, Batlle chose to accomplish labor incorporation without developing links between the Colorado Party and the unions, while seeking to minimize labor mobilizations. Indeed, this attitude can be related to the very image Batlle had of an ideal polity, but there are also good reasons to believe that a Colorado intervention in union politics would have failed.[13] First, the foundation of the FORU (Uruguayan Regional Workers Federation) in 1905 marked the end of the formative stage of the labor movement and consolidated an Anarchist leadership composed mainly of European immigrants.[14] These leaders, who had probably witnessed the hard struggles for political and social rights of the European working class, could not but see Batlle as a "temporary exception" within the Uruguayan bourgeoisie, and remained reluctant to engage in any kind of alliance with him or his party.

Second, the creation of organizational links between the unions and the Colorados would have seriously altered the party's internal equilibrium and power mechanisms. Originating in the early civil wars that followed Uruguayan independence, the Colorado Party largely preceded organized labor and did not rely on union support to win elections, but rather maintained strength through an extensive network of local leaders. Moreover, Batlle drew much of his political strength from skillful coalition-making among rather different social sectors, some of which might have strongly opposed engaging in alliances with an organized force such as the unions. Besides these powerful structural constraints, an expensive incursion into union politics might have seemed unnecessary for Uruguayan political elites. The affluent economy of the country at the beginning of the century allowed for an effective increase of the working-class living standard without significant transformations in the socioeconomic structure, which usually require the active support of organized labor.[15]

The unique characteristics of the Uruguayan process had three main consequences for labor politics. First, since the state political elites that championed "initial incorporation" had failed to generate their own ideological space within organized labor, the latter developed with total independence from the state apparatus, a feature that distinguished Uruguayan unions from almost all other Latin American experiences. Second, the prevalence of radical union leadership, either Anarchist or Marxist-Leninist, took place under structural conditions that constrained both the generation of an authentically revolutionary movement and the possibility for leftist parties to obtain electoral profit from a rank-and-file support virtually devoid of political meaning. Third, having no formal link with powerful political parties, organized labor became a "pressure group," using its mobilization and lobbying capabilities between elections rather than influencing the political choices of union members in those elections.[16]

This tacit division of labor between the left and the traditional parties was an efficient controlling mechanism during much of modern Uruguayan history. Nevertheless, the arrangement was potentially destabilizing, since it relied largely on the continuation of the prosperous economic conditions of the first half of the century, where distributive policies did not produce major harm to the interest of the upper class. To be sure, it was an arrangement utterly dependent upon prosperity. The structure of the Uruguayan political system lacked any formal ties between the party in government and the labor movement. Moreover, exchanges between actors often involved incommensurable power resources: mobilization and ballots. In a hypothetical context of economic crisis and radicalized politics, this very incommensurability left the door open for the emergence of two alternative legitimation claims. By the mid-1950s, this context became real with the development crisis that led to sustained devaluation and inflation rates in a stagnant economy, combined with growing popular mobilization and the crisis of the party system. The weakness of such a unique political arrangement soon became evident.[17]

These economic and political changes had important effects on labor politics. The almost constant decline in real wages after 1956, together with the conflict between unions and government and the strategy of electoral coalitions pursued by the left, were crucial factors in the unification of the labor movement in the 1960s. The trend toward unification, present since the beginnings of "dual" unionism, reached its peak when the CNT (National Convention of Workers) was founded (1964) and ratified as the sole central a year later. The fledgling CNT was the first authentically comprehensive labor organization of its type. Its structure integrated preexisting federations of unions organized within particular economic activities, where white collar workers — especially teachers and bank and public employees — were acquiring significant strength.[18] Among the leadership, the Communist Party had secured a majority which gave them a substantial degree of control over the movement. The broad CNT platform was mostly defined in the 1964 *Congreso del Pueblo*, a gathering of various leftist groups that included both the Communist and Socialist parties. The platform included short-term economic demands together with other programmatic ones, such as agrarian reform and the nationalization of banks and foreign commerce. The close connection between the unification processes in both the political and the union arenas was clearly evident in the electoral platform of the *Frente Amplio*, the electoral coalition formed by the left in 1971, whose agenda basically reproduced the CNT programmatic demands.[19]

Although the CNT had a unified character, its structure and statutes tacitly acknowledged the existence of conflicting tendencies within the leadership. By the late 1960s, the appearance of radical groups, which criticized what in their view was a conservative and short-run strategy imposed by the Communist majority, gave new shape to the tensions among different political orientations within the leadership. These new and increasingly coordinated groups identified themselves as "The Combative Tendency" and managed to control three important federations within the CNT at the same time it became an active minority in most of the other unions.[20] The Combative Tendency also had strong links to the student movement, where it successfully challenged the Communists. Its strategy was inspired by a particular interpretation of the new approaches to revolutionary action resulting from the Cuban experience and from the principles settled by the Latin American Solidarity Organization (OLAS) conference, which had met in Havana during 1967. In particular, the labor movement was intended as a political instrument to fight for the programmatic demands raised by the broad CNT program. This strategy was based on an optimistic evaluation of the rank-and-file's commitment to the program and entailed a strong criticism of what were perceived as demobilizing and electoralist tactics pursued by the Communist-controlled leadership.[21] Some of the "combative" groups, such as the *Movimiento 26 de Marzo* and the *Resistencia Obrero-Estudiantil* — an Anarchist group which did not join the *Frente Amplio* — developed close links with urban guerrillas, such as the *Movimiento de Liberación Nacional-Tupamaros* and the marginal *Organización Popular Revolucionaria-33*.

By the early 1970s the Uruguayan labor movement had acquired a profile of growing mobilization. Conflicts escalated in tandem with state repression, the government repeatedly resorted to a constitutional clause which allowed the executive to suppress certain individual rights under emergency conditions. This measure was consistently used to repress workers' mobilization, and it accompanied the progressive strengthening of civil authoritarianism. Turned into a structure of permanent mobilization, the once functional opposition subsystem increasingly became a "dysfunctional obstacle," hindering the incipient economic and political style which would later tend toward authoritarianism.[22] However, labor conflicts cannot be seen as the main factor in the breakdown of Uruguayan democracy, although available data suggest that they were indeed perceived as a threat by business elites.[23]

The coup d'état of June 1973 brought the conflict to a decisive point. When the CNT began a general strike, the government replied with several resolutions and decrees declaring the CNT illegal and ordered both its dissolution and the imprisonment of all prominent leaders.[24] A major concern of the civic-military coalition was the effects of the strike on the strategic state-owned fuels enterprise, whose prolonged stoppage would have economically paralyzed the country. Several executive decrees forcing the staff of the fuels enterprise to work and prohibiting the discontinuity of both public and private activities were promptly enforced by military troops.[25] At the same time, labor leaders were arrested (beginning a process that would not end until after early 1976) when members of the Communist Party and clandestine union activists systematically jailed. The repressive action of Uruguayan authoritarianism was characterized by its high efficacy, higher than that of other "hard" authoritarian regimes. The dismantling of the labor movement was complete, and thus union activity from 1974 to 1982 was almost nonexistent. Formally, individual unions in the CNT were not declared illegal, but, in practice, repression made their activities impossible. Furthermore, the great majority of Uruguayan unions lacked dependent social security programs comparable to the *obras sociales* of Argentinian labor, which could have been used to subsidize the activities of a militant group.[26]

The authoritarian government did not systematically promote alternative, pro-regime labor organizations, and the few attempts it made ended in failure. The most important of these took place only a month after the CNT dissolution when an executive decree regulating the creation of new unions and the right to strike was issued.[27] Through the establishment of a secret ballot for electing union delegates, the regime aimed toward the replacement of existing leaders by new more democratic ones. However, the few elections that were actually held confirmed the old leadership, and the project was promptly dropped. The second of these attempts took place in 1977 with the creation of factory commissions representing both labor and capital, which were supposed to discuss working conditions and wages.[28] Perhaps as a means of avoiding what happened in 1973, the new decree established that status as a worker's delegate was to be revoked if individuals acted ". . . in organizations contrary to our democratic and republican form of government" — a clear reference to the CNT and leftist political organizations. But after a few initial trials, the initiative was equally forgotten. A year and half later, and probably in response to pressures from the International Labour Organization in Geneva, the Ministry of Labor and Social Security announced ten criteria upon which a "Project of Law for the Constitution of Professional or Labor Associations" would be elaborated. The slow evolution of the law finally concluded three years later in a period seen as already transitional to the reestablishment of democracy.[29] These feeble attempts seemed to have been the initiative of certain groups of persons within the regime, rather than the product of a definite political will to reorganize the unions. Apart from these short-lived efforts, governmental action was reduced in practice to hinder, through both direct and dissuasive repression, the appearance of new labor organizations.[30] Perhaps the single most important element of authoritarian labor policy was the military-instituted Bureau of Labor Affairs of the Joint General Staff, where private sector workers could address their claims when they thought their rights had been violated by their employers. The Bureau offered actual service to the worker (seen as an individual but not as a member of some larger group). Workers frequently resorted to the Bureau, although wages were excluded as a basis for complaint.

The legacy of authoritarianism for the Uruguayan labor movement can be summarized as having two major effects. First, the absence of any successful attempt to generate alternative unions left the situation prior to 1973 in a state of "suspended animation," likely to be restored once repressive conditions were relaxed. Second, the 15-day general strike, which had been the response of the CNT to the coup, became a milestone in the history of the Uruguayan labor movement. The strong discrepancy between the ways the Communists and the radical "tendencies" viewed both the conduct and the outcome of the strike deepened a cleavage that would reappear 13 years after the events, thus constituting a major source of tension among the leadership during the resurgence of the labor movement.

LABOR MOVEMENT RESURGENCE DURING THE TRANSITION TO DEMOCRACY

After the military failed in its attempt to impose a semi-authoritarian constitution through the 1980 plebiscite, the country slowly entered the process of political transition back to democracy. As has been emphasized, the Uruguayan military was not by then under any significant pressure from civil society to initiate a liberalization process.[31] The political opening appeared, first as a consequence of a unilateral military will to legitimate authoritarian institutions, and second, as a result of the electoral rejection of an initiative that had been promoted from above.[32] In Uruguay, mobilization in civil society did not constitute a prime cause for political opening. Rather, such mobilization grew as a consequence of the cautious and often reversible liberalizing measures taken by the regime after the plebiscite was lost, reaching a significant role only by mid-1983. In this setting, the resurgence of the labor movement should be seen as more a consequence than a cause of the political transition.

The Process of Resurgence
Labor resurgence took place initially within the framework provided by the Law of Professional Associations, promulgated in May 1981 and formally put into effect after October of that year. Although the law had a restrictive character, and in spite of continual bureaucratic hindrance, the very dynamics of the transition generated a legitimate sphere of action which was promptly occupied by labor.[33] After the first moves to create company-level unions during 1982, a group of leaders representing a so-called *Plenario Intersindical de Trabajadores* (PIT) obtained police authorization to celebrate Labor Day in 1983. Under the auspices of various political parties and other organizations, some 80,000 persons congregated in front of the Legislature building on the first of May, under the motto "Freedom, Work, Salary, Amnesty." Since then, the newly formed PIT has embodied the representative top leadership of the reorganizing labor movement. The political inspiration of the initiative was made evident in the official speech read at the meeting, where the recovering of democratic liberties was a central topic. Later on, some of those leaders ran for Congress within different groups of the *Frente Amplio* coalition.[34]

The presence of the historical legacy discussed in the first part of this chapter can be seen in the reorganization process that Uruguayan labor has undergone in recent years. Post-authoritarian unionism once again has close ties with the political left, is totally independent from the state apparatus, and has adopted a unitary internal organization. From the very beginning the PIT has defined itself as a continuation of the "unitary working class movement," thus making a clear reference to the organization that existed up to 1973. Such a continuity was ratified during the 1984 Labor Day meeting, celebrated under the unitary motto: "PIT-CNT: A Single Labor Movement." However, the two-part acronym actually reflected the resurgence of leadership struggles between the so-called CNT historical majority of Communist orientation and those who proclaimed the necessity of producing a deep transformation in the organization of the movement.

The key issue reflecting the course of the controversy was the planning of a congress to decide upon the structure and future political strategy of the movement. Initially programed for the end of 1983, it was repeatedly postponed because of internal rivalry. Finally, the Third CNT Congress — now under the PIT-CNT designation — was held in November 1985. The meeting was preceded both by arguments about the actual number of affiliates which would determine how many delegates particular unions would be granted, and by disagreement about what some leaders considered an insufficient previous discussion of the documents submitted. Tensions grew deeper throughout the meeting, prompting unsatisfied participants to propose a recess. After the motion had been rejected intemperately by the Communist majority, the losers (507 out of 1,154 delegates) withdrew from the congress.[35] (See Table 9.1) Although later, successful negotiations saved the threatened unity of the movement, the incident had a significant impact on the internal life of the unions and on their public image.

Ideological Tendencies within the Unions

The leadership of the Uruguayan labor movement in the mid-1980s encompasses four major ideological lines, although their levels of distinctness and significance for the dynamics of the unions are quite disparate.[36] Three of these lines correspond to trends within the left, while the fourth stems from an attempt by the Blanco Party to gain a presence in the labor arena.[37] To characterize these lines, I have considered three variables. The first estimates their power resources by assessing their ideological and strategic consistency and the development and coordination of their militants. The second describes different perspectives on the relationship between labor and society, emphasizing their evaluation of existing political institutions and of the role of the unions in the polity. Finally, the third variable considers preferences regarding the internal organizational structure of the unions.

TABLE 9.1
Unions and Representatives in the III PIT-CNT Congress, by Economic Sector, Prevalent Class Composition, and Behavior in the Internal Conflict

Union or Federation	Sector	Composition[a]	Representatives[b] Withdraw	Stay	Total
SUANP (harbor workers)	Public	Blue/White	12	5	17
ANCAP (fuels)	Public	Blue/White	18	6	24
AUTE (electricity)	Public	Blue/White	26	15	41
SUTEL (state telecommunications)	Public	Blue/White	14	13	27
State railroad union	Public	Blue/White	19	15	34
ADEOM Montevideo (local government)	Public	White/Blue	13	26	39
ADEOM interior (local governments)	Public	White/Blue	4	65	69
COFE (central government)	Public	White/Blue	62	50	112
Judicial employees	Public	White	7	0	7
Teachers unions	Both	White	79	35	114
Sports Federation	Both	White	5	7	12
FUS (health services)	Both	White	35	27	62
AEBU (bank employees)	Both	White	47	21	68
CUPIP (fishing industry)	Both	Blue	4	10	14
SUA (clothing industry)	Private	Blue	1	54	55
COT (textile industry)	Private	Blue	27	18	45
SAG (graphic industry)	Private	Blue	4	6	10
FENARU	Private	Blue	1	18	19
SAT (tobacco industry)	Private	Blue	2	0	2
SUNCA (construction industry)	Private	Blue	4	71	75
FOEB (beverage industry)	Private	Blue	17	3	20
UNTMRA (metal industry)	Private	Blue	6	44	50
SUNTMA (sea transportation)	Private	Blue	3	10	13
SUOPA (bread bakers)	Private	Blue	5	0	5
FOT (ground transportation)	Private	Blue	14	31	44
UTAA[c] (sugar cane industry)	Private	Blue	2	0	2
Cement Industry Federation	Private	Blue	2	0	2
Rubber Industry Federation	Private	Blue	8	2	10
Paper Industry Federation	Private	Blue	5	6	11
Sweets Industry Federation	Private	Blue	1	3	4
Meat Industries Federation	Private	Blue	6	20	26
Milk Industry Federation	Private	Blue	11	4	15
Tanners' Union	Private	Blue	1	9	10
Chemical Industry Union	Private	Blue	2	9	11
General Electric Union	Private	Blue	2	0	2
Confectioners	Private	Blue	2	0	2
Household workers[c]	Private	Blue	1	0	1
SIMA (medical drugs)	Private	Blue/White	6	3	9
Regional groups (interior)	Both	Blue/White	9	2	11
FUECI (shop employees)	Private	White	17	33	50
APU (journalists)	Private	White	3	6	9
TOTAL			507	647	1,154
			(44%)	(66%)	(100%)

Source: Centro Uruguay Independiente, *El Tercer Congreso.* vol. II *Desarrollo y consecuencias* (Montevideo: Centro Uruguay Independiente, 1986).
[a] Estimated occupational category that prevails among members.
[b] Each representative corresponds to 200 union members approximately.
[c] Representatives not formally accepted in the Congress.

The line that presents the most distinct ideology, along with the largest organized groups of militants, is linked to the Communist Party of Uruguay (PCU) and its allies. This group accounted for 56 percent of the delegates to the conflict-ridden Third Congress. However, this support was unequally distributed: Communist leaders controlled almost all of the major blue-collar unions, including metal, clothing and construction workers, but they were in the minority in several of the most important white collar unions, including those for high-school teachers and bank and government employees. Although the orthodox Marxist-Leninist inspiration of the PCU should have made it an anti-system party, its actual strategy has been constantly supportive of democratic institutions, and the party was a strong opponent of the Tupamaro guerrillas during the 1960s. As great advocates of "unity," the Communists seek primarily to achieve the expansion of the labor movement, while keeping party hegemony within the leadership. In the past, the practical outcome of this strategy had been unions mostly devoted to economic demands which, although often expressed through radical discourse, did not pose, per se, a challenge to the legitimacy of the political system. Communists support centralized internal organization, which enables them to take advantage of the strength and discipline of their militants, thus more efficiently achieving the necessary equilibrium among different economic demands, opposed ideological tendencies among leaders, and the tensions between rank-and-file demands and the tactical options of the leadership.

The second line is formed by several radical groups whose immediate affiliation can be traced back to critical opposition to the Communist strategy during the 1960s. Given the heterogeneous composition of this group, as well as its comparatively smaller and more weakly coordinated support, its power within the labor movement is quantitatively and qualitatively less than that of the PCU. The actual strength of the radicals is difficult to estimate, for they tend to join other non-Communist groups on many controversial issues, among which we should include the withdrawal from the Third Congress. However, it seems safe to argue that radical groups are the second major force among labor leaders, being particularly strong in white-collar unions and in some sectors of public administration. Among blue-collar workers, radicals control the rubber industry, which was their historical bastion during the 1960s.

Even though finer distinctions can be drawn between relatively moderate and more radicalized groups, they all share a similar view of the role of the movement as a critical political instrument in the struggle for social transformation. This position is reflected both in their understanding of the struggle and in their praising of mobilization as an alternative to electoral support as a source of legitimacy. These are expressed in a discourse that sometimes comes closer to the radical criticism of the formal, "bourgeois," democracy which characterized radicals in the sixties.[38] In accordance with their stress on the political role of labor, groups in this line pursue a strengthening of rank-and-file organizations as a way of increasing the capacity to resist confrontations and to raise class consciousness, as well as to accommodate workers' economic demands to the broader goals of the struggle. Thus, radicals are decidedly supporters of a participative internal structure with strong rank-and-file, intermediate, and regional organizations.

The third leftist line has an even less-defined ideological profile and weaker organization. This line is a product of an alliance among politically moderate socialists, Christian-Democrats, and militants of the newborn *Partido por el Gobierno del Pueblo*.[39] This alliance could only achieve major support among bank employees (the majority in their union) whereas it is almost absent in blue-collar unions. Its still vague ideological definition, together with the weakness of its militant apparatus, constitute serious obstacles to its growth, although it should not be underestimated. Though often imprecise and not always representative of the views of the union leaders, the political rhetoric of the parties in this coalition seems to approach a moderate socialism which has been identified with leftist tendencies in other Latin American countries.[40] This moderation implies a gradualist view of capitalist transformation and acceptance of the rules of the democratic game. In such a view, labor appears as one component within larger political coalitions of popular forces, seeking the construction of hegemonic popular majorities within a democracy without challenging the legitimacy that results from electoral procedures. However, labor leaders associated with this line have focused mainly on internal issues such as reorganization and reassessment of the role of its rank-and-file and leadership. Although the image behind that reassessment might appear to set them apart from radicals, in practice they have joined the latter in most internal conflicts, opposing Communist, centralized rule within the movement.

Finally, the post-authoritarian period has seen the emergence of an effort by the Blanco Party to coordinate its supporters within the labor movement. Although none of the top labor leaders are aligned with the Blancos, the effort has proved fruitful in certain white-collar unions, especially among government and bank employees. These moderate gains do not make Blanco leaders serious contenders within labor, but it may make them important players in strategies of coalition-formation, particularly on internal issues. Inspired by the ideology of one of the two traditional parties, this line combines a substantial support for liberal democracy with a conception of the union as an instrument for the defense of working conditions, a characteristic in which it clearly differs from all other leftist tendencies. Sympathizers of the Blanco Party add their voices to the demand for participation and decentralization within the labor movement.

Internal Composition of the Unions

Key elements which may influence the evolution of Uruguayan labor reorganization are the size and the composition of its membership. The early stage at which these variables are observed makes it difficult to estimate the degree to which the unions succeeded in incorporating different sectors of the working class. However, available information suggests that the unions of the 1980s are generally smaller and weaker than their counterparts during the heyday of the CNT in the early 1970s. According to membership lists submitted to the III Congress, 246,530 associates were represented, or only 60 percent of the CNT estimated membership.[41] Given the active recruitment campaign conducted prior to the Congress and a covert leadership concern about a tendency among members to withdraw support thereafter, the figure can be seen as representative of a peak recruitment capacity at the present stage. Available data (mid-1985) from Montevideo, where the great majority of unionized workers is concentrated, show that 45 percent of the economically active population indicated the existence of unions in their work-place.[42] Among these workers, 68 percent were actually members of the union, which amounts to approximately 30 percent of the economically active population in the capital. Since the active population is estimated to be about 44 percent of the total, we may conclude that some 165,000 workers were unionized in Montevideo at the beginning of the democratic period.

The analysis of workers' involvement in the unions, measured by membership and by their support of mobilization, reveals that both variables reach their highest level in manual occupations and in lower income strata. Table 9.2 shows that the inverse relation between income and involvement in unions is almost linear, with the sole exception of the medium-high group, which scores less than the high income group in both variables. Regarding political preferences, both indicators of involvement follow a similar pattern, with the highest found among *Frente Amplio* voters. However, differences in membership across political preferences are smaller than differences in the support of mobilization, thus suggesting that leftist voters tend to endorse mobilizations even when they are not union members. The opposite tendency is observed for Colorado members, among whom only half regularly support mobilizations. In both cases, Blanco members occupy an intermediate position.

Another important discussion to be considered is the relation between unions and the political orientation of the workers. Analyzing these same data, González has shown that 58 percent of the workers having unions in their work-place voted for the *Frente Amplio* in 1984.[43] His interpretation of this finding is that unions were accomplishing an effective political socialization favorable to the left. Although the cross-

TABLE 9.2
Views on Union Involvement in Montevideo, by Occupation, Income, and Political Preferences[a] (1985)

	Regular support for mobilization[b] (%)	Membership in the union (%)
Occupation		
Techno-professional	51	59
White collar	63	61
Blue collar	84	79
Income		
High	60	71
Medium-high	56	50
Medium-low	69	73
Low	83	81
Political preference		
Colorado Party	28	45
Blanco Party	56	63
Frente Amplio	86	79

Source: Equipos Consultores Asociados, *Informe Trimestral*, July, 1985.
[a] Percentages computed over total workers in each category who acknowledged the existence of unions in their workplace.
[b] Regular support includes workers who claimed to join mobilizations "always or almost always." Other choices were "sometimes" and "never or almost never."

sectional nature of the data and the timing of the poll (about four months after the national elections) makes it impossible to identify the causal direction of the relationship, at least two important conclusions may be drawn. First, if this association between support for the left and union membership observed in 1984 becomes permanent, it may precipitate important changes in the relationship between the unions and the party system. Second, given the observed tendency of leftist voters to partici-pate more actively in union life and the lesser weight of the more passive traditional party voters among members, the new situation may bring about pressures for a higher rank-and-file participation at all levels of the movement. Such a situation might generate new tensions between an active rank-and-file and a centralized leadership where most of the important decisions are made. While the traditional tensions between leaders and rank-and-file have resulted primarily from the need to make different economic demands compatible with the overall strategy of the movement, the new setting may introduce tensions stemming from political concerns of the unionized workers, on both internal and external matters.

THE SOCIOECONOMIC CONTEXT OF UNION RESURGENCE

During the 1970s, income distribution in Uruguay underwent a process of significant concentration, manifested in a steady growth of the Gini index. Considering family income derived from earnings, this index rose from 0.369 to 1973 to 0.473 in 1984. Between these years, income concentration in the richest 10 percent passed from 27.35 percent to 34.53 percent of the total while, for the poorest 10 percent it went from 2.13 percent to 0.64 percent. All families but those in the top 20 percent lost income in that period.[44] At the same time, real wages experienced a sharp decline: the value for December 1984 was 51.5 percent of that in 1968, having decreased by 20.8 percent since 1981. The magnitude of the figures does not leave room for doubt about the impact of the authoritarian period on income concentration and wage decline, a process that was aggravated in its final stage by economic stagnation.

The economic depression characteristic of the last years of authoritarian rule caused unemployment to rise to 15 percent of the economically active population in Montevideo in 1983, the year after the breakdown of the pre-announced currency exchange control in November 1982 and the subsequent strong devaluation.[45] Unemployment has only slowly declined thereafter. This reduction accelerated during the first year of democratic rule, when it came down from 14.01 percent to 13.08 percent. The reduction was unequally distributed among the different economic sectors, even fluctuating markedly within some of them. Unemployment affected young people particularly: the ratio for the population under 25 was 3 times higher than the one for people over that age.[46] However, the tendency for unemployment to decline has been maintained in subsequent years, falling to 8.73 percent in August 1987, a figure that is similar for both Montevideo and the rest of the country.[47]

The economic policy of the new Colorado government has been repeatedly rejected by the union leaders, who have criticized it as being a simple continuation of previous authoritarian economic tendencies. The dominant issue has been the heavy burden imposed by external debt which, in May 1985, reached $1,562 per capita, or $4.7 billion. By then, the debt represented 5.1 times the value of exports, and 90 percent of the GDP.[48] Given that situation, the government decided to seek an agreement with the IMF in order to settle conditions for payment and to ease the way toward getting new loans. Such resolution was strongly criticized by the unions and, in various degrees, by several opposition groups. The criticism focused mainly on the basic guidelines for economic policy that the agreement with the IMF and foreign banks entailed, and particularly on its likely effect on income policy. According to the Memorandum of the Agreement, the goal of steady economic reactivation should be achieved by means of reduction of both the inflation rate and the fiscal deficit, as well as by a strengthening of the balance of payments.[49] The goals thus defined implied that the determination of wages for the public sector — approximately one third of all salaried workers and 23 percent of the economically active population – would depend upon the evolution of inflation and fiscal deficit. Within the private sector and notwithstanding some governmental intervention, wage policy was limited to some basic guidelines for state representatives in institutionalized wage bargaining. Such guidelines, as clearly expressed in the Memorandum, were supposed to agree with the public sector policy, with these geared to the achievement of anti-inflationary goals.

In spite of both the restrictive effect of this policy and the fact that the rate of economic growth was almost zero in 1985,[50] real wages in the whole country rose 13 percent from December 1984 to December 1985.[51] The rise in the private sector in Montevideo was particularly important, amounting to 19.1 percent, while the figure for the whole country was 11.7 percent. Public salaries, on the other hand, only experienced a rise in real terms of 12.7 percent. The 83.0 percent inflation rate in 1985, although above the level anticipated in the government plan, was also much lower than what could have been expected from an economy that by March showed a prospective fiscal deficit of 11 percent of the GDP — a deficit which by the end of the year had almost disappeared. Real wages rose again in 1986 by 4.1 percent, and by September 1987 they had shown an increase of 5.0 percent with respect to the same month in 1987. However, this last increment is completely accounted for by increases in the private sector, given the stagnation observed in the salary levels in the public sphere.[52] The gap between real wages in the public and private sectors began to grow in September 1986. If confirmed as a trend, it may be an important element affecting the level of conflict in each sector and introducing tensions within the unified structure of the labor movement.

The labor policy of the new government has been focused on the creation of bargaining mechanisms, combined with a situation where salary increases would be unilaterally determined by administrative decree. Within the public sector, negotiations take place directly between each union and the authorities of various parts of the state. Bargaining in the private sector takes place within a framework similar to the so-called — salary councils, — which were active between 1943 and 1968. Reestablished with minor modifications by executive decree in May 1985, the councils received support from political groups, union leaders, and management. Each council is composed of representatives of the Ministry of Labor and Social Security, as well as those of capital and labor. Although not formally stipulated, the appointment of labor representatives is controlled by the union in each branch of economic activity. According to an internal report of the Ministry of Labor, the councils have defined occupational categories and minimum wages affecting approximately 346,700 workers during the first two series of negotiations.

As was foreseeable given the low level of real wages, liberalization in the political context allowed for an outburst of labor demands that were already present during the last three months of authoritarian rule. According to official data, during the first two years of democratic government, 1,114 labor conflicts took place. Only 394 of these conflicts were in the private sector, while 716 took place in the public sphere, thus reflecting the effects of budgetary constraints on public salaries. Finally, the total figure includes four one-day general strikes.[53] Looking at their characteristics, these conflicts can be classified into two types depending on the method for determining salary increases.[54] The period prior to the establishment of the salary councils was characterized by the proliferation of conflicts focused on wages, encompassing the whole branch or sector and supported by extended strikes.[55] Beginning in June 1985 when the councils started to work, conflicts decreased progressively in scope, just as partial stoppages and low-performance became more frequent as a means of exerting pressure upon the negotiators. Within the public sector, however, strikes have tended to last longer.

Although government spokesmen (including the President himself) insinuated several times their desire to pass a law regulating the constitutional right to strike and the internal affairs of the unions — even submitting the issue to a plebiscite if necessary — the thesis of self-regulation prevailed during the first two years of democratic government. With very few exceptions, such as the declaration of "essential services" that cannot be discontinued by labor conflicts, or the imposition of a referendum among private health workers to decide about a strike, government has not interfered to end any conflict by authoritative decree. However, this attitude seems to be related to the effective progress of "self-regulation," which in practice means the capacity and will of union leaders to curb radical conflicts.

THE URUGUAYAN LABOR MOVEMENT IN DEMOCRACY: MAJOR TRENDS AND PERSPECTIVES FOR FUTURE RESEARCH

The analysis I have presented shows a labor movement in transition within a society which is itself in transition. By the second half of the 1960s, the traditional pattern of incorporation of the unions as a pressure group that regularly participated in collective bargaining had come to a crisis. The dissolution of the salary councils in 1968 marked the formal end of an approach to labor relations that had become incompatible with the government's economic policy. The breakdown of the subtle equilibrium that provided the foundations for an institutionalized opposition paved the way for a growing confrontation between mobilized social sectors and repressive forces, a confrontation which would end in the total destruction of the former in the 1973 coup. Ten years later, the transition to democracy created a political space for the resurgence of the labor movement. The important role of the unions in the final stages of the transition allowed labor to recover its position within the polity. In the months that preceded the 1984 national elections, the importance of the participation of labor leaders together with politicians and businessmen in consultation within the corporatist-oriented *Concertación Nacional Programática* should be stressed. However, the newly elected Colorado government has not continued neo-corporatist mechanisms at the national level; as a result, the actual influence of labor on policy-making has been limited, at best.

The long-standing leftist tradition of labor leadership and the thorough repression during authoritarian rule (which raised the risks that came with union membership) had promoted highly politicized and often radicalized activists, thus contributing to the maintenance of a continuity between pre-authoritarian unionism and the movement of the 1980s.[56] However, caution should be used when speaking of "restoration" in Uruguayan labor — as with the Uruguayan political system as a whole — because such restoration might well be just a temporary resurgence. Three interrelated variables which may have a crucial effect on the future evolution of labor in Uruguay are: (1) the economic situation; (2) the confrontation of different tendencies within the leadership; and (3) the structure of ties between labor and the political left.

The first variable affects the availability of resources and their distribution among groups in the social structure. The income policy and labor relations under authoritarian rule contributed to the development of radical wage demands among rank-and-file, often escaping the control of the more moderate sectors of union leadership. Persistence of such short-run radicalism, however, depends on the outcome of wage conflicts. In a rather tight economic situation, those outcomes are likely to be below expectations, if not nil, and possibly harmful to the maintenance of jobs. Moreover, some gains have been achieved, which may raise the marginal cost of further radicalism. In this sense, it is significant that radicalism has persisted longer among white collar workers in the public sector, where lower risk of job loss is combined with a relative stagnation of real wages.

The examination of the second variable reveals another cause for radicalism stemming from political conflicts within the union leadership structure. Leaders of the extreme left have tried to take advantage of short-term economic radicalism in order to mobilize the rank-and-file.

The Communist Party, in spite of its moderate political position, does not always act this way in the unions, where Communist leaders have to compete against the radicals for the support of the rank-and-file. Rather, they have often pretended to follow radicals in conflicts which present few possibilities of success. This state of affairs can be understood in terms of the competition between "tendencies" to control the unions. Given the difficulties imposed by the economic context, the resort to radicalism can turn against the leaders themselves, especially if the outcome repeatedly frustrates worker efforts and expectations. Thus, Communist "radicalism" in settings where radical leaders are in control can be explained as a mechanism to erode existing noncommunist leadership, while in those unions where Communists are the majority, radicalism is reduced in scope and becomes merely a defensive response to criticism from the extreme left.[57]

Given the additive effects of the first two variables on radicalism, two alternative developments can be expected. First, radicalization could evolve in an explosive process as happened in the 1960s, when economic and political factors positively reinforced each other. Second, the process could decline to some point of equilibrium, even though the bottom limit of such a decline may be relatively high and variable for different sectors of labor. Although it is still early for making accurate predictions, it seems likely that Uruguayan labor politics will follow the second option. An economic situation per se does not necessarily foster radical politics; rather, collective violence requires formulation of alternatives, actual political strength and, most important, the lack of regular channels to transmit demands.[58] None of these factors seems to be present in the Uruguay of the 1980s. Yet other factors generating opposite effects do exist. Although successive polls have shown a decrease in the perceived risk of a coup d'état, both union and political leaders know that military intervention is probably the most likely outcome of radicalism. On the other hand, the great majority of the left supports democratic institutions, and the significant 22 percent obtained by the *Frente Amplio* in the last national elections makes electoral politics more feasible and attractive. In the arena of labor, the evolution has been toward a decreasing influence of radical leadership, mostly favoring moderate Communists. Thus, rather than a coincidence of factors that might lead to collective violence, the Uruguayan situation might tend toward the effective incorporation of a moderate left into the political system and toward a decline in the strength of radical leaders within labor.

This last point leads to a third variable, the structure of ties between unions and the political left. Given the changes that seem to be taking place, this area presents one of the most interesting topics for further research. In post-authoritarian settings, the consolidation of democracy becomes a central concern, and it poses challenges for actors who were either incorporated into the polity or whose position in it had undergone significant changes during the political transition. The Uruguayan left is one such group.

The concern with democracy in the discourse of the Latin American left is more recent than that of its European counterpart, and its origin is rather different. In Europe, the political and social broadening of democracy within the framework of capitalism presented "anti-system" leftist parties with a need to back a program in which the advance of "substantial" democracy would not entail the decline of "formal" democracy; the very distinction between the two became meaningless. In Latin America, this concern with democracy did not originate in a progressive broadening of democratic life, but rather in its complete destruction by authoritarian regimes. The contemporary reflection on democracy generates a cleavage between moderate and revolutionary tendencies, which has been detected in the Chilean left and which can also be recognized, broadly speaking, in Uruguay.[59] The major difference lies in the method for transforming the capitalist system. Moderates advocate a gradualist approach that comes closer to the Eurocommunist model and to the idea of democratic socialism. Revolutionary socialists, in turn, stick to Marxist-Leninist orthodoxy, defending the idea of class-based action and the significance of the revolutionary moment as a turning point in the political process.

In the Uruguay of the late 1980s, the moderate/revolutionary cleavage corresponds to the division between the political and union branches of the left.[60] The 1984 national elections produced significant changes in the relation of forces within the *Frente Amplio* coalition.[61] In the comparison of electoral support gained by various groups within the coalition in 1971 and 1984 (Table 9.3), three facts appear notable. First, the share of radical groups dropped from 23.3 percent to 6.7 percent.[62] Second, the moderate *Movimiento Por el Gobierno del Pueblo* (now transformed into a party) climbed from 10.3 percent to 39.3 percent. Third, although the less significant reduction in the Communist share from 32.0 percent to 28.2 percent may have been due to circumstantial factors, the party has lost its electoral predominance in the coalition, lagging considerably behind the moderates.

The close relation between the structures of the political left and labor limits moderate hegemony in the political arena, especially as long as moderates fail to make their presence strong within the unions. Although consolidated labor parties are frequently more conservative than their supporters in the unions, the emergence of a leftist party that would leave labor to its left does not seem historically likely, either in terms of the Uruguayan political reality or from a comparative perspective.[63] As noted above, moderate labor leaders do not pose a serious challenge to the dominant Marxist-Leninist orientation, since they

TABLE 9.3
Distribution of "Frente Amplio" voters, by Sectors in the Coalition (1971 and
1984 National Elections)

Party or Sector	1971		1984	
	Voters	%	Voters	%
Communist Party				
and allies[a]	100,211	32.93	113,116	28.20
Socialist Party	35,927	11.82	61,278	15.27
Christian Democratic				
Party	61,527	20.22	39,203	9.77
"Por el Gobierno del				
Pueblo"	31,479	10.34	157,808	39.34
Radical left				
coalitions[b]	70,944	23.32	26,783	6.68
Without specification	4,457	1.37	2,916	0.74
TOTAL	304,275	100.00	401,104	100.00

Sources: For 1971, Julio Fabregat, Elecciones uruguayas (Montevideo: Cámara de Senadores,
1972); for 1984, Juan Rial, Uruguay: Elecciones de 1984 (Montevideo: Ed. de la Banda Oriental,
1985).
[a] The Communist Party was formally banned in 1984, but participated under the motto
"Democracia Avanzada."
[b] Ballots for radical coalitions correspond to "Patria Grande" in 1971 and to "Izquierda
Democratica Independiente" in 1984.

presently lack the power resources to attain real consolidation and
subsequent hegemony.[64] Although a decline of the radical "tendencies"
within labor may be expected, the future balance of power is most likely
to favor Communist leaders, whose strategy sees hegemony in the
unions as essential. Indeed, Communists are likely to maintain a moderate political strategy, favoring broad alliances in the electorate. Although
this strategy might attenuate the cleavage between a moderate, middle-
class supported political left and an orthodox, Marxist-Leninist union
leadership, the Communist Party of Uruguay remains closely identified
with Moscow and distant from any "bourgeois deviation," in the
Eurocommunist sense.[65]

When analyzed from the perspective of the historical legacy of the
Uruguayan left, this ideological cleavage between its major basis of
mobilized support and its political elite poses a twofold challenge. From
the standpoint of the unions, the problem is to search for a new strategy
of linkage between economic and political goals in a context open to
electoral politics, where the old pattern of differences between union and
electoral behavior of the rank-and-file may also be changing. From the
point of view of the political leadership, the problem seems to lie in a
redefinition of the relation with organized labor, which in the past has
been its main source of power in the polity. In this search for new

strategies, neither political nor labor leaders can disregard two important constraints posed by the social structure and spatial distribution of the Uruguayan population. First, unionized workers account only for 19 percent of the adult population in Montevideo, and is almost insignificant in the rest of the country. Second, the very concentration of unions in Montevideo prevents them from being an efficient agent of political socialization in the rest of the country where traditional parties have managed to maintain an efficient network of local leaders for more than a hundred years. In 1984, the Frente Amplio was supported by 33 percent of the voters in Montevideo, but got only 9 percent in the rest of the country. This uneven distribution suggests that electoral growth in the so-called "interior" should be a priority in any electoral strategy of the left. If the future political role of the Uruguayan labor movement depends on its alliance with parties that are likely to gain increasing electoral support, union leaders must be aware of the serious constraints that the structure of the country imposes on any political action based on a class perspective while simultaneously aiming to control the government though democratic procedures. A moderate political left, on the other hand, may have to learn how to manage a coalition with actors in the unions who may make strange bedfellows.

NOTES

This article is based on research I carried out in Montevideo between 1983 and 1985 at the *Centro Latinoamericano de Economía Humana*. Funds were provided by a research grant from the *Consejo Latinoamericano de Ciencias Sociales* (CLACSO). This chapter was translated from the Spanish original by Daniel Videla.

    1. Apart from the work done by Alfredo Errandonea and Daniel Costábile, *Sindicato y sociedad en el Uruguay* (Montevideo: Fundación de Cultura Universitaria, 1969) discussed here, the few available pieces are mostly insider accounts, often influenced by the political views of the author. On this point, see Francisco Pintos, *Historia del movimiento obrero del Uruguay* (Montevideo: 1960); German D'Elía, *Los Sindicatos* (Montevideo: Nuestra Tierra, 1969); Héctor Rodríguez, "El arraigo de los sindicatos," *Enciclopedia Uruguaya*, vol. 51 (Montevideo: 1973). This situation has now been somewhat reversed. Two studies covering different periods by D'Elía and Armando Miraldí, *Historia del movimiento obrero en el Uruguay: Desde sus orígenes hasta 1930* (Montevideo: Ed. de la Banda Oriental, 1984) and Jorge Luis Lanzaro, *Sindicatos y sistema político: Relaciones corporativas en el Uruguay, 1940–1985* (Montevideo: Fundación de Cultura Universitaria, 1985) have reintroduced the topic in the 1980s. A group of historians coordinated by Carlos Zubillaga has recently undertaken a major research project on the history of Uruguayan unionism, involving systematic archival research among the working class press, with initial results now already available. See Zubillaga and Jorge Balbis, *Historia del movimiento sindical uruguayo, Vol. 1: Cronología y fuentes hasta 1905* (Montevideo: Ed. de la Banda Oriental, 1985). Among non-

Uruguayans, I should mention a stimulating article by Howard Handelman, "Labor, Industrial Conflict and the Collapse of Uruguayan Democracy," *Journal of Inter-American Studies and World Affairs*, 23:4 (1981), pp. 371–394, although he focuses exclusively on the effect of labor mobilization on the breakdown of democracy.

2. Errandonea and Costábile.

3. Pooled together, groups on the left received 67,900 votes in 1962 (or 5.9 percent of the electorate), and 84,100 in 1966 (or 6.8 percent). See Julio T. Fabregat, *Elecciones uruguayas* (Montevideo: Cámera de Senadores, 1972). Even assuming that all these voters did belong to the unionized working class, such figures suggest that only a tiny minority of workers supported leftist groups in national elections. Analyzing polls taken in November 1971 only a few days before the national elections of that year, César Aguiar found that electoral identification with groups on the left correlated with education (0.637) and age (−0.598), and to a lesser extent with social strata (0.363), using gamma statistical coefficients, "La doble escena: Clivajes sociales y subsistema electoral," vol. 1 in Charles Gillespie, Louis Goodman, Juan Rial, and Peter Winn, eds., *Uruguay y la democracia* (Montevideo: Ed. de la Banda Oriental-The Wilson Center, 1984). This finding suggests that leftist voters were mostly young, medium to highly educated members of the middle and lower middle classes, a profile that strongly differs from that of the typical member of the working class.

4. In this chapter, the concept of "anti-system party" is used as in Giovanni Sartori, *Parties and Party Systems. A Framework for Analysis* (Cambridge: Cambridge University Press, 1976).

5. The 1942 *Consejos de Salarios* law established trilateral salary councils representing the state, capital, and the workers within similar branches of economic activity which were empowered to determine job classifications and minimum wages in each such area. The councils gradually lost their effectiveness as bargaining mechanisms, although they continued to function until 1968 when wage levels were frozen and the *Comisión de Productividad, Precios, e Ingresos* (COPRIN) was created. From that time on, salary increments were determined exclusively by the state.

6. For Uruguay's industrial development during the twentieth century, see Henry Finch, *A Political Economy of Uruguay since 1879* (London: Macmillan, 1980) and Raúl Jacob, *Uruguay, 1929–1938: Depresión ganadera y desarrollo fabril* (Montevideo: Fundación de Cultura Universitaria, 1981).

7. Errandonea and Costábile.

8. Among the vast bibliography about the Batllista period, one should note the works by Milton Vanger, *José Batlle y Ordóñez of Uruguay, 1902–1907* and *The Model Country: José Batlle y Ordóñez of Uruguay, 1907–1915* (both Cambridge, MA: Harvard University Press, 1963 and 1980, respectively). For a hypothesis stating the populist character of Batllismo and its relationship with the labor movement, see Zubillaga, "El Batllismo. Una Experiencia populista," *Cuadernos del Centro Latinoamericano de Economía Humana*, 27 (1984), pp. 25–27. Finch dedicates parts of his book to this topic.

9. David Collier and Ruther Berins Collier, "The Initial Incorporation of the Labor Movement in Latin America. A Comparative Perspective," a paper read at

the annual meetings of the Western Political Science Association, Eugene, Oregon, March 1986.

10. The common traits identified were (1) the scarce (or null) importance of the labor movement during the time party elites had access to power; (2) the attempt to gain support from the working class and to control the labor movement; (3) the subsequent mobilization of the workers exclusively in terms of electoral aims; and (4) the limited attempt to reorganize social and economic relations.

11. Seymor Martin Lipset, "Radicalism or Reformism: The Sources of Working-Class Politics," *American Political Science Review*, 77:1 (1983), pp. 1–18.

12. Miguel Urrutia, *Historia del sindicalismo en Colombia* (Bogotá Ed. Universidad de los Andes, 1969) emphasizes the broad support that López received from union leaders. Edgar Caicedo, *Historia de las luchas sindicales en Colombia* (Bogotá: Ed. CEIS, 1971) also points to the intervention of the Liberal Party in the union arena through young leaders in what he — from the Communist perspective — calls the period of "the rise and deviationism" of the Colombian labor movement. It is worth noting that, unlike in Uruguay, Colombian labor did not have a strong radical component prior to the initial incorporation, probably due to the relative lack of European immigrants holding anarchist ideas.

13. My analysis is based on J. Samuel Valenzuela's discussion, "Labor Movement Formation and Politics: The Chilean and the French Cases in Comparative Perspective, 1850–1950," unpublished Ph.D. dissertation, Department of Sociology, Columbia University, 1979; and "Movimientos obreros y sistemas politicos: Un análisis conceptual y tipológico," *Desarrollo Económico*, 23:91 (1983), pp. 339–368 about the effect of "freezing" ideological "tendencies" in the unions that results from the strengthening of a specific leadership and about the tensions derived from the links of labor movements with pre-existing political parties.

14. This classification is that of Zubillaga and Balbis.

15. Germán Rama, "Las clases medias en la época de Batlle," *Tribuna Universitaria*, 11 (1963); Finch.

16. The importance of pressure groups in the Uruguayan political system was emphasized by Aldo Solari, *Estudios sobre la sociedad uruguaya*, vol. 1 (Montevideo; Arca, 1964), and recently taken up by Aguiar. Exhaustive research on these groups for the business sector can be found in William Berenson, "Group Politics in Uruguay. The Development, Political Activity and the Effectiveness of Uruguayan Trade Associations," unpublished Ph.D. dissertation, Department of Political Science, Vanderbilt University, Nashville, TN, 1975. It should be noted that, as a pressure group, Uruguayan labor might be considered a "purer" case than that of American unions, given the links of the AFL-CIO with the Democratic Party.

17. For a good synthesis of the Uruguayan economy in the 1960s and 1970s, see Walter Cancela and Alicia Melgar, *El desarrollo frustrado* (Montevideo: Centro Latinoamericano de Economía Humana, 1985) and Jorge Notaro, *La política económica en el Uruguay, 1968–1984* (Montevideo: CIESU, Ed. de la Banda Oriental, 1985).

18. The organization of Uruguayan unions is that of one per industry rather than one per craft. Although blue and white collar workers in the same firm are

members of the same union, one of these categories normally prevails as a result of the nature of the type of economic activity.

19. The emergence of the *Frente Amplio* in 1971 constituted the first significant attempt to unify the left, broadening both its ideological base and its electoral weight. The *Frente Amplio* was preceded by two electoral coalitions formed in 1962, the Communist-controlled *Frente Izquierda de Liberación* (FIDEL) and the ill-fated *Unión Popular*, itself the result of an alliance between the dissident nationalist Enrique Erro and the radicalized Socialist Party. Unlike its predecessors, the *Frente Amplio* included almost all Marxist groups, the left-oriented Christian Democratic Party, and several splinters from the traditional parties. In spite of their participation in the electoral struggle, important sectors of the coalition regarded mass mobilization as the true expression of popular will, thus diminishing the importance of elections. Often caught in the revolutionary discourse of its extreme left wing and dismissed by the traditional parties, the new coalition remained in a sense outside the party system, despite its participation in the 1971 elections.

20. In 1973, the unions controlled by the Combative Tendency were the Uruguayan Federation of Health Workers (FUS), the Federation of Workers and Employees of the Beverage Industry (FOEB), and the union of the rubber industry workers (FUNSA). Also included was the largest portion of the important Association of Uruguayan Bank Employees (AEBU).

21. A good example of these polemics can be found in the collection edited by one of its protagonists, Héctor Rodríguez, *Polémica. El movimiento sindical: ¿Factor de cambio?* (Montevideo: Tierra Nueva, 1973). The book reproduces the extended polemic that Rodríguez, a radical former Communist textile union leader, participated in with Communist leaders Mario Acosta, César Reyes Daglio, and Vladimir Turiansky. The notes by Rodríguez were originally published in the independent weekly, *Marcha*, while those by his rivals were printed in the Communist newspaper, *El Popular*.

22. Martín Gargiulo, "Movimiento sindical y estabilidad democrática," *Cuadernos del Centro Latinoamericano de Economía Humana*, 30 (1984), pp. 17–38.

23. Handelman; Guillermo O'Donnell, "Reply to Remmer and Merkx," *Latin American Research Review*, 17:2 (1982), pp. 41–50. On the process of democratic breakdown in Uruguay, see Gillespie, "Desentrañando la crisis de la democracia uruguaya," in Gillespie, et al., vol. 1.

24. Executive Resolution 1102/73, June 30, 1973.

25. Executive Decree 500/73, July 3, 1973; Decrees 518/73 and 548/73, July 4 and July 6, 1973.

26. The main exception was the Association of Bank Employees which runs one of Montevideo's most important sports clubs. This union had a key role in the resurgence of labor during the democratic transition of the early 1980s.

27. Decree 622/73, August 1, 1973.

28. Decree 87/77, February 15, 1977.

29. Apart from these formal attempts, evidence is available of secret conversations promoted by Navy officers aiming to obtain support from more moderate labor leaders. Those attempts did not succeed, being hindered by a foreseeable lack of support from both the other sectors in the government (where the Navy lacked substantial power) and from union leaders.

30. For a more detailed account of authoritarian measures against labor, including an unsuccessful attempt to recreate unions without any participation from leftist leaders, see Gargiulo.

31. Luis E. González, "Uruguay, 1980–82: An Unexpected Opening," *Latin American Research Review*, 18:3 (1983), pp. 63–76; Alfred Stepan, "State Power and the Strength of the Civil Society in the Southern Cone of Latin America," in Peter Evans, Dietrich Rueschemeyer, and Theda Skocpol, eds., *Bringing the State Back In* (Cambridge: Cambridge University Press, 1985).

32. Juan Rial, *Partidos políticos, democracia y autoritarismo* (Montevideo: CIESU-Ed. de la Banda Oriental, 1984).

33. A good example of this restrictive character can be seen in Decree 513/81 implementing the law. This decree established that workers' representatives would be ousted in the case of any previous participation "in organizations that are contrary to our democratic and republican form of government," thus maintaining the proscription that impinged on the old leftist leadership originally introduced in Decree 87/77 promoting Bilateral Commissions in 1977.

34. Such is the case of Juan Pedro Ciganda (the Association of Bank Employees) and Andrés Toriani (the Health Federation) who were elected first and second deputies for Montevideo within the *Democracia Avanzada*, a front group of the Communist Party and its allies. Another of the PIT founders, Carlos Pereyra, was the candidate in third place for *Izquierda Democrática Independiente* (IDI), but where the low voting support of this group within the *Frente Amplio* coalition was not sufficient to secure his election.

35. The dissident sectors were composed of workers close to the Socialists, the Christian Democrats, and the *Por el Gobierno del Pueblo*; independent leftist leaders; and by radical sectors like the Movimiento 26 de Marzo (pro-Tupamaro) and the *Partido por la Victoria del Pueblo*. Representatives linked to the Blanco Party also withdrew from the Congress. Subsequent changes due to internal elections altered the previous Communist weakness in several unions, most notably among the textile, health, and railroad workers, thus giving the Communists an even larger majority.

36. For a detailed survey of the different leftist factions in the union movement, see Gargiulo, "El movimiento sindical uruguayo en los 80: ¿Concertación o confrontación?", in Comisión de Movimientos Laborales *El sindicalismo latinoamerican en los 80* (Santiago: CLACSO, 1986).

37. Although the Colorados have made some attempts to organize workers linked to the party, such efforts were marginal, not receiving strong support from the party organization.

38. This position was clearly exemplified by early statements from Juan Carlos Pereyra, a member of the PIT-CNT executive secretariat and a *Frente Amplio* candidate for Congress. Referring to the relations between the unions and the future civilian government, Pereyra pointed out that "a government without popular support can last very little time, and we may face serious consequences if there is a confrontation at the very beginning." In his speech, the electoral support eventually obtained by the future government did not mean "popular support," which was identified as only that coming from mobilized groups. See the interview in *Aquí* (Montevideo), January 10, 1984.

39. The *Partido por el Gobierno y el Pueblo* originates in the *Movimiento por el*

Gobierno del Pueblo founded by Senator Zelmar Michelini. After his assassination, under the moderate leadership of Senator Hugo Batalla, this sector became the single largest faction in the *Frente Amplio*, obtaining almost 40 percent of *Frente* votes in 1984.

40. Rodrigo Baño, *Lo social y lo político: Un dilema clave del movimiento popular* (Santiago: FLACSO, 1985).

41. At the beginning of the 1970s, Thomas Weil, the *U.S. Area Handbook* (Washington, D.C.: American University, 1971) estimated that 400,000 workers were affiliated to the CNT (Berenson, p. 219). CNT leaders, however, usually spoke of 500,000 members.

42. Data from a report prepared by Equipos Consultores Asociados, *Informe Trimestral: Situación Sindical* (July 1985).

43. González, "Los sindicatos en la arena politica," *Cuadernos de Marcha*, Third Epoch, 9 (1986).

44. Alicia Melgar and Fablo Villalobos, *La desigualdad como estrategia* (Montevideo: Centro Latinoamericano de Economía Humana-Ed. de la Banda Oriental, 1986).

45. The American dollar was valued at N$ 19.00 in November and rose to N$ 33.75 in December (average monthly exchange rates).

46. Eduardo Cobas, Alicia Melgar, and Jorge Notaro, *Evolución reciente de los ingreso y el empleo et el Uruguay* (Montevideo: CEPAL, 1986)

47. Official information published in *Búsqueda* (Montevideo), October 8, 1987. *Búsqueda* is an independent, elite-oriented weekly which regularly includes comprehensive and accurate data on economic indicators and information on national politics.

48. Compared with other member countries of the Asociación Latinoamericana de Integración (ALADI), the situation faced by the new government was one of the most critical. In per capita terms, the Uruguayan foreign debt is only surpassed by Venezuela ($2,047), Chile ($1,670), and Argentina ($1,613). When expressed in GNP terms, Uruguay was only exceeded by Chile, where the foreign debt is equal to 98.4 percent of the national product (data for June 1985 published in *Búsqueda*, January 30, 1986).

49. The Memorandum was published in *Búsqueda*, September 12, 1985.

50. In 1985, the GNP amounted to 5.13 billion dollars, reflecting zero growth in respect to the previous year. The Uruguayan GDP had sharply declined in the last years of authoritarian rule, falling 16.8 percent between 1981 and 1984. In 1986, GDP experienced a notable increase of 6.3 percent (data from *Búsqueda*, November 12, 1987).

51. Cobas, et al.

52. Information published in *Búsqueda*, November 12, 1987.

53. Data released by the Ministry of Labor and Social Security and published in *Búsqueda*, December 31, 1986.

54. Cobas, et al.

55. Those were the textile industry strike, lasting approximately 45 days, that in paper manufacturing (30 days), and that in the clothing industry (30 days, but with interruptions). Other groups like the state-run harbor stevedores, fishermen, and bus drivers have to be included in this category, although these conflicts were of lesser duration. In the public sector, the main wave of conflict

took place during the last two months of the authoritarian government. During the democratic period, it is worth noting that prolonged strikes occurred among the justice, post office, and railroad workers. The government's inflexible position led to clear union defeats in the justice and railroad strikes, although post office workers did manage to obtain some of their demands.

56. Valenzuela ("Labor Movement Formation") has emphasized the negative correlation between the emergence of moderate union leaders and the level of anti-labor repression. This relation was confirmed by Robert Fishman in his "Working Class Organization and Political Change: The Labor Movement and Transition to Democracy in Spain," Ph.D. dissertation, Department of Sociology, Yale University, New Haven, CT, 1985) in the case of Spain and would seem to apply to Uruguay where new leaders tend to be highly radicalized. The argument is based on the high cost of militancy which discourages moderates.

57. This pattern seems to apply to conflicts that involved the state-owned railroads and to those in the private sector health services. In both cases, strike failures led to a serious erosion of the radical leadership, thus favoring the Communists.

58. Charles Tilly, *From Mobilization to Revolution* (New York: Random House, 1978).

59. Baño.

60. For a similar analysis of the dynamics of the left in the post-authoritarian period, see Gargiulo, "El desafío de la democracia. La izquierda política y sindical en el Uruguay post-autoritário," *Cuadernos de Centro Latinoamericano de Economía Humana*, 38 (1986), pp. 17–45. The monthly magazine *Cuadernos de Marcha* included several notes on these issues in 1987.

61. In 1985, with the exception of the Movimiento 26 de Marzo and other minority groups like the Trotskyist *Partido de los Trabajadores*, the Uruguayan left was entirely represented within the *Frente Amplio*.

62. The IDI is composed of the following groups: *Núcleos de Base Frenteamplista, Los Grupos de Acción Unificadora* (GAU), *Pregón, Patria Grande*, and the Marxist-Leninist *Partido por la Victoria del pueblo* (PVP). Both the GAU and the ROE were founders of the Combative Tendency discussed earlier. Unlike the 1971 radicals, the IDI excluded the Movimiento 26 de Marzo and included the PVP whose predecessor, the ROE, was not in the original 1971 *Frente*. In 1971, radical groups pooled votes under the *Patria Grande* voting list.

63. Valenzuela, "Movimientos obreros."

64. Gargiulo, "Movimiento sindical."

65. Given this identification, the transformations taking place in the Soviet Union under Gorbachev's *Perestroika* may have important effects on the line of the Uruguayan Communist Party, although probably not in the short run. Whatever the case, Uruguay in recent years has significantly increased its commercial, cultural, and scientific links with the USSR, a factor also likely to affect the Uruguayan Communist Party.

Chapter 10

Political Control of Organized Labor in a Semi-Consociational Democracy: The Case of Venezuela

Charles L. Davis
Kenneth M. Coleman

Charles Anderson's metaphor of "the living museum" is helpful in understanding the construction of Venezuela's post-1958 competitive democratic regime. According to Anderson, the opening of the political arena to new power contenders in typical Latin American countries does not lead to the demise of traditional power contenders.[1] Indeed, the entry of new contenders, such as labor and peasants, often generates no significant redistribution of political power. This stands in contrast to what occurred in the countries first to industrialize during the nineteenth century as suffrage was expanded. Privileged groups in Latin America, however, generally have managed to retain political power and the capacity to determine public policy even when the political arena has been opened to new groups.

Nevertheless, occasional restructurings of power relationships have occurred in contemporary Latin America, manifested either in the exclusion of previous power contenders or in a redistribution of political power. Rearrangement of the political landscape can occur either through a popular revolution or a demobilizing coup. In demobilizing coups, less privileged groups and the left are generally excluded from the political arena or stripped of their power.[2] In the case of revolutions, less privileged groups or revolutionary movements seek to exclude privileged groups after gaining control of the state.[3] The contemporary Venezuelan state can be viewed as an attempt to prevent either of these two outcomes from occurring. State builders in Venezuela sought to remove the temptation of any group to seek the exclusion of other groups via revolution or a demobilizing coup. The democratic regime in Venezuela was set up by a series of social pacts after the downfall of the Pérez Jiménez dictatorship in 1958. These pacts sought not only to incorporate newly emergent groups, but also to protect an existing distribution of political and economic resources that was favored by traditional power contenders. How these pacts have shaped the role of organized labor in the post-1958 era is the main focus of this chapter.

THE FORMATION OF A SEMI-CONSOCIATIONAL DEMOCRACY IN VENEZUELA

To understand the formation of the current democratic state in Venezuela, it is first necessary to examine how competing power contenders emerged in previous decades. The Spanish loss of the Americas in 1820 and Simón Bolívar's failure to achieve a regional federation created a void of centralized authority in the emergent nation-states of northern South America. Into this void moved local strong men, or *caudillos*, who sought to gain control of the state by eliminating rival caudillos, usually by force. As a consequence, *caudillismo* introduced a high level of political instability into the region. Political stability could only be achieved when a caudillo imposed a dictatorship in which rival caudillos were effectively excluded from power. Economic growth was delayed partly by political instability, with some growth occurring primarily during periods of dictatorship. In effect, political stability and economic change depended on effective *exclusion* of rival caudillos from the political arena. But no formula for institutionalized *inclusion* was ever found.

With the exception of the *trienio* (1945–1948), these general observations characterize Venezuelan history from independence until 1958. Caudillo politics during this period led to a great deal of political instability. It is estimated that 39 major and 127 minor revolts occurred between 1830 and 1900, lasting a total of 8,847 days.[4] However, these were periods in which a dictator would emerge by using the coercive and cooptive resources at his disposal to eliminate or control rivals.[5] Strong man rule provided Venezuela with periods of political stability in which economic growth could proceed.

During the brutal dictatorship of Juan Vicente Gómez (1908–1935), Venezuela was transformed from a nation based on a coffee export economy to one with a contemporary petroleum-based export economy. It was during this era that new power contenders, including organized labor and political parties, emerged. During the 1920s, a wave of strikes occurred in the oilfields. These strikes marked the beginning of labor's role as a significant political actor in Venezuelan politics. In 1928 a famous student strike also occurred in which over 200 students at the Central Venezuelan University were briefly jailed.[6] From the student movement emerged three of Venezuela's contemporary political parties — *Acción*

Democrática (AD), *Unión Republicana Democrática* (URD), and the *Partido Comunista Venezolano* (PVC). The Social Christian Party emerged slightly later. It was known as COPEI, for the *Comité de Organización Política Electoral Independiente.*[7]

Gómez, as well as his immediate successors, Eléazar López Contreras (1936–1941) and Isaías Medina Angarita (1941–1945), tried to manage emergent power contenders with a combination of repression and cooptation. Repression was the primary tool for managing conflict, but inducements were used as well. For example, the labor law of 1928 extended such privileges and rights as an eight and one-half-hour day, but provided no mechanisms for collective bargaining or for enforcement of the law. A *Banco Obrero* was also created to provide cheap loans for housing.[8] However, the few "carrots" proffered did little to quell popular unrest and labor agitation.[9]

In 1945, young military officers overthrew the Medina government and turned power over to *Acción Democrática*. This began Venezuela's first short-lived experience with competitive democracy, lasting only until 1948.[10] During the *trienio*, AD tried to forge a broad-based coalition of indigenous industry, labor, and peasants. The *Corporación Venezolano de Fomento* was created in 1946 to channel oil revenues into industrialization.[11] AD tried to capture labor support by expanding unionization, by forming the Confederation of Venezuelan Workers (CTV),[12] and by taking advantage of a schism that had weakened the Communist presence in the trade union movement.[13] Also, the number of peasant associations was expanded dramatically and a Peasant Federation was formed.[14]

In the end, the attempt to build a grand coalition among major power contenders failed in the 1940s. Virtually all groups except labor and peasants became progressively alienated from AD: the Church and COPEI were disgruntled over efforts to secularize education;[15] multinational corporations were unhappy about threats of nationalization and increased taxes; the landowners were frightened by land reform; and industrialists were threatened by increasing unionization and by having to accede to real wage increases.[16] By 1948, the traditional major power contenders, who had not been eliminated from the political process, were ready to support a demobilizing coup. The coup ushered in ten years of brutal dictatorship, most of them under Marcos Pérez Jímenez. Even though the AD party won over 70 percent of the vote in three elections between 1945 and 1947, the coup occurred because in the "living museum" of power capabilities, only partial legitimacy was accorded to electoral mandates.[17] The use of force to determine who would govern Venezuela remained equally legitimate as late as 1948.

The 1948 *golpe* represents a classic case of a demobilizing coup in which power contenders recently admitted to the political arena, particularly the reformist AD party which was closely linked to labor and peasant associations, were stripped of power. For our purposes, we need not examine the dictatorship except to note one of its most enduring legacies: the suffering it engendered bred a spirit of compromise and a commitment to an inclusive polity. By 1958, elites throughout Venezuelan society were committed to building a state in which another demobilizing coup would be unlikely to occur. Conversely, this also meant the creation of a state in which popular revolution would also be difficult. The goal was to avoid polarization that would give either the right or the left a pretext to impose a political "solution" via force. To avoid these extremes, special agreements had to be negotiated.

During the Betancourt years (1958–1963), elites from all sectors of Venezuelan society attempted to negotiate agreements that would provide the basic operating norms for the new regime. Two specific accords were fundamental in laying the basis for the new political order: (a) "The Statement of Principles and the Minimum Program of Government" and (b) the Pact of Punto Fijo. Interestingly, both pacts were negotiated before Venezuela's first national elections in 1959, thereby removing fundamental economic and political issues from the arena of electoral politics.[18] These pacts were signed by party elites from three of the major parties of the time — AD, COPEI, and URD.[19] The Communists were excluded, perhaps contributing to a subsequent guerrilla insurrection.

Terry Karl has identified three basic operating norms established for the new regime by these two agreements. The first norm was that public policy ought to recognize the economic interests of all major power contenders. Domestic capitalists were guaranteed the right to pursue private capital accumulation and were offered state assistance in capital formation through development banks and tariff protection. Large landowners were assured that there would be no expropriation of land without adequate compensation. The multinational oil companies were reassured by AD's dropping of its prior demand for nationalization. For political parties there was an agreement that they could distribute benefits to lower and middle class constituencies. For the popular sector classes, the Minimum Program committed the state to "pursuit of full employment, freedom to organize unions, a new labor code, and widespread social legislation in health, education, and social security."[20] Obviously this program was beyond the resources of most third-world nations, but Venezuelan elites hoped that revenues from petroleum exports would provide the needed revenues without having to impose new costs on any sector of Venezuelan society.[21]

The second norm stipulated that power sharing agreements would obtain among major political parties. By the Pact of Punto Fijo, three major parties (AD, COPEI, and URD) agreed to respect election results and to contain conflict. Also the parties agreed to form coalition governments based on election results. While formal coalitional arrangements for cabinets were dropped after the Leoni administration (1963–1968), informal *concertación* practices between parties and power-sharing arrangements (such as proportional representation) have continued.[22]

The third norm was "to defeat militarily any force which would not accept the first two rules."[23] This norm was put into practice when a leftist insurrection in the early 1960s was crushed. It was also invoked when the Betancourt administration moved to expel the militant wing of AD and the Communists from leadership in the unions.[24] These efforts facilitated the imposition of state control over the union movement.

The Venezuelan state that was established by these pacts is best understood as a semi-consociational democracy. According to Lijphart's conceptualization, a consociational democracy is characterized by: (1) "government by a grand coalition of the political leaders of all significant segments of the plural society;" (2) "the mutual veto or 'concurrent majority' rule, which serves as an additional protection of vital minority interests;" (3) "proportionality as the principal standard of political representation, civil service appointments, and allocation of public funds;" and (4) "a high degree of autonomy for each segment to run its own internal affairs."[25]

The Venezuelan state is clearly designed to provide elite accommodation via a "grand coalition." Since 1959, much attention has been devoted to mending fences among elites and to keeping open the channels of intra-elite communication. In this sense, Venezuela fits Lijphart's characterization of consociational democracy very well. However, in two important respects, the Venezuelan case does not fit the ideal type. There is relatively little subsystem autonomy for popular sector organizations such as labor unions, peasant associations, or student associations. As Levine explains:

> Party ties became a central kind of social affiliation, knitting together and often overriding more limited group and sectoral loyalties. Thus, for example, peasant, trade union, and student activists were simultaneously group leaders and party militants. As such, they could be called upon by party leaders to modify strategies, tactics, or goals in order to accommodate the long-range political interests of the party. In this way, party organization *per se* became strong and complex because it incorporated and reinforced other kinds of loyalties and affiliations. In addition to cutting across group ties, AD penetrated the society vertically as well, creating organizational ties from the national level through regions to blocks and precincts — in cities, towns, and countryside alike.
>
> This set of party-based structures took root in the 1940s and, after surviving a decade of brutal military repression after the 1948 coup, became firmly established in the democratic period as the major channel of political action. To be effective in Venezuelan politics, groups and interests have been largely required to work through the matrix of party organization.[26]

Parties provide the mechanism by which subsystem autonomy is avoided. Moreover, there is little equality in the distribution of political and economic resources among power contenders (or segments). Labor and peasants are subordinated to political parties and have no "mutual veto power." This is a second reason why the fit is imperfect. Thus, we label the Venezuelan post-1958 regime as a semi-consociational democracy.[27]

The semi-consociational nature of the polity does not imply that Venezuelan politics will tend toward instability. We would argue that the subordination of the popular sector to political parties is vital for maintaining the original social pacts upon which the stability of the Venezuelan polity rests. Understanding the vertical relationships between *Acción Democrática* and labor unions is vital to understanding Venezuela's quasi-consociational system.

In order to perpetuate the original pacts, the Venezuelan state has been forced to play a delicate balancing act. On the one hand, the state must maintain an "attractive climate" for private capital accumulation in order to benefit from continuing support of entrepreneurial groups. Such a climate is contingent on guarantees of labor peace and on the political demobilization of the trade union movement so as to preclude a labor coalition with parties of the left. On the other hand, consistent with the Minimum Program, the state must seek to accommodate the demands of labor elites. Yet entrepreneurial groups impose limits on what the state can deliver to unions. The state is caught in the middle. Lucena has shown that the capacity of the Venezuelan state to deliver benefits to labor within these constraints has been dependent on the oil bonanza.[28]

THE INCORPORATION OF ORGANIZED LABOR AND THE IMPOSITION OF POLITICAL CONTROL

To maintain the semi-consociational system, Venezuelan political leaders have tried to minimize labor-management conflict. The state has sought to regulate labor-management relations, to deactivate politically the trade union movement and to provide unions with concrete benefits.

State Regulation of Labor-Management Relations
A favorable climate for private capital accumulation depends in large part on the domestication of labor and the containment of labor costs. In the case of Venezuela's export model of economic development, it is especially vital that organized labor not disrupt the flow of petroleum, Venezuela's most essential export. In other words, strike activity and other disruptions to the export economy need to be minimized. The Venezuelan state has contained labor costs and maintained a *paz laboral*

(labor peace) in three ways: (a) specific accords between labor and management, (b) state regulation of union formation and of collective bargaining, and (c) partisan control over the labor movement by AD.

A pact between labor and management was signed in April 1958. The *Pacto de Avenimiento Obrero-Patronal* was signed by both leftist as well as AD/COPEI labor elites. In this pact, labor was committed to maintaining democratic stability by agreeing to seek conciliation of conflicts with management. For its part, management agreed to avoid layoffs.[29] In effect, organized labor accepted the regime norm of *concertación*, or accommodation, with management. At the same time, the right to strike was seriously compromised as any strike could be portrayed as a betrayal of Venezuelan democracy.[30]

The labor law and its administration has provided another mechanism to ensure labor peace. The labor code formulated in 1936 provided the basic mechanisms for state regulation of unionization and collective bargaining. It has been reformed in 1945, 1947, 1966, 1974 and 1975, 1983 and is currently being reconsidered.[31]

The right to unionize was officially guaranteed by the Labor Law of 1936. The 1936 law also gave unions the right to strike, provided that the government did not find the strike to be dangerous to the economic well-being of the nation.[32] Article 177 of the current Labor Law provides that a company workforce must contain 20 members before official recognition to a union can be given. Boeckh estimates that as of the late 1960s, this requirement precluded 35 percent of the economically active population from forming unions.[33] By his estimate, only 20.9 percent of Venezuelan workers at this time were covered by collective contracts – that is, were unionized.[34] As a general rule, unionized workers were found to be concentrated in the oligopolistic, capital intensive sector of the economy.[35]

The labor code details how unions are to gain official recognition. The labor ministry is to be provided a detailed application by the union seeking recognition, including a list of members and governing statutes.[36] The latter must conform with legal standards in the code. In addition, the union must implicitly accept close supervision of union affairs by the labor ministry.[37] The labor ministry can deny registration, although appeals are available through the courts.[38] Union registration can also be cancelled for failure to comply with the labor law.[39]

The extent to which these provisions of the labor law are administered for partisan purposes is not clear.[40] Certainly the party in control of the presidency and the labor ministry could use these powers for partisan advantage by rewarding unions affiliated with the party and by punishing unions controlled by opposition parties. It is certain, however, that the labor code provides the Venezuelan state a formidable mechanism for controlling the rate of unionization. Interestingly, the level of unionization continued to expand during the 1970s and 1980s.[41] Continual growth of the union movement might indicate elite acceptance of the trade union movement as an effective device for the cooptation and control of labor.[42] By contrast, elites in bureaucratic-authoritarian regimes generally seek to contain or suppress unionization.[43] When such regimes come to power some unions are disbanded, and the rate of unionization slows.

The Venezuelan labor law also provides for effective control over collective bargaining. Workers are not permitted to strike until conciliation and arbitration have been attempted. Before a "legal" strike can occur, a petition of grievances (*el pliego de las peticiones de los obreros*) has to be submitted to the appropriate *Inspectoría del Trabajo*[44] that is responsible for setting up a Conciliation Board (*Junta de Conciliación*). In turn, this board can turn the case over to an Arbitration Board (*Junta de Arbitraje*) that presumably has the power of binding arbitration, a power rarely used.

However, Héctor Lucena notes that mediation by a Labor Inspector is more prevalent than either conciliation or compulsory arbitration.

> Mediation is carried out by the initiative of the Labor Inspector . . . , Labor Ministry policy is to promote this. Mediation occurs when the Labor Inspector calls upon one or both parties for discussion, doing so of course before a formal grievance petition is filed, because when that occurs only two things can happen. One, the most frequent, is that a petition will be "admitted for study and review," which implies that it is not fully recognized by the Inspector. This . . . is an illegal practice, since nowhere in the Labor Law is such a status contemplated. The other alternative is the exceptional case of a petition being recognized by the Inspector, in which case the time lapses for constituting a Conciliation Board begin to run, as was contemplated in the Labor Law and its Regulations.
>
> Generally, before accepting the grievance petition, the Labor Inspector has engaged in some mediation; admitting it for "study and review" gains time for further mediation.
>
> Now, what is this business of admitting grievance petitions for "study and review?" In labor circles, it is widely believed that this is a strategy to undercut the right of workers to strike. . . . Admitting petitions "for study and review" simply postpones the legal remedy of conciliation which *must* be traversed before strikes can be declared legal.[45]

López and Werz note that the labor law makes legal strikes "almost impossible in Venezuela."[46] Table 10.1 demonstrates the point well. Note that in 1977 and 1978 there were no legal strikes. Many strikes have occurred, but most strikes have been declared illegal by the Ministry of Labor in recent years. Once a strike is declared illegal, the government has the legal authority to use police and military force to quell the strike.[47] Such authority has rarely been used recently, but has been deployed occasionally when buildings have been occupied by strikers.[48]

TABLE 10.1
Legal versus Illegal Strike Activity in Venezuela: 1961–1985

	Number of Legal Strikes	Number of Illegal Strikes	Total Work Stoppages
1961	5	9	14
1962	8	11	19
1963	5	4	9
1964	7	20	27
1965	4	20	24
1966	1	11	12
1967	5	29	34
1968	4	9	13
1969	3	83	86
1970	2	64	66
1971	5	228	233
1972	7	172	179
1973	4	250	254
1974	3	116	119
1975	3	100	103
1976	1	171	172
1977	0	214	214
1978	0	140	140
1979	2	145	147
1980	4	185	189
1981	3	129	132
1982	2	100	102
1983	0	200	200
1984	0	39	39
1985	6	11	17

Sources: Héctor Lucena, "Papel del sindicalismo venezolano antes de la crisis económica," *Revista Relaciones de Trabajo*, 6 (September 1985): Table 3, p. 130; Jennifer L. McCoy, "The Politics of Adjustment: Labor and the Venezuelan Debt Crisis," *Journal of Interamerican Studies and World Affairs*, 28:4 (Winter 1986–7): Table 5; also, personal communication from Héctor Lucena, October 10, 1986.

These measures have aided the post-1956 state in maintaining the *paz laboral*. Low labor conflict is shown by the data in Table 10.2 which details strike frequency between 1970 and 1985. The date show that strikes, considering both legal and illegal types, occurred infrequently in each of the years between 1970 and 1985. In most Venezuelan unions strikes did not occur, although it should be noted that strike activity tended to increase after 1969.[49] The number of strikes occurring never surpassed three percent of the total number of unions existing at any given point in time (1971 and 1973 were years in which the incidence was circa three percent).

Our empirical study of selected Venezuelan labor unions revealed a similar pattern of low strike frequency even among leftist unions. We

TABLE 10.2
Strike Frequency in Venezuela: 1970–1985[a]

	Number of Work Stoppages[b]	Number of Legalized Unions	Number of Strikes Per 1000 Unions
1970	66	7,678	8.59
1971	233	7,857	29.66
1972	179	7,996	22.39
1973	254	8,186	31.03
1974	119	8,379	14.20
1976	171	8,843	19.34
1977	214	9,069	23.60
1978	140	9,235	15.16
1979	147	9,569	15.69
1980	189	9,541	19.81
1981	132	9,967	13.24
1982	100	10,228	9.77
1983	200	10,353	19.32
1984	39	10,523	3.71
1985	17	10,851	1.57

[a] Figures were compiled from Tables 1 and 3, Héctor Lucena, "Papel de sindicalismo venezolano . . .," 127, 130; Jenifer McCoy, 'The Politics of Adjustment . . .,' Table 5; and personal communication from Héctor Lucena, October 10, 1986.
[b] Includes both legal and illegal strikes, as reported in table 10.1.

interviewed officials in four leftist unions in 1979–1980. Among two leftist unions in the oilfields, only two wildcat strikes had occurred since 1970, neither of which lasted more than two days. The other two leftist unions in less strategically important industries revealed the same pattern. A Communist union in a Barquisimeto plastics manufacturing firm had never struck. The other leftist union, located in a distillery in La Miel, had engaged in strike activity only three times since 1970, and even then only for a few days.[50]

Infrequent strike activity combined with decentralized collective bargaining contributes to the containment of labor costs.[51] Still, organized workers were able to achieve real wage gains until the late 1970s, despite the beginnings of serious inflation in 1974. Lucena has shown that workers were not in a strong enough bargaining position to obtain real wage increases via collective bargaining during the inflationary era. Therefore, they had to depend on the first minimum wage law signed by Carlos Andrés Pérez in 1974 and on an emergency wage increase the same year to avoid loss of purchasing power.[52]

We do not wish to leave the reader with the impression that collective bargaining has been entirely futile in contemporary Venezuela. Large unions in strategic industries have continued to bargain effectively, and prior to 1974, unions generally managed to procure real wage increases for their members.[53] Bargaining has rarely been highly conflictual. The Venezuelan trade union movement has contributed to relatively peaceful, non-conflictual labor-management relations in the contemporary democratic era. Furthermore, as we shall see, wage demands have posed no serious problems for capital accumulation.

The Political Deactivation of the Trade Union Movement

A politically powerful and independent trade union movement is a potential source of social and political conflict. Such a movement can generate conflict with management by demanding public policies that would lead to greater worker input in management decisions, greater allocation of resources to wages and benefits, government regulation of the workplace, and redistribution of wealth. The political power of the trade union movement depends on the capacity to compel political parties to bargain for its support and/or to exercise significant political influence within the dominant party. If labor unions become politically powerful, they might compel political parties to favor policies that are in the interests of labor, but in conflict with the interests of management. An independent, politically powerful trade union could thus pose a serious threat to the consociational arrangements upon which political stability in Venezuela rests.

Form distinguishes *job unionism* from *political unionism*.[54] In the former case, unions focus on maximizing labor's immediate benefits through collective bargaining. In the case of political unionism, unions seek to maximize the collective political power of labor so as to structure public policy choices made by political leaders. It is only through political unionism that labor could hope to challenge and to modify elite-preferred strategies of state capitalist economic development. To preclude such challenges, elites in bureaucratic-authoritarian regimes generally seek to exclude labor unions altogether from the political arena. In Venezuela's semi-consociational democracy, elites have not sought to exclude, but rather, have tried to limit the political power of labor and to channel the labor movement into job unionism.

The political deactivation of the trade union movement in Venezuela has never been complete and remains somewhat tenuous. Yet the labor movement has never fully enjoyed the independence or unity needed to compel parties of the hegemonic center to compete for labor's support with parties of the left. To the contrary, *Acción Democrática* (and to a lesser extent COPEI) has managed to capture the trade union movement, thereby reducing the autonomy of labor as a major power contender.

AD Control Over The Trade Union Movement

AD hegemony in the trade union movement has its origins in the post-Gómez period in the late 1930s and early 1940s. During this era, AD and the Venezuelan Communist Party both developed close ties with the nascent labor movement. The Venezuelan labor movement was still passing through what has been labeled "the heroic phase,"[55] in which unions tended to be militant in face of stiff entrepreneurial and government opposition.[56] Additionally, the labor movement maintained a high degree of autonomy from party control—a situation that could have led to labor becoming a power broker in Venezuelan politics.[57]

In 1944, a year before the *trienic* began, the Communist Party's influence in the labor movement was to receive a crippling blow from which it would never recover. At a national labor conference in Caracas that year, the Medina government withdrew official recognition from 93 Communist dominated unions and 3 labor federations on grounds that these unions, in violation of the 1936 Labor Law, had illegally affiliated with a political party.[58] After this the Venezuelan Communist Party would never again become a serious factor in Venezuelan labor politics.[59]

This event paved the way for AD to solidify its control over organized labor during the *trienio*. During this era Raúl Leoni, the labor minister, moved to consolidate AD control over labor by a series of generous wage increases, improved benefits, and favorable strike settlements. For its part, labor agreed to limit strike activity to extreme circumstances. Additionally, AD founded the Confederation of Venezuelan Workers in 1947.[60] It is noteworthy that many of the features of the current system of labor relations were established during this era, including party control of the labor movement, *paz laboral*, and the state as benefactor of organized labor.

After the democratic regime was reconstituted in 1958 following the downfall of Pérez Jiménez, AD moved to reconsolidate its hegemony over the labor movement. As Karl explains:

> Before the insurrection [of the left in the early 1960s], AD youth and the Communist Party exerted important influence in the union structure. The unions had been militant under this leadership, raising economic demands and demonstrating the willingness to strike. The only redistribution of income which took place during the democracy occurred under the pressure of strong leadership within the mass organizations. The expulsion of AD's youth wing in 1960 removed aggressive leadership in the unions. In November 1961, militants of the Communist Party and the URD were also purged under the auspices of the government, which moved quickly to consolidate its hold over the unions.[61]

AD also moved to consolidate its control of the Confederation of Venezuelan workers (CTV), by far the most powerful and largest of four labor confederations in Venezuela.[62] As the data in Table 10.3 show, AD has managed to control the majority of delegates to every CTV congress since 1959 (except the Sixth Congress in 1970).[63] In the case of the 1970

TABLE 10.3
Partisan Composition of CTV Congresses, 1959–1980

	Third CTV Congress 1959	Fourth CTV Congress 1961	Fifth CTV Congress 1964	Sixth CTV Congress 1970	Seventh CTV Congress 1975	Eighth CTV Congress 1980	Ninth CTV Congress 1985
Party Affiliation of Delegates:							
AD	52.2%	70.0%	70.6%	34.5%	50.8%	53.6%	61.4%
COPEI	14.5	30.0	19.0	18.8	21.5	24.4	20.6
URD	10.0	—	12.0	11.7	8.0	2.3	3.8
PCV	23.3	—	—	—	—	—	—
MEP	—	—	—	32.0	16.7	12.6	8.9
MAS	—	—	—	—	—	3.7	3.4
Others	—	—	—	—	—	2.8	—

Sources: Héctor Lucena, "Papel del sindicalismo venezolano ante la crisis económica," *Revista Relaciones de Trabajo*, 6 (September 1985) pp. 124–125, for years from 1959–1980. For 1985 see *El Nacional* (Caracas), 20 May 1985, D-4.

congress, AD confronted a strong challenge from the leftist *Movimiento Electoral del Pueblo* (MEP), a party that had split from the AD in 1967 over the presidential candidacy of Luis Beltran Prieto. AD gained control of the 16 member CTV executive committee by forming a coalition with COPEI.[64] Thus, the threat of leftist control of Venezuela's largest labor confederation was ended.

Until 1980, the CTV could be counted on to endorse elite-preferred strategies of development, although strike activity tended to increase after 1969, particularly during the administrations of COPEI presidents (see table 10.2, especially the periods between 1968 to 1973 and 1978 to 1983, the respective presidencies of Rafael Caldera and Luis Herrera Campíns). The CTV supported the status quo not only because of AD domination of the organization, but also because of other factors as well. The CTV was and continues to be heavily subsidized by the government, although less so now than in the past.[65] Not only does the CTV enjoy far more subsidy than other labor confederations, it also enjoys privileged access to the labor ministry.[66]

Party control at the local level is maintained in large part by the nomination process for local union leaders. In Venezuela, union leadership is determined by competitive elections in which all political parties represented in the union are free to present a *plancha*, or slate of candidates. Seats on the union directorate are divided after elections on the basis of proportional representation. Each political party has a "multi-level labor bureau" to which partisan factions within unions are responsible.[67] Party labor bureaux can presumably impose guidelines on the formation of coalition slates and in some cases can impose their own nominees in local union elections. "In order to achieve its electoral objectives in local unions, a national labor bureau works through its factional heads in the federation — or, more infrequently, the bureau hierarchy at the regional or local level."[68] Federation leaders, in turn, work actively in local union elections to ensure the election of their preferred slate. The fusion of union/party leadership roles represents a pattern of cooptation by political parties. Consequently, as several observers of the Venezuelan scene have noted, union leaders have been willing to shape union demands so as not to disrupt elite goals of rapid import substitution industrialization.[69]

The available evidence does not allow us to determine precisely the extent to which Venezuelan labor unions respect democratic norms. Our impression is that consociational norms are widely diffused through all segments of organizational life in Venezuela and are generally respected. Our research on a selected number of unions in 1979–1980 did reveal the existence of tendencies toward oligarchy in some local unions. Unfortunately, we could not determine how extensive oligarchy is in all Venezuelan union structures. To illustrate, we studied one local union of *copeyano* oil workers in which the same secretary general had been reelected every two years since 1971. No opposition slate had ever challenged the official COPEI slate for seats on the union's executive committee.[70] It seems that such unions are not the norm, but clearly they do exist.

It may be that oligarchy and authoritarianism are not necessary to preserve AD and COPEI hegemony in the majority of unions. These parties have greater resources than do leftist parties in seeking to gain control of the union governing apparatus. Still leftist parties have managed to win control of a few unions, but never in sufficient numbers to challenge AD control at the federation and confederation level. *Acción Democrática* remains in control of the CTV, while the communist left contents itself with the much smaller CUTV.

Domination of the labor movement by hegemonic parties has not only contributed to the *paz laboral* that has characterized labor relations since 1958, but it also has led to a weakening of the political left. A strong leftist-labor coalition is unlikely as long as AD controls the CTV.[71] Consequently, the trade union movement has traditionally been in a weak position to bargain over issues of national policy. It is not surprising, therefore, that the Venezuelan labor movement traditionally rejected "political unionism."

Until the Eighth Congress of the CTV in 1980, the mainstream of the Venezuelan trade union movement has been solidly committed to job unionism rather than to political unionism. This commitment reflected labor's weakness as a power contender as well as acceptance of the incorporative social pacts. The trade union movement hoped to take advantage of a growing economic pie so as to secure better wages and benefits for workers rather than to pressure political elites for immediate distribution largesse.

Interviews that we conducted with local union leaders in 1979–80 showed that both AD/COPEI/URD union leaders as well as leftist leaders were committed principally to job unionism. Moreover, the union leaders that we interviewed almost universally perceived political union-ism to be a risky strategy.[72] Their primary concerns were with collective bargaining so as to obtain improved wages and benefits for workers. They did tend to see partisan electoral activity as normal for individual labor leaders and for workers, but as a general rule, local leaders tended to be skeptical of the value of overtly political activity by unions as organizations. They did not see politics as highly useful in generating material benefits for workers or in improving other working conditions. Indeed, overtly political activity on the job was portrayed as being potentially divisive and a threat to unity that was necessary in collective bargaining. Therefore, union leaders generally drew a sharp distinction between their *political* and *sindical* roles. Proselytizing for parties is carried out as an individual *adeco* or a *mepista*, but not as a part of one's union leadership responsibilities.

Nonetheless, in 12 of 13 Venezuelan unions, leaders that we inter-viewed acknowledged that they do work actively in political campaigns. They claim to do so as individuals. Interestingly, while Venezuelan union leaders work actively for their respective parties, unions generally do not endorse candidates officially. Only in a communist-dominated union in a plastics company in Barquisimeto were formal endorsements made. Nonendorsement of candidates seems to be a practice by which to avoid inflaming partisan divisions within the union.

The State As Benefactor Of Organized Labor

The Minimum Program of 1958 committed the Venezuelan state to look after the interests of organized labor. This was not a novel role; previous regimes from Gómez to the *trienio* had also provided induce-ments to organized labor. From the time of Gómez to the present, the benefits and privileges extended to organized labor often indicate a cooptive or preemptive intent on the part of the state. These initiatives generally did not result from labor conflict or pressures.[73] As such, these elite-initiated actions can be seen as efforts to strengthen the original incorporation bargain with labor.

The primary vehicle for extending privileges and benefits to organized labor has been reform of the labor law. We will focus in particular on the reforms that were introduced in the early 1970s as illustrative. Most of these measures were designed not only to implement Andrés Pérez's populist campaign promises, but also to preempt labor dissatisfaction with rising inflation. We shall also see a familiar pattern in Venezuelan labor history repeated — with "new carrots" came "new sticks" by which labor relations could be regulated more effectively.

Earlier we mentioned the first minimum wage law and the emergency wage increase of 1974. In the previous year, a reform of the labor law had provided for eight months of unemployment insurance and a vacation bonus by which one day of vacation would be added for each year of work. By a 1974 executive decree, President Andrés Pérez modified Article 37 of the Labor Law to require indemnity to fired workers under contract *regardless* of the reason for dismissal. Later that year, the law was changed to require payment of double indemnity if a worker was dismissed for "unjustifiable cause."[74] As a further carrot to labor, the rate of unionization was allowed to expand during the early years of the Andrés Pérez presidency.[75]

These inducements to labor were coupled with new measures to increase the state's capability to regulate labor relations. The revised Labor Law of 1973, for example, introduced binding arbitration in industries (like petroleum) that have a single collective contract when industry-wide (*rama de industria*) negotiations break down. A presidential order of 1975 provided for mandatory arbitration without appeals for all labor disputes involving public employees. Included under this order were workers in the nationalized petroleum industry. In addition, the Organic Law for Defense and Security gave the president the power to use the armed forces in security zones to preserve order.[76]

Yet the contemporary democratic state has provided real and substantial gains to organized labor, even if the intent was cooptive or preemptive and even if ample devices for social control exist. The state guarantee of access to collective bargaining along with favorable wage policies enabled wages of workers to keep up with inflation until the late 1970s. Collective bargaining enabled organized workers to negotiate benefits that otherwise would not have been forthcoming. Furthermore, through revision of the labor law, the state has secured for labor profit-sharing plans, subsidized retirement plans, social security, paid vacations, the eight-hour work day, and health and safety regulations.[77]

While these gains are very real and should not be overlooked, it is important to take into account constraints that are imposed on the labor movement by the original incorporative bargain. The labor movement poses no serious threat to private capital accumulation and, until 1980, never challenged the petroleum export model of economic development. Nor have unions in the past fought for redistributive policies or social programs to aid the rural and urban poor. Zero-sum redistributive policies that are likely to produce conflict are generally avoided in the Venezuelan semi-consociational system.

TABLE 10.4
Profit Margins of Selected Venezuelan Industries, 1971

Sector	(in percentages) Over Sales Venezuela	USA	Over Added Value Venezuela
Food	14.8	3.6	40.7
Beverages	33.5	12.2	47.7
Tobacco	14.8	4.1	31.1
Textiles	21.6	2.0	37.2
Leather Products	12.3	3.0	27.8
Footwear	12.4	7.4	28.9
Wood Products	11.2	6.2	24.2
Paper Products	23.2	11.2	49.1
Chemical Products	17.3	10.2	28.7
Petroleum Derivatives	4.1	5.0	22.7
Plastics	15.6	9.0	30.5
Basic Metals	16.5	7.0	31.5
Metal Products	22.9	3.4	42.0
Machinery	19.1	11.0	34.1
Total for Manufacturing	16.4	6.2	37.0

Source: Terry Karl, "The Political Economy of Petrodollars: Oil and Democracy in Venezuela" (Vol. 1), Unpublished Ph.D. Dissertation, Stanford University, 1982, p. 135.

To illustrate the innocuous character of the Venezuelan labor movement, one has to only look at the profit margins for Venezuelan industry. Data on profits in 1971 (Table 10.4) show that virtually all sectors of Venezuelan industry received substantially higher profit margins than their counterparts in the United States. The high profit margin can be explained by industrial concentration which increases the opportunity for price-fixing, by low labor costs, by low income taxes and nonexistent import taxes for capital goods and raw materials, and by state subsidies.[78] Labor has been unable to change any of these conditions.

The relative incapacity of the trade union movement to reorient state development strategy toward greater equity is revealed by data on (1) the distribution of national income to salaries and on (b) income distribution to the richest and poorest sectors of Venezuelan society. Table 10.5 provides data on the distribution of national income between salaries and capital profits over three decades in Venezuela. Additional data are provided for comparative purposes on the United States, Germany, and Belgium. These data show that the trade union movement in Venezuela has not produced any significant reallocation of income from capital formation to salaries. In fact, during the 1970s, there was a slight shift of income toward capital in Venezuela. By contrast, in all three cases of advanced industrial nations the shift over time has been consistently away from capital formation toward salaries.

TABLE 10.5
Distribution of National Income Between Salaries and Capital Profits

Country	Year	% Salaries	% Capital Profits
Venezuela	1950–1960	51.1	48.9
	1961–1970	51.1	49.0
	1971–1981	45.6	55.4
United States	1900–1924	55.8	44.2
	1925–1953	64.6	35.4
	1954–1963	69.9	30.1
	1964–1980	74.3	25.7
West Germany	1950	58.6	41.4
	1963	64.8	35.2
	1980	72.3	27.7
Belgium	1953	53.8	46.4
	1962	58.6	41.4
	1980	68.6	31.4

Source: Kenneth M. Coleman, "La politización de la clase obrera: Datos comparativos y el caso venezolano," Revista Relaciones de Trabajo, 6 (September 1985) Table 2, p. 149.

It is also instructive to examine trends in income distribution. Table 10.6 shows: (a) the percentage of salaries received by the richest 20 percent of the Venezuelan population from 1962 to 1981, (b) the percentage of salaries received by the poorest 20 percent during the same period, (c) the percentage of salaries received by the richest 5 percent, (d) the percentage of salaries received by the poorest 5 percent and (e) the differentials between the salaries of the richest and poorest sectors of society. It is apparent that there has been some redistribution of income from top income groups in the period from 1962 to 1981. However, very little redistribution has trickled down to the poorest 5 percent or the poorest 20 percent of the population. What redistribution has occurred has gone almost entirely to middle-income groups.[79] We cannot say if income gains by the middle sector are related to effective bargaining by unions representing skilled and technical workers or to a growing demand for such workers in an increasingly capital intensive economy. These, however, would be plausible inferences. What is apparent from table 10.6 is that there has been no significant redistribution of income to the large informal proletariat (bottom 40 percent) that might pose a real threat to profits and to capital formation. Additionally, it should be noted that Venezuela retains a highly uneven distribution of income even by Latin American standards.[80]

In sum, the trade union movement in Venezuela has achieved some significant gains for organized labor in the post-1958 era, but it has also

TABLE 10.6
Salary Distribution in Venezuela: 1962–1982

Year	Percentage of Salaries Received by Richest 5% of Population	Percentage of Salaries Received by Poorest 5% of Population	Number of Times Salaries of Richest 5% Exceed Poorest 5%	Percentage of Salaries Received by Richest 20% of Population	Percentage of Salaries Received by Poorest 20% of Population	Number of Times Salaries of Richest 20% Exceed Poorest 20%
1962	22.1	0.6	35.8	51.1	4.1	12.6
1970	19.7	0.6	33.9	48.8	4.6	10.6
1977	16.7	0.6	24.6	48.0	3.1	9.4
1978	14.5	0.7	22.3	47.6	4.8	9.8
1979	13.1	0.7	18.7	47.4	5.3	8.8
1980	11.2	0.7	15.4	45.1	5.3	8.5
1981	15.2	0.8	19.8	45.4	5.4	8.5

Source: Asdrúbal Baptista, "Más allá de optimisimo y del pesimismo: las transformaciones fundamentales del país," in Moisés Naím and Ramón Piñango, eds., El caso venezolano: una ilusión de armonía (Caracas: Ediciones IESA, 1984), pp. 32–33.

confronted structural limitations linked to the original incorporative bargain. These gains, however, have depended on an expanding economy with low inflation and on continuation of the oil bonanza.[81] By the late 1970s these favorable conditions began to deteriorate. How recent macroeconomic crises have strained the incorporative bargain and exposed cracks in the system of control shall now be examined.

ECONOMIC CRISIS AND CRACKS IN THE SYSTEM OF CONTROL

Organized labor was incorporated into the democratic state with the intent of minimizing labor conflict with capitalists and with political elites committed to a capitalist state. Through explicit agreements, elites hoped to hold together the semi-consociational state that they constructed in 1958. Success depended on economic expansion without inflation and on an oil bonanza. Without these conditions, resources would not be available for real wages to rise and simultaneously for capital formation to expand. Furthermore, without such conditions the state would confront greater difficulty in managing collective bargaining and in extending new benefits and privileges to labor. Thus, resource scarcity could generate the type of conflict that Venezuela's consociational arrangements were designed to preclude.

Suffice it to note that Venezuela has experienced various economic crises since the late 1970s. Since 1979, the annual GNP in Venezuela has shown virtually no change or has experienced negative growth. From 1979 to 1984, the nation experienced double-digit inflation in every year except 1983, while real wages declined.[82] The worldwide recession of 1982, the weakening of the OPEC cartel, and the debt crisis all have contributed to Venezuela's economic woes.

These economic conditions contributed to a shift in strategy on the part of the Venezuelan trade union movement toward greater political unionism. Such a development clearly implies the possible emergence of labor conflict with management and with political elites over public policy and development strategy. We shall examine more specific reasons for the development of political unionism and then show how it has been manifested in the 1980s.

What is surprising about the shift to political unionism is that it occurred in the Confederation of Venezuelan Workers (CTV) in which AD had consolidated its control. Thus it occurred in the mainstream of the Venezuelan labor movement that previously was committed to *concertación* with other major power contenders and to a strategy focused primarily on collective bargaining. We would suggest three reasons for the shift in strategy: (1) the failure of collective bargaining to protect the real wages of workers, (2) the increased financial independence of the CTV, and (3) rising rank-and-file political discontent.

Throughout the late 1970s, it became apparent that collective bargaining could not protect the real wages of workers. Even generous wage increases could be wiped out by inflation. Government wage and price policies offered the only hope.[83] Wage and price controls, along with automatic adjustment of wages to the cost of living, become major policy proposals of the CTV.

Political unionism requires a certain degree of autonomy of unions from external control. Union organizations are not likely to criticize prevailing public policies and to propose alternative visions of economic development if they are closely tied to ruling parties. By the 1980s, the CTV had seemingly become thoroughly controlled by AD. Yet, while still dependent on state subsidy, the CTV had also created its own financial empire beginning with the Workers' Bank established in 1966. According to one source, the CTV by 1980 was the owner of "banks, shipping companies, laundries, gypsum companies, automatic parts supply companies, prefabricated housing, urban housing, and dozens of private businesses."[84] This implied that the apparent subjugation to AD preferences might have been lessened, given the new financial autonomy.

The principal factor leading to a reorientation of strategy on the part of the CTV was likely the rising discontent on the part of rank-and-file workers. Our survey of workers in selected unions in 1979–1980 revealed considerable discontent with the policies of both Carlos Andrés Pérez (AD) as well as with the incumbent Social Christian President, Luis

Herrera Campíns.[85] Other studies have documented a steady erosion of support for government performance among the general populace during this era, although interestingly, support for the democratic regime remains high.[86] Rank-and-file discontent among workers created pressures on union elites to reconsider basic questions of union strategy. Given the relatively democratic structure of Venezuelan unions, it would not have been wise for leaders to disregard rank-and-file pressures. Unresponsiveness could well have created new opportunities for the left to capture control of the union movement.

Evidence of worker discontent increased during the presidency of Luis Herrera Campíns (1978–1983). Discontent was manifested not only against his conservative economic policies, but also against general economic conditions. President Herrera encountered: (1) an occupation of the National Cathedral by workers of a leftist textile union (*la Unión de Trabajadores de la Industria Textil*), (2) a general strike in the fall of 1979 to protest disinflationary policies that sacrificed jobs without containing the rise in prices for basic necessities, and (3) the disorder created when the labor minister refused to recognize the victory of the left in a steel workers union (SUTISS) in Ciudad Guayana.[87]

Certainly it was not surprising that leftist unions engaged in political activism at this time. What was surprising were the actions taken by the labor wing of AD and by the CTV in 1980. The labor wing of the party developed the *Proyecto de Tésis Sindical de Acción Democrática* (the Sindical Thesis of the Democratic Action Party) and the Eighth Congress of the CTV adopted the *Manifesto de Porlamar*. These documents went beyond critique of the incumbent COPEI administration and called into question the basic state capitalist model of economic development. Both documents called for a greater state role in regulating Venezuelan capitalism and in providing for mass welfare. Specific measures called for included the incorporation of workers into management (*cogestión*), industry-wide organization of unions, and semi-annual adjustments of salaries to reflect changes in the cost of living index.[88]

Since 1980, the CTV has continued to speak out on major policy issues. In 1982, the organization publicly stated that it would not accept "the imposition of sacrifices of the workers via unjustified reductions of the workforce, freezing of salaries or the repudiation of policies designed to improve work and living conditions for public service workers."[89] In 1983 and 1984, the CTV fought unsuccessfully to give greater regulatory powers to the Price Regulatory Commission set up in 1982. The reforms proposed by the CTV called for a tripartite commission that would have binding powers to regulate salaries and prices.[90] These actions illustrate the increasing use of "political unionism" by the CTV in the 1980s.[91] To adopt the strategy of political unionism does not mean, however, that political success will be attained. The new assertiveness of the CTV has yet to produce a dramatic reorientation of public policy and cannot be expected to do so in the near future.

CONCLUSIONS

It is clear that Venezuela's prolonged economic crisis has severely crippled the traditional consociational system upon which political stability has rested since 1958. Rising worker discontent in the context of relatively open and democratic union structures propelled the leadership of the union movement into political activism designed to protect the interests of workers. The resultant political unionism could result in a transformation of the Venezuelan state to one characterized by greater pluralism, social conflict, and possibly toward policy immobility.

On the other hand, it is possible that a new incorporative bargain can be worked out that will provide new forms of *concertación* between labor, capitalists, and the Venezuelan state. The fact that the Venezuelan labor movement has sought reforms such as *cogestión* and tripartite commissions within the context of existing state capitalism and competitive democracy suggests this possibility. In an environment of resource scarcity, however, it remains to be seen if state capitalism can coexist with any form of consociational democracy that permits genuine labor movement autonomy.

NOTES

We have benefited from the comments of Edward Epstein, Gilbert Merkx, and Jennifer McCoy. We are also grateful to the National Science Foundation (Grant SES 079-01798), to the University of Kentucky Research Foundation, and to the Council for International Exchange of Scholars for financial assistance in carrying out our research. The authors accept sole responsibility for all facts and interpretations presented herein.

   1. Charles W. Anderson, *Politics and Economic Change in Latin America* (New York: Van Nostrand and Reinhold Company, 1967), pp. 87–114.

   2. See David Pion-Berlin, "The Defiant State: Chile in the Post-Coup Era," paper delivered at the 1982 Annual Meeting of the American Political Science Association, Denver, Colorado.

   3. Control of the state may be "seized" via extra-legal means or "earned" via the mobilization of consent. In either case, the distinguishing feature of revolutionary change is the reorientation of public policy so that new interests are represented.

   4. See John D. Martz, "The Evolution of Democratic Politics in Venezuela," in Howard R. Penniman, ed., *Venezuela at the Polls: The National Elections of 1978* (Washington: American Enterprise Institute, 1980), p. 3.

   5. These included Generals José Antonio Pérez, Antonio Guzmán Blanco,

Juan Vicente Gómez, and Marcos Pérez Jímenez. See John V. Lombardi, *Venezuela: The Search for Order, The Dream of Progress* (New York: Oxford University Press, 1982), pp. 172, 189–190.

6. See Daniel Levine, *Conflict and Political Change in Venezuela* (Princeton, NJ: Princeton University Press, 1973), pp. 21.

7. On the formation of COPEI, see Donald L. Herman, *Christian Democracy in Venezuela* (Chapel Hill: University of North Carolina Press, 1980), pp. 1–22; 23–42.

8. Gene E. Bigler, *La política y el capitalismo de estado en Venezuela* (Madrid: Editorial Técnos, 1981), p. 67.

9. The truly essential source on this era is Steven Ellner, *Los partidos políticos y su disputa por el control del movimiento sindical en Venezuela, 1936–1948* (Caracas: Universidad Católica Andrés Bello, 1980), available in English via University Microfilms (No. 8012544) as a 1979 doctoral dissertation in history from the University of New Mexico. See note 16 below.

10. See Terry Karl, *The Political Economy of Petrodollars: Oil and Democracy in Venezuela*, 2 vols., unpublished Ph.D. dissertation, Stanford University, 1982, p. 93.

11. *Ibid.*, p. 94.

12. The *Confederación de Trabajadores de Venezuela* (CTV) is today the largest and dominant labor confederation with an estimated one million affiliates. Secondary confederations include the Social Christian CODESA (*Confederación de Sindicatos Autónomos de Venezuela*), with an estimated 60,000 affiliates; the communist CUTV (*Confederación Única de Trabajadores Venezolanos*), whose enrollment has been estimated at 80,000; and the *Confederación General de Trabajadores*, or CGT, whose membership was estimated recently at 30,000. See Bernard Lestienne, *El sindicalismo venezolano: curso de formacion socio-política* (Caracas: Centro Gumilla, 1981), p. 12.

13. On the events leading to a 1961 schism within AD and the labor movement, see Julio Godio, *El movimiento obrero venezolano, 1945–1964* (Caracas: Instituto Latinoamericano de Investigaciones Sociales, 1985), vol. 3, p. 227.

14. Karl, *The Political Economy*, p. 97.

15. See Terry Karl, "Petroleum and Political Pacts: The Transition to Democracy in Venezuela," (Working Papers of the Wilson Center, Latin American Program, Washington, D.C., 1984), pp. 9–10.

16. It should be noted that AD acquiesced to a labor policy that forbade strikes except in exceptional circumstances. See Steve Ellner, *Acción Democrática-Partido Comunista de Venezuela: Rivalry on the Venezuelan Left and in Organized Labor 1936–1945*, Ph.D. dissertation, University of New Mexico, 1979, p. 105.

17. Herman, *Christian Democracy*, pp. 27–31.

18. See Karl, "Petroleum and Political Pacts."

19. The *Unión Democrática Republicana* (URD) was the personalistic vehicle of Jóvito Villalba, a student leader of the generation of 1928 and perpetual figure in Venezuelan politics.

20. Karl, *Political Economy*, p. 114. See also Charles Bergquist, "Nuevos enfoques para el estudio del movimiento obrero en América Latina," *Revista Relaciones de Trabajo*, 3–4 (1984), p. 29, who argues that "the capitalists converted the labor movement into a partner."

21. See Karl, "Petroleum and Political Pacts." Also Hector Lucena, "Concertación y revision en las relaciones laborales," *Revista Relaciones de Trabajo*, 5 (1985), pp. 6–9.

22. Karl, "Political Economy," pp. 116–119.

23. *Ibid.*, p. 120.

24. *Ibid.*, pp. 120–122.

25. Arend Lijphart, *Democracy in Plural Societies: A Comparative Exploration* (New Haven: Yale University Press, 1977), p. 25.

26. Daniel H. Levine, "Venezuelan Politics: Past and Future," in Robert D. Bond, ed., *Contemporary Venezuela and Its Role in International Affairs* (New York: New York University Press, 1977), pp. 14–15. See also Andreas Boeckh, *Organized Labor and Government Under Conditions of Economic Scarcity: The Case of Venezuela*, unpublished Ph.D. dissertation, University of Florida, 1972, pp. 97–98.

27. As originally applied by Lijphart, the concept of consociational democracy assumed that plural segments of society would often be defined on the basis of ascriptive characteristics (religion, race, language). Social differentiation in Venezuela is less frequently based on ascriptive characteristics than in Belgium or the Netherlands, societies to which Lijphart originally applied the label. For this reason also, the label of semi-consociational is appropriate. However, the norms of "agreeing to disagree" and "letting leaders negotiate for subgroups" that characterize consociationalism *are* found in Venezuela.

28. *Inter alia*, Lucena, "Papel del sindicalismo venezolano."

29. See Margarita López and Nikolaus Werz, "El estado venezolano y el movimiento sindical (1958–1980)," *Revista Relaciones de Trabajo*, 2 (1983), p. 60.

30. *Ibid.*, note 14, p. 60.

31. See various analyses in *Revista relaciones de Trabajo*, 7 (1986).

32. This was Article 178. See Boeckh, *Organized Labor and Government*, p. 170.

33. Boeckh, p. 136.

34. Boeckh argues that percentage of workers covered by a collective contract provides a better estimate of unionization in Venezuela than does the actual number because of large numbers of nonexistent paper unions.

35. Boeckh, Chapters 4 and 5.

36. See Title 6, Article 180–200, *Ley de Trabajo*. See Juan Garay, *Legislación laboral práctica, con la reforma de 1983* (Caracas: Librería Ciafre, 1985), pp. 44–49. Multiple unions are permitted in a given industry and even in a given worksite. The petroleum industry is a good example; we studied six separate unions at two refineries in Puntio Fijo, Falcón, in 1979–1980.

37. See Title 6, Article 189 as illustrative. The executive committee of each union is required to submit at least every six months a detailed account of revenues and spending to a general assembly of the union. This report is required to be sent to the Labor Inspector, an officer from the Labor Ministry.

38. See Title 6, Article 185, *Ley de Trabajo* in Garay, *Legislación laboral*.

39. See Title 6, Article 199, *Ley de Trabajo* in Garay, *Legislación laboral*.

40. See examples cited in Boeckh, *Organized Labor*, 204–209. Various authors note that in the *trienio* union registration was granted more rapidly to AD unions than to those affiliated with other parties.

41. See Table 2 in Lucena, "Papel del sindicalismo venezolano," p. 128.

42. See Kenneth M. Coleman, "La politización de la clase obrera: datos comparativos y el caso venezolano," *Revista Relaciones de Trabajo*, 6 (1985), pp. 145–167.

43. See Guillermo O'Donnell, *Modernization and Bureaucratic-Authoritarianism* (Berkeley, California: Institute of International Studies, 1972).

44. The petition is submitted to the local office of the Labor Ministry.

45. Personal communication of May 24, 1986, to Kenneth Coleman. See also Title VIII, Articles 216–240, *Ley de Trabajo* in Garay, *Legislación laboral*.

46. López and Werz, "El estado venezolano," pp. 62–63.

47. See Boeckh, *Organized Labor and Government*, pp. 203–204.

48. As, for example, when the National Cathedral was taken over by textile union strikers in the late seventies. See López and Werz, "El estado venezolano," p. 65.

49. McCoy argues that increased labor militance after 1969 led to increasing utilization of the state, rather than political parties, to regulate and to control the union movement. See Jennifer L. McCoy, "From Party to State: Inducements, Constraints and Labor in Venezuela," *Latin American Research Review* (forthcoming).

50. See Charles L. Davis "Political Control and Working Class Mobilization: Venezuela and Mexico" (unpublished manuscript) Chapter 2.

51. On the tendency of collective bargaining to be carried out at the plant level in Venezuela, see Hector Lucena, "Concertación y revisión en las relaciones laborales," *Revista Relaciones de Trabajo*, 5 (1985), pp. 11–12.

52. See Lucena, "Papel del sindicalismo," pp. 137–138.

53. See Lucena, "Papel del sindicalismo." Even after 1974, real wages continued to increase until the late 1970s. See Table 9 in Julio Godio, *El movimiento obrero venezolano, 1965–1980* (Caracas: Editorial Ateneo de Caracas, 1984), vol. 3, p. 33.

54. William H. Form, "Job Unionism vs. Political Unionism in Four Countries," in Irving L. Horowitz, John C. Leggett, and Martin Oppenheimer, eds., *The American Working Class: Prospects for the 1980s* (New Brunswick, New Jersey: Transaction Books, 1979), pp. 214–230.

55. See Francisco Zapata, "Las organizaciones sindicales," in Rubén Katzman and José Luis Reyna, eds., *Fuerza de trabajo y movimientos sindicales en América Latina* (Mexico City: El Colegio de México, 1979), p. 196.

56. See Charles Bergquist, *Labor in Latin America: Comparative Essays on Chile, Argentina, Venezuela, and Colombia* (Stanford: Stanford University Press, 1986), pp. 191–273.

57. See Ellner, *Acción Democrática-Partido Comunista de Venezuela*, chapters 3 and 4.

58. See Bergquist, *Labor in Latin America*, pp. 251–254. Also Ellner, *Acción Democratica-Partido Comunista de Venezuela*.

59. See López and Werz, "El estado venezolano," pp. 60–61.

60. Raúl Leoni was subsequently to become President under the AD label, 1963–1968. On the foundation of the CTV see Ellner, *Los partidos políticos*, and John D. Martz, "Growth and Democratization of the Venezuelan Labor Movement," *Inter-American Economic Affairs*, 17:2 (1963), p. 8.

61. Karl, *Political Economy*, p. 122.

62. See Lucena, "El papel del sindicalismo," p. 125.

63. AD was aided by the expulsion of the Communists in 1961. See data presented in table 10.3.

64. See Godio, *El movimiento obrero*, p. 59.

65. See Boeckh, *Organized Labor and Government*, pp. 201–202. Also López and Werz, "El estado venezolano," p. 64.

66. Karl, *The Political Economy*, p. 122.

67. Stuart I. Fagan, *The Venezuelan Labor Movement: A Study in Political Unionism*, Unpublished Ph.D. dissertation, University of California at Berkeley, 1974, p. 120.

68. *Ibid.*, pp. 121–122.

69. See José A. Silva Michelena and Heinz Rudolf Sonntag, *El proceso electoral de 1978* (Caracas: Editorial Ateneo de Caracas, 1979), pp. 37–53; Boeckh, *Organized Labor and Government*, pp. 212–217.

70. See Davis, *Political Control*, chapter 2.

71. Even if such an alliance were formed, "traditional leftist" parties might opt for a more conciliatory political strategy. The moderation and passivity of the 'traditional left' has caused a recent fission within the leftist union movement. A splinter group of more militant leftists developed in the 1980s and has been highly critical of unions affiliated with "traditional leftist" parties. See Daniel Hellinger, "Venezuelan Democracy and the Challenge of the 'Nuevo Sindicalismo'," paper presented at the Meeting of the Latin American Studies Association (LASA), Boston, Massachusetts, October 1986. In this context, "traditional left" includes parties that reentered the democratic political process after the Caldera amnesty program in the late 1960s or after the Soviet invasion of Czechoslovakia.

72. *Ibid.*, Chapter 9.

73. See López and Werz, "El estado venezolano," pp. 61, 67. They suggest that some signs of independent action by the CTV were occurring in the early 1980s.

74. See Godio, *El movimiento obrero*, pp. 38–39.

75. *Ibid.*, pp. 37–39.

76. Lopez and Werz, "El estado venezolano," p. 82.

77. See Title III, Chapter III, Section II of the *Ley de Trabajo* in Garay, *Legislación laboral*, 25–28. The importance of these provisions is suggested by a recent analysis indicating that the most important determinant of job satisfaction among Venezuelan workers was their degree of satisfaction with the way profit-sharing had been implemented in their company. See Kenneth M. Coleman, Carolina Codetta and Adolfo Vargas, "Condiciones de trabajo y satisfacción en el empleo," paper presented at National Tripartite Seminar on Work Conditions, sponsored by the Venezuelan Ministry of Labor and the International Labor Organization, January 27–29, 1986, Caracas.

78. See Karl, *The Political Economy*, p. 127.

79. Also size of middle sectors expanded significantly suggesting that there was significant upward mobility during the 1960s and 1970s. See Table 7 in Godio, *El movimiento obrero*, p. 30.

80. See Table 9 in Asdrúbal Baptista, "Más allá del optimismo y del pesimismo: las transformaciones fundamentales del país," in Moisés Naím and

Ramon Piñago, eds., *El caso Venezuela: una ilusión de armonía* (Caracas: Ediciones IESA, 1984), p. 35.

81. See Lucena, "El papel del sindicalismo," pp. 123–144.

82. See Table 4 in Lucena, *ibid.*, p. 131. See also figures on real incomes in Norelius Betancourt, "Empleo y salario en Venezuela," *Sic*, 125 (1985), pp. 197–203.

83. This argument is developed in Lucena, "El papel del sindicalismo," pp. 123–144.

84. See López and Werz, "El estado venezolano," p. 64.

85. See Tables 4 and 5 in Charles L. Davis, "The Labor Aristocracy Thesis and the Political Quiescence of Labor," *Social Science Quarterly*, 67:2 (1986), pp. 328–429.

86. See Arístides Torres, "Evaluación política y deterioro del proceso democrático," paper prepared for a meeting of the Study Group on Comparative Public Opinion, Maracaibo, Venezuela (June 21–23, 1984). Also Enrique A. Baloyra, "Public Opinion and Support for the Regime: 1973–83," in John D. Martz and David J. Myers, eds., *Venezuela: The Democratic Experience* (New York: Praeger, 1986), pp. 34–71.

87. The role of the new militant left in these activities is discussed in Hellinger, "Venezuelan Democracy."

88. See Godio, *El movimiento obrero*, pp. 120–135, 141–175.

89. Lucena, "El papel del sindicalismo," p. 139.

90. *Ibid.*, p. 140.

91. Numerous other examples of CTV political activism in the post-1980 era are presented in Lucena, p. 138.

Chapter 11

Conclusion: The Question of Labor Autonomy

Edward C. Epstein

*I*n the discussion of the relation between trade unions and the state found in the nine case countries under study here, a prevailing theme has been the repeated attempts of state elites to subordinate organized labor. What has differed has been the ability (and willingness) of union leadership to resist and the resulting degree of labor autonomy attainable in any one country at any particular moment. The various shifts experienced in the relationship in these countries are seen as directly reflective of the respective power resources each side is able to call upon. If autonomy is to be measured in terms of more or less, rather than by its absolute presence or absence, it is also likely to fluctuate because of the political conditions in each country at any historical conjuncture. The purpose of this concluding chapter is to depict the differing configuration of autonomy found in the cases examined in the contemporary period and, in so doing, to offer preliminary explanations for the comparative success or failure of individual labor movements in asserting their relative political independence vis-à-vis the state.

The concept of labor autonomy, especially autonomy from state control, elicits a variety of normative responses in different types of social theory. In what might be called liberal pluralism, the autonomy of interest groups (including economic ones, like organized labor and business) is posited as a good, given the preconception that only where the various groups are free to seek to maximize the interests of their members will the general welfare be enhanced. In this view, the role of the state in the political process is limited to that of being a guarantor for a set of commonly agreed to rules on inter-group competition.[1] The notion of interest group pluralism, however, has tended to have far fewer advocates in Latin America than alternatives like Marxism or corporatism.

Such theoretical alternatives to pluralism share neither its stress on the value of group autonomy nor its deemphasis of the role of the state in politics. The Marxist view that the state is controlled by particular social

275

classes rather than being politically neutral suggests that isolated worker organizations will achieve little in terms of realizing their economic interests as long as the state is dominated by their class enemies; led by a politically aware vanguard party, groups of workers ought to actively support the revolutionary struggle to confront and seize state power in order to transform class relations and end exploitation. Marxism is vague about the possible role of trade unions in the socialist society to come.[2] The corporatist view, in its turn, stresses the need to channel group expression through a limited number of official structures controlled by the state if the disruptive conflicts endorsed by pluralism and, *a fortiori*, by Marxism, are to be avoided. Group interests are to be consciously subordinated to those of the nation as perceived by the state elite. In theory at least, a presumption exists that state behavior will not systematically favor any one sector of society at the expense of others.[3]

In practice, labor leaders find that trade union autonomy has been subject to considerable pressure from virtually all governments regardless of their particular ideological inspiration. Democrats and authoritarians; conservatives, reformers, and radicals; populists and technocratic elites: all have felt that organized labor occupies too strategic a place in the economy to be allowed unrestricted use of its major means of influence, the threat to strike. Naturally, the limits sought by populist social democrats in terms of direct or indirect controls are far more modest than those of an exclusionary bureaucratic-authoritarian dictatorship. Where the former might rely on mechanisms like the right to grant official recognition to unions before they are able to engage in collective bargaining, or the establishment of mandatory state-supervised worker/management conciliation talks prior to a strike, the latter may impose officially decreed wage levels, suspend the right to strike, and/or exercise a veto over the choice of all union leaders.

If, from their common perspective of being responsible for the economy, all governments have seen the utility of imposing limits on labor autonomy, not all have been equally successful in implementing this objective. Those which are politically weak and lack resources (like unified military support and widespread popular legitimacy), are certainly in no position to induce labor compliance. Trade union resistance, in turn, is more likely to be forthcoming where strong partisan loyalties separate the major portion of organized labor from the government. Where such partisan cleavage is reinforced by strong ideological differences — especially those based on unmuted class antagonism – labor's opposition is likely to become militant. For both labor and government, however, internal unity seems a precondition for effective political action.

By the contemporary period under discussion in the present volume, most labor leaders had accepted the necessity of an alliance between labor and particular political parties capable of intervening in politics in their behalf so as to attenuate the effects of what might otherwise be suffocating restrictions placed on union behavior. Although such an alliance itself would result in limits on labor's freedom to act, it could offer important compensation. Under the best of conditions where a party allied to the labor movement as a whole, or to some of its constituent parts controlled the state, clientelistic arrangements typically have resulted in the unions exchanging their political support for the government for economic and political favoritism. On the other hand, should the union's ally be in the opposition, its ability to win significant government concessions as the price of labor peace would be less likely, unless those in power felt specially vulnerable.

The type of political integration achieved by labor varied significantly, depending on the existing political regime.[4] Although corporatist in requiring worker affiliation with state-controlled labor organizations, bureaucratic-authoritarian regimes sought to exclude labor and its partisan allies from any meaningful political participation. The state attempted to impose a ban on party ties and usually forbade the existence of any single national-level representative body which could possibly rival the labor ministry. In the socialist regime studied, union membership only gradually became universal as political organizations in general were revitalized after 1970. While the single national labor confederation is not officially part of the state, financing itself entirely from dues, the most important leadership positions are indirectly elected with little or no opposition; the presumption here is that such top leaders must all be acceptable to the ruling Communist Party. Populist authoritarianism shares with socialism a degree of worker input in policy making, but lacks consistency in how this is structurally organized. For those populist authoritarian regimes which incorporate organized labor through a single official party, there are others which have favored a direct non-mediated link to the state bureaucracy, or even a multitude of contacts via several rival labor confederations (each sponsored by a different political party or by the regime itself). Under a democratic regime, the unions have been free to develop a variety of ties with one or more parties, ranging from centrist populists of the Social Democrat and Christian Democratic type, to the Marxist Socialists and Communists on the left. The frequent competition — and the resulting divisions — within the labor movement between populists and Marxists have weakened the unions' political impact, but have guaranteed a maximum of autonomy. Confederations thought to be too subservient to any government face the prospect of losing affiliates to groups more demonstrative of their support for worker concerns.

The degree of political integration with any regime and concurrent loss of labor autonomy then varies both with the nature of the regime and with the political fortune of any specific administration holding office. What follows in the next section is an attempt to measure such autonomy quantifiably and to rank the particular counties included here for study along the continuum of high to low labor independence from state control. Again, the present discussion will conclude with an attempt to explain such variation both by country and over time.

COMPARING LABOR AUTONOMY IN NINE COUNTRIES

While autonomy can be conceptualized in terms of institutional independence (versus integration) as well as by any resulting conflict emerging between organized labor and the state, the approach adopted in this section favors the conflict approach due to the availability of quantifiable data on strikes which are seen as particularly useful in facilitating objective comparison.[5] The degree of union integration is likely to be much harder to measure over time with any precision. An operationalization utilizing strikes rests on the assumption that autonomy is a relational term resulting from the respective power capacities of union and state actors. The withholding of labor in organized strikes is the workers' major political weapon; most governments are presumed, under normal conditions, to want to avoid strikes given their costs to the national economy.[6] The resulting strike activity or its absence can be seen as a direct indication of the union's ability to demonstrate its power capability as against the government's ability to prevent that from occurring.

Given that several different types of strike statistics exist, the problem to be resolved is which is best to use for the purposes of measuring levels of labor autonomy. The three major categories available consist of the total number of strikes per year, the number of strikers participating per year, and the number of general strikes. At first glance, the incidence of general strikes would seem the most relevant for the present concern. Such strikes, by their very nature, have a direct political impact since they are intended to publicly pressure the government to respond to a list of grievances raised by a major labor body, usually a national confederation. The typical practice of limiting in advance such actions to a specified number of hours of work stoppage suggests that they are intended as a demonstration to the authorities of the extent of popular support for these demands rather than as an effort to undermine the government.[7] In a sense, the general strike represents an invitation to those in power to negotiation, but one where labor has a position of some strength. Although problems occur in defining what constitutes an authentic general strike (for example, must it be called by a truly national labor organization? must it be reasonably successful in terms of the actual number of participants?), the major difficulty consists in the lack of any single central recorded source in which to find general strike figures and the resulting variable reliability of the information obtainable through the perusal of the relevant monographic literature. The figures used here may include or omit some seemingly doubtful cases.

The statistics for what are nominally economic strikes might seem a somewhat curious measure of union political autonomy. What is argued here, however, is if an individual strike may not have much direct political reverberation on its own (although that may not be true where the strike occurs in a particularly important industry), the mass of all economic strikes and strikers involved in any specified period will have a noticeable indirect political impact where it is large enough to lead to significantly lowered economic production and services. Such an effect can become directly political should a wave of strikes be perceived as resulting from worker militancy encouraged or centrally organized by a particular labor confederation. Given that the historical experience of many countries finds increases in strikes and strikers coinciding with the calling of one or more general strikes, reason exists to include these data along with those for the political general strike. One final reason for the use of the total number of strikes and strikers relates to cases where general strikes are rare, but where the existence of other strikes would indicate some — if, admittedly, much less — union autonomy.

Similar problems exist as to reliable sources for the number of strikes and strikers. While the International Labor Organization publishes figures for a number of countries provided by their governments, not all countries are included, information is often missing for particular years, and governments themselves distort the data they report to suit their own ends. In some cases, such gaps can be filled from unofficial sources. On the other hand, cases exist of more than a single numerical estimate and, embarrassingly, the two data series may not be consistent either numerically or in terms of overall upward or downward trends. Despite these data problems, the inclusion of more rather than fewer indicators of union autonomy will yield a more complete account and, hence, will be better for the purposes of describing the configuration to be found in the nine case countries discussed in this volume.

The figures on general strikes for the recent 1970–1986 period found in Table 11.1 are thought to be the most important in terms of measuring autonomy from the state, given their directly political nature as discussed earlier. Representing the average number of general strikes per year, the figures at the bottom of the table allow us to group the nine countries on autonomy into five categories: (1) high — Brazil (plus Uruguay in 1985–1986); (2) medium-high — Argentina; (3) medium — Peru (plus Chile in 1970–1973); (4) medium-low — Chile, Uruguay, Colombia, Mexico, and Venezuela (plus Chile after 1980); and (5) low — Cuba.[8] In

TABLE 11.1
General Strikes, 1970–1986

	Arg.	Braz.	Chile	Col.	Cuba	Mex.	Peru	Urug.	Ven.
1970	3	0	0	0	0	0	0	0	0
1971	1	0	0	1	0	0	0	0	0
1972	2	0	1[a]	0	0	0	0	0	
1973	0	0	2[a]	0	0	0	0	1	0
1974	0	0	0	0	0	0	0	0	0
1975	1	0	0	0	0	0	0	0	0
1976	1	0	0	0	0	0	0	0	0
1977	0	0	0	1	0	0	1	0	0
1978	0	0	0	0	0	0	3	0	0
1979	1	0	0	0	0	0	2	0	1
1980	0	0	0	0	0	0	0	0	0
1981	1	0	0	1	0	0	2	0	0
1982	1	0	0	0	0	0	0	0	0
1983	1	2	1	0	0	1[b]	2	0	0
1984	1	5	1	0	0	1[b]	2	0	0
1985	2	15	0	1	0	0	—[d]	2[c]	0
1986	4	25	1	0	0	0	—[d]	2[c]	0
Totals:	19	47	6	4	0	2	12	4	1

Sources: Argentina, Edward Epstein chapter in this volume; Brazil: Leigh Payne, "The Brazilian Labor Movement and the New Republic," paper presented at the meetings of the Latin American Studies Association, New Orleans, 1988, p. 13; Chile: Jaime Ruiz-Tagle chapter in this volume; Colombia: Rocío Londoño chapter in this volume, and Edgar Caicedo, *Historia de las luchas sindicales en Colombia* (Bogotá: Ed. CEIS, 1982), p. 181; Mexico: Kevin Middlebrook, "The Sounds of Silence: Organized Labor's Response to Economic Crisis in Mexico," paper presented at the meetings of the American Political Science Association, Washington, D.C., 1988, p. 11; Peru: Isabel Yepes and Jorge Bernedo, *La sindicalización en el Perú* (Lima: Universidad Catílica, 1985), p. 33, Denis Sulmont, *El movimiento obrero peruano, 1890–1980* (Lima: Tarea, 1980), pp. 112–125 and Nigel Haworth chapter in this volume; Uruguay: Martin Gargiulo chapter in this volume. Venezuela: Charles Davis and Kenneth Coleman chapter in this volume. There is no indication of any general strikes having taken place in Cuba from 1970 to the present.
[a] Includes truckers/shopkeepers strikes.
[b] Includes "paros civicos" of those years.
[c] 1985–86 figure of 4 was arbitrarily divided in half for each year.
[d] No data available.

discussing the two countries with the most general strikes per year, Brazil and Uruguay (in 1985–1986), it is important to note that these cases only occur after the restoration of national-level labor organizations — in Brazil from 1983 when the CUT and what was to become the present CGT were organized as the first national labor organizations permitted since the 1964 military coup, and in Uruguay, with the reestablishment of the old CNT in the restored democracy. As a rule, general strikes in military regimes occur mainly when authoritarian governments are declining in popular support and political legitimacy. Among those countries with the lowest number, the two Mexican strikes (the *paros cívicos*) and two of those in Chile (one each in 1972 and 1973) were organized by minority elements in the local labor movements and had a smaller number of adherents. It is again worth noting that no general strikes occurred in Uruguay during the military regime or in Chile for almost the first ten years of that country's military rule. The conclusions suggested by the data relate to the difficulty of organizing a mass labor protest against a well intrenched military regime that, as a result of considerable support from parts of the population, is willing to use repressive force to dissuade opposition from protesting government anti-worker policies.

Table 11.2 provides information on both the number of ordinary strikes occurring in the 1970–1986 period and estimates of the number of strikers participating. Of the two sets of data included, that on the number of participants may be somewhat more revealing since it indicates the unions' ability to demonstrate their capacity to mobilize the workers at different times. As was done with general strikes, the case countries can be comparatively ranked on this measure of labor autonomy: (1) high — Peru (and Chile in the years immediately prior to the 1973 coup); (2) medium-high — Argentina (plus Brazil after 1978); (3) medium — Brazil and Chile for the whole period studied (plus, probably, Uruguay before and after its military government); (4) medium-low — Venezuela and probably Uruguay for the entire period; (5) and low — Colombia, Cuba, and Mexico (as well as Brazil prior to 1978, Chile since 1974, including the post-1980 period, and Uruguay from 1974 to 1984).[9] Cuba is placed in the lowest category given the view of most observers that there has been little or no strike activity there during the Castro years.[10] While the figures used for Mexico only include strikers in local jurisdictional strikes, a doubling (or even a tripling) of these to take into account participants in federal jurisdiction strikes does not change the overall evaluation to any significant degree. Although there are no figures available on strike participation in Uruguay, the level on the other indicators suggests a moderately high strike participation before and after the military government, but with virtually no strikes during harshly authoritarian rule.[11]

The average number of strikes per year is seen here as the crudest measure of labor autonomy from the state given the likely variation in interpretation of its impact on the political atmosphere, a rather subjective matter at best. The nine countries can once again be grouped from the highest to the lowest in terms of the overall frequency of strikes: (1) high — Chile, Mexico, and Peru (plus Uruguay in 1985–1986); (2) medium-high — Argentina (and Brazil after 1978); (3) medium — Brazil, Colombia (based upon a weighted average of the two data sets), and Venezuela; (4) medium-low — Uruguay (and Chile after 1980); and (5) low — Cuba.[12]

In terms of labor autonomy as that concept has been operationally

TABLE 11.2
Number of Strikes (in 1000s) & Number of Strikers/EAP[a], 1970–1986

Year	Argentina Stri	Kers	Brazil Stri	Kers	Chile Stri	Kers	Colombia A[b] Stri	Kers	Colombia B Stri	Kers
1970	0116	—	—	—	1819	223.7	—	—	—	—
1971	0237	—	—	—	2696	099.3	037	—	—	—
1972	0187	—	—	—	3325	127.6	067	—	—	—
1973	0214	—	—	—	2050	224.6	053	—	—	—
1974	0543	027.5	—	—	—	—	075	—	—	—
1975	1266	—	—	—	—	—	109	—	—	—
1976	0154	018.9	—	—	—	—	058	—	—	—
1977	0100	050.0	—	—	—	—	093	—	—	—
1978	0040	020.3	0137	014.2	—	—	068	—	266	02.8
1979	0188	030.1	0224	081.9	—	—	060	—	137	03.5
1980	0261	033.9	0081	016.5	0089	007.9	049	—	261	03.5
1981	—	—	0079	—	—	006.4	—	—	219	02.6
1982	—	—	0126	—	—	000.5	—	—	149	06.4
1983	—	—	0312	061.3	0041	001.0	—	—	146	05.6
1984	0717	401.1	0407	035.7	0038	001.0	—	—	147	03.1
1985	0344	—	0689	131.2	0042	002.1	—	—	087	01.0
1986	0563	—	1128	110.0	0041	000.9	—	—	—	—
Ave.	352		187[c]		1127[d]		67		177	
Ave.		83.1		64.5		47.0[d]		—		3.6

Year	Cuba Stri	Kers	Mexico[e] Stri	Kers	Peru Stri	Kers	Uruguay Stri	Kers	Venezuela Stri	Kers
1970	—	—	0206	01.0	345	026.0	—	—	064	07.8
1971	—	—	0204	00.6	377	036.6	—	—	106	12.1
1972	—	—	0207	00.2	409	028.9	—	—	172	07.4
1973	—	—	0211	00.5	788	089.2	—	—	250	13.1
1974	—	—	0742	01.1	570	075.8	—	—	116	04.6
1975	—	—	0236	00.6·	779	125.4	—	—	100	06.8
1976	—	—	0547	01.4	440	050.8	—	—	171	08.5
1977	—	—	0476	00.7	234	251.0	—	—	214	15.3
1978	—	—	0758	00.8	364	258.9	—	—	140	05.7
1979	—	—	0795	00.9	653	151.3	—	—	145	05.1
1980	—	—	1339	02.2	739	084.1	—	—	195	14.4
1981	—	—	1066	01.6	871	145.0	—	—	129	06.1
1982	—	—	1925	01.2	809	093.8	—	—	102	02.9
1983	—	—	0216	02.1	643	124.9	—	—	067	03.2
1984	—	—	0427	02.9	509	107.5	—	—	073	02.2
1985	—	—	0159	02.4	566	035.2	557[f]	—	099	02.3
1986	—	—	0312	03.4	642	034.8	557[f]	—	—	—
Ave.	—		539		573		86[f]		134	
Ave.		—		1.4		101.1		—		7.3

Sources: Strike statistics. Argentina: those for 1970–1972 are from Guillermo O'Donnell, *1966–1973: El estado bureaucrático autoritario* (Buenos Aires: Ed. del Belgrano, 1982), p. 439; for 1973, from Elizabeth Jelin, "Conflictos laborales en la Argentina," *Estudios Sociales*, 9, (1977), p. 46; for 1974–1975, ILO, *Yearbook of Labour Statistics*, 1978, p. 622; for 1976–1980, Jelin [for the first three months of 1976] and Ronaldo Munck, et al., *Argentina from Anarchism to Peronism* (London: Zed Books, 1987), p. 229, for the remaining time; for 1984, *El Bimestre*, January–February 1985, p. 15; for 1985–1986, Héctor Palomino, "Los conflictos laborales de 1986," *El Bimestre*, January–February, 1987, p. 11. Brazil: for 1978–1979, Maria Herminia Tavares de Almeida, "Sindicalismo brasileiro e pacto social," in Comisión de Movimientos Laborales (ed.), *El sindicalismo latinoamericano en los ochenta* (Santiago: CLACSO, 1985) p. 113. 1980–1982, from ILO, 1986, p. 924; and for 1983–1986, Leigh Payne, "The Brazilian Labor Movement and the New Republic," Paper presented at the meetings of the Latin American Studies Association, New Orleans, 1988, p. 19. Chile, Colombia B, Mexico, Peru, and Venezuela: from ILO, 1986, pp. 924–927. For Colombia A, from Alvaro Delgado, *Politica y movimiento obrero, 1970–83* (Bogota: Ed. CEIS, 1984), p. 122. For Uruguay, Martín Gargiulo chapter in this volume.

For Strikers. Argentina: sources listed above for 1974, 1976–1980 — except those of 1976 which begin in April after the coup — and 1984. Brazil: for 1978–1980, Maria Helena Alves, *State and Opposition in Military Brazil* (Austin: University of Texas Press, 1985), pp. 197, 199, 208; for 1983–1986, Payne. Chile, Colombia, Mexico, Peru, and Venezuela: same as above.

Stri   = The number of strikes in 1000s.
Kers   = The adjusted number of strikers participating in strikes.
—   = No figures available.
[a] The number or strikers/year has been divided by the size of the economically active population so as to control for the differences in population between the countries; large countries are seen as likely to have more strikers than small countries, all other things being equal. The number of strikes, however, is seen as more a factor of the number of individual unions able to strike rather than population.
[b] While the figures for Colombia A seem too low as compared with those of Colombia B for the years where they overlap, they probably are internally consistent and, hence, show strike trends for the entire 1970s when the more reliable official figures are not available.
[c] The Brazilian figures are for the entire period, not just those from 1978. Excluding the earlier period, the averages for the last ten years are 354 strikes per year and 64.5 score on the number of strikers.
[d] The average presented for Chile is for the entire time period. Taking just that interval from 1980 characterized by far lower union autonomy, the average number of strikes falls to 50 and that of strikers to 2.8. The averages for the more active period prior to the 1973 coup correspondingly rise to 2473 for strikes and to 168.8 for strikers.
[e] The figures for Mexico represent only local jurisdiction strikes.
[f] The figures presented for Uruguay in 1985–1986 were presented as a single figure for the two year period in the source used; they have been divided arbitrarily in half here to get the figures in the table. The figure presented for average strikes is for the 1974–1986 period.

defined here, the case countries discussed in this volume can be compared either for the most recent 1970–1986 period taken as a whole, or for any subpart where the behavior of organized labor has been atypical. To facilitate such comparison, I propose the combined use of all three measures in a weighted index. Given their greater importance as measures, rankings on the number of general strikes will be given three times the weight and those on strike participants twice the weight of the average total of all ordinary strikes. The weightings are admittedly arbitrary, but in general conformity with the argument developed earlier in this section. Table 11.3 provides the results of such averages. The cases fall into four categories of autonomy: (1) high — Argentina, Brazil, and

TABLE 11.3
Weighted Labor Autonomy Scores, 1970–1986

	General Strikes (× 3)	Strikers (× 2)	Strikes (× 1)	Scores
Cases				
A.Entire Period:				
Argentina	4 × 3 = 12	4 × 2 = 8	4 × 1 = 4	24
Brazil	5 × 3 = 15	3 × 2 = 6	4 × 1 = 4	25
Colombia	2 × 3 = 6	1 × 2 = 2	3 × 1 = 3	11
Chile	2 × 3 = 6	3 × 2 = 6	5 × 1 = 5	17
Cuba	1 × 3 = 3	1 × 2 = 2	1 × 1 = 1	6
Mexico	2 × 3 = 6	1 × 2 = 2	5 × 1 = 5	12
Peru	3 × 3 = 9	5 × 2 = 10	5 × 1 = 5	24
Uruguay	2 × 3 = 6	2 × 2 = 4	2 × 1 = 2	12
Venezuela	2 × 3 = 6	2 × 2 = 4	3 × 1 = 3	13
B. Sub-Periods:				
Brazil				
1978–1986	5 × 3 = 15	4 × 2 = 8	4 × 1 = 4	27
Chile				
1970–1973	3 × 3 = 9	5 × 2 = 10	5 × 1 = 5	24
Chile				
1980–1986	2 × 3 = 6	2 × 2 = 4	2 × 1 = 2	12
Uruguay				
1985–1986	5 × 3 = 15	3 × 2 = 6	5 × 1 = 5	26

Sources: See cites for individual countries in tables 11.1 and 11.2.
Scoring Explanation: For each of the three measures of labor autonomy, a high ranking = 5, medium-high = 4, medium = 3, medium-low = 2, and low = 1. All such general strike evaluations were weighed by a factor of 3, those for strikers by 2, and those for ordinary strikes by 1, to reflect their relative importance as argued in the text.

Peru (plus Chile in 1970–1973 and Uruguay in 1985–1986); (2) medium-high autonomy — the period average for Chile; (3) medium-low — Colombia, Mexico, Uruguay, and Venezuela (plus Chile in 1980–1986), and (4) low — Cuba.[13]

A POSSIBLE EXPLANATION FOR LABOR AUTONOMY

How can autonomy be best explained? One strategy is to single out those cases where its presence is the strongest in order to look for commonalties. At first glance, the three countries exhibiting the highest level of long-term trade union autonomy — Argentina, Brazil, and Peru — would appear to have relatively little in common. Taking just the factor of union organization, while Argentina has had a single national labor confederation going back to 1930, Brazil banned any such organizations over most of the last 50 years, and Peru saw a plurality of rival groups competing in those years when they were not underground. Nevertheless, important similarities are there, as, indeed, there are for those cases with the lowest autonomy levels.

The focus adopted in this volume has been to stress the linkages between organized labor and the society in which it operates, with particular emphasis both on the institutions of the state itself and on the political parties. What is suggested here as a general hypothesis is that relative labor autonomy results when those controlling the state are either politically weak or under strong challenge from groups not sharing their overall policy preference, and where the existing class-based social cleavage finds increasingly visible expression through politicization of the question of income distribution. The first factor leads to an indecisive, sporadic use of the state power necessary to keep the unions politically subordinate, while the second increases the likelihood that as the result of rank-and-file pressure for better wages, the labor elite will become more confrontative.

The political party linkage with organized labor plays an important role in structuring the resulting conflict. Where party leaders hold positions as members of governmental bodies, they are likely to be able to use such an institutional platform to create a broader audience for union claims and, therefore, to lend them somewhat more legitimacy than if they were just presented as the direct expression of the unions. Should it be strategically useful to find a peaceful resolution of labor conflict the status afforded party leaders may allow them to serve as mediators with state officials. Perhaps, most importantly, the ideological perspective of a specific party often predisposes workers who are party activists to particular styles and strategies of political conflict. In this regard, populists might be more conciliatory to the state than those imbued with a more militant, openly Marxist class-oriented frame of mind.

The above interpretation is perhaps best explained by direct reference to the individual country cases discussed in this volume. In reviewing such cases, those providing examples of greater autonomy will preceed those with relatively little independence from the state.

Cases of Greater Autonomy

As presented in table 11.3, the countries with the highest indicators of labor autonomy are Argentina, Brazil since 1978, and Peru, as well as Chile in 1970–1973 and Uruguay in 1985–1986 during those quite short time periods. As is suggested in the second chapter, Argentina represents a case of deep hegemonic crisis where neither of two rival class-based political coalitions — one populist and one elitist — has been able to achieve more than temporary control of the state and the policy-making process. Because of long-term economic stagnation, politics has been conceived by all major interest groups, including organized labor, largely in zero-sum terms, where sectoral income distribution is of primary concern. Imbued with the populist traditions of Peronism, the mass-based unions have been able to mobilize large numbers of protestors whenever those running the state pursue policies seen as anti-worker and, critically, appear vulnerable to a politically astute if often divided union leadership.

In her chapter on Brazil, Alves discusses the sudden emergence in 1978 of an independent labor movement after years of repression and cooptation. What seems central here is the weakening of the military regime under the influence of the worsening economic crisis at a time when the post-1974 *abertura* created a space in which political protest could take place. Under the leadership of the metalworkers of the ABC suburbs of São Paulo, the unions focused on the twin issues of income disparity and job insecurity, both acerbated by the continuing economic deterioration of the early 1980s. The transition to democracy under the New Republic, in turn, hastened the creation of rival national-level labor confederations with ties to the political parties of the left and center-left. With no real linkage to the traditionalist José Sarney administration, labor was totally free to fight for the abrogation of the old restrictive labor laws in the Constitutional Assembly, but lacked any government support in so doing.

Haworth describes a similar growth of vigorous labor protest in the Peruvian case, fed by the expectations aroused and then frustrated by the military populism of the Velasco presidency. The concurrence over the subsequent decade of increasingly conservative economic policies and a radicalized Marxist-led trade union movement created an explosive labor climate. With the decay of military power and the shift to a democratic regime soon besieged by guerrillas, state power weakened; the level of strikes was kept in partial check only due to the initial sectarianism of contending union groups and, by the early 1980s, with sharply rising levels of unemployment.

The high level of labor militancy in Chile just before, and in Uruguay just after, extremely repressive military governments conforms with this pattern of explanation for union autonomy. In his discussion of pre-1973 Chilean events, Ruiz-Tagle discusses the effects of competing party loyalties within the divided labor movement as well as the relative absence of state repression in stimulating union efforts to maintain the buying power of the wages of particular groups of workers. The increasing political polarization and loss of state authority to which the unions responded did, of course, play a key role in precipitating the 1973 coup. In the Uruguayan chapter, Gargiulo notes the similarity of the reemerging unions of the early 1980s with those that had existed before the military seized power ten years earlier. What remains noteworthy is the divided loyalty of workers who support Marxist-affiliated unions, but vote for the traditional political parties. The weakness of the dominant

political elite in the labor movement leads to the creation of an oppositional mentality in the unions; in the largely unfettered atmosphere of
the new regime, the many strikes in behalf of wage recovery strain the
economy and, with it, the bases of the still fragile new democracy. High
labor autonomy has its costs.

Cases of Low Autonomy

In addition to bureaucratic-authoritarian military regimes like Brazil
before 1978, Chile between 1973 and 1979, and Uruguay from 1973 to
1984, where political repression made strikes and other forms of
independent union activity virtually impossible, other cases of low union
autonomy consist of Chile in the recent 1980–1986 period, Colombia,
Cuba, Mexico, and Venezuela. The latter five are more complicated and,
therefore, more in need of the explanation that follows.

Cuba, Mexico, and Venezuela exhibit a similar close integration
between regime and labor movement based upon the exchange of
benefits provided by the state in return for union cooperation. In these
cases, the unions have become, ipso facto, an official or semi-official part
of the ruling political alliance. While repression may be used on occasion,
the cooperative nature of these relationships is based more on the bonds
of obligation and dependency felt by the union elite, bonds which may
also extend to certain elements of the organized workers as well. Fuller's
chapter on Cuba emphasize the social accomplishments of the socialist
state in alleviating inequality and providing stable employment and a
host of social services for most workers. (Such a massive redistribution of
national resources clearly goes far beyond the labor populism of Mexico
and Venezuela.) If the initial Cuban government action in naming and
removing labor leaders without consultation led to widespread worker
apathy in the unions of the 1960s, efforts have been made since to
rekindle rank-and-file interest in union activities by allowing them to
become a more authentic channel for worker concerns. Zapata's account
of Mexican unions emphasizes the steady wage improvements received
from the late 1940s through the early 1970s by the urban workforce as a
means of reinforcing regime legitimacy. In his discussion of the economic
difficulties of more recent years, he points to official efforts to provide
compensation for declining income levels in the form of attempts to
minimize unemployment and to provide job retraining. The emergence
of leftist 'independent unions' which might challenge the dominant CTM
has so far been contained, but if the officially-imposed austerity is
continued, the regime may be required to use more force than has been
customary in order to maintain the present social pact. For Venezuela,
Davis and Coleman have emphasized the creation of similar pacts at the
time of the restoration of the democratic regime in the late 1950s. They
point out that the nature of labor peace in that country has rested on the

availability of an oil bonanza to provide jobs and steady improvements in worker income. The close ties between the rival centrist political parties and specific elements of the labor movement did not lead to greater militance because political and union leaders possessed common assumptions about what constitutes acceptable worker behavior. With the economic problems of recent years, labor relations have remained remarkably tranquil as most union leaders still believe that it is possible to accomplish more by working through their ties with the established political system than to risk any direct challenge to the status quo.

The final cases of low labor autonomy, Colombia and recent Chile respectively, seem to reflect the increased instability of the regimes in which they operate: major changes in regime will obviously have serious implications for labor relations there. In both countries, the use of force has alternated with such "market mechanisms" as massive unemployment to maintain relative labor quiescence.[14] Londoño focuses her discussion of Colombia on the replacement in importance of the traditional unions (whose links with the two dominant political parties have steadily eroded) by an alliance of the Communists with the rapidly growing 'independents' of a similar Marxist perspective. While attempts at joint labor protest, such as the 1977 *paro cívico*, resulted in official hostility and repression, the unions nonetheless continued their effort to promote labor unification. At the present time, the CUT can be said to speak for the greater part of the labor movement, but it remains shrunken in size due to the growth of mass unemployment and subject to increasing predations by the death squads. Ruiz-Tagle's account of recent Chile points to the prominent role assumed by labor in the anti-regime protests that surfaced with the economic collapse of the early 1980s. Although initially fragmented after the new institutionalization process imposed with the Labor Plan, the requirements of opposition to the military regime have led to considerable organizational unity among the unions. While less dependent than in pre-coup times on party allies (equally likely to suffer from official harassment and intimidation), labor exhibits low autonomy as measured by strike activity due to the effects of widespread joblessness.

FINAL REMARKS

This volume has stressed the frequent efforts using state power to limit labor autonomy throughout the Latin American region. Union resistance, in turn, has depended for success both on the existence of a weakened state incapable of using force in a sustained fashion and the salience of income distribution as an issue capable of mobilizing workers to protect their organizations. If in a few countries labor has developed an oppositional mentality inspired by supportive political party ties, cases of subordination to the state have been more common over a large number of years. Such cases of low autonomy themselves can be divided into ones based on clientelist types of state/union pacts where the use of force has been relatively unnecessary and those where labor dependency results from a combination of repression and fear of unemployment.

NOTES

1. Among the better known discussions of such interest group liberalism are Arthur Bentley, *The Process of Government* (Chicago: University of Chicago Press, 1908); David Truman, *The Governmental Process* (New York: Knopf, 1951); and Robert Dahl, *Polyarchy* (New Haven, CT: Yale University Press, 1971).

2. The classical Marxist statement is found in such works of V. I. Lenin as his *What Is to Be Done?* and *State and Revolution* (both New York: International Publishers, various editions).

3. Two somewhat different descriptions of corporatism can be found in Philippe Schmitter, "Still the Century of Corporatism?" *The Review of Politics*, 36:1 (1974), pp. 85–121; and Alfred Stepan, *The State and Society* (Princeton, NJ: Princeton University Press, 1978), part 1.

4. Here one might see Ruth Collier's article, "Popular Sector Incorporation and Political Supremacy," in Sylvia Hewlett and Richard Weinert, eds., *Brazil and Mexico* (Philadelphia: ISHI, 1982).

5. See Linda Fuller's comments at the beginning of her chapter in this volume.

6. An exception to this assumption of normal government opposition to strikes is where a pro-labor government threatened by business seeks to use strikes as a means to intimidate its enemies through the mobilization of labor support. Given the economic costs involved, such action will be avoided except in a moment of perceived political threat. The goal of transferring income to a government's labor ally can usually be accomplished less disruptively through administrative action.

7. For the notion of the general strike as a demonstration of labor's power capability, see Charles Anderson, *Politics and Economic Change in Latin America* (Princeton, NJ: Van Nostrand, 1967), p. 98. The open-ended strike, on the other hand, clearly has a directly destabilizing purpose.

8. In categorizing the scores, anything above an average of 2.0 general strikes per year was seen as high; anything above 1.0 but below 2.0 as medium-high; between 0.5 and 1.0 as medium; between 0.1 and 0.5 as medium-low; and the absence of any general strikes as low.

9. A score of 10 or above on the number of strikers/EAP was seen as high; one between 50 and 100 as medium-high; one between 20 and 50 as medium; one of 5 to 20 as medium-low; and any score less than 5 as low.

10. On this point see Susan Eckstein, "Transformación socialista y clase obrera cubana," p. 325, in Rubén Katzman and José Luis Reyna, eds., *Fuerza de*

trabajo y movimientos laborales en América Latina (Mexico City: El Colegio de México, 1979).

11. For the 1985–1986 period, see Martín Gargiulo's chapter in this volume; for the period before the 1973 coup, see Vladimir Turiansky, *El movimiento obrero uruguayo* (Montevideo: Eds. Publos Unidos, 1973).

12. Any score above 500 strikes per year is ranked as high; one between 200 and 500 as medium-high; one above 100 but less than 200 as medium; one between 0 and 100 as medium-low; and the absence of any as low.

13. On this comprehensive measure of labor autonomy, high was scored as 20 or above; medium-high as 15 to 19; medium-low as 10 to 14; and low as below 10.

14. The distinction between corporatist controls and "market mechanisms" is made in J. Samuel Valenzuela, "Labor Movements in Transitions to Democracy," Working Paper 104 (Notre Dame, IN: The Kellogg Institute of International Studies, University of Notre Dame, June 1988), p. 5.

Contributors

Maria Helena Moreira Alves (Brazil) teaches Political Science at the State University of Rio de Janeiro where she is the coordinator of Latin American Studies. Her book *State and Opposition in Military Brazil* has been published in Portuguese (Vozes, 1984) and English (Texas, 1985).

Kenneth Coleman (Venezuela) is an Associate Professor of Political Science at the University of Kentucky, Lexington, where he heads the Latin American Studies Program. In addition to two monographs on Mexico and his co-edited volume with George Herring, *The Central American Crisis* (Scholarly Resources, 1985), he has written a number of articles on unions in Venezuela and Mexico.

Charles Davis (Venezuela) is an Associate Professor of Political Science at the University of Kentucky, Fort Knox. He has written articles on a variety of topics including trade unions, voting and legitimacy, and public opinion.

Edward Epstein (Argentina), Associate Professor of Latin American politics at the University of Utah, Salt Lake City, has written a number of articles on unions and income distribution in Argentina, as well as others on the effect of regime type on economic policy outcome.

Linda Fuller (Cuba) is an Assistant Professor of Sociology at the University of Southern California. She is the co-editor (with Nora Hamilton, Jeffrey Frieden, and Manuel Pastor) of *Crisis in Central America* (Westview, 1988) and author of several articles on Cuban labor.

Martín Gargiulo (Uruguay) is a doctoral candidate in Sociology at Columbia University as well as a researcher in the Sociology Program at the Latin American Center for Human Economics (CLAEH) in Montevideo. He has published a number of articles in Spanish on Uruguayan unions.

Nigel Haworth (Peru) teaches in the Department of Management Studies and Labour Relations at the University of Auckland in New Zealand. He is the author of a monograph, *Labour and Politics in Peru Revisited* (University of Glasgow, 1987) and several articles about the Peruvian working class.

Rocío Londoño Botero (Colombia) teaches Sociology at the National University in Bogotá. She is the author (with Hernándo Gómez and Guillermo Perry) of *Sindicalismo y política económica* (FEDESARROLLO-CEREC, 1986) and other works on Colombian unions.

Jaime Ruiz-Tagle P. (Chile) is the Assistant Director of the Program of Labor Economics (PET) at the Academia de Humanismo Cristiano in Santiago. Among his monographs are *Los trabajadores del Programa de Empleo Mínimo* (PET-PISPAL, 1984) and *El sindicalismo chileno después del Plan Laboral* (PET, 1985).

Francisco Zapata Schaffeld (Mexico) is a professor and researcher at the Center for Sociological Studies at the Colegio de México. Among his many publications on trade unions are his edited volume, *Clases sociales y acción obrera en Chile* (Jornadas, El Colegio de México, 1986) and co-authored with José Luis Reyna, Marcelo Miquet, and Silvia Gómez-Tagle, *Tres estudios sobre el movimiento obrero en México* (Jornadas, El Colegio de México, 1976).

Index